# GCSE
# ECONOMICS

ROBERT PAISLEY & JOHN QUILLFELDT

Longman

**LONGMAN GROUP UK LIMITED,**
*Longman House,*
*Burnt Mill, Harlow, Essex CM20 2JE, England*
*and Associated Companies throughout the world.*

© Longman Group UK Limited 1987
*All rights reserved; no part of this publication*
*may be reproduced, stored in a retrieval system,*
*or transmitted in any form or by any means, electronic,*
*mechanical, photocopying, recording, or otherwise,*
*without the prior written permission of the Publishers.*

First published 1987
Second impression 1988
ISBN 0 582 00520 5

*Edited by Stenton Associates*
*Design and illustration by Ken Vail Graphic Design*
*Cartoons by David Lock*

**Acknowledgements**
The authors wish to thank Carolyn Quillfeldt, Linda Thomas, and the students of Haydon, Northwood and Dame Alice Owen's schools for their invaluable help in the preparation of this book.

We are grateful for permission to reproduce copyright material. It has not been possible to identify the sources of all the material used and in such cases the publishers would welcome information from copyright holders. The sources of text extracts are given as the texts appear. Photograph acknowledgements are listed below:

Chris Davies/Network p1, p39, p144; The Press Agency (Yorkshire) Ltd p3 (left); Mike Goldwater/Network p3 (right); Sally & Richard Greenhill p4 (top right), p16, p31, p32 (top right), p34 (top right), p38, p44 (right), p173 (bottom), p216 (top), p249 (top); Cement and Concrete Association p4 (bottom right); Laurie Sparham/Network p4 (bottom left), p32 (left), p234, p257 (bottom); Camera Press Ltd/John Moss p5 (top left); John Sturrock/Network p5 (top right), p117, p237 (right); Jenny Matthews/Format p5 (bottom right), p29, p66, p75, p99, p180, p237 (left); Popperfoto p5 (bottom left), p135; Val Wilmer/Format p6 (left); Sunil Gupta/Network p6 (right); Maggie Murray/Format p9; Ford Motor Company Ltd p20 (left), p36; Vauxhall Motors Limited p20 (right); Camera Press Ltd p27; Brenda Prince/Format p32 (bottom right), p34 (bottom right), p216 (bottom); British Steel p33 (top); Telegraph and Star Studios p33 (middle); Mappin and Webb Ltd p33 (bottom); Pam Isherwood/Format p34 (top left); Malcolm Pendrill/Camera Press p34 (bottom left); Mike Abrahams/Network p43, p44 (left); Weidenfeld & Nicolson Ltd p55, p243; Financial Times p78 (left); Gordon Ridgewell/Stenton Associates p78 (right), p195; The Post Office p151 (top); British Aerospace p151 (bottom left); BP Oil Ltd p151 (bottom middle); John Cole/Network p151 (bottom right); British Steel/Owens of Wishaw p172; Roger Taylor/Financial Times p173 (top right, top left); British Tourist Authority p248, p292 (bottom); Roger Hutchings/Network p249 (bottom), p257 (top); Frank Spooner Pictures p263.

Produced by Longman Group (FE) Ltd
Printed in Hong Kong

# CONTENTS

| | | | |
|---|---|---|---|
| **PART 1** | **THE ECONOMIC SYSTEM** | 1 | |
| Unit 1.1 | Economic decisions and the economic problem | 2 | |
| Unit 1.2 | Demand, supply, markets and prices<br>▶ Elasticity | 10 | |
| Unit 1.3 | Different types of economy | 21 | |
| **PART 2** | **WORK** | 29 | |
| Unit 2.1 | Why and how people work | 30 | |
| Unit 2.2 | Finding work and training for work | 37 | |
| Unit 2.3 | Trade unions and employers | 43 | |
| **PART 3** | **MONEY AND BANKING** | 55 | |
| Unit 3.1 | Money | 56 | |
| Unit 3.2 | The value of money | 61 | |
| Unit 3.3 | The banking and financial system | 66 | |
| **PART 4** | **MANAGING YOUR MONEY** | 75 | |
| Unit 4.1 | Getting paid | 76 | |
| Unit 4.2 | Planning your spending | 82 | |
| Unit 4.3 | Saving | 89 | |
| Unit 4.4 | Borrowing money | 97 | |
| Unit 4.5 | Insurance | 103 | |
| Unit 4.6 | Buying and renting a home | 111 | |
| **PART 5** | **POPULATION** | 117 | |
| Unit 5.1 | Population size and why it changes<br>▶ Theories of population | 118 | |
| Unit 5.2 | The structure of the population | 124 | |
| **PART 6** | **PRODUCTION** | 135 | |
| Unit 6.1 | Production and costs | 136 | |
| Unit 6.2 | Private sector firms | 142 | |
| Unit 6.3 | Nationalised industries and privatisation | 149 | |
| Unit 6.4 | The financing of firms | 156 | |
| Unit 6.5 | Large and small firms<br>▶ Competition and monopoly | 163 | |
| Unit 6.6 | The location of firms | 172 | |
| Unit 6.7 | Retailing, wholesaling and advertising | 179 | |
| Unit 6.8 | Protecting the consumer | 187 | |
| **PART 7** | **THE GOVERNMENT AND THE ECONOMY** | 195 | |
| Unit 7.1 | The public sector and government spending | 196 | |
| Unit 7.2 | Government income<br>▶ The Public Sector Borrowing Requirement<br>▶ The National Debt | 205 | |
| Unit 7.3 | The National Income<br>▶ Factor incomes | 214 | |
| Unit 7.4 | Managing the economy<br>▶ The money supply and bank lending | 222 | |
| Unit 7.5 | Unemployment | 234 | |
| Unit 7.6 | Inflation | 242 | |
| Unit 7.7 | Economic growth | 248 | |
| Unit 7.8 | The distribution of income and wealth | 256 | |
| **PART 8** | **BRITAIN AND THE WORLD ECONOMY** | 263 | |
| Unit 8.1 | Why countries trade<br>▶ The principle of comparative advantage | 264 | |
| Unit 8.2 | The UK's balance of payments<br>▶ The terms of trade | 273 | |
| Unit 8.3 | The value of the pound<br>▶ Different types of exchange rate | 283 | |
| Unit 8.4 | Trade agreements and the EEC | 290 | |
| Unit 8.5 | Developing economies & world economic organisations | 296 | |

# Introduction

## Aims and objectives

▶ To provide a comprehensive coverage of GCSE syllabuses.
▶ To provide a textbook which is of practical use in the classroom for the majority of economics teachers.
▶ To provide material suitable for use with a wide range of abilities, with the average student in the range GCSE grades C–E, while meeting the needs of students that could achieve the highest or lowest grades.
▶ To provide (after some of the basic concepts such as opportunity cost and the price mechanism have been introduced), a progression of economic ideas, from the more accessible world of the consumer and worker to the world of producers, and the UK and world economies.
▶ To ensure that the language is suitable for the target ability range and becomes progressively more sophisticated in the use of economic terms.
▶ To provide stimulus material and exercises which meet the assessment objectives of the national criteria for GCSE Economics, particularly in the development of skills in the application of economic concepts to real-world situations and issues.

## A guide for the teacher

*GCSE Economics* follows a specific format. This is designed to cover the broad range of key ideas, skills and attitudes required for GCSE. The book is divided into eight parts, which are in turn divided into smaller Units (38 in all), each with a common structure.

**Focus:** The Focus section at the beginning of each Unit raises questions on the key ideas covered in each Unit. It has two purposes: the first is to provide the students with an idea as to the content of the Unit. The second is to give the students an opportunity to reflect on what they have learnt by testing what the students *know*. In each Unit the Activities section begins with 'Go back and answer the questions raised in the Focus'. Students could make a variety of responses to these questions (e.g. 'Why do countries trade?'), from short answers to longer more analytical answers (differentiation by outcome). The Focus questions are not exhaustive – basic knowledge may also be tested in other activities.

**Background text:** The main text and activities are designed to be accessible to students with a wide range of abilities as stated in the aims and objectives. Many of the cartoons, diagrams and photographs can be used as stimulus materials as they are often accompanied by a question which is intended to generate discussion about economic concepts dealt with in the text. After looking at the Focus, the cartoons, photographs and diagrams may be used as a lead-in to the main text.

**Database:** The databases provide stimulus data represented in a variety of ways without questions or comment, to encourage students to 'select, interpret and apply data' (GCSE National Criteria – assessment objective). They often extend the discussion beyond the main themes in the text. Teachers could use the Databases in a variety of ways. They could set exercises based on the data, they could be used for discussion, or as a possible stimulus for coursework, including a means of increasing students' awareness of alternative methods of data presentation. They can also be used to demonstrate that statistical data can be used to present a particular point of view, and that the interpretation of data may not be value-free. The use of the Databases remains, therefore, very much up to teachers and students.

**Activities:** As well as the Focus questions there are two other types of activity included in this section:

**Stepped questions:** These are graded questions on an *incline of difficulty* to provide differentiation. The higher level stepped questions are often designed to question attitudes, thus not all the stepped questions will be directly answerable from the text. The teacher's input is particularly important here.

**Data-response questions:** The data-response questions are also usually stepped, and stimulate the interpretation of data, as well as testing students' knowledge, understanding, attitudes and analytical skills.

The stepped questions and data-response sections are designed to test what students *understand and can do* as well as basic knowledge. The data-response questions also stimulate the interpretation of data. In some cases activities from one Unit may be appropriate for use with other Units.

**Extension material:** Some Units have an Extension Material section covering more complex concepts. This enables the main text and activities to be accessible to the majority of students.

At the end of each part there is:

**Coursework:** There are different coursework requirements for different boards, and it is not the intention of this textbook to deal with coursework in a comprehensive manner. The suggestions for coursework made in the book are designed as much to stimulate other ideas about coursework projects as they are to provide specific tasks which students can undertake.

**Dictionary of economic terms:** There are a variety of new words and terms introduced in Economics. The list of words and terms provided at the end of each part include many of those that are essential for GCSE Economics. Students could be encouraged to make their own dictionaries, possibly in a separate small notebook.

# Using *GCSE Economics* with *Understanding Economics*

You may well be familiar with '*Understanding Economics*' (Longman 1985) which you may be using already in the classroom. This page suggests where Units in '*Understanding Economics*' can be used with Units in '*GCSE Economics*' to reinforce the skills and key ideas developed in this book.

### UNIT REFERENCES

| GCSE Economics | Understanding Economics (Young Person as Consumer/Producer/Citizen |
|---|---|
| THE ECONOMIC SYSTEM | |
| 1.1 | Consumer – A; Producer – F. |
| 1.2 | Consumer – B, H; Producer – B, E, J. |
| 1.3 | Consumer – D. |
| WORK | |
| 2.1 | Producer – C,D. |
| 2.3 | Producer – G. |
| MONEY AND BANKING | |
| 3.1 | Consumer – E. |
| MANAGING YOUR MONEY | |
| 4.2 | Consumer – F,H,K. |
| 4.4 | Consumer – E. |
| PRODUCTION | |
| 6.1 | Producer – A,B,E. |
| | Citizen – A,B. |
| 6.3 | Consumer – H,K. |
| 6.5 | Producer – F. |
| 6.6 | Citizen – I. |
| 6.7 | Consumer – C. |
| THE GOVERNMENT AND THE ECONOMY | |
| 7.1 | Citizen – A,C,E,F,H. |
| 7.2 | Citizen – F,G. |
| 7.3 | Producer – H. |
| 7.8 | Consumer – G. |

# Part 1
## The economic system

# UNIT 1.1 Economic decisions and the economic problem

**FOCUS**

▶ What is an economic problem?

▶ What economic problems are faced by individual people, firms and other organisations, and governments?

▶ How are **scarcity**, **choice**, and **opportunity cost** related to economic problems?

▶ What is meant by a **marginal** decision?

▶ What are **factors of production** or **economic resources**?

▶ What is the difference between **capital goods** and **consumer goods**, and how do they relate to opportunity cost?

## The basic economic problem

Economic problems arise because people nearly always want more than they already have. This is obviously true of a starving child in a developing country, but it is just as true of a nurse in the UK, or even of a film star in Hollywood.

There would be no problem if there was an unlimited amount of the **resources** – things like land, workers, machinery, oil, crops, etc. – that are needed to produce goods and services. However, these resources are limited in supply (or **scarce**), so people, organisations and governments have to make economic decisions, or **choices**. They have to choose which goods and services to make or buy, and which goods and services they will go without.

Some people have wider choices than others in making their economic decisions. Think again about the examples at the beginning of this section.

### Economic decisions and the individual

There are many goods and services that we would like, but we have not got the money to buy all of them. Most of us would like to spend more on clothes, holidays and going out, but our money is limited. Because our money is limited we have to choose, and every time we choose something, we have to give something up. For example, if you choose to spend £5 on a record, you can't spend that same £5 on a book.

In economics we use the term **opportunity cost** to refer to the amount of one good or service that we have to give up when we choose another. In our example, the opportunity cost of buying the record was the book that we had to give up.

Sacrifices like this don't always have to be made. If you live by the sea and you decide to collect a bucket of sea water, then you simply go out and get it. There has been no sacrifice by you or by anybody else. You did not have to give up anything else when you chose to collect the water, and you took nothing of use to anyone else. Things like sea water, sand in the desert and air are called **free goods** because they can be used at no opportunity cost.

Most goods, however, do involve an opportunity cost. These goods are called **economic goods**. You have to sacrifice something so that you can buy them. Usually you give up something else that you could have bought instead.

In addition, the resources used to make economic goods could have been used to make something else, so there is also an opportunity cost in making them. Economics is about the **production** (or 'making') and the **consumption** (or 'using up') of economic goods.

We have seen that sea water is a free good, but what about tap water?

### Economic decisions and organisations

An organisation is a group of people who get together to do something. Churches are organisations; they are groups of people who get together to worship. Businesses are organisations; they are groups of people who get

**Figure 1.1a**
How is opportunity cost involved here?

together to produce something to sell.

Organisations receive money, and their money does not usually buy all the things they want. They are faced with the basic economic problem of choice, just as individuals are. Here are some examples of choices that could be faced by organisations:

▶ A church may receive most of its money from donations, and it has to choose how to spend that money. If it decides to repair a church building, for example, the opportunity cost could be the money that could have been given to the poor.

▶ A business, or **firm**, has to make choices when it receives income from selling the things it produces. It could give workers a large pay rise, but the opportunity cost may be that it delays buying some new machinery which it needs. Alternatively, it could buy the new machinery, but then it may not be able to afford to reduce prices to try to attract new customers.

## Economic decisions and governments

Governments have the same basic problem as the individuals and organisations they govern. There are only limited means available to produce the things people want. Here are some examples of the choices the government may need to make:

▶ The government may decide that defence is particularly important. This could mean an increase in the number of soldiers. Young people who could have worked in other jobs will join the army. More money will need to be found for weapons, and this could mean cutting spending on, for example, education and health.

▶ The government may decide to spend a lot of money on improving and expanding the road network. This could mean taking valuable farmland for a new motorway. It may mean increasing taxes to pay for the new roads, leaving people with less to spend on food, clothing, household goods, holidays etc.

**Figure 1.1b**
How is opportunity cost involved here?

Economic decisions may also be made by firms and governments which affect people in other countries, for example setting up factories abroad and reducing or increasing aid to the Third World.

## Marginality

You may have heard a commentator on a cricket or football match say that an umpire's or referee's decision was **marginal** – it could have gone one way or another. Economic decisions are often marginal. For example, you might go browsing in a record shop and see a record you like priced at £5. Although you can afford it you think the £5 would be better spent on something else. But if the price was reduced to £3, you would probably buy it. Another example would be where a council decides to build a hospital instead of four council houses, but when it finds out that it could actually build five council houses for the same cost as a hospital, it decides to build the houses. So you can see that economic decisions, involving opportunity cost, are made at the margin.

## The factors of production

The production of goods and services for individuals, organisations, and the economy as a whole needs the use of other goods and services.

For example, in order to make simple wooden chairs for sale, someone would have to provide the money for the business. Someone would have to hire and organise workers to produce the chairs. The workers would need a factory and some tools and machinery for sawing, sanding, and gluing the chairs. And, of course, they would need wood and varnish to make and finish the chairs.

**Figure 1.1c**
What difficult choices does the government face when deciding the goods and services it wishes to produce?

The goods and services needed to produce other goods and services are called **factors of production**. They can also be called **economic resources**, or simply **resources**. As our example shows, a lot of resources are needed to make even the most simple product.

Factors of production fall into four groups: land resources, labour, capital and enterprise.

**Land resources** are the natural resources used to produce something. Some of these are shown in Fig 1.1d.

All of the people who contribute to the production of a good or service are called **labour**. This includes production line workers, managers, secretaries, miners, railway guards and accountants.

The manufactured resources used to produce goods and services are called **capital**. Some capital, like steel or glue, is used up during the production process. Other capital, like machinery and tools, can be used again and again.

**Figure 1.1d**
Which factors of production are illustrated here?

None of the other factors of production would be of any use unless someone was willing to provide the money to buy or hire land resources, labour and capital and organise them to produce something. The person (or group of people) who does this is called an **entrepreneur** and it is the entrepreneur who supplies the factor of production called **enterprise**.

## Producers and consumers

People are involved in the economy as **consumers** and **producers**. They are consumers when they are buying goods and services and producers when they are making and distributing goods and services. The workers in a car factory, for example, are consumers when they buy a television set for their homes; they are producers when they are involved in turning steel into cars.

Economists make a distinction between **consumer goods** and **capital goods**. Consumer goods are produced for sale to the consumer. Capital goods form one of the factors of production and include factories, machinery and materials. There is often an additional opportunity cost in producing consumer goods: if we want consumer goods in the future, we must produce the capital goods needed to make them.

Figure 1.1f shows a **Production Possibilities Curve** (PPC). It shows all the possible combinations of capital goods and consumer goods that can be produced in an economy with all its economic resources used to their full capacity. For example, in the diagram the opportunity cost of producing 10 extra capital goods is 50 consumer goods. However, in the future the extra capital goods can be used to produce more consumer goods, which would move the PPC to the right. Which would you prefer, more consumption now and less in the future, or less now and more in the future?

**Figure 1.1e**
In a large firm the factor of production called enterprise is supplied by the shareholders who put their money into the business, and the directors who organise and run the business for the shareholders. In smaller firms the same person usually provides the money and runs the business.

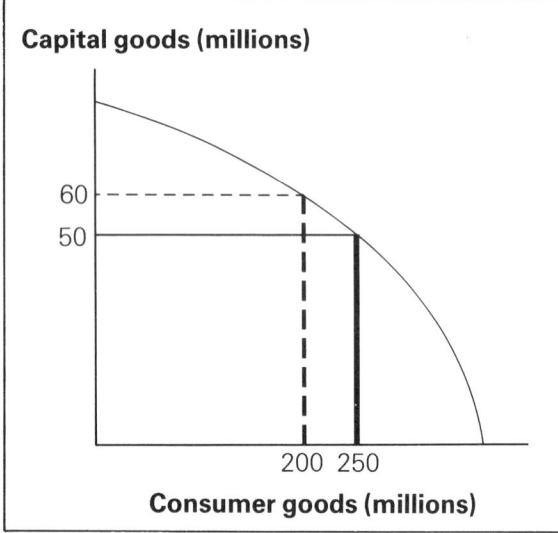

**Figure 1.1f**
A production possibilities curve

## DATABASE

# Making economic decisions
(Approximate figures for 1986)

### £10 could buy:

100 Ballpoint pens
**or**
60 Small cans of soft drink
**or**
50 Days supply of *The Sun* newspaper
**or**
30 Small loaves of bread
**or**
11 Pints of beer
**or**
8 Hamburgers
**or**
2 Cut-price LPs
**or**
1 Half-hour's labour at a garage

### £1 billion could buy:

487,000 Jobs using special employment measures, e.g. community programme. (Includes saving on benefits)
**or**
66 New general hospitals
**or**
45 Boeing 757 jets
**or**
8 Type 22 frigates
**or**
5 Large reservoirs
**or**
4 Nuclear-powered submarines

**ACTIVITIES**

## SECTION A: FOCUS ON UNIT 1.1

Go back and answer the questions raised in the Focus.

## SECTION B: STEPPED QUESTIONS

1 **a** Describe some problems involving opportunity cost that may have to be faced by:
   ▷ yourself in your weekly spending (use the Database to help you)
   ▷ a young couple with little money who have just bought their own flat
   ▷ a firm
   ▷ the government (use the Database to help you)
   ▷ a poor family in Ethiopia.
   **b** For each example in (a) explain how each person or group would decide which goods and services to choose, and which to go without.

2 **a** Put a heading 'Some Factors of Production Used in the Supply of Bread'. Taking about half a side of paper, divide the paper into columns. Head the columns 'Land Resources', 'Labour', 'Capital' and 'Enterprise'. Put the items in the list below into the correct columns.

   Lorries
   Bakers
   Cash tills
   Flour
   Company chairperson
   Ovens
   Salt
   Lorry drivers
   Water
   Mills
   Shop keepers
   Slicing machines
   Baking trays
   Shareholders

   **b** Draw a flow diagram to show how the four factors of production are used by a firm to produce goods and services for consumers.
   **c** Explain how the production of capital goods and consumer goods involves opportunity cost, and explain the effects of deciding between these two types of goods.

## SECTION C: DATA RESPONSE QUESTION

### The wounds that fester in Africa

The most serious problem in Africa is posed by the failure of agriculture, which is the main cause of malnutrition, unemployment and the growing number of imports. A great deal of hard work has gone into developing rice growing in West Africa, and output almost doubled between 1962 and 1977. But as consumption grew much faster than output, imports had to be stepped up at the same time. Few African countries have given priority in their investment programmes to agricultural development. Very small amounts of government expenditure were earmarked for agriculture, since the lion's share went on administrative buildings and other equipment, the urban areas and industry. Food crops have received – and are still receiving – the least attention of all.

(Adapted from *The Guardian* 20/5/83)

a  Why have African countries been importing (buying goods from abroad) more and more?
b  Give a possible reason for consumption growing faster than the supply of food in many African countries.
c  What kind of things have many African governments spent money on, and what has been the opportunity cost of that spending?
d  What would you expect to happen to the standard of living of agricultural workers in future years in Africa? Give reasons for your answer.
e  How does the economic problem of scarcity differ between West Africa and Western Europe?

# UNIT 1.2 Demand, supply, markets and prices

**FOCUS**

▶ What is a **market**?

▶ How does the **market mechanism** work?

▶ What factors affect the **demand** for a product?

▶ What factors affect the **supply** of a product?

▶ What are **demand and supply curves**?

▶ What is the **equilibrium price**, and what factors cause it to change?

## Markets and the price mechanism

If you ask someone why house prices are higher in the south-east of England than in the north-east, or why a footballer can be sold from one club to another for more than £1 million, you may well get the answer, 'demand and supply'.

For demand and supply to exist there must be buyers and sellers. Economists say there is a **market** when buyers and sellers exchange money for goods and services. For example, there is a market for houses and a market for eggs. So a market need not be a fixed place. We often talk about 'putting something on the market' when we want to sell it.

In a market, price is used by consumers to 'signal' to producers what they want produced. If consumers start to demand more of a good there will be a temporary shortage and its price will tend to rise. Producers will then want to make more of the good and will move factors of production into its manufacture. So markets are one way in which scarce resources are **allocated** to the production of different goods and services. This process of allocating scarce resources through markets is called the **market mechanism**, although it is sometimes called the **price mechanism**, because of the importance of prices.

Sometimes governments can decide how to allocate resources, but in the UK this decision is left largely to the market mechanism. We will consider the allocation of resources by governments a little later in the book.

For now we will look at the connection between demand, supply and prices in more detail.

## The demand for goods and services

The **demand** for a good or service is the amount of that good or service that people are willing and able to buy in a given period of time at a particular price. As the price of a good rises, the demand for it tends to fall, and as the price of a good falls, so the demand for it tends to rise. This can be shown as a **demand curve**. Figure 1.2a shows a possible demand curve for records. You can see that at high prices relatively few records are demanded each month by consumers. For example, at £16 per record only 100,000 records are demanded each week by consumers. If the price of records was only £2 per week, however, the demand for records would rise to 800,000 per week.

We must be careful not to confuse demanding and wanting. The demand curve in Fig 1.2a shows that when the price of records is very low, people will buy huge numbers of records. As the price rises, however, many people who may

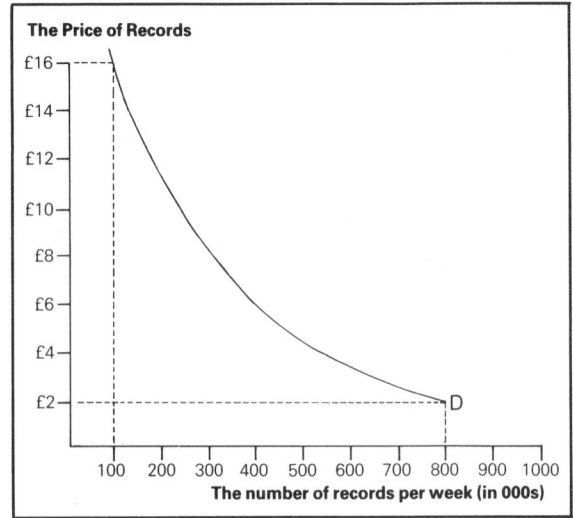

**Figure 1.2a**
A demand curve
The demand curves for most products possibly have the shape shown in Fig 1.2a. However, for simplicity demand curves are often drawn as straight lines and this will be the case further on in this book.

want the records are not prepared to pay the higher prices; their wants are unfulfilled.

**Changes in the conditions of demand**

Figure 1.2b shows a rise in demand. The whole demand curve moves to the right. More records are demanded at each and every price. Changes in demand are caused by changes in the **conditions of demand**.

▶ **1 A change in incomes**

For most goods and services a rise in incomes leads to a rise in demand. For example if people have more money they will buy more records. For some goods, like bread and potatoes, a rise in income will lead to a fall in demand. These goods are called **inferior goods**.

▶ **2 A change in fashions, tastes and habits**

In some industries demand can change considerably according to the latest trends. Health food shops have done very well in recent years with the increasing interest in a healthy diet. A new pop star can lead to a big increase in the demand for records.

▶ **3 Advertising**

The whole point of advertising is to increase the demand for goods and services. Firms spend huge sums on advertising in order to raise demand.

▶ **4 A change in the price of other goods**

As the price of a good changes, and the demand for it changes, the demand for some other goods will change as well. Some examples will show the way this happens.

If butter becomes cheaper, there will be an increase in the demand for butter, and a decrease in the demand for margarine. Butter and margarine are **substitutes**, and as the price of one of them falls, so the demand for the other falls at every price. Butter and margarine are said to be **in competitive demand**. Records and cassette tapes are also in competitive demand. If the price of cassette tapes rises, the demand for records will rise, as shown in Fig 1.2b.

If the price of video recorders falls, there will be an increase in the demand for them. There will also be an increase in the demand for video tapes. Video recorders and video tapes are **complements**, and as the price of one of them falls, so the demand for the other rises. Video recorders and video tapes are said to be **in joint demand**. Other complementary goods are records and record players. If the price of record players falls, the demand for records will rise, as shown in Fig 1.2b.

▶ **5 A change in credit facilities**

If it becomes easier or cheaper to borrow money, the demand for many goods and services will rise. The increased use of credit cards in recent years has boosted the sale of electrical goods like videos and home computers.

▶ **6 Changes in population size and structure**

Any change in the total number of people in the country, or in the numbers in different age groups, will affect demand. There are at present many people in the UK in their mid to late twenties and this has increased the demand for housing.

## The supply of goods and services

The supply of a good or service is the amount that suppliers are willing to put on the market over some given period of time at a particular price. As the price of a good rises, the supply of it tends to rise, and as the price of a good falls, so the supply of it tends to fall. This is because in most cases it is more profitable to sell a good at a higher price than at a lower one.

Figure 1.2c shows a supply curve. You can see

**Figure 1.2b**
A rise in demand

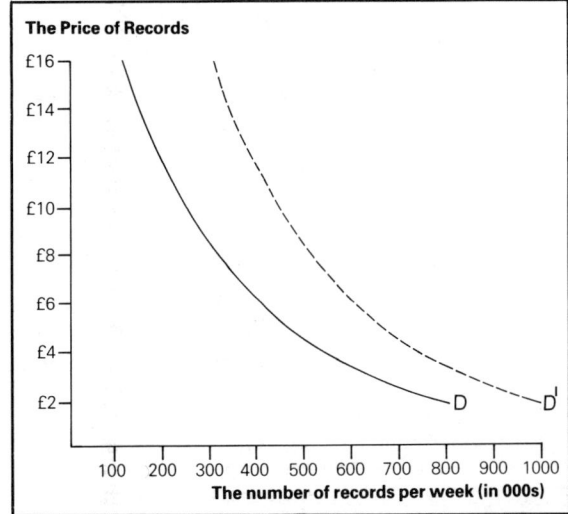

**Figure 1.2c**
A supply curve

Supply curves possibly have the shape shown in Fig 1.2c for most products, but for simplicity they are shown later in the book as straight lines

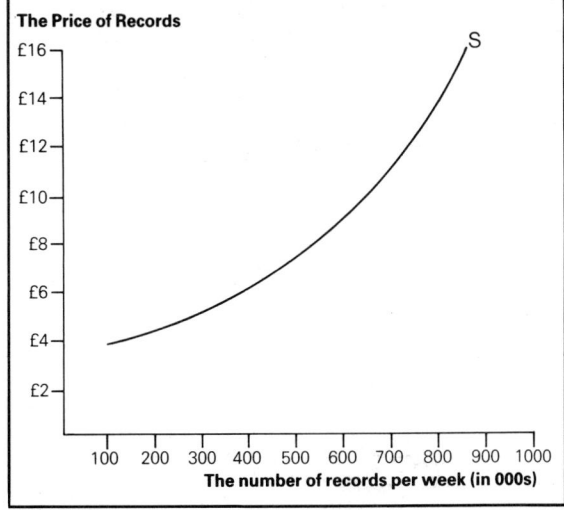

that as the price of a good falls, suppliers are willing to put less on the market than when the price is high.

### Changes in the conditions of supply

Figure 1.2d shows a rise in supply. More records are supplied at each and every price. The whole supply curve has moved to the right. Changes in supply are caused by changes in the **conditions of supply**.

▶ **1 A change in the costs of factors of production**

A rise in the price of labour (wages), for example, will cause a rise in the cost of the good and this will cause a fall in supply. A fall in the price of factors of production will cause a rise in supply.

▶ **2 Taxes and subsidies**

If the government places a tax on a good, for example by charging Value-Added Tax, this will cause a fall in supply and thus a rise in price. If it gives a payment to a producer for every good produced (a subsidy) this will cause a rise in supply.

▶ **3 Changes in the weather and discoveries of minerals**

The supply of farm products is particularly affected by the weather; a bad harvest will reduce supply and a good harvest will increase it. The supply of a mineral such as oil can be increased greatly by the discovery of a new oil field.

▶ **4 The time period involved**

If a rise in demand causes a rise in price, we have seen that the suppliers will be prepared to supply more of the good. If the price then remains high, however, not only will existing suppliers be prepared to continue to supply more of the good, new producers will enter the market. The effect of this is that the industry as a whole is now prepared to supply more of the good for a given price than it was before. We show this by moving the whole supply curve to the right, as in Fig. 1.2d.

▶ **5 Technical progress**

New ways of producing goods can also lead to an increase in the amount that producers are willing to sell at a given price, moving the supply curve to the right. For example, technical developments in the manufacture of microchips have enabled producers to make microcomputers more cheaply, and this has led to a large increase in the supply of computers.

## The market or equilibrium price of goods and services

The **market price** or **equilibrium price** of a good is the price at which demand for the good is equal to the supply of it. This is the point where the demand and supply curves cross. Equilibrium means 'balance', and the market price balances out the forces of supply and demand.

Figure 1.2e shows us that if the price of records was above £6 the supply of records would exceed the demand for them and there would be a **surplus**. Suppliers would reduce the price until they were selling all their records at £6. If the price was lower than £6, the demand for records would exceed the supply of them, and there would be a **shortage**. Suppliers would increase the price of records to increase profit until the shortage disappeared, so that the price would rise to £6.

### Changes in market price

Changes in price are caused by changes in either the conditions of demand or changes in the conditions of supply.

Figures 1.2f and 1.2g show us that the movement **of** one curve causes movement **along** the other curve. In Fig 1.2f an increase in the

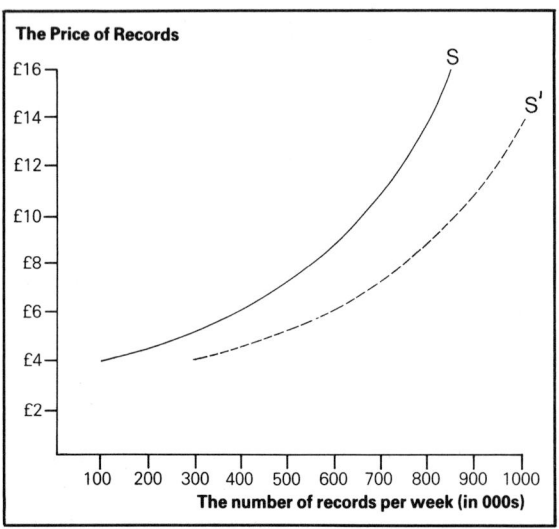

**Figure 1.2d** A rise in supply

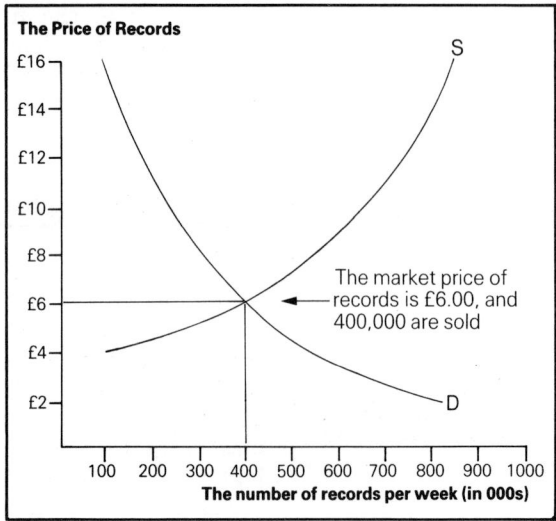

**Figure 1.2e** The market price of records

*Unit 1.2 Demand, supply, markets and prices*

demand for records, from D to D′, has caused an increase in the quantity of records supplied, from 400,000 to 510,000. In Fig 1.2g an increase in the supply of records, from S to S′, has caused an increase in the quantity of records demanded, from 400,000 to 480,000.

A movement to the right along a curve is called an **extension** in supply or demand, and a movement to the left along a curve is called a **contraction** in supply or demand.

**Figure 1.2f**
**Figure 1.2g**
The effect of changes in demand and supply on market price. Diagram (a) shows a rise in demand leading to a rise (or extension) in quantity supplied. Diagram (b) shows a rise in supply leading to a rise (or extension) in quantity demanded.

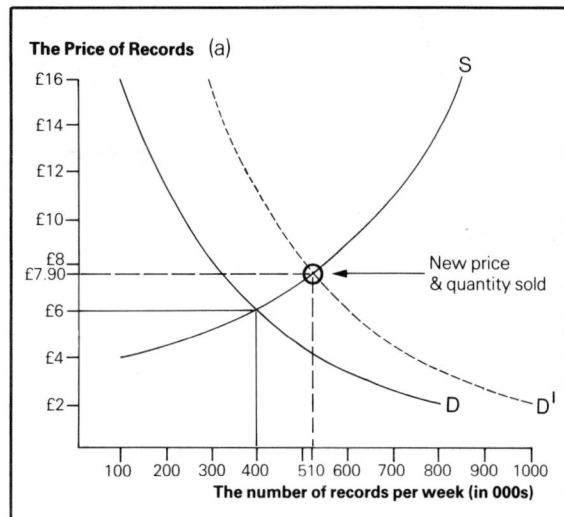
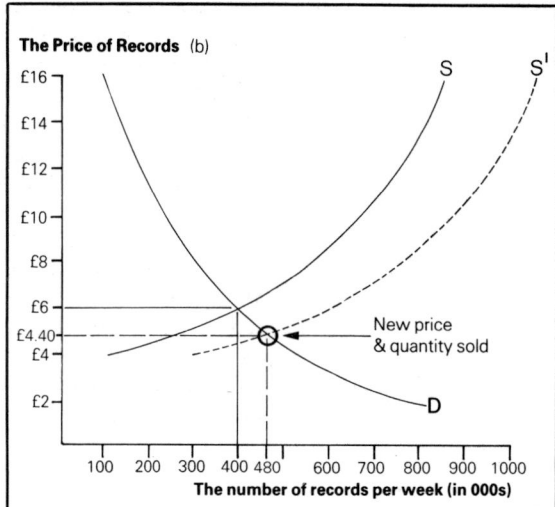

**Unit 1.2** *Demand, supply, markets and prices*

## DATABASE

## Average House Prices 1986

| | |
|---|---|
| United Kingdom | **£39,640** |
| Greater London | **£60,100** |
| South East | **£53,945** |
| East Anglia | **£40,180** |
| North | **£27,550** |
| Yorks & Humberside | **£27,320** |
| Scotland | **£33,740** |
| Wales | **£29,810** |
| North West | **£29,760** |
| East Midlands | **£30,880** |
| West Midlands | **£31,140** |
| South West | **£41,470** |
| Northern Ireland | **£28,350** |

(Source: Nationwide Building Society, 3rd quarter 1986)

Unit 1.2 Demand, supply, markets and prices

**ACTIVITIES**

## SECTION A: FOCUS ON UNIT 1.2

Go back and answer the questions raised in the Focus.

## SECTION B: STEPPED QUESTIONS

1. a Explain the meaning of:
   ▷ joint demand
   ▷ competitive demand.
   b List five pairs of products that are in:
   ▷ joint demand
   ▷ competitive demand.
   c ▷ Explain how the demand for and supply of Rover Group cars would be affected by goods which are in joint demand and competitive demand with them.
   ▷ Use demand and supply diagrams to illustrate your answer.
2. a The price of butter is affected by the prices of certain other goods such as margarine, milk and bread. How will a rise in the price of each good affect the demand for butter?
   b Use three separate demand and supply diagrams for butter to illustrate your answers to (a). Show the new equilibrium prices and quantities sold.
   c Use demand and supply diagrams to show the effect on the price and quantity sold of butter if a major health report comes out suggesting that butter can cause heart disease, while at the same time the price of milk purchased by butter producers rises.

## SECTION C: DATA RESPONSE QUESTIONS

**Figure 1.2h**
The diagram shows the market for Turbo chocolate bars before and after a successful advertising campaign for them.

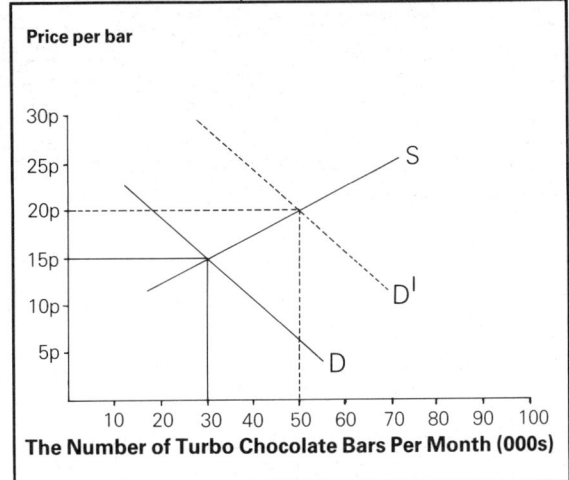

1 The Market for Turbo Chocolate Bars
   a ▷ What was the market price and quantity sold of Turbo chocolate bars before the advertising campaign?

▷ What was the total revenue received by the sellers before the advertising campaign? (Total revenue = price × quantity sold)
b ▷ What was the market price and quantity sold of Turbo chocolate bars after the advertising campaign?
▷ What was the total revenue received by the sellers after the advertising campaign?
c Name three other changes in the conditions of demand that could have caused the rise in demand.
d Sketch a demand and supply diagram to show what happens in the market for Turbo chocolate bars if there is a successful advertising campaign for a different, substitute brand of chocolate.

2

## New 4p tea rise, another increase brewing

BRITAIN'S biggest tea seller Brooke Bond yesterday slapped a 4p increase on packet tea prices, and said that another 4p rise may be only weeks away if auction prices continue to soar.

Tea prices in the shops have already risen by around 4p this week, in response to an earlier wholesale price increase announced by the tea companies early in December. The latest rise to around 42p for a 125 gram packet is expected to be seen in the shops within the next few weeks.

Other main tea sellers, including Cadbury-Schweppes (Typhoo) and Allied-Lyons (Tetley) said they would follow Brooke Bond's lead and put up the prices of their own popular brands. Tea bag prices are expected to rise by 11½ per cent, or 9p on a 500 gram box.

The sudden rise in the London auction price, which is a barometer of world demand, has been caused by the Indian government's decision on Christmas Day to ban the export of common grades of tea for at least three months in an effort to maintain supplies, and to hold down the price for its burgeoning population, which is consuming tea in record quantities.

India supplies 25 per cent of world demand. Brokers believe prices will reflect the fear of shortages and rise again at the weekly auction on Monday.

"If prices continue to rise, or even if they do not come down very much I cannot see how we can avoid another increase very shortly," a Brooke Bond spokesman said.

The latest rise means that tea in the shops will have increased in price by 20 per cent since November.

A spokesman for Sainsbury's, the supermarket firm, said that tea sales had been brisk, but the store had seen no evidence of panic buying by customers and there were no plans to ration supplies.

(From *The Guardian* 12.1.84)

a Why did India decide to ban the export of some common grades of tea?
b How much of the tea in the world is supplied by India?
c What was the effect of India's decision on tea sold in the UK? Quote one or two figures in your answer.
d What is 'panic buying', and what might Sainsbury's have done if there had been panic buying?
e Draw supply and demand diagrams to show the equilibrium price of tea before and after India decided to restrict the world supply of tea.
f Explain the main factors that would affect the demand and supply of tea.

## Elasticity

Elasticity is a measure of the extent to which something changes in response to a change in something else. **Price elasticity of demand** measures the responsiveness of the demand for a good to a change in the price of that good. **Price elasticity of supply** measures the responsiveness of the supply of a good to a change in the price of that good.

### Price elasticity of demand

Price elasticity of demand is calculated by the following formula:

Price elasticity of demand =

$$\frac{\% \text{ change in quantity demanded of good}}{\% \text{ change in the price of good}}$$

For example, the price of sweets rises by 10 per cent, and the quantity demanded falls by 20 per cent:

Price elasticity of demand = 20/10 = 2

**Figure 1.2i**

| Price of Sweets per 4oz bag (pence) | Quantity Demanded (4 oz bags per day) |
|---|---|
| 10 | 100 |
| 11 | 80 |

$$\frac{\frac{\text{Change in quantity}}{\text{Original quantity}}}{\frac{\text{Change in Price}}{\text{Original Price}}} = \frac{\frac{20}{100}}{\frac{1}{10}} = 2$$

If price elasticity of demand exceeds 1, it is **elastic**.

If price elasticity of demand equals 1, it is of **unit elasticity**.

If price elasticity of demand is less than 1, it is **inelastic**.

In the example of the sweets the price elasticity of demand is 2, and we would therefore say that demand is elastic; it is very responsive to a change in price.

If, however, the quantity demanded had fallen by only 5 per cent:

Price elasticity of demand = 5/10 = 0.5

Price elasticity of demand is 0.5, and we would therefore say that demand is inelastic; it is not very responsive to a change in price.

(N.B. price elasticity of demand will actually always be negative, because quantity demanded falls when price rises. The minus sign is usually left out.)

### The factors affecting price elasticity of demand

▶ **1 The availability of substitutes**

If a good has a close substitute available, people will switch to the substitute in large numbers if the price of the good changes. The good will therefore tend to have elastic demand. One brand of cigarettes is a close substitute for all other brands, and each brand of cigarettes is likely to have elastic demand. The total market demand for cigarettes is likely to be inelastic, however, as there are no close substitutes for cigarettes as a whole.

▶ **2 The percentage of income consumers spend on the good**

If a good is relatively cheap, even a large percentage price rise may seem of little consequence to consumers, and demand will tend to be inelastic. If matches rose in price by 50 per cent, for example, this would represent only a few pence a week to many consumers, and it is unlikely that demand would fall by 50 per cent. If cars went up by 50 per cent, however, the increase could be thousands of pounds for most consumers. Demand could well fall by over 50 per cent, other things being equal.

▶ **3 The durability of goods**

Goods which can be used more than once are called **durable goods**. They are likely to have more elastic demand than goods which you use up in the act of consumption. If car prices rise, for example, demand could fall heavily because people will choose to hang on to their old cars for a little longer. This option is not available in respect of **non-durable goods** such as food.

### Price elasticity of demand and total revenue

A firm's **total revenue** is the money it makes from selling its goods. It is found by multiplying the price of the good by the quantity sold. A firm that sells 100 goods at £10 each will have a total revenue of £1,000. The effects of a change in price on the total revenue of the firm depend on whether the demand for the good is elastic or inelastic.

Figure 1.2j shows what happens when the firm reduces the price by 10 per cent. There is an increase in demand of 5 per cent. Price elasticity of demand is therefore 0.5, and demand is inelastic. Total revenue at the new price is 105 × £9 = £945, so the firm has lost money by reducing the price.

## EXTENSION MATERIAL

**Figure 1.2j**
**Figure 1.2k**
The effect of changes in price on total revenue with different price elasticities of demand

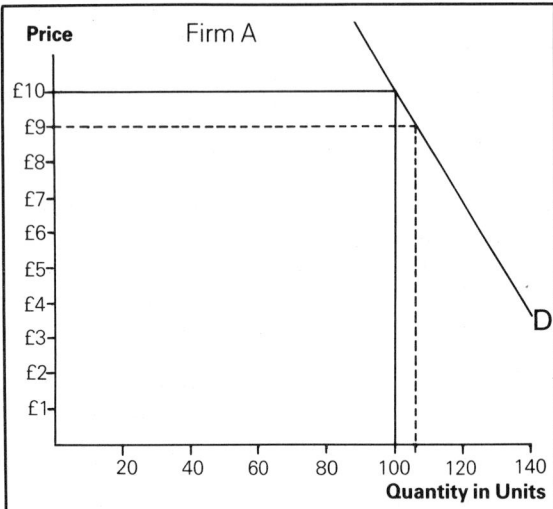

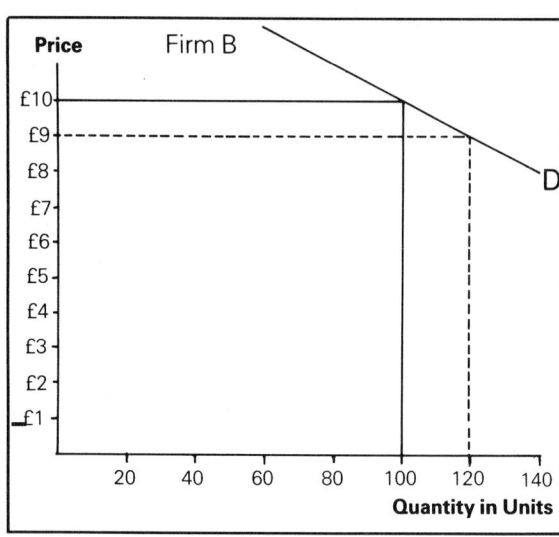

Figure 1.2k shows us what happens to a similar firm. It sells 100 goods at £10 each for a total revenue of £1,000. If it reduces the price by 10 per cent there is an increase in demand of 20 per cent. Price elasticity of demand is therefore 2, and demand is elastic. Total revenue at the new price is 120 × £9 = £1080, so this firm has gained revenue by reducing the price.

So, when demand is elastic, a decrease in price will increase total revenue, and an increase in price will decrease total revenue.

When demand is inelastic, a decrease in price will decrease total revenue, and an increase in price will increase total revenue.

These two examples show us that the concept of price elasticity of demand is vital if we are to understand what happens to the total revenue of a firm, or an industry, when prices change.

### Income elasticity of demand

Income elasticity of demand measures the way in which demand for a good changes as people's incomes change. Put more formally, it measures the responsiveness of changes in the demand for a good to changes in the income of consumers.

Income elasticity of demand is calculated by the following formula:

Income elasticity of demand =

$$\frac{\text{\% change in the demand for good X}}{\text{\% change in income}}$$

For normal goods like records, income elasticity of demand will be a positive figure. As people have more money to spend, they will tend to buy more records. For example, if consumers' incomes rise by 10 per cent, and the demand for records rises by 5 per cent as a result:

Income elasticity of demand = +5/+10 = +0.5

For inferior goods like potatoes, income elasticity of demand will be a negative figure. As people have more money to spend, they will tend to buy less potatoes and more higher-priced or luxury foods. For example, if consumers' incomes rise by 10 per cent, and the demand for potatoes falls by 5 per cent as a result:

Income elasticity of demand = −5/+10 = − 0.5

### Cross elasticity of demand

Cross elasticity of demand measures the way in which demand for a good changes as the price of another good changes. Put more formally, it measures the responsiveness of demand for a good to changes in the price of another good.

Cross elasticity of demand is calculated by the following formula:

Cross elasticity of demand =

$$\frac{\text{\% change in the demand for good X}}{\text{\% change in the price of good Y}}$$

For substitute goods like butter and margarine, cross elasticity of demand will be a positive figure. As the price of one rises, so the demand for it falls and demand for the other rises. For example, if the price of butter rises by 10 per cent, there will be a rise in the demand for margarine of 5 per cent as a result:

Cross elasticity of demand = +5/+10 = +0.5

For complementary goods like cars and tyres, cross elasticity of demand will be a negative

# Unit 1.2 Demand, supply, markets and prices

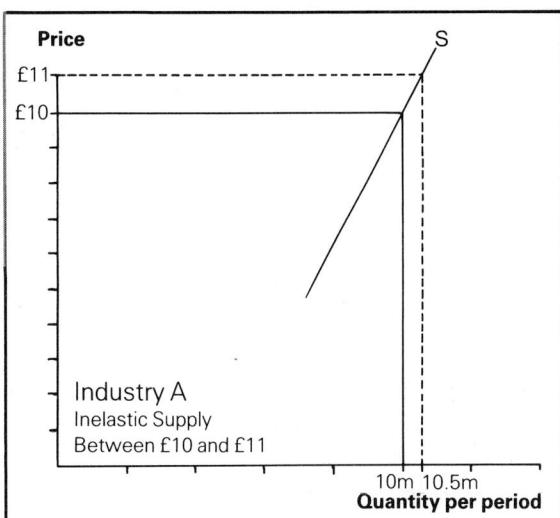

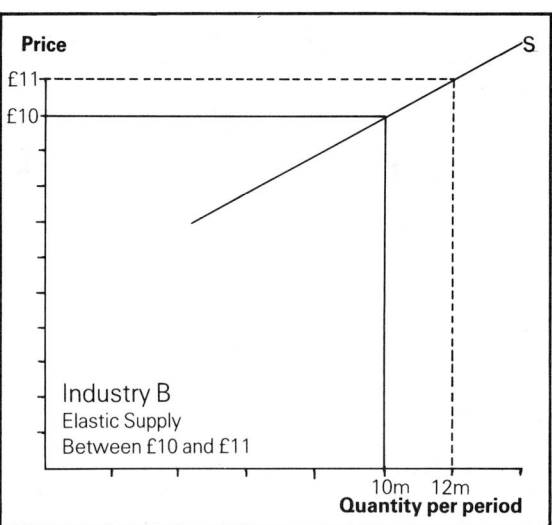

**Figure 1.2l**
**Figure 1.2m**
The effects of changes in price or quantity supplied in an industry with inelastic supply and in an industry with elastic supply

figure. As the price of cars increases, there will be a fall in the demand for cars, and therefore a fall in the demand for tyres. For example, if the price of cars rises by 10 per cent, there will be fall in the demand for tyres of 10 per cent as a result:

Cross elasticity of demand = −10/+10 = −1

**Price elasticity of supply**
Price elasticity of supply measures the responsiveness of the supply of a good to a change in the price of that good. It is a measure of the ability of a supplier to put more goods on the market when the price goes up.

Price elasticity of supply is calculated by the following formula:

Price elasticity of supply =

$$\frac{\% \text{ change in quantity supplied}}{\% \text{ change in the price}}$$

If price elasticity of supply exceeds 1, it is **elastic**.
If price elasticity of supply equals 1, it is of **unit elasticity**.
If price elasticity of supply is less than 1, it is **inelastic**.

For example, the price of steel bars rises by 10 per cent, but the quantity supplied increases by only 5 per cent:

Price elasticity of supply = 5/10 = 0.5

In this example the price elasticity of supply is 0.5, and we would therefore say that supply is inelastic; it is not very responsive to a change in price (see Fig. 1.2l).

If, however, the quantity supplied had increased by 20 per cent:

Price elasticity of supply = 20/10 = 2

Price elasticity of supply is 2 and we would therefore say that supply is elastic; it is very responsive to a change in price (see Fig 1.2m).

**The factors affecting price elasticity of supply**
▶ **1 The time period involved**
Over a very short time period the industry may be unable to raise production, and if the price rises they will have to rely on stocks of goods in shops and factories. If there are no stocks, supply will be completely inelastic (or **perfectly inelastic**). Over a longer period of time production can be increased and supply will become more elastic.

▶ **2 The availability of factors of production**
If the industry cannot easily obtain extra workers, raw materials and other resources when the price rises, then supply will tend to be inelastic. If they are readily available, however, supply will be more elastic.

▶ **3 The level of employment in the economy**
If there is a 'boom', then factors of production will be in short supply and supply for products will be more inelastic. If there is a 'slump', factors will be readily available and supply will tend to be more elastic. Obviously this point is related to the previous one, but it should be noted that individual industries can run short of vital factors of production even in a slump.

**EXTENSION QUESTION 7**

A market analyst working for a particular car manufacturer produces the following figures for estimated average monthly demand for its small hatchback model:

| PRICE(£) | AVERAGE MONTHLY DEMAND |
|---|---|
| 7,000 | 2,000 |
| 6,000 | 6,000 |
| 5,000 | 10,000 |
| 4,000 | 15,000 |

(a) What happens to customers' total spending on this make of small hatchback when the price rises from £5,000 to £6,000?
(b) What would an economist conclude about the price elasticity of demand for the price change in (a)? Check the answer by working out the price elasticity of demand.
(c) Would you expect the demand for small hatchbacks as a whole to be less or more price elastic than for one particular make? Give reasons for your answer.
(d) Would you expect the income elasticity of demand for small hatchbacks to be positive or negative? Explain your answer.
(e) Would you expect the cross elasticity of demand of small Ford hatchbacks with small Vauxhall hatchbacks to be positive or negative? Explain your answer.
(f) What other information might the car manufacturer require apart from the demand figures before deciding on a price?

# UNIT 1.3 Different types of economy

**FOCUS**

▶ What does **model economy** mean?

▶ What are the main features of a **free-market economy**?

▶ What are the main features of a **centrally-planned economy**?

▶ What are the benefits and disadvantages of these types of economy?

▶ What is a **mixed economy**?

The market mechanism is just one way in which scarce resources can be allocated to produce goods and services. There are very many ways in which countries can decide how to use their factors of production. To describe the economy of every country in the world would take far too long so economists usually refer to two imaginary, simplified **model economies**, the free-market economy and the centrally-planned economy. These two model economies are not the same as any real-world economies, but most real-world economies are partly like one and partly like the other.

## A free-market economy

In this model economy the allocation of resources is determined by the market mechanism, by the forces of demand and supply. The government plays no part in economic activity.

**The main features of a free-market economy**

▶ 1 Producers will provide those goods and services that are profitable and for which there is a demand.

▶ 2 Consumers can choose to buy whatever they can afford. We assume that consumers will try to maximise their total **satisfaction** or **utility**, i.e. they will spend their money in a way which gives greatest benefit to themselves.

▶ 3 People are able to buy or hire the factors of production so that they can become producers and supply the goods and services demanded by the market.

▶ 4 Changes in the demand for or the supply of goods result in changes in the price of the goods. Prices bring supply and demand into balance or equilibrium.

**Some possible benefits of a free-market economy**

▶ 1 People are able to choose to produce and consume whatever they can afford.

▶ 2 The price system makes sure that shortages and surpluses of goods and services do not last for long.

▶ 3 The price system does not need officials and civil servants to decide what should be produced. The government has no part to play in running the economy so there is less bureaucracy and 'red tape'.

▶ 4 People have a financial incentive to be productive. If they successfully produce what consumers wish to buy, they can become very rich.

**Some possible disadvantages and problems of a free-market economy**

▶ 1 It is not possible to produce some goods and services through the price system. For example, it would not be easy to charge prices for street lighting, roads or defence. Goods and services for which it is not practical to charge a price are called **public goods**.

Figure 1.3a
How does this illustrate a disadvantage of a model free-market economy?

▶ 2 People might choose to spend their money on goods and services giving short-term benefits, like videos and holidays, and choose not to spend on things like education and health which give longer-term benefits. Goods and services which a government considers are important to the welfare of the community but which may not be adequately provided through the price system are called **merit goods**.
▶ 3 With no government control on the economy, manufacturers would seek to maximise profits, and may pay little attention to whether they cause pollution (like smoke or smells from factories), whether their workers work in safe and healthy conditions and are paid good wages, and whether the goods and services they produce are of a good quality.
▶ 4 Small firms may be taken over by big firms until consumers have no choice about who they buy certain goods from. A model free-market economy can only work when there is **competition** between producers.
▶ 5 Some people could become very rich and powerful because of their success in business, while other people, especially the sick, the old and the unemployed would remain very poor. Economists call this situation an **unequal distribution of wealth**.

### The centrally-planned economy

In this model economy the allocation of resources is determined by the government. The forces of demand and supply play no part.

#### The main features of a centrally-planned economy
▶ 1 The state owns all of the factors of production and the government decides what to produce, and how to allocate that production.
▶ 2 The government will make a plan for production for, say, a five-year period on what it considers an appropriate use of resources. For example a government might decide to use many resources on hospitals and schools, and use very few resources producing pop records, fashionable clothing and television sets.
▶ 3 All workers are employed by the state.

#### Some possible benefits of a centrally-planned economy
▶ 1 Factors of production can be organised to produce public goods, and merit goods and services like education and health.
▶ 2 The distribution of wealth is more equal, because goods and services can be priced so that everyone can afford them, and because no individual can become very rich by making a profit.
▶ 3 Because the state owns all of the factors of production, any 'profit' can be re-distributed so that the people who contribute to the profit can benefit from it.
▶ 4 The government can make sure that factories do not cause pollution, and that people work in healthy and safe conditions.

#### Some possible disadvantages or problems of a centrally-planned economy
▶ 1 People cannot bring about the production of goods and services through demand.
▶ 2 Because there is no price system (prices are fixed by the government), shortages of some goods and surpluses of others could be a constant problem.
▶ 3 Because all 'profits' go to the state people may have little financial incentive to work efficiently and productively. As a result the quality of goods and services could be low.
▶ 4 The government may be out of touch with the wants and needs of people in factories and shops, and there could be long delays and inefficiency in providing goods and services.

**Figure 1.3b**
How does this illustrate a disadvantage of a model centrally-planned economy?

### A mixed economy

A mixed economy is a mixture of a free-market economy and a centrally-planned economy. Individual people create demand and so determine some of the goods and services that are produced by the way that they spend their money. The government determines other goods and services that are produced.

In the UK, which is a mixed economy, consumers determine the production of goods and services like clothing, restaurant meals and home computers by the way in which they choose to spend their money on them. All these goods are sold through the market mechanism.

**Figure 1.3c**
How does this show that a mixed economy is like a free-market economy in some ways, but more like a centrally-planned economy in others?

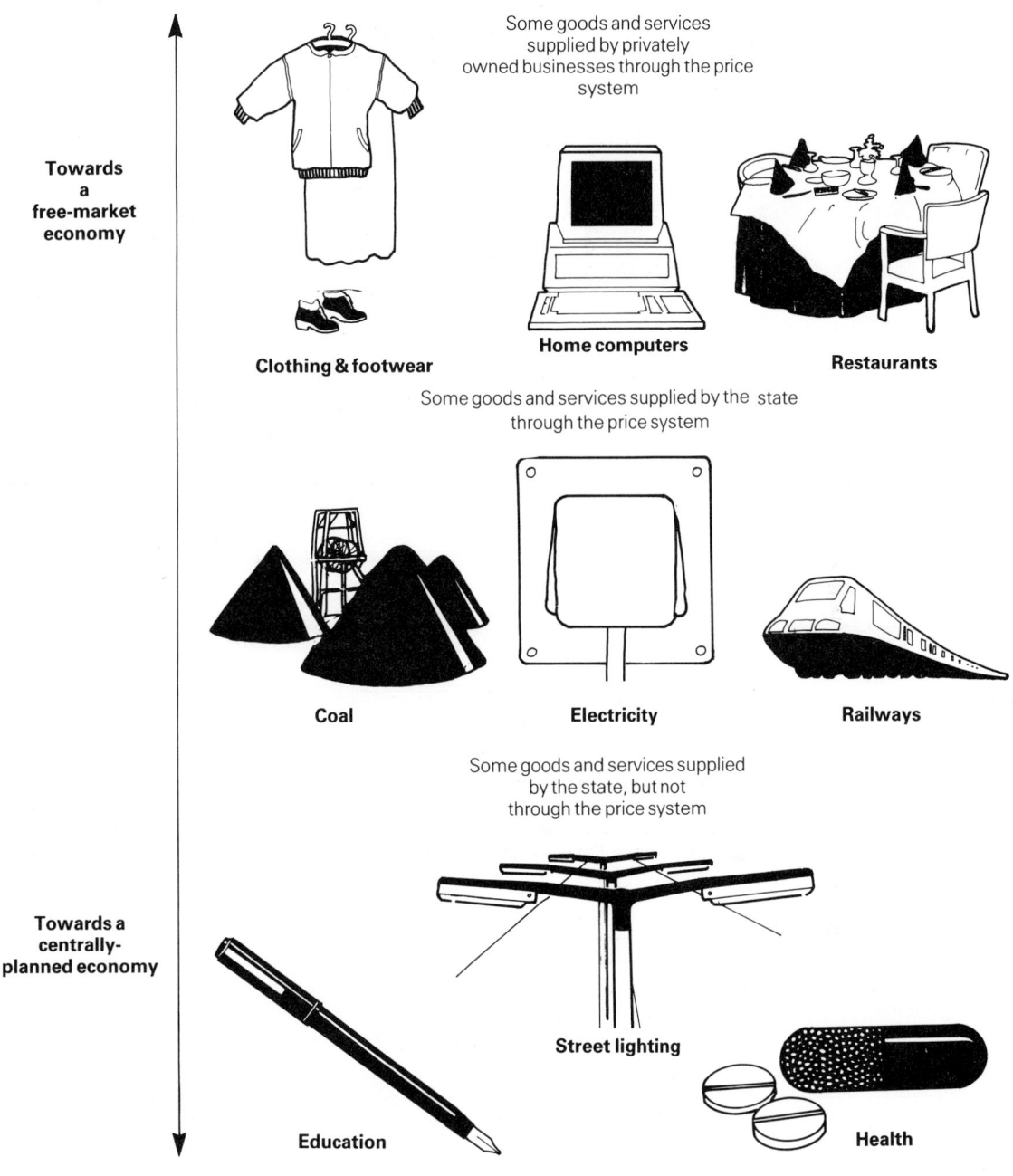

The government determines the production of some merit goods like education and health and some public goods like street lighting and defence. People do not have to pay a 'price' for them, but they have to pay for them out of general taxation. Some goods and services are provided by the government but through the market mechanism. Examples of these are coal, railways and electricity. All goods and services provided through the market mechanism, whether by the government or by private firms, are called **private goods**.

Most economies are mixed economies, but some are nearer free-market economies and others are nearer centrally-planned economies. The USA government provides fewer goods and services than the government in the UK, and its economy is more like a free-market economy. In the USSR, however, the government produces nearly everything, and the USSR is said to have a centrally-planned economy.

## DATABASE

## 1. Comecon in the world

**Population (% of world total – 4.7bn in 1983)**

COMECON: Soviet Union 6% | other COMECON 4% — 10%

EEC: 6%

United States: 5%

Japan: 3%

These are the member countries of Comecon:

SOVIET UNION
BULGARIA
CUBA
CZECHOSLOVAKIA
EAST GERMANY
HUNGARY
MONGOLIA
POLAND
ROMANIA
VIETNAM

**Exports**

COMECON*: $47bn (of which Soviet Union $29bn)

EEC*: $275bn

United States: $200bn

Japan: $147bn

*Excluding intra-group trade

NOTE: Comecon is the Council for Mutual Economic Assistance.

## DATABASE

## 2. Growth of national production
(average annual percentage charge)

|  | 1971–80 | 1981–85 |
|---|---|---|
| Eastern Europe | 5.7 | 2.4 |
| USSR | 4.9 | 3.8 |

|  | 1970–79 | 1981–85 |
|---|---|---|
| UK | 2.2 | 1.7 |
| USA | 2.4 | 2.3 |
| Japan | 5.4 | 3.9 |
| France | 3.9 | 1.2 |
| W. Germany | 2.9 | 1.1 |

Sources: *The Economist*, 20.4.85 for Comecon Countries
*Barclays' Review* May 1986 for others.

NOTE: The table shows the net material product for the USSR and Eastern Europe, and GDP for the other countries.

**ACTIVITIES**

## SECTION A: FOCUS ON UNIT 1.3

Go back and answer the questions raised in the Focus.

## SECTION B: STEPPED QUESTIONS

1 **a** Give examples of an economy which is most like:
   ▷ a free-market economy
   ▷ a centrally-planned economy
   ▷ a mixed economy.
   **b** Describe how resources are allocated in a free-market economy compared to a centrally-planned economy.
   **c** Economists who would like to see the UK move further towards a free-market economy criticise the mixed economy by saying that the large size of the government-owned part of the economy brings with it the disadvantages of a planned economy. Explain this view, and say whether you think that it is justified. Give reasons for your point of view.

2 **a** What are:
   ▷ private goods
   ▷ public goods
   ▷ merit goods?
   **b** The market mechanism can only provide private goods. What would be the effects of only private goods being available?
   **c** ▷ In what ways does the government restrict people's ability to earn high salaries and make profits in mixed economies like the UK?
   ▷ Is the government justified in doing this? Explain your answer.

# SECTION C: DATA RESPONSE QUESTION

## Streetwise Mikhail

Russia now faces an economic crisis. A major problem is that production has been concentrated in making things that most advanced countries no longer make.

The Russian leader, Mikhail Gorbachev, has decided that drastic change is necessary. He has to find something, call it what he likes, which can do for the Soviet economy what the market does under capitalism: create a link between what people want to buy and the most efficient means of producing it. That will involve a radical change of the pricing system. Until now the central planners have fixed prices of raw materials, goods and services without fully taking into account forces of demand and supply.

Mr Gorbachev will not abandon price-fixing entirely, since he will not want to change the basic economic system of central planning. However, a far wider range of prices will have to be allowed to be set by what the market wants. To make sure that happens, party officials will have to be stopped from interfering with business decisions.

Many of the Communist Party will fight the loss of power and privilege that management by the market will mean. Workers at the bottom of the new pay scales with greater differences in pay will resent the success of smarter colleagues working their way up. With so many problems the question is whether Mikhail Gorbachev is streetwise enough to make such changes within the existing system.

**Adapted from** *The Economist* **26.7.86**

a Describe the main economic problems faced by the Soviet Union according to the article.
b Write out the phrase in the article which means 'matching the wants of consumers and producers'.
c What disadvantages of the centrally-planned economy does the article suggest?
d Why will it be difficult to bring about the changes that the article suggests are necessary?
e What disadvantages might arise from reducing state control over the decisions of businesses and consumers?

## PART 1: COURSEWORK SUGGESTION

### A DEMAND SURVEY

1. Conduct a survey among at least ten people to find out how many long-playing records they would purchase each month over a range of prices.
2. Use the same survey to find out what other factors affect the number of long-playing records that the people buy.
3. Carefully record your findings in tables and by drawing a demand curve.
4. Using your data write a report to a record company explaining what is likely to happen to their total revenue if they charge different prices for long-playing records. Advise them what measures they could take to increase sales of their records. Use graphs, charts, tables etc. extensively in your report.

### EXTENSION COURSEWORK

5. Calculate the price elasticity of demand for the different price levels along the demand curve. Use your answers in the first part of your report to the record company.

---

In this chapter we have introduced a number of new words and phrases that are often used in the discussion of economics, and that we will continue to use throughout this book. We have listed these words below so that you can start your own Dictionary of Economic Terms. If you write a short definition of each term in your own words, you will find this a useful revision aid when you come to your exam.

allocation of resources
capital goods
centrally planned economy
competitive demand
complements
conditions of demand/supply
consumer goods
consumption
contractions in demand/supply
demand
distribution of wealth
economic goods
economic resources
extensions in demand/supply
factors of production: land, labour, capital, enterprise

free goods
free market economy
inferior goods
joint demand
margin
market
market mechanism
market (equilibrium) price
merit goods
mixed economy
private goods
public goods
supply
opportunity cost
scarcity
substitutes

### EXTENSION MATERIAL
cross elasticity of demand
income elasticity of demand
price elasticity of demand
price elasticity of supply

# Part 2
## Work

# UNIT 2.1 Why and how people work

**FOCUS**
- ▶ Why do people want to work?
- ▶ What is the **division of labour**?
- ▶ Why do people specialise at work?
- ▶ How is work different in different industries?

## The reasons for working

In modern Britain people tend to be very clearly **employed** or **unemployed**. In Britain in the past this difference was by no means so clear, and in many countries throughout the world today, millions of people work in farming, in small cottage industries (where manufacturing takes place at home), and in other sorts of work based on the family unit. In these circumstances the available work is shared out within the family rather than some people working and some remaining unemployed. In modern economies most people are employees: they work for someone else rather than for themselves or their families. If employers wish to reduce their labour force, then they tend to make people redundant rather than share out the available work.

In Britain most adults can make a clear choice between taking paid employment or remaining out of paid work. There are several reasons why people may prefer to take a paid job:

### ▶ 1 People in paid employment enjoy higher living standards

In Britain the social security system gives cash benefits to people in need, and this would include most adults who are not in employment. People who have paid jobs tend to enjoy a much higher living standard in terms of the goods and services they have available to them than would be the case if they were unemployed. Very few people actually choose to remain unemployed.

### ▶ 2 People work for social reasons

In recent years there has been an increasing proportion of married women taking up part-time and full-time paid employment. Undoubtedly they do this to increase their standard of living. However they also work to get out of the house and make new friends. It also reduces the extent to which they need to rely on their husbands financially. Many women consider that housework, because it is unpaid employment, is not held in sufficient regard and that it offers insufficient job satisfaction.

### ▶ 3 People work because they enjoy their jobs

Many people are fortunate to have interesting employment. Businesswomen and men, for example, often enjoy the challenge of building up their businesses and trying to increase profits. People can enjoy manufacturing goods or providing a service for others. Jobs tend to become more enjoyable when, for example, they are varied, challenging, require skill, and allow people to take individual responsibility for what they do.

### ▶ 4 People work for status

The way in which other people look at you depends to a large extent on the job that you do. We probably regard someone more highly if they are a doctor than if they are a road sweeper, however unfair that is to the people concerned. A major problem of unemployment is said to be the loss of self-esteem that people feel when they are labelled as 'unemployed'. It is interesting that jobs enjoy different status in different countries: in the Soviet Union, for example, doctors have lower status than they do in Britain.

## The division of labour

When workers specialise in doing one job, or part of a job, this is called the **division of labour**. In a country like the UK in the 1980s, nearly everyone who works specialises. Many people never use the goods and services they produce. For example, non-smokers who work in a cigarette factory will never use what they are making. Some people specialise so much that they never make a whole product, they just make a small part of it. This happens especially when goods are made on a production line. On a production line (or assembly line) the workers stay in one place, and they do their bit of the work as the product moves past them, usually on a conveyor belt.

For example, on a production line in a car factory one person may put on wheels, while another puts in windscreens.

**Figure 2.1a**
What examples of the division of labour can be found in a car factory?

The division of labour has many advantages, but also some disadvantages. The lists below give some of them.

### The advantages of the division of labour

▶ **1 People become faster or more skilled at what they are doing**
An experienced typist, for example, may type at more than 60 words per minute, and make few errors.

▶ **2 Specialisation leads to the production of many more goods and services**
When cars were built by hand with each worker using a variety of skills, relatively few could be produced. Modern car factories, which are organised on the basis of huge production lines, where each worker concentrates on one task, can produce well over half a million cars a year.

▶ **3 Specialised, more efficient machinery can be employed**
Large-scale production makes the fullest and most efficient use of machinery and equipment, and allows the use of specialist machinery that would not be economic if production took place on a smaller scale. The cost per unit of production usually falls when production increases. (There are several reasons for this which are explained in Units 6.1 and 6.5.) In a big office, for example, a word processor can be employed because it will be in use constantly. A small office might made do with a typewriter because the amount and variety of work would not justify the expense of a word processor. Specialised machinery and equipment may be expensive at first but save money in the long-run.

▶ **4 If goods are cheaper to produce they can be sold at low prices**
The cost of production is one of the main factors affecting the supply of goods. If costs fall the supply curve moves to the right and prices come down. Simple products which can be produced in huge numbers, like some ball-point pens, can be sold for a few pence each.

▶ **5 If people do only one job they waste no time moving around**
In a well-organised workplace, if people do only one task, there will be less waste of tools and time. The greater the degree of specialisation, the less time people will spend moving around and therefore not producing. The worker doing a variety of tasks will have to use a variety of tools, and many tools will be idle for most of the time.

▶ **6 People can be employed in the jobs to which they are more suited**
This applies equally to people who already have a particular skill or profession. For example, a solicitor can specialise in a particular aspect of law.

### The disadvantages of the division of labour

▶ **1 Workers can become bored**
The division of labour can mean that people do the same jobs, day in, day out. This can lead to poor quality work because people lose interest. Mistakes can happen when people take no pride in their work.

▶ **2 Goods and services may lack variety**
The division of labour can lead to large outputs of more or less identical products. For example,

**Figure 2.1b**
What jobs would we have to do ourselves without the division of labour?

in restaurants owned by large hamburger producers there would be little variety in what was sold from restaurant to restaurant. Customers could not necessarily ask for special menus to be prepared.

▶ **3 If one or a small group of people stop work it could hold up everyone**
With the division of labour, everyone depends on everyone else. A record factory relies on supplies from a plastics factory. If the plastics factory supplies a faulty batch or has a machine breakdown, then this could halt production in the record factory.

▶ **4 The danger of unemployment**
Workers who have been trained in only one skill may find it difficult to get another job if the demand for that kind of labour falls.

**The limitations of the division of labour**
Division of labour has no use, or only limited use, in some circumstances. These are as follows:

▶ **1 The division of labour is limited by size of the market**
A firm producing high quality, expensive jewellery would produce a relatively small output, because there would be a small market.

▶ **2 The division of labour is limited by the nature of the produce or process involved**
For example, a best-selling novelist, even if he or she had a huge market, would be unable to divide the task of writing a book into a number of tasks that could be shared out between a number of different people. There is limited scope for specialisation in the process of writing a novel.

▶ **3 The division of labour is limited by the amount of labour available**
When factories developed in Britain in the eighteenth and nineteenth centuries large labour forces were needed to enable the principle of the division of labour to be used extensively. Workers were drawn from agriculture to provide this labour, and without it the division of labour would have been limited.

▶ **4 The division of labour is limited by the extent to which money is used in exchange**
If money did not exist, people who specialised would have to **barter** the goods and services they produced for the goods and services they needed. The problems with barter are dealt with in Unit 3.1.

▶ **5 The division of labour requires transport**
If people are to produce for other people to consume, there must be transport to take the goods from producers to consumers, as the consumers may be distributed over a very wide area.

Because of the division of labour we can buy a large number of different goods and services and we can work in a variety of different jobs. Some of the most boring jobs created by the division of labour, particularly those found on factory production lines, are rapidly disappearing as machines and robots take over. People will have to find work providing services rather than making goods. The amount of work that is available could fall. People may either have to accept longer periods of unemployment, or share work, or work shorter hours.

**Unit 2.1** *Why and how people work*

## Work in different industries

The work that people do depends to some extent on the industry in which they are working. As there are a large number of different industries economists tend to group them together for convenience under three headings. The first group of industries are called **primary industries** and they are concerned with the extraction of raw materials. They include mining, agriculture, fishing and farming. In **secondary industries** something is manufactured from the goods produced by the primary industries, or by other secondary industries. They include furniture, vehicles, and food processing (canning, freezing, etc.). **Tertiary industries** provide services to the general public, the government and to other industries. They include banking, window cleaning, transport and restaurants.

**Figure 2.1d**
Which type of industry is shown in each of the pictures?

### Work in the primary industries

Work in the primary industries is often outdoors or underground, for example in coal mining or North Sea oil extraction. Such work can be dangerous and therefore rates of pay can be high. Much of the work is unskilled and needs little if any training. The use of more and more sophisticated machinery has increased the level of skill, and many jobs would now be classed as semi-skilled. In fact many jobs are being lost as a result of mechanisation. Modern coal cutting equipment in mining and combine harvesters in farming have greatly reduced the number of unskilled and semi-skilled jobs in the coal and agriculture industries.

### Work in the secondary industries

Work in secondary industries is usually indoors, in factories and workshops. Much of the work is simple and repetitive, for example, on production lines. It can involve doing the same small task over and over again. For this reason many of the jobs require little training and few, if any, qualifications. Such work tends to be poorly paid and increasingly done by machines and robots. As machines take over the direct production of the goods so more and more people in secondary industries are employed in providing services. In a modern factory more people may be employed in administration, catering, cleaning and security, for example, than will be employed on a production line.

### Work in the tertiary industries

There is a great variety of work in the tertiary sector, the only sector which in the 1980s is growing in terms of employment. Jobs range from typists to professional sports people, from waiters to doctors. Some tertiary workers like cleaners, waiters and waitresses require little training and are very poorly paid. Some tertiary sector jobs require long training and many academic qualifications, and they may be very well paid. Chartered accountants, for example, train for many years and they can expect high salaries when they qualify.

## DATABASE

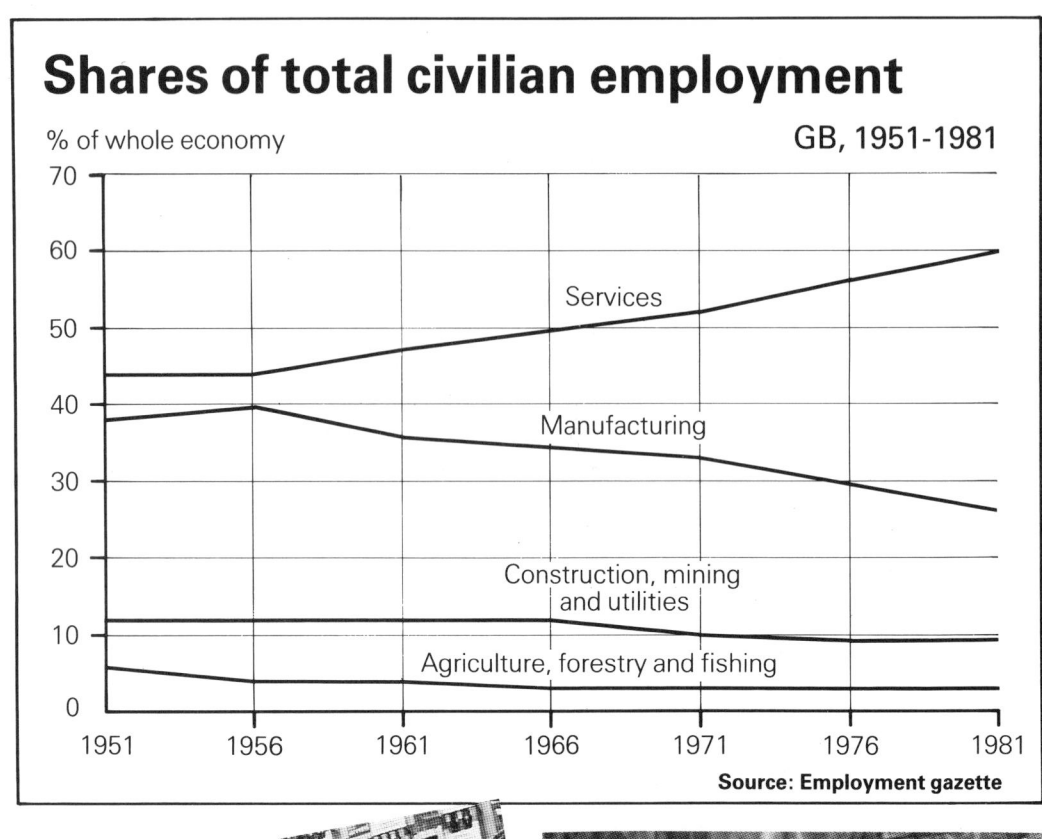

**Shares of total civilian employment**

% of whole economy  
GB, 1951-1981

- Services
- Manufacturing
- Construction, mining and utilities
- Agriculture, forestry and fishing

Source: Employment gazette

**Unit 2.1** *Why and how people work*

## ACTIVITIES

### SECTION A: FOCUS ON UNIT 2.1

Go back and answer the questions raised in the Focus.

### SECTION B: STEPPED QUESTIONS

1. **a** Make a list of TEN jobs created by the production of record players. Here are some examples of the areas in which workers might be involved:
   ▷ building and running the factory
   ▷ providing the materials needed
   ▷ selling and promoting the record player
   ▷ the production, sale and promotion of records.
   **b** Draw three columns headed 'Primary', 'Secondary' and 'Tertiary' and put the jobs you have listed in (a) into the correct columns.
   **c** Explain what you think would be the effects on (i) firms, (ii) workers, (iii) consumers, if record player manufacturers gave up the division of labour, with each worker producing the whole record player.

2. **a** ▷ List five products you think would be unsuitable for the division of labour.
   ▷ Explain why you think they would be unsuitable.
   **b** If you had a free choice of which job to do, what kind of job would you choose and which aspects of the job would influence your choice?
   **c** In a town in the north east recently some people were offered jobs for about the same money as their unemployment benefit. All the jobs were taken up. How can you explain this?

## SECTION C: DATA RESPONSE QUESTION

### The Mass Production of Cars

Henry Ford introduced motoring for the population at large. Before he began mass producing Model T cars, motoring was an activity enjoyed only by the very rich. Ford believed that the way to make motoring accessible to all was by producing cars that were all identical, "just like one pin is like another pin when it comes from the pin factory ... When you get to making the cars in quantity, you can make them cheaper, and when you make them cheaper you can get people with enough money to buy them".

Ford launched his famous Model T in 1908. Prices quickly fell as output rose from 20,000 in 1910 to 200,000 in 1913. The car cost $850 in 1909 and only $440 in 1915. Production of the Model T continued until 1927 by which time 15 million had been produced.

Ford's cars were manufactured on a production line. Workers no longer moved around from job to job but they remained in one place while the car in its various stages moved slowly past them. Each worker had a very specific task to do like fitting a wheel onto the car or bolting down a seat. This production method led to an enormous fall in the number of man-hours needed to make a car.

**a** How many Model T Fords were made between 1908 and 1927?
**b** Why did Henry Ford think people would buy these cars?
**c** ▷ Describe what happened to prices of the Model T between 1909 and 1915 and output between 1910 and 1913.
  ▷ Using your knowledge of economics and the division of labour, explain the reasons for the trend.
**d** What would have been the likely effects of the introduction of mass production methods in the vehicle industry on (i) firms, (ii) consumers and (iii) workers?

# UNIT 2.2 Finding work and training for work

**FOCUS**
- ▶ How can people find work?
- ▶ In what different ways can people train for work?

## Finding work

Most adults will attempt to find paid employment at some time during their lives. Unfortunately they may have little choice about which job they accept. Those who have a choice will need to consider carefully what academic and personal qualities will be required in different jobs. Academic qualifications include all paper qualifications such as GCSE examination certificates. Personal qualities include such things as health, self-confidence, appearance, punctuality and reliability. They will also need to consider what features of a job might be important to them such as rates of pay, hours, holidays and opportunities for training, promotion, and taking individual responsibility.

There are various ways of finding paid employment. To find a job someone may need to try many of them. The section that follows looks mainly at the various services available to help school leavers find work.

### ▶ 1 Friends and relatives

This is the way in which many school leavers find work. Often employers will consider someone in a particular family if they are already satisfied with a member of the family that they already employ.

### ▶ 2 The school or college careers teacher

Here are some of the ways in which the schools and college careers services assist young people looking for work:

▷ **a** They interview young people to assess their strengths and weaknesses, and what work might be available for them. They tell them what training and qualifications they require.

▷ **b** The careers teacher will have many books, magazines and pamphlets giving information about jobs. These may be kept in a special careers room.

▷ **c** Visits to careers fairs, films about employment, and visiting speakers may be arranged by careers teachers.

▷ **d** Careers teachers may give help with filling in application forms and preparing for interviews.

### ▶ 3 The careers service

This will be run by the local authority. It provides the same kind of help as the school or college careers teacher, but the people in the careers service spend their whole time on careers matters concerning young people.

▷ **a** They help schools organise their own careers departments.

▷ **b** They have plenty of up-to-date information on careers.

▷ **c** They organise talks by experts from industry. They also organise careers conventions and exhibitions, visits to employers, and so on.

▷ **d** They interview young people on their own, in groups, and with their parents.

▷ **e** They can arrange places on the Youth Training Scheme (see below).

The careers service offers help and assistance to employers, as well as to young people looking for a job. It does the following for employers:

▷ **a** It provides information on the law affecting the employment of young people.

▷ **b** It helps with recruitment procedures including the preparation of selection tests and the distribution of publicity material and application forms.

▷ **c** It gives advice on interviewing arrangements and suggestions on interviewing techniques.

▷ **d** It provides private interviewing facilities at careers offices.

▷ **e** It helps and advises on schemes of induction and training for young workers.

### ▶ 4 Jobcentres

You will find Jobcentres in the middle of many busy high streets. They are run by a department of the Government called the **Manpower Services Commission** (MSC). Inside the Jobcentre you will find lots of jobs displayed on boards. If you want to know more about any of them, you go to the desk and ask about it. If you are suitable for the job, you will be given the name and address of the employer, and an interview will be fixed up for you.

### ▶ 5 Professional and Executive Recruitment

Highly qualified people can take advantage of a special scheme called Professional and Executive Recruitment when they are looking for employment. If you have A-levels or higher qualifications, PER may be able to find you work in areas that require high qualifications.

PER can be contacted through some of the larger Jobcentres, or at their own offices.

### ▶ 6 Private employment agencies

An **agency** is an organisation that works for someone else. Private employment agencies work for firms who are looking for people to employ. Unlike the Jobcentres, they charge the employer when they have found someone to fill the job. In most other ways they are similar to Jobcentres. Jobs are often displayed on cards, and there is someone there to help you when you want it. There are many private employment agencies. One of the most famous is the Brook Street Bureau.

### ▶ 7 Newspapers and the radio

Newspapers, magazines, radio and TV are sometimes called the **mass media**, and the mass media is often a way of finding a job. Local newspapers, including the free papers that often fall through letter boxes, contain many jobs near where you live. You can also find out about jobs through local radio stations.

### ▶ 8 Writing directly to employers

Some people get jobs by sending a letter to an employer telling them something about themselves. A letter should be carefully written and it should contain full details about yourself, and why you want the job.

## Training for work

When you learn the things necessary to do a particular job you are said to be **training**. Training courses, and courses aimed specifically at preparing someone for the world of work, are often called **vocational** courses. On such courses, you may be taught the skills you need for a specific job, or for the world of work in general.

### ▶ 1 Vocational education in schools

Most education in schools is general education. This means that you are learning things that could be useful at work, but they are not related specifically to the world of work. The things you learn in mathematics, for example, are equally useful to a nurse measuring medicine doses, or to an engineer working on the precise measurements for a new bridge. Languages are useful for firms selling abroad.

Courses preparing pupils for the world of work in general, or for specific occupational areas, are becoming more common all the time in schools. In 1982 the Government launched the **Technical and Vocational Education Initiative** (TVEI) aimed at developing vocational education for fourteen to eighteen year olds.

From 1986 many schools started to run **Certificate in Pre-Vocational Education** (CPVE) courses which are designed to provide a general introduction to the world of work. These courses include some work experience, and often school students attend a local college for part of the course.

### ▶ 2 Training at college

There are an enormous number of training and general vocational courses offered at colleges. Most of these could be put in one of three groups:

▷ **a** *Pre-vocational courses* Many colleges now do courses, usually lasting for one year, which are designed to teach you the basic skills expected in a number of jobs, often in a particular industry. For example, many colleges now run courses leading to a **City and Guilds of London Institute** (CGLI) qualification in areas like Engineering, Commercial Studies and Information Technology. Many colleges also offer CPVE courses. After a pre-vocational course you can either try to find a job, or go on to a higher level course.

▷ **b** *Vocational courses leading to qualifications for specific jobs* Colleges offer a large number of courses leading to diplomas, certificates, degrees and other qualifications which will make you fully or partly qualified to take up a job in a particular industry. The **Business and Technician Education Council** (BTEC) course in Electrical and Electronic Engineering is one example.

**Figure 2.2a**
In what sense is a Jobcentre a 'market' for labour?

*Unit 2.2 Finding work and training for work*

▷ **c** *General courses* Colleges offer a large number of courses which are not aimed at particular jobs, but which continue teaching you general skills that could be useful in many jobs. These courses may allow you to go on with a school subject, or try something quite new. Many colleges offer you the opportunity, for example, to try for GCSE and A-levels in subjects that you cannot take at school.

There are several ways in which you can study at colleges:

▷ **a** *Evening classes* Many courses can be taken in the evening, and these are filled mainly by people with full-time jobs during the day.

▷ **b** *Day release* Employers often give workers one day off each week to study at a local college.

▷ **c** *Block release and sandwich courses* These are courses which allow you periods off work to study, or they allow you periods away from college for work experience. Foreign language courses, for example, often involve the student going abroad for a year to work in the country whose language he or she is learning.

▷ **d** *Full-time courses* These are courses where you spend all of your time at college, with no work experience element.

▶ **3 Training at work**

If you get a job when you leave school, the chances are that you will receive some training at work. The training may involve working alongside an experienced worker, and learning as you do the job. If you work for a big firm, they may have their own training section. Training at work is called **on-the-job training**. Many firms send young workers on day release or block release courses (see above). Training received away from your place of work is called **off-the-job training**. An **apprenticeship** is when a firm undertakes long-term training for a specific trade or skill, for example as a motor mechanic.

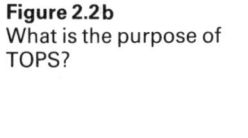

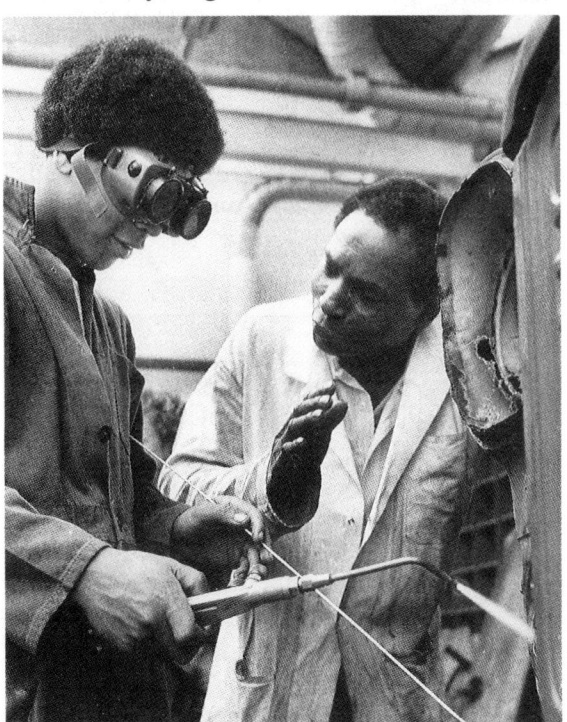

▶ **4 The Youth Training Scheme (YTS)**

This scheme started in 1983, and it is run by the Manpower Services Commission through managing agents such as employers, local authorities, voluntary organisations, colleges of further education and training organisations. From 1986 it was open to all 16-year-old school leavers as a two-year course and to all 17-year-olds and a few older students as a one-year course. The YTS aims to link training with work experience leading to a vocational qualification.

All trainees on the two-year programme must have 20 weeks off-the-job training. From April 1986, trainees on the two-year programme were paid £27.30 in their first year, and £35 a week in their second year, without deductions. Those on one-year programmes received the lower rate for the first 13 weeks and the higher rate for the rest of the time. Lodgings and travelling expenses were also payable.

Trainees receive a YTS certificate which includes information about their training and what they have actually achieved during it. It also lists any additional qualifications that they may have received during the one or two years.

▶ **5 The Training Opportunities Programme (TOPS)**

This scheme is organised by the Manpower Services Commission, and it is mainly for people over the age of 18. Trainees take courses that can last from a few weeks to a year. The courses take place at special **Skillcentres**, and at some colleges and places of work. Trainees receive an allowance. There are courses in many occupations like plumbing and clerical work. Courses are very practical and they are mainly for retraining people who have worked before.

▶ **6 Industrial Training Boards**

In the 1964 Industrial Training Act, 24 industrial training boards and six non-industrial training boards were set up to organise training in their industries. The boards are financed by payments from the firms in their industry, as well as by the government. At present, following government spending cuts, there are only seven boards left of which the Construction Training Board and the Hotel and Catering Training Board are two examples.

Industrial training boards are responsible for organising and promoting the training within their industry. They help to set up college courses, and training courses at work. They provide grants, and give general advice about training to the firms in their industry.

**Figure 2.2b**
What is the purpose of TOPS?

## DATABASE

### YTS
High-quality training and planned work experience for school leavers.
**OPEN TO** – 16 and 17-year-old school leavers, including those who are employees, with a higher age limit in certain cases. There are special arrangements for disabled young people and some others. Employers and other suitable groups can provide training or work experience.
**CONTACT** – Your local Careers Office, Jobcentre or (for employers) MSC Training Division Area Office.

### Job Training Scheme
Training for unemployed adults who wish to add to or learn new skills.
**OPEN TO** people who are over 18, unemployed and who have been away from full-time education for at least two years.
**CONTACT** – your local Jobcentre.

### Training for Enterprise
Full- or part-time training for the business owner or manager.
**OPEN TO** – suitable employed, self-employed or unemployed people over 18.
**CONTACT** MSC Training Division Area Offices.

### Training Grants for Employers
A wide range of practical and financial help for training employees and new recruits.
**OPEN TO** – employers.
**CONTACT** – your local Jobcentre or MSC Training Division Area Office.

### Access to Information Technology
Evening or weekend training to provide an introduction to Information Technoilogy.
**OPEN TO** – employed, self-employed or unemployed people.
**CONTACT** – your local Jobcentre.

### Wider Opportunities Training Programme
A wide range of training to help adults get back into work.
**OPEN TO** – unemployed people and Community Programme participants.
**CONTACT** – your local Jobcentre.

### Open Tech Programme
Improved access to training, especially for those at technician and supervisory levels.
**OPEN TO** – employers, employed and unemployed.
**CONTACT** – Open Tech Directory available at your local Jobcentre, public library or MSC Training Division Area Office.

### Career Development Loans
Pilot scheme offering loans for training or vocational education courses in four areas.
**OPEN TO** – people over 18 living in or intending to train in Aberdeen, Bristol/Bath, Greater Manchester or Reading/Slough.
**CONTACT** – Jobcentres in the pilot areas.

Source: *Action for Jobs*, Department of Employment, 1986.

## ACTIVITIES

### SECTION A: FOCUS ON UNIT 2.2

Go back and answer the questions raised in the Focus.

### SECTION B: STEPPED QUESTIONS

1. **a** What is meant by 'vocational courses'?
   **b** Give examples of such courses:
   - in schools
   - in colleges
   - at work
   - for people who want to retrain for another skill.
   
   (Use the Database to help you.)
   
   **c** What would be the economic effects on firms, workers and consumers of governments spending less on vocational courses?

2. **a** Why will you not have a completely free choice in deciding on a job when you leave school?
   **b** What factors will determine the type of job you will be able to obtain?
   **c** How might you go about making sure that you have as wide a choice of jobs as possible?

## SECTION C: DATA RESPONSE QUESTION

# £1bn drive launched to train youth for jobs

### By David Felton
### Labour Correspondent

The Government last night approved a £1,000 million two-year Youth Training Scheme which will give an extended period of training to school leavers and is planned to result in a new system of job qualifications.

Mr Tom King, Secretary of State for Employment, who outlined the scheme in the Commons yesterday, said that extra funds will be made available to encourage schemes in deprived areas such as Merseyside and the North-east.

The two-year scheme, which can accommodate up to 550,000 young people a year replaces the present YTS which has a maximum intake of 350,000. Mr King also announced that the £26.25 weekly allowance for young people will be increased to £27.30 for the first year. The allowance for the second year will be £35.

The minister told MPs: "The proposals represent a major step forward in improving the opportunities for young people both in training and work experience."

The scheme would give broad-based training in the first year with a greater emphasis on more specific training in the second year.

The issue of whether trainees would receive a certificate at the end of their training period is still to be decided but the Government's aim is that school leavers would become more employable as a result of spending time on the scheme.

The minister dismissed suggestions at a press conference later that the proportion of young people finding work after leaving the scheme had fallen to 48 per cent. He said that figure was based on one month's statistics last year and the present figure was about 60 per cent.

Source: *The Times* 2.7.85

**a** How much will the two-year YTS cost the government?
**b** Why will extra funds be available for areas like Merseyside and the north east?
**c** What are the main differences between the 1985 YTS and the present two-year YTS (the proposed scheme in the article) in terms of:
  ▷ number of trainees
  ▷ allowances?
**d** What is the main difference between the first year and second year of the training course in the new YTS?
**e** ▷ What is the government's aim in extending the scheme?
  ▷ Does the last paragraph suggest that this aim will be achieved? Give reasons for your answer.
**f** Do you think the allowances are high enough? Give reasons for your answer.

# UNIT 2.3 Trade unions and employers

**FOCUS**

▶ Why do people join trade unions?

▶ What different types of trade union are there?

▶ How are trade unions organised?

▶ What is **collective bargaining**?

▶ How is agreement reached in industrial disputes?

▶ What types of industrial action can trade unions take?

▶ What is a **closed shop**?

▶ How are employers organised?

## Trade unions

When you go to work one of the other workers may come up to you and ask you whether you want to join a trade union. A trade union will look after your interests in matters which involve your employer, other unions, and the government.

### Benefits of joining a trade union

If you join a trade union you will get some or all of the following benefits:

▶ 1 The union will try to get you a good wage when it talks about pay to your employer.
▶ 2 The union will make sure that you do your work in healthy and safe conditions, and that you have, for example, a proper safety guard on dangerous machinery.
▶ 3 The union will try to see that your working conditions are good and that you have, for example, clean toilets, reasonable tea and lunch breaks, and a good canteen.
▶ 4 The union will try to get shorter working hours and longer holidays.
▶ 5 The union may arrange for you to receive sums of money in special circumstances, for example, if you go on strike or extra money on top of state sickness benefit if you are sick.
▶ 6 The union will keep you informed on a large number of matters like pensions, and your rights if you are threatened with redundancy.
▶ 7 The union may offer a large number of other services like educational courses, its own insurance company, cheaper goods and services for union members, and so on.
▶ 8 The union will try to make sure that laws

**Figure 2.3a**
Why is an individual worker in a stronger position if he or she is part of a union?

**Figure 2.3b**
Why may you want union support if an employer wants to introduce new machinery?

passed by Parliament will benefit you, and they will try to get changes in the law to help workers.

▶ 9 The union will try to protect your position when new machinery and equipment, for example computers and robots, and new ways of working are suggested by your employer.

▶ 10 The union will protect you if there is an argument between workers or unions about who does what job. These arguments are called **demarcation disputes**.

### Different types of union

Unions are often grouped together as craft unions, industrial unions, and general unions. Sometimes you will also hear people talk about white collar unions. Many white collar unions are also craft unions.

A **craft union** is for workers who do the same or very similar work in a number of different industries. The Amalgamated Union of Engineering Workers (AUEW) and the National Graphical Association (NGA) are both craft unions.

An **industrial union** is open to all the workers in an industry whatever job they do, for example the National Union of Mineworkers (NUM).

A **general union** is for workers doing different jobs in different industries. The workers are usually unskilled or semi-skilled, and mostly fairly low paid. The Transport and General Workers Union (TGWU) is a general union, and it includes workers such as lorry drivers and school caretakers.

A **white-collar union** is for workers who do non-manual jobs. Some white collar unions are craft unions, like the National Union of Teachers (NUT) and some are general unions, like the Association of Scientific, Technical and Managerial Staffs (ASTMS).

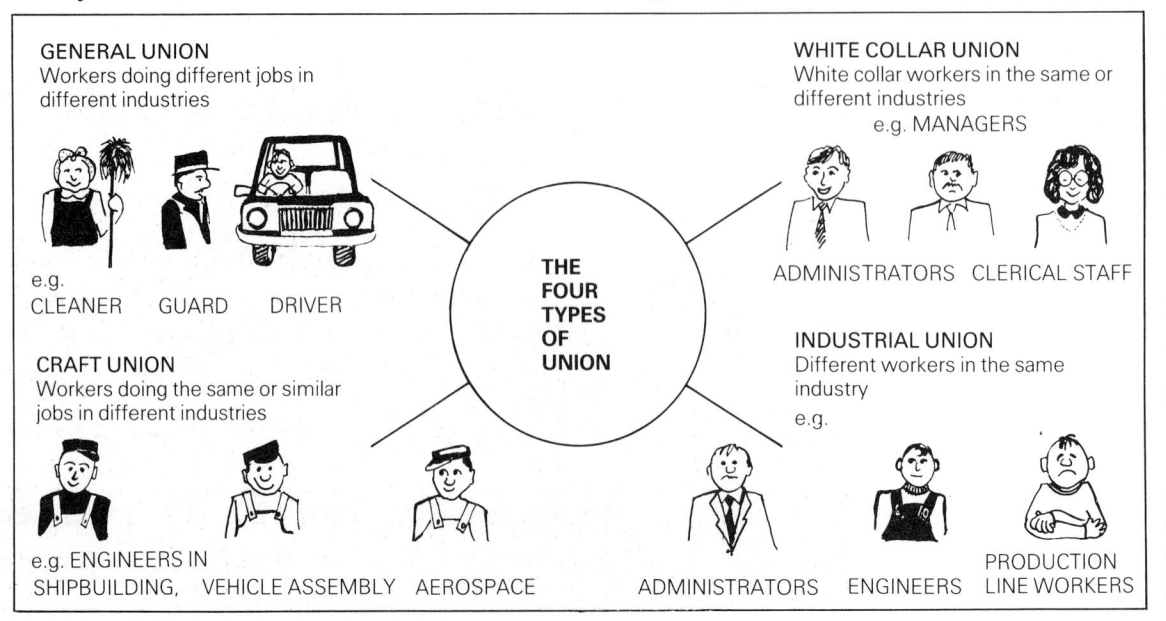

**Figure 2.3c**
The four main types of trade union

GENERAL UNION
Workers doing different jobs in different industries
e.g. CLEANER   GUARD   DRIVER

CRAFT UNION
Workers doing the same or similar jobs in different industries
e.g. ENGINEERS IN SHIPBUILDING,   VEHICLE ASSEMBLY   AEROSPACE

THE FOUR TYPES OF UNION

WHITE COLLAR UNION
White collar workers in the same or different industries
e.g. MANAGERS   ADMINISTRATORS   CLERICAL STAFF

INDUSTRIAL UNION
Different workers in the same industry
e.g. ADMINISTRATORS   ENGINEERS   PRODUCTION LINE WORKERS

### How unions are organised

Many people are involved in running a trade union. This section looks at how the union is organised from the basic place of work, right up to the annual conference of the union which takes the most important decisions.

▶ **1 The shop steward or representative**

This person is voted in by groups of workers in a **shop** (the name given to part of a large factory, small factory, office, or other place of work). He or she is not paid, but might get some time off work to do the job. Some of the things a shop steward will have to do are:

▷ **a** Collect the annual subscriptions or dues – the amount members of the union pay each year for membership.
▷ **b** Try to persuade new workers to join the union.
▷ **c** Give out information on union matters.
▷ **d** Keep the union informed of members' opinions.
▷ **e** Keep in contact with the management over working conditions, the introduction of new methods of work, and so on.

▶ **2 The local branch**

If you join a union you will be asked to go to meetings of the local branch of the union. The branch is for all members of the union in a local area. Unfortunately branch meetings are often poorly attended because they are held after work, and some members will have to travel from where they work to where the meeting is held. The branch may do some or all of the following jobs:

▷ **a** They accept new members into the union.
▷ **b** They elect **delegates** to go to the annual conference to represent their branch.
▷ **c** They talk about some of the things that have been decided at the annual conference, and they talk about pay agreements.
▷ **d** They look after union matters generally in their area.

▶ **3 The district/area/regional committee**

Big unions have a committee which looks after a number of branches in a certain area. These district committees often have full-time officials working for them. These are usually union members who have stopped their normal work to do union work full-time. These officials are paid from union funds, and they should be able to help union members with their problems. If there is, for example, a serious dispute between

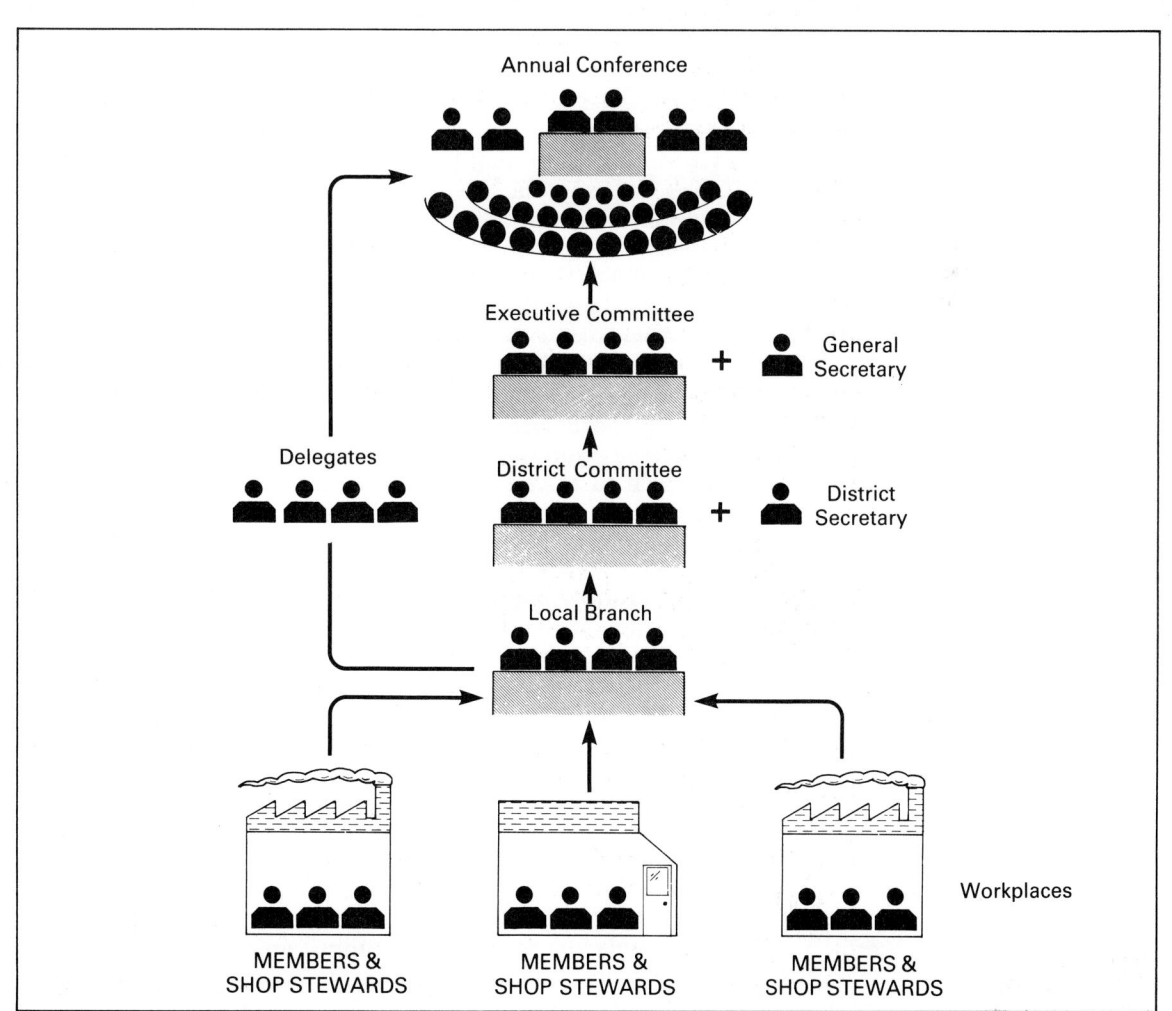

**Figure 2.3d**
The organisation of many larger trade unions

management and employees about putting in new machines, then the union members might contact an official from the district for help.

▶ **4 The annual conference**

Every year each branch will send one or more members chosen by the branch (and called delegates) to the annual conference of the union. Conferences often last a few days, and take place in a large conference hall or hotel. Branches can suggest things they want to talk about, and if they want the union to accept an idea, they can ask for a vote. Putting forward an idea for a vote is called **putting down a motion**. If the idea is accepted by the conference the motion is said to be passed, and it becomes union **policy**. This means that it will be supported by all members of the union. A branch might propose for example, that union members do not use certain new machinery unless there is extra pay. If the conference votes in favour of the motion, then all members of the union will support the demand for extra pay for using the new machinery.

▶ **5 The national executive committee**

The union will elect a national executive committee to look after union affairs between conferences. The national executive committee usually has the following jobs:

▷ **a** It negotiates pay rates with employers.
▷ **b** It calls a strike if the union thinks that one is needed.
▷ **c** It makes sure that the union has enough money by deciding, for example, the amount for the members' annual subscriptions.
▷ **d** It sends a report to the annual conference, and makes recommendations about what it thinks the conference should talk about.

▶ **6 The general secretary or president**

This person is the most important single member of the union. He or she is normally voted in by the members. The general secretary is responsible for the day-to-day running of the union, and he or she tends to have a great deal of influence with the national executive committee and the annual conference.

## Changes in union membership

Union membership reached a record high in 1979. Over 13,200,000 workers were in trade unions, 52 per cent of the working population. Since that time the total number of union members declined to just over 11,000,000 in 1985. There have been two main reasons for this:

▶ 1 The depression in the early 1980s increased unemployment, particularly in large general and craft unions whose members are found mainly in manufacturing industries.

▶ 2 Machinery is replacing workers in many manufacturing industries, and this has caused a loss of members in unions like the AUEW, the engineers' union.

Before 1979 the fastest growing unions were white-collar unions like NALGO (the National and Local Government Officers' Association), the local government officers' union, and BIFU (the Banking Insurance and Finance Union). One of the main reasons for the rapid growth in white-collar unions was the fact that very few white-collar workers were in unions before 1970. White-collar workers noticed how members of large unions like the NUM, the miners' union, had the strength and influence to negotiate good pay and conditions, and this encouraged them to join unions. When unemployment rose steeply after 1979, even some white-collar unions lost members.

## The Trades Union Congress (TUC)

The TUC is not a trade union. It is an organisation including most trade unions that speaks on behalf of the whole trade union movement.

### How the TUC is organised

▶ 1 *The annual congress* Over 100 unions send delegates every year to the annual conference (known as the annual congress) of the TUC. Matters of interest to all trade unions, like government laws concerning trade unions, are discussed.

▶ 2 *The general council* The general council runs the TUC between congresses. It is made up of members of the individual unions that are **affiliated to** (joined to) the TUC. Members of the general council sit on many committees that need the opinion of trade unionists represented.

▶ 3 *The general secretary* The general secretary works full-time for the TUC, and he or she is in charge of the other full-time members. The advice of the general secretary to the general council is very important. The general secretary often appears on the radio and television giving opinions on various matters on behalf of the whole trade union movement.

▶ 4 *TUC officials* The TUC has a number of other full-time workers who find out about various matters for the TUC committees. The TUC has several committees dealing with matters like health and safety, and the education of workers and trade union officials.

## Reaching agreement

This section looks at how unions try to reach agreement with employers. Although you always seem to read about strikes in the paper, in the vast majority of cases unions and employers reach agreement about things like pay without any difficulty or bad feeling.

▶ **1 Collective bargaining**

Collective bargaining is where two groups, such as trade unions and management, try to reach an agreement that satisfies the aims of both groups, on matters like pay and working conditions. The discussion between the two groups, which usually aims to reach a compromise, is called **negotiation**. Collective bargaining can take place at different levels. Three of these are where:

▷ **a** The shop steward talks to the management in the place of work about matters like the state of the canteen, or the use of new machines.

▷ **b** The executive committee of the union negotiates with a group of employers about national pay rates.

▷ **c** The TUC talks to the government about laws which could affect trade unions.

▶ **2 Advisory, Conciliation and Arbitration Service (ACAS)**

ACAS is an organisation set up by the government. One of its main jobs is to help unions and employers reach agreement where collective bargaining has not worked for some reason. ACAS tries not to take sides in a dispute. ACAS provides advice to unions and employers about conducting negotiations. It also provides a conciliation and arbitration service.

**Conciliation** is where someone not involved in a dispute between an employer and a union comes in and acts as a sort of referee, trying to bring the two sides together.

**Arbitration** is where someone not involved in a dispute between an employer and a union comes in and acts as a sort of a judge, hearing what both sides have to say, and making a decision which is binding on both of them. If the union and the employer cannot reach a decision, then they can call in an arbitrator from ACAS to make one for them.

▶ **3 Industrial action**

Industrial action refers to the actions that a union might take to put pressure on an employer if collective bargaining, and possibly also conciliation has failed. Some of the forms of industrial action that a union can use are as follows:

▷ **a** *Non-co-operation* The shop stewards might, for example, cancel weekly meetings with the management.

▷ **b** *Work-to-rule* The workers might decide to follow every single rule about working, even those that everyone knows to be out of date. This usually means that things happen much more slowly. This way they go on getting paid, but they stop work running smoothly.

▷ **c** *Overtime ban* Workers will only work normal hours and they will refuse to do any extra work.

▷ **d** *Strikes* Strikes are where workers stop work. They can last from a few hours, to many months. To be **official** they must be approved by the union's executive committee. The union might pay strike pay.

▷ **e** *Picketing* Up to six workers can stand outside their own place of work and tell people about their grievances. If a strike is in progress,

**Figure 2.3e**
What name is given to the process of negotiation shown here?

they can peacefully try to stop workers going in to the place of work by telling them about the dispute, and asking them not to co-operate with management.

**The closed shop**

If you want to do some jobs, you must join the union. A closed shop is where all the workers in a particular place of work must be members of the union.

### Advantages of a closed shop
▶ 1 The union has more power because it speaks on behalf of all the workers in a place of work.
▶ 2 If there is industrial action, all workers are involved. Sometimes union members who take industrial action for a pay rise get very upset with non-union workers who take no action but still accept the pay rise. This is unlikely to happen in a closed shop.
▶ 3 The management has to deal with only one union, and this can make reaching agreement much easier.

### Disadvantages of a closed shop
▶ 1 It takes away a worker's freedom of choice about whether to join a union.
▶ 2 The union that the worker has to join may not be very good at its job and, given a choice, the worker might prefer another union.

### One-union agreements
A one-union agreement is where the management recognises only one union for the purposes of collective bargaining. Workers need not join the union at all, but if they want to be represented collectively they must join the recognised union. An example of a one-union agreement is that between Nissan and the Amalgamated Union of Engineering Workers (AUEW) at the Sunderland factory.

### Employers' associations
In some industries, like engineering, there are many firms but only one or a few big unions. Employers who own these businesses will often join together in associations in local areas. Sometimes the associations will get together in even bigger organisations called **federations**, like the Engineering Employers' Federation. These federations will often have a general council which can negotiate basic pay for all their workers with the executive committee of a large union.

### The Confederation of British Industry (CBI)
This organisation is the employers' version of the TUC. Many large companies and employers' associations belong to the CBI, which speaks on behalf of employers. Like the TUC, the CBI has an annual conference. Its most important official is called the director-general.

Unit 2.3 *Trade unions and employers*

## DATABASE

### 1. The number of strikes in the UK since 1962

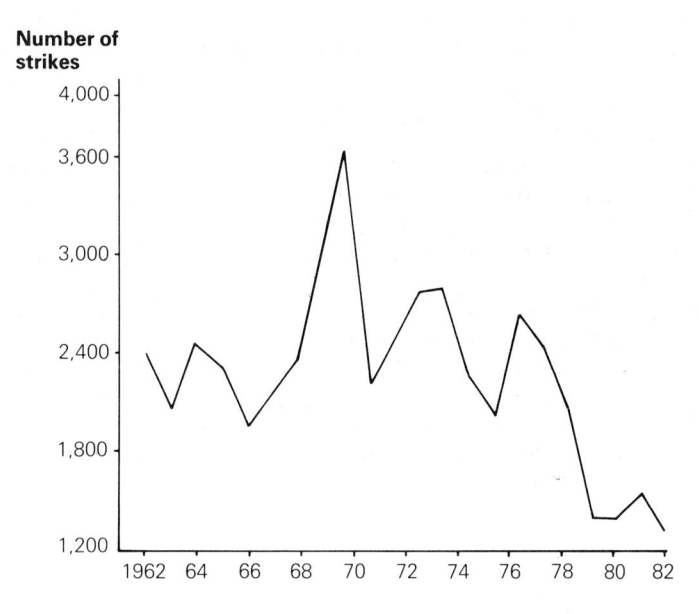

Source: *The Economic Review*, Jan. 1985, Philip Allan

## DATABASE

### 2. The causes of strikes in the UK in 1982

| Cause | Number of strikes | % of total | Duration (days) | Days lost (000's) | % of days lost | Days lost per dispute (000's) | Workers involved per dispute |
|---|---|---|---|---|---|---|---|
| Pay | 654 | 43 | 5.5 | 2,826 | 61 | 4.321 | 781 |
| Redundancy | 122 | 8 | 2.7 | 839 | 18 | 6.770 | 2,510 |
| Working conditions: hours of work, manning and work organisation | 518 | 34 | 4.9 | 658 | 14 | 1.270 | 261 |
| Dismissal and discipline | 143 | 11 | 3.7 | 155 | 4 | 1.084 | 287 |
| Trade union matters | 91 | 6 | 4.9 | 125 | 3 | 1.373 | 283 |

Source: Department of Employment *Gazette*, July 1983

## DATABASE

# 3. Changes in trade union membership

| Trade Union | Membership ('000) 1979 | 1983 |
|---|---|---|
| Transport Workers (TGWU) | 2,070 | 1,633 |
| Engineers (AUEW) | 1,200 | 1,001 |
| Municipal Workers (GMBWU) | 965 | 940 |
| Local Government (NALGO) | 729 | 784 |
| Public Employees (NUPE) | 712 | 702 |
| Shopworkers (USDAW) | 462 | 417 |
| Managerial Staff (ASTMS) | 471 | 410 |
| Electricians (EETPU) | 420 | 380 |
| Builders (UCATT) | 321 | 261 |
| Miners (NUM) | 255 | 245 |

(The Economist; 10/9/83)

*Unit 2.3* Trade unions and employers

## ACTIVITIES

### SECTION A: FOCUS ON UNIT 2.3

Go back and answer the questions raised in the Focus.

### SECTION B: STEPPED QUESTIONS

1  a  What is meant by 'negotiation'?
   b  In what ways might the aims of trade unions and employers be:
      ▷ different?
      ▷ similar?
   c  What would be the economic effects if trade unions were abolished?
2  a  ▷ What kinds of issues can cause disputes between trade unions and employers? (Use Database 2 to help you.)
      ▷ Which are the most common causes of disputes?
   b  Why did the number of strikes fall in general between 1979 and 1983?
3  a  Draw a bar chart to show the changes in trade union membership in recent years. (Use Database 3 to help you.)
   b  Explain the trends shown in your graph.

### SECTION C: DATA RESPONSE QUESTIONS

1  Industrial disputes in different countries

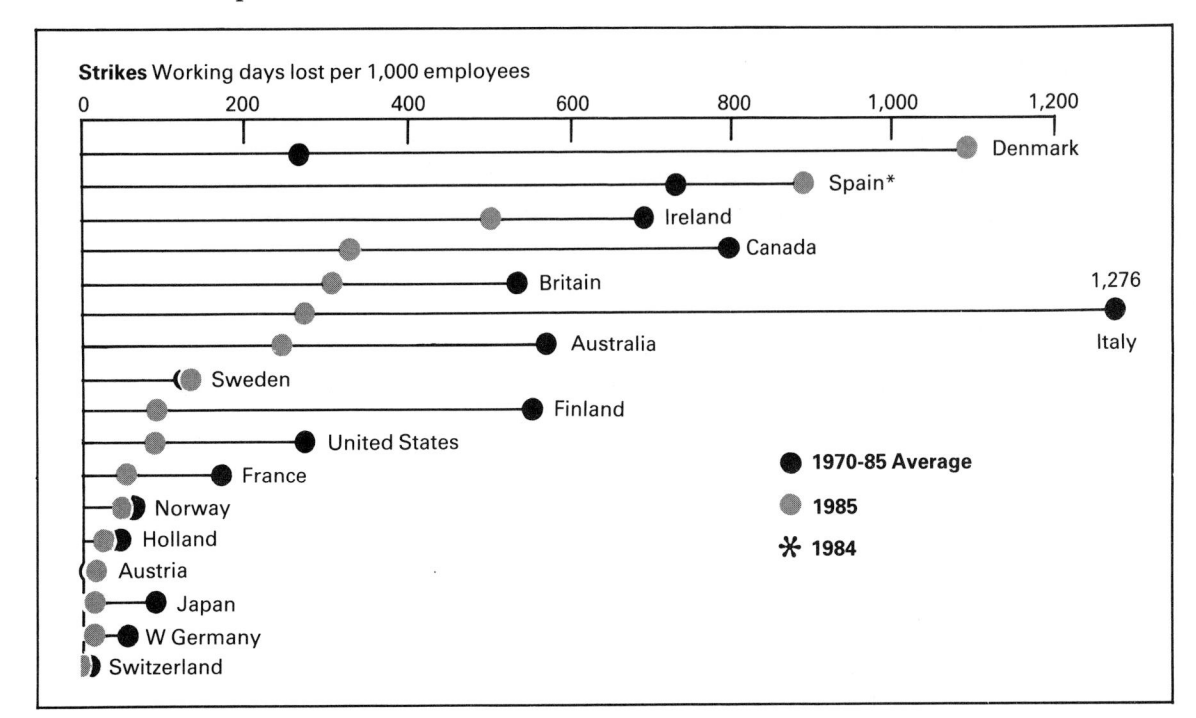

**Strikes** Working days lost per 1,000 employees

Countries shown (top to bottom): Denmark, Spain*, Ireland, Canada, Britain, Italy (1,276), Australia, Sweden, Finland, United States, France, Norway, Holland, Austria, Japan, W Germany, Switzerland

Legend:
● 1970-85 Average
● 1985
* 1984

Source: *The Economist* 14/6/86

a Which three countries had the largest number of strikes:
  ▷ in the period 1970–85 (on average)?
  ▷ in 1985?
b How many days were lost per 1000 workers in Britain:
  ▷ in the period 1970–1985 (on average)?
  ▷ in 1985?
c How would a large number of strikes affect an economy?
d If an economy is performing badly and there are a large number of strikes, is the poor economic performance the fault of the trade unions? Explain your answer.

2 The 1984 Trade Union Act

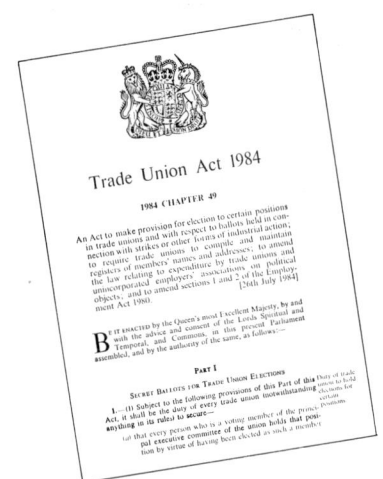

The Act:
  requires trade unions to ensure that all voting members of their executive committees are directly elected at least once every five years;
  provides that all elections for voting members of union executives must be conducted by secret postal ballot unless the trade union can be satisfied that a workplace ballot (the only permitted alternative to a postal ballot) will:
  (a) be secret and free from any interference or constraint;
  (b) provide a convenient opportunity for members to vote during, or immediately before or after working hours without direct cost to themselves;
  (c) be one in which voting is by the marking of a ballot paper and in which votes are fairly and accurately counted.

**Source:** *Employment News* Aug. 1984 No. 122 (DoE)

a This passage describes part of an Act of Parliament passed by Parliament to try and control one activity within a trade union. Which activity does the Act try and control?
b How often must a union hold elections for members of their executive committee?
c What is meant by a 'secret postal ballot'?
d If a postal ballot is not held, what is the alternative?
e Can workers who work Monday to Friday be asked to go into work on a Saturday to vote in a union election? Explain your answer.
f Do you think that the government has the right to intervene in trade union matters? Give reasons for your answer.

Unit 2.3 Trade unions and employers

## PART 2: COURSEWORK SUGGESTION

THE LOCAL JOB SITUATION

1. Use local sources of information to find out what jobs are available in your local area.
2. Analyse each job under the same group of headings e.g. by salary, by type of industry (primary, secondary, etc.), by qualifications required etc.
3. Use different methods of presentation to show the results of your analysis, e.g. bar charts, tables, pie charts etc.
4. Write a report which highlights any trends and patterns in job vacancies in your local area.

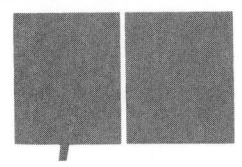

---

Here are some more words and phrases for your Dictionary of Economic Terms. Remember to look for each word or phrase in the text and then write your own definition for it.

closed shop
collective bargaining
Confederation of British Industry (CBI)
craft union
division of labour
employers' association
general union
industrial action
industrial union
Manpower Services Commission (MSC)
primary industry
secondary industry
tertiary industry
trade union
Trades Union Congress (TUC)
white-collar union

# Part 3
## Money and banking

# UNIT 3.1  Money

**FOCUS**

▶ How did money develop?

▶ What are the different qualities possessed by money?

▶ What are the functions or uses of money?

## The development of money

In many countries the most important types of money that people use are **notes**, **coins**, and **bank deposits**. Later in the Unit we tell you why these things are called 'money', but first we will look briefly at the development of money.

### Barter

We saw in Unit 2.1 how people in Britain many thousands of years ago swapped goods that they specialised in making for the other goods that they wanted. This swapping is called **barter**. Sometimes children use barter when, for example, they swap stickers for sweets. Barter is still very common in countries in the world which have less developed economies than the UK.

Barter has several problems:

▶ 1 A person who has something to swap must find someone who has what he or she wants, and who wants what he or she has to offer in exchange. If you want a particular record, you must find someone who not only has the record you want, but who also wants the record you are offering in exchange.

▶ 2 People involved in barter argue over the value of things compared to each other. Exactly how many singles is an LP worth?

▶ 3 People argue about the quality of things offered in exchange. Would you swap a Frank Sinatra LP for a Madonna LP?

**Figure 3.1a**
What problem with barter is illustrated here?

These and other problems led people to using just one or two things that were generally acceptable to everyone in exchange for goods and services.

### Coins

Precious metals like gold and silver were accepted by most people in exchange for goods and services, and because they were generally acceptable they became the earliest forms of money. People still argued about the weight and quality of gold and silver so rulers stamped the weights of the metal upon it. They also stamped on the metal their own likenesses to show that the metal was of proper quality. This is how the first coins came into existence.

**Figure 3.1b**
Why were precious metals used as money?

### Banknotes

Coins were heavy to carry around, and there was always the risk of being robbed, so some people stored coins with goldsmiths. In return the goldsmith gave them an IOU or 'promise to pay'. Soon people started to accept the IOUs of trustworthy goldsmiths in exchange for goods and services, and the IOUs themselves became 'money'. Eventually banks replaced goldsmiths as the place where people would store their gold and silver, and banknotes became the modern version of goldsmiths' IOUs.

**Figure 3.1c**
The top of a modern banknote still has similar words to the IOUs given out by goldsmiths. A modern bank would not, however, give you one pound of gold for a £1 note. One pound of gold nowadays could cost you about 5000 £1 notes!

### Bank deposits

These are the most important form of money in a country like the UK. If you put money into a bank current account you will receive a cheque book in exchange. If you pay someone with a cheque you are telling your bank to take some money out of your account and pay it to someone else. The person who accepts your cheque is accepting part of your current account – your bank deposit – in exchange for goods and services. Bank deposits are 'money' because, like notes and coins, they are generally acceptable in exchange for goods and services.

### Credit cards

Credit cards such as Access and Visa are an increasingly used form of money. They are now accepted in exchange for a wide range of goods and services. We will look at credit cards in more detail in Unit 4.4.

## The qualities of money

Throughout the world different things have been used at different times as money. We use pieces of paper, bits of metal and things we cannot even see (bank deposits) as money. In other countries sharks' teeth and precious shells have been used as money. For people to accept something as money it must have certain qualities. They are as follows:

▶ **1 Acceptability**
The thing used as money must be generally acceptable in exchange for goods and services. This means that nearly everyone will take it in exchange for something that they give you in return.

▶ **2 Portability**
Anything used as money must be portable, easy to carry around. You can, for example, easily carry about enough banknotes or a cheque to buy a car.

▶ **3 Durability**
Money should not perish or rot away if you store it. It must be durable. Food, however rare, could not become a common form of money because you could not easily and cheaply store it until needed.

▶ **4 Scarcity**
Anything used as money should be fairly scarce in supply. Nobody would accept pebbles in exchange for goods and services because there are too many around.

▶ **5 Divisibility**
Money should be easily divided up (easily divisible). This was the great advantage of precious metals in the past. They could be divided up into smaller and smaller amounts so that each part had some value, and the total value remained the same.

## The functions of money

Money isn't used just to buy goods and services. It has several uses or functions and these are listed below:

▶ **1 A medium of exchange**
Money is used to make possible the exchange of goods and services. It is a **medium of exchange**. For example, a plumber receives money for the services he or she provides. The plumber then exchanges the money for goods and services. Without money the plumber would have to work for the farmer for food, for the builder for a home, for the clothes manufacturer

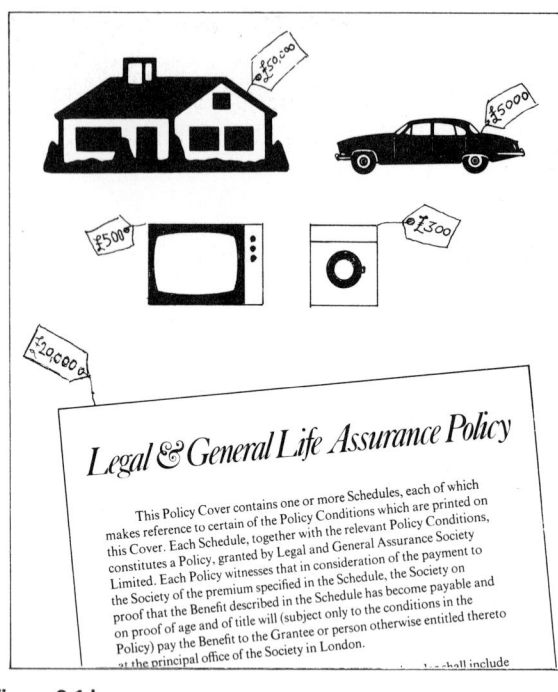

**Figure 3.1d**
When people die, a money value is put on what they owned.

for clothes, and so on. Money helps to make life much simpler!

▶ 2 **A measure of value**

Money is a way of putting a value on things. It is a **measure of value**. If the government wants to tax someone when they die, it has to work out the value of what the person has left: the value of their 'estate'. It could just list all the things they left, but it is much easier to put a money value on everything, add up what it is all worth, and take part of it in tax.

▶ 3 **A store of value**

Money is a way of storing up something of value for the future. We may have savings of money sufficient to buy records, clothes and holidays in the future. It is much more convenient to hold on to the money rather than to store up the things we want to use at some future date.

▶ 4 **A means of deferred payment**

Money can be used as a 'promise to pay'. Money can be used to obtain goods and services now, while putting off the actual payment for them until some future date Money is a means of postponing or deferring payments.

## DATABASE

## Disappearing coins

| COINS | Coins available in: | | | |
|---|---|---|---|---|
| | 1955 | 1965 | 1975 | 1986 |
| ¼d | ✓ | | | |
| ½d | ✓ | ✓ | | |
| 1d | ✓ | ✓ | | |
| 2d | ✓ | ✓ | | |
| 3d | ✓ | ✓ | | |
| 6d | ✓ | ✓ | | |
| 1s | ✓ | ✓ | | |
| 2s | ✓ | ✓ | | |
| 2/6d | ✓ | ✓ | | |
| ½p | | | ✓ | |
| 1p | | | ✓ | ✓ |
| 2p | | | ✓ | ✓ |
| 5p | | | ✓ | ✓ |
| 10p | | | ✓ | ✓ |
| 20p | | | | ✓ |
| 50p | | | ✓ | ✓ |
| £1 | | | | ✓ |

### NOTES (up to £50)

| | 1955 | 1965 | 1975 | 1986 |
|---|---|---|---|---|
| 10 sh | ✓ | ✓ | | |
| £1 | ✓ | ✓ | ✓ | |
| £5 | ✓ | ✓ | ✓ | ✓ |
| £10 | ✓ | ✓ | ✓ | ✓ |
| £20 | ✓ | ✓ | ✓ | ✓ |
| £50 | ✓ | ✓ | ✓ | ✓ |

**ACTIVITIES**

## SECTION A: FOCUS ON UNIT 3.1

Go back and answer the questions raised in the Focus.

## SECTION B: STEPPED QUESTIONS

1. **a** What is meant by 'barter'?
   **b** What advantages does exchange using money have over exchange by barter?
   **c** What is the difference between money and cash?
   **d** ▷ What kinds of money exist in an industrialised economy like the UK?
      ▷ Explain the advantages of using a current account rather than cash to pay for goods and services.
2. **a** A major change in UK coinage took place in 1971. Look at Database 2 and work out what it was.
   **b** Why do you think this happened?
   **c** Using your knowledge of the qualities of money explain:
      ▷ why the ½p coin disappeared
      ▷ why the £1 note was replaced by a coin.

## SECTION C: DATA RESPONSE QUESTION

Study the information below and answer the questions which follow it.

**Croesus Makes a Mint**
A major development in the history of money came with a decree issued by Croesus, King of Lydia, in the sixth century BC. (Lydia is now part of modern Turkey, on the east Mediterranean coast.)

The decree stated that all coins would have a standard weight, size and shape for each value so they would be quickly recognised and easily acceptable. The only way to be sure that all coins met the standard was for Croesus to have total control (or a 'monopoly') over gold mining and the production of coins.

This created great confidence in the coinage, and trade increased rapidly as people no longer had to rely on barter and this resulted in greater wealth for the kingdom.

Croesus is said to have developed the first standard coinage.

   **a** How did the decree make coins more easily acceptable?
   **b** Explain which other characteristics of money you think the Lydian coins possessed.
   **c** What is meant by a 'monopoly'?
   **d** Why was the king's monopoly over the supply of money necessary?
   **e** ▷ How did the coinage result in increased trade?
      ▷ What modern forms of money have developed in recent years which have helped to increase trade?
   **f** Are so many different forms of money desirable?

# UNIT 3.2  The value of money

**FOCUS**
▶ How does a rise in the cost of living affect the value of money?
▶ What is **inflation**?
▶ How are changes in the value of money measured?
▶ What is the **Retail Prices Index**?

## The value of money

The value of money is the goods and services we can buy with the money. The value of a £5 note is the same to everyone in the sense that it will buy the same amount of goods and services for everyone. It is different, however, in the sense that an extra £5 may be valued more highly by a poorer person than by a richer person.

## Changes in the value of money

If the amount of goods and services you can buy with a given sum of money changes, then there has been a change in the value of the money. If prices are rising, we say that there has been a 'rise in the cost of living'. This means that a given sum of money is buying less and less each year, that is, there is a fall in the value, or purchasing power, of money. If prices are falling, we say that there has been a 'fall in the cost of living'. This means that a given sum of money is buying more and more each year, and there is an increase in the value, or **purchasing power**, of money.

**Figure 3.2a**
What happened to the purchasing power of money between 1974 and 1984?

A £1 note put in a piggy bank in 1974 would be worth only 28p at the beginning of 1984. In other words you could buy well over three times as many goods and services for £1 in 1974 as you could in 1984

## Measuring changes in the value of money

The value of money changes when prices change. If the **cost of living** (prices in general) goes up it does not mean, however, that people are necessarily worse off. The amount of goods and services you can buy – your **standard of living** – depends not only on the value of a given sum of money, but also on the total amount of money that you get from wages, social security and other places. If prices rise by 10 per cent and your wages rise by 20 per cent, then the cost of living has gone up, but so has your standard of living. If prices are rising, therefore, the value of money is going down but standards of living could be rising, falling or staying the same. Measuring changes in the value of money is therefore all about measuring changes in prices.

**Figure 3.2b**
What will happen to this man's standard of living if his wages stay the same and there is inflation?

## The Retail Prices Index

The **Retail Prices Index** (RPI) is the main way in which the government measures changes in the value of money. It measures over a number of years the price of a fairly typical 'basket' of goods that an ordinary family spends its money on.

If there is a general rise in prices, then the index will rise, and the country will experience **inflation**, a rise in the cost of living, and a fall

**Weights, 1986**

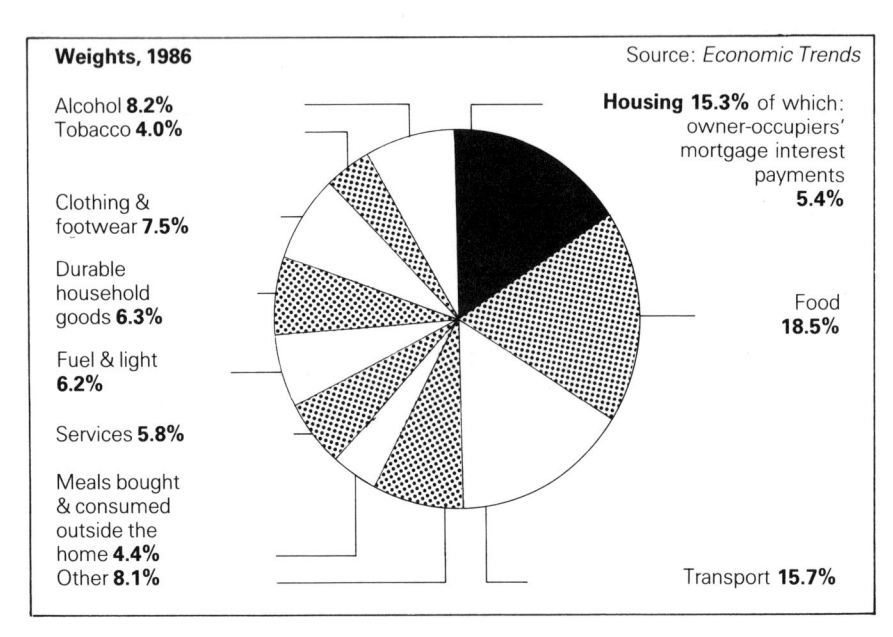

Source: *Economic Trends*

- Alcohol **8.2%**
- Tobacco **4.0%**
- Clothing & footwear **7.5%**
- Durable household goods **6.3%**
- Fuel & light **6.2%**
- Services **5.8%**
- Meals bought & consumed outside the home **4.4%**
- Other **8.1%**
- Housing **15.3%** of which: owner-occupiers' mortgage interest payments **5.4%**
- Food **18.5%**
- Transport **15.7%**

**Figure 3.2c**
The main groups of goods and services in the RPI, and the percentage of a typical family's income spent on each in 1986.

in the value of money. If the index is falling, the country is experiencing a fall in prices, a fall in the cost of living, and a rise in the value of money.

However, remember that even if the rate of inflation is falling, prices are still rising. They are just rising at a slower rate than previously.

The Retail Prices Index is worked out in the following way:

▶ 1 The government chooses a particular date, and calls that date the **base date**. The year in which the base date occurs is called the **base year**.

▶ 2 The price of each item in the basket is found out, and given a **weight**. This means that the importance of the items in the basket shows up in the calculation of the index. For example, if food makes up 20 per cent of the average household budget, then a rise in the price of food will have a bigger effect on the index than a rise in the price of, say, cigarettes.

▶ 3 The price of the entire basket, allowing for the importance of different items, is worked out, and it is given an index number of 100 in the base year.

▶ 4 The price of the basket in future years is shown as a percentage change from the base year. For example, if the RPI in the year after the base year was 105 it means that the cost of the basket has risen in price by 5 per cent. If the RPI stood at 110 the following year, it means that the cost of the basket has risen by 10 per cent since the base year.

**Problems in constructing the Retail Prices Index**

▶ 1 There is no such thing as a 'typical' family. Inflation affects different people differently according to what they spend their money on. If food is rising in price more rapidly than the RPI as a whole, for example, poorer people, who spend a much larger proportion of their money on food than do richer people, will be affected by rising prices more than the RPI suggests.

▶ 2 The items in the basket need to be changed constantly. New items appear, for example home computers and videos, and the weight given to existing items has to be adjusted. As well as revising the basket, the government rebases the RPI from time to time.

▶ 3 Prices vary from area to area and from shop to shop. The price of a tin of baked beans, for example, could cost twice as much in an expensive London store as in a large supermarket in a poorer district.

▶ 4 Changes in shopping habits make it difficult to find out the typical price of an item. Many people now buy meat in large quantities for the freezer, and they will pay less per kilo than people who buy meat in small amounts.

These, and other problems, mean that the RPI should be treated with caution. It does provide for most people, however, a reasonable guide as to changes in the general level of prices.

YEAR 1... PRICE: £20 INDEX: 100

YEAR 2... PRICE: £24 INDEX: 120

**Figure 3.2d**
What is the rate of inflation in Year 2?

Unit 3.2 *The value of money*

## DATABASE

# The falling value of money

In 1930, £1 would buy this much: **(£15.17 worth of goods in 1985)**

In 1940, £1 would buy this much: **(£14.48 worth of goods in 1985)**

In 1950, £1 would buy this much: **(£10.97 worth of goods in 1985)**

In 1960, £1 would buy this much: **(£7.39 worth of goods in 1985)**

In 1970, £1 would buy this much: **(£5.11 worth of goods in 1985)**

In 1980, £1 would buy this much: **(£1.47 worth of goods in 1985)**

## ACTIVITIES

### SECTION A: FOCUS ON UNIT 3.2

Go back and answer the questions raised in the Focus.

### SECTION B: STEPPED QUESTION

1  **a**  A worker earns £6,000 a year and receives no wage rises for three years. Over the same period the RPI rises, at a faster rate each year. Decide whether each of the following has risen, fallen, or stayed the same:
- ▷ the value of money
- ▷ the purchasing power of money
- ▷ the worker's standard of living
- ▷ the worker's real income
- ▷ inflation
- ▷ the cost of living.

  **b**  Explain in detail how the changes in the general level of prices are measured using the RPI.

  **c**  What problems are involved in measuring price changes using the RPI?

  **d**  A newspaper headline says 'Prices are rising but inflation is falling'. Can this be true? Explain your answer.

**Unit 3.2** *The value of money*

## SECTION C: DATA RESPONSE QUESTION

### The Cost of Living with the RPI

The annual inflation rate has fallen to 3 per cent, its lowest level for 18 years – or has it?

A new report by the independent think-tank, the Institute for Fiscal Studies, claims that the Retail Prices Index (RPI) generally overstates price rises, while at the same time underplaying their effect on the lives of the poor.

The RPI is a central figure in the government's economic thinking, and a trigger for much government expenditure. The value of social security benefits and state pensions, personal tax allowances, public sector pensions, and index-linked national savings and gilts are now automatically pinned to rises in the index. Every 1 per cent increase in the RPI adds more than £500 million to public expenditure.

The first problem identified by the IFS researchers is the time that elapses between each fine-tuning of weightings in the index. The weights used in the calculations of the annual RPI are adjusted each January, but they reflect the quantities of goods and services purchased on average 12 months before the January base. This tardiness means the index does not accurately reflect current spending patterns.

If the cost of beef soars, for instance, the thrifty or penny-pinched will be inclined to eschew steak, and stick their knives and forks into a leg of lamb instead. The weighting for expenditure on beef in the RPI, following this change in budgeting, should therefore be reduced, but it may be almost two years before the new data is reflected in the index.

'The effect is to over-estimate inflation, because people adjust their spending when prices go up,' says Vanessa Fry, one of the report's authors.

The highest margin of error unearthed by the IFS came in 1978. The authors reckon the inflation rate then was actually 9.1 per cent, not the official 9.9 per cent.

(Source: *The Observer* 18.5.86)

1 a ▷ What is measured by changes in the Retail Prices Index?
  ▷ Which organisation wrote the new report that the newspaper extract above is all about?
 b ▷ What are the two main problems about the RPI which are written about in the new report?
  ▷ Which of the two problems is the newspaper extract about?
  ▷ Name three different items of government spending that are automatically increased in line with rises in the RPI.
 c ▷ What problem is suggested by the sentence: 'This tardiness means the index does not accurately reflect current spending patterns'?
  ▷ How do people react when the price of a particular product rises steeply, and how does this affect the accuracy of the RPI as far as they are concerned? Explain your answer.
  ▷ What in particular concerned the organisation that wrote the new report about 1978?

# UNIT 3.3  The banking and financial system

## FOCUS

▶ What are the functions of banks?

▶ What banking services are available?

▶ What are the functions of the Bank of England?

▶ How does the clearing system work?

▶ What other organisations are there in the financial system?

## Using banking services

Banks are places which help you deal with your money. They offer their customers a wide range of financial services. Many of the services offered by banks are now also offered by other organisations not actually called banks, such as building societies.

**Figure 3.3a** How might consumers benefit from so many banks and building societies?

### The functions of banks

The five services (or 'functions') of banks are: taking deposits; transacting; lending; safe-keeping; and providing other services such as financial advice. The way in which banks perform these functions is summarised in Fig 3.3b. The specific services provided by banks will now be explained in more detail:

▶ **1 The current account or cheque account**

When you have money in a bank you are said to have an **account** or **deposit**. When you actually put money into your account you are said to be 'depositing' money or **crediting** your account. When you withdraw money you are said to be **debiting** your account. Whether you have to pay for a current account depends on the bank that you use. You will have no charges with most banks if you keep the account **in credit** (do not take out more than you have in). Some cheque accounts even pay you interest if you keep large sums in them.

The following examples show some of the services available with a current account:

▷ **a** *Paying-in or credit slips* Rosie has a current account with the Midland. When she wants to pay money into her account she may use a Bank Giro credit slip. She can use these slips to pay money through other branches of her bank, or even through other banks as well, into her own account.

▷ **b** *The payment of your wages directly into your current account – direct credit* Glen works for an engineering company, and they pay his wages directly into his current account through the Bank Giro system. Glen has a chequebook for when he wants to draw money out of his account. This is a convenient and safe way to pay wages, because the company doesn't have to put cash into a weekly wage packet, and Glen doesn't have to carry a large sum of money around with him when he gets paid. Glen knows how much money has gone into his bank account because the company still gives him a pay slip with all the details on it.

▷ **c** *Cheques* These are instructions to your bank to take money out of your account and pay you or the person to whom the cheque has been made out (the **payee**).

▷ **d** *Cheque guarantee cards* Angela likes to shop with her chequebook, but some shops didn't accept her cheques because they didn't know if she had enough money in her account. So the bank gave Angela a **cheque guarantee card**. She shows this to the shop assistant, who writes her number on the back of the cheque, and checks her signature and the date. The bank now guarantees to pay the shop any sum up to £50, even if Angela doesn't have the money in her account. The card guarantees that the cheque will be **honoured**.

▷ **e** *The payment of several bills with one cheque* Edward always seems to get his gas and electricity bills at the same time. The bills have attached to them a completed Bank Giro credit slip made out to the gas and electricity boards. Edward just fills in the right amount

*Unit 3.3 The banking and financial system*

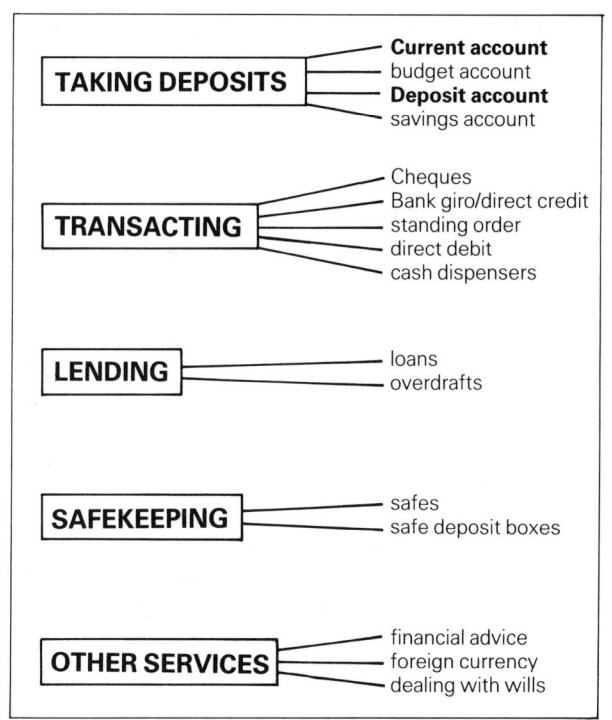

**Figure 3.3b**
The functions of the banks

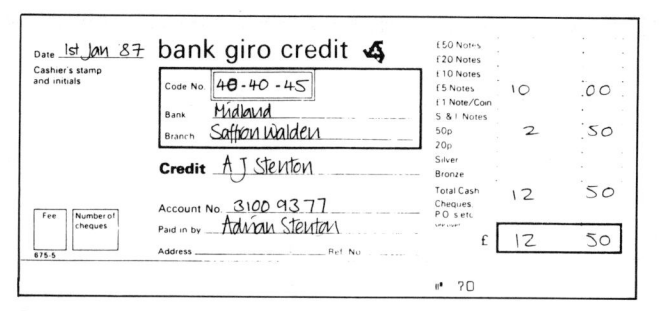

**Figure 3.3c**
A completed credit slip

**Figure 3.3d**
A completed cheque

on each one, and then writes a single cheque made out to his bank for the total amount. He then takes the cheque and the Bank Giro credit slips to his bank, and they make the separate payments for him. This saves Edward the cost of several cheques and the postage. The National Girobank's Transcash service works in a similar way.

▷ **f** *Standing orders* Barbara decided to take out a subscription to her favourite monthly computing magazine so that she got it before it was in the newsagents. She filled in a **standing order** form at the bank. This form enabled her to make regular payments for a fixed sum of money. Barbara told the bank who to pay, how much to pay, the dates on which the payments should be made, and when to start and stop making the payments. The bank now sends the subscription to the magazine each month, and Barbara gets her magazine through the post.

▷ **g** *Direct debit* Robin prefers to pay her electricity bill by **direct debit**. This is a service very much like that for standing orders, but is for paying bills which are usually a different amount of money each time. She filled in a form at the bank which allows the bank to pay the electricity board however much they need for each quarter. The electricity board still sends a statement to Robin (which, of course, she doesn't pay), and a notice to the bank, asking them to pay the amount on the bill.

▷ **h** *Budget accounts* John pays his bills out of a **budget account**. He worked out how much he needed to pay all his regular bills for one year, then divided it by twelve. He now pays that sum into a budget account every month from his current account, and pays his bills with a special chequebook from his budget account. This means that sometimes his budget account is in credit, and sometimes it is in debit, but over the year as a whole it should balance. Meanwhile, he is able to keep his current account in credit because he knows exactly how much he has to pay out of it each month, no matter how many bills he has to pay.

▷ **i** *Cash dispensers* Many banks have machines that let you get cash out without using a cheque. You put a special cash card in the machine, type in your secret number, and type in the amount that you want. The dispenser will be linked to the bank's main computer. It will check that you have enough in your account before paying you. It may also tell you your **current balance**, the amount that you have in your current account. **Cash dispensers**, or **automated teller machines** (ATMs), are an aspect of the banks' use of the new technology. Over 5,000 ATMs had been installed by the end of 1983, mostly outside bank branches. However, some of the banks have been placing ATMs in petrol stations, supermarkets and other locations away from their branches.

Unit 3.3 *The banking and financial system*

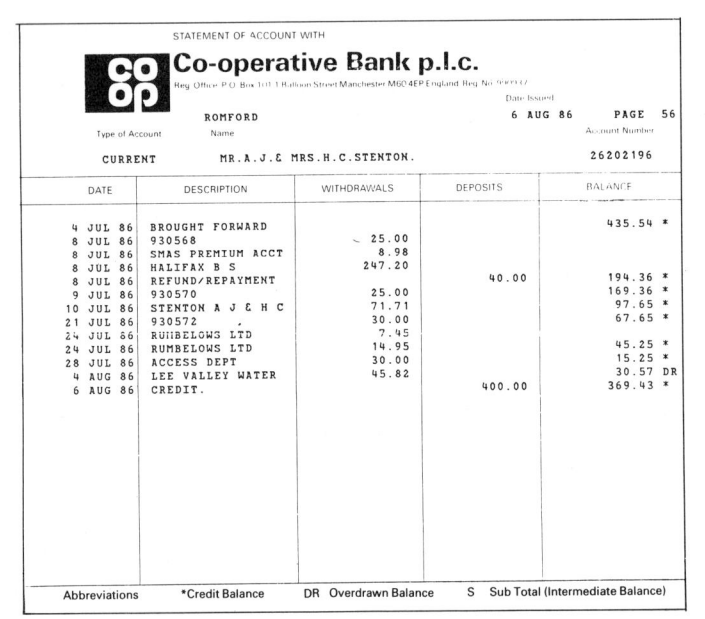

**Figure 3.3e**
In what way is a bank statement useful in a consumer's economic decision-making?

**Figure 3.3f**
You can use one cheque to pay several bills at the same time

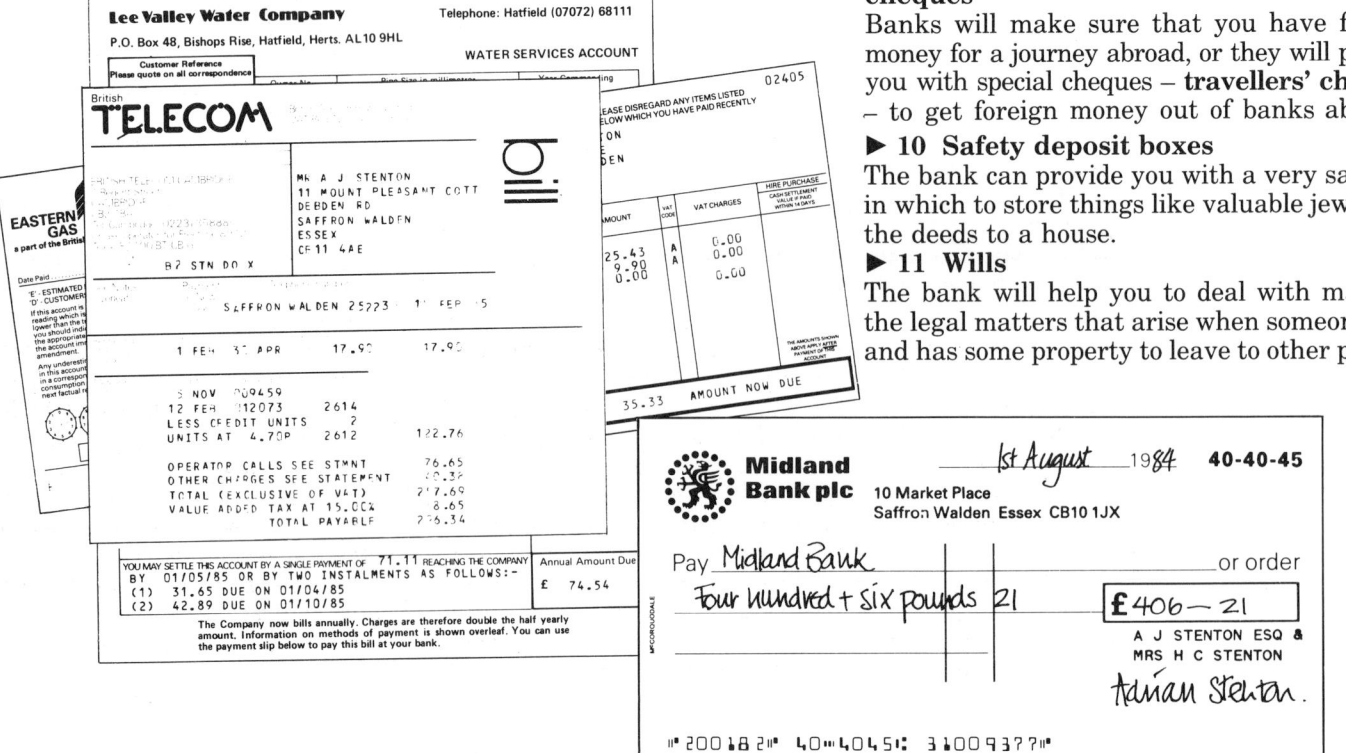

▷ **j** *Bank statements* Bank customers get a **statement** regularly from their banks. This is a list showing all of the money that has been credited to or debited from the account over the period, and the balance at the end of the period.

▶ **2 Overdrafts**
With the agreement of your bank manager you might be allowed to take more money out of your current account than you have in it. You can usually **overdraw** up to a certain limit, and you can take out the extra money and repay it as and when you want to. The extra money is called an **overdraft** and you have to pay the bank interest for the money they are lending you.

▶ **3 Personal loans**
Banks will lend money to customers for things like buying new cars, or improving a home. The loans are given in a fixed sum to be repaid in regular instalments (regular amounts, usually each month) by a certain date. You will need to pay interest on the loan. Borrowing money is treated in more detail in Unit 4.4.

▶ **4 Deposit and savings accounts**
Banks offer a variety of savings schemes, the most important of which is called a **deposit account**. If you put your money in a deposit account you will be paid interest. You will not get a cheque book, and it may not be as easy to get the money out as it is with a current account. Some banks offer **savings accounts** for people who want to save the same amount each month.

▶ **5 Investment services**
Banks will advise you how to invest large sums of money so that they earn you high interest.

▶ **6 Taxation advice**
Banks will give you advice on how to keep your income tax as low as possible.

▶ **7 Insurance**
You can go to your bank to get insured against, for example, death, or difficulties on a holiday.

▶ **8 Mortgages**
Many banks will now lend you money for very long periods of time to buy or improve a home. These loans are called **mortgages**.

▶ **9 Foreign currency and travellers' cheques**
Banks will make sure that you have foreign money for a journey abroad, or they will provide you with special cheques – **travellers' cheques** – to get foreign money out of banks abroad.

▶ **10 Safety deposit boxes**
The bank can provide you with a very safe box in which to store things like valuable jewels, or the deeds to a house.

▶ **11 Wills**
The bank will help you to deal with many of the legal matters that arise when someone dies and has some property to leave to other people.

## The banking and financial system

### Clearing banks and the clearing system

Everyday, individuals and organisations pass cheques to each other. These cheques are drawn on many different banks and in order to sort out the payments that must be made each day between them the banks use the Clearing House system at the Bank of England. The Clearing House works out how much each bank owes every other bank at the end of a day's business, and credits and debits their accounts at the Bank of England accordingly.

The Clearing House is used by Barclays, Lloyds, National Westminster and the Midland banks (known collectively as 'The Big Four Clearing Banks'), and by smaller clearing banks. Although not called clearing banks, the Co-operative Bank, the Trustee Savings Bank, and the National Girobank also use the system.

### Other financial institutions

#### ▶ 1 The Bank of England

The Bank of England has a few personal customers, but most of its work is involved with the banking and financial system as a whole. Some of its functions include:

▷ **a** The issue of bank notes for England and Wales. It is the only bank allowed to do this.

▷ **b** The government's bank. The Bank of England manages the accounts of government departments. It also manages the **Public Sector Borrowing Requirement** (PSBR) and the **National Debt**. The PSBR is the total amount of money that the government has to borrow in a year if its spending exceeds its tax revenue. The National Debt is the total outstanding debt accumulated by the government over the years. The bank borrows funds on behalf of the government, and it pays interest and repays past debt.

▷ **c** The Bank of England is the 'bankers' bank'. Other banks hold the equivalent of current accounts with the Bank of England which are used to settle debts between them through the Clearing House system. The other banks can also make payments to the government through the Bank of England.

▷ **d** Management of monetary policy. The Bank uses the supply of bank notes and its ability to affect how much money is lent to customers by the clearing banks to control the amount of money in the economy. This matter is considered in more detail in Unit 7.4.

▷ **e** The management of foreign exchange. This includes the purchase and sale of currencies and gold on foreign exchange markets.

▷ **f** Supervision of the banking system. The Bank makes sure that other banks act in a proper fashion, and carry out the various banking laws that have been passed by the government.

The Bank of England will also rescue the banking system if a shortage of cash appears. The major clearing banks have short-term deposits with other institutions called **discount houses**. If the banks need cash they can withdraw these deposits at any time. If the banks need a lot of cash, the discount houses may run short, and the Bank of England can supply extra cash to the discount houses.

#### ▶ 2 The National Girobank

This is a banking service offered by the Post Office. It offers very similar services to the clearing banks, and it operates through the 20,000 post offices throughout the country.

#### ▶ 3 The Trustee Savings Bank

These banks originally offered mainly savings services, but now they offer many of the services available at clearing banks, including cheque accounts and personal loans.

#### ▶ 4 Merchant banks

These banks offer a variety of services to commerce and industry. These include **accepting** (which means 'guaranteeing') **bills of exchange**. These bills are basically IOUs given by an import trader in return for goods received from someone in a foreign country. The bills, promising payment at some future date, were often not acceptable to the seller abroad unless a merchant bank had investigated the buyer and accepted the bill.

Merchant banks also guarantee **finance bills**. These are similar to bills of exchange in that they are IOUs issued by large companies when they wish to raise very large sums of money.

Merchant banks provide many services to companies wishing to issue new shares. These include **underwriting**, which means undertaking to buy any shares that may remain unsold when a company sells shares to the public in order to raise finance. Examples of merchant banks are N M Rothschild and Hill Samuel.

#### ▶ 5 Building societies

The main role of building societies is to accept deposits, and make loans for house purchase and home improvements. In recent years people have used building society share accounts to transact their day-to-day business. Some societies even have a cheque account. More recently, building societies have been given increasing freedom to compete with banks, for example by giving loans not specifically for house purchase. Britain's two largest building societies are the Halifax and the Abbey National.

**Unit 3.3** *The banking and financial system*

## DATABASE

### Non-cash methods of payment by households

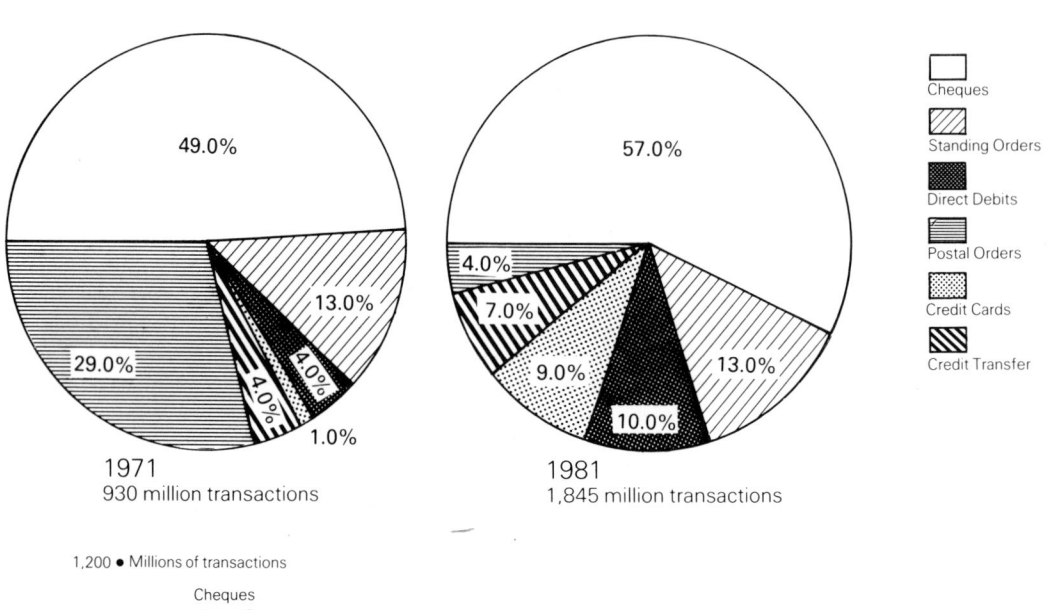

**1971** — 930 million transactions
- Cheques: 49.0%
- Standing Orders: 13.0%
- Direct Debits: 4.0%
- Postal Orders: 29.0%
- Credit Cards: 1.0%
- Credit Transfer: 4.0%

**1981** — 1,845 million transactions
- Cheques: 57.0%
- Standing Orders: 13.0%
- Direct Debits: 10.0%
- Postal Orders: 9.0%
- Credit Cards: 7.0%
- Credit Transfer: 4.0%

Millions of transactions (bar chart, 1971 vs 1981): Cheques, Standing Orders, Direct Debits, Postal Orders, Credit Cards, Credit Transfer.

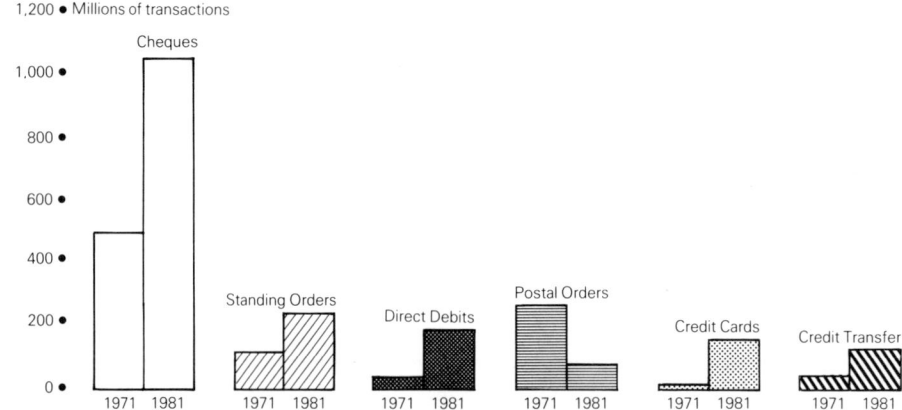

(Source: *Barclays Review*: November 1985)

Unit 3.3 *The banking and financial system*

## ACTIVITIES

### SECTION A: FOCUS ON UNIT 3.3

Go back and answer the questions raised in the Focus.

### SECTION B: STEPPED QUESTIONS

1. **a** Describe the following methods of transaction:
   - ▷ Bank Giro (credit slips and direct credit)
   - ▷ Cheques and cheque guarantee cards
   - ▷ Standing orders
   - ▷ Direct debit.
   
   **b** Give TWO examples of occasions when EACH method would be used.
   
   **c** Draw up a bank statement showing the transactions taking place in one month for a young couple with a small car renting a council house. Use Fig. 3.3e to help you.

2. **a** Explain the difference between a personal loan and an overdraft.
   
   **b** Give TWO examples of occasions when EACH type of loan would be used.
   
   **c** Explain the factors that a bank manager would take into account when deciding whether to grant a personal loan.

### SECTION C: DATA RESPONSE QUESTIONS

## Changes in the holding of bank current accounts

|  | 1976 | 1981 | 1983 |
|---|---|---|---|
|  |  | per cent |  |
| Proportion of adult population with account | 45 | 61 | 62 |
| Proportion of working population with account | 51 | 72 | 75 |

*Source:* Inter-Bank Research Organisation
(working population: those in paid employment and the registered unemployed)

(Source: *A Guide to the British Financial System*, Banking Information Service, 1984)

1. **a** Describe the trends shown in the data.
   
   **b** Explain why these trends have taken place.
   
   **c** ▷ What effects do you think these changes have had on the proportion of payments made using cash?
   
   ▷ What alternatives to cash could be used for making payments?

2  Transcash

> **Transcash**
> This is an easy and economical way to pay bills such as electricity, gas, and many others at a post office or to send money to anyone who has a Girobank account.
> When you next have to pay a bill or send money, check whether the organisation or person you are paying has a Girobank account. This information is often on the bill. If not, ask to see the Girobank Directory of account holders at your post office.
> Then pick up and complete the special Transcash slip (or use the stub attached to the bill) and hand it in at a post office together with the correct money plus the handling fee.
> You will certainly save time and trouble and could save money.

(Source: *National Girobank*)

**a** Transcash is a service of the National Girobank. Where would you go to open a National Girobank account?
**b** What is the purpose of the Transcash service?
**c** What do you do if you do not know the Girobank account number of someone you wish to pay?
**d** How do you pay bills using Transcash?
**e** How could using Transcash save you time and money?

Unit 3.3 *The banking and financial system*

## COURSE WORK

## PART 3: COURSEWORK SUGGESTION

### BANKING AND BUSINESS

1. Visit some local banks and collect leaflets about services which banks offer to businesses. Contact the head office of some banks to see whether there is any additional information available.
2. Use a grid to analyse which banks offer which services. For example, down the side list the different services and across the top write the names of the banks. Tick the boxes to show the availability of services.
3. Design a leaflet which could be used to persuade small businesses to make greater use of banking services.

### EXTENSION COURSEWORK

4. Find out how a local business or businesses have used banking services. Write a report which highlights the benefits and problems that the businesses have found when using banks.

## DICTIONARY

Here are some more words and phrases for your Dictionary of Economic Terms. Remember to look for each word or phrase in the text and then write your own definition for it.

Bank of England
barter
building society
clearing bank
clearing system
cost of living
current account
deposit account
discount house
inflation
merchant bank
Retail Prices Index (RPI)
standard of living
value of money

# Part 4
# Managing your money

# UNIT 4.1 Getting paid

**FOCUS**

▶ What are the different ways in which people can receive an income?

▶ What is **gross pay** and **net pay**?

▶ How do rising prices affect the value of incomes?

▶ What is **real income**?

During your life, you may receive money from many different places and in many different ways. These are just some of the ways in which you might receive **income** (money coming to you):

▶ **1 Earnings from employment**
If you go to work for someone else you will be an **employee**. For giving them your services you will receive wages or a salary. This section is mostly about getting paid as an employee.

▶ **2 Earnings from self-employment**
If you are your own boss you are said to be **self-employed**. You will decide your own earnings from the profits made by your business.

▶ **3 Earnings from investments**
Some people own stocks and shares in companies which earn them interest and dividends each year. Many people have savings which earn interest.

▶ **4 Pensions and social security benefits**
Many people nowadays receive a pension from the company they have worked for when they retire. Everyone who has retired and has paid National Insurance contributions can receive a pension from the state. Many people receive other benefits from the state through the social security system, for example when they are very poor, or unemployed.

**Figure 4.1a**
In what ways might a person receive income throughout his or her life?

### The pay packet

If you are an employee you will usually get paid weekly, in which case your money will probably be called a **wage**, or monthly in which case your money will probably be called a **salary**. You will receive a pay packet. In it you will find a pay slip and, if your money has not been paid straight into the bank, a cheque or cash.

Some important words connected with your pay packet are as follows:

▶ **1 Gross pay**

This is all the income you have earned and it includes all or some of the following:

▷ *Basic pay* This is the minimum amount you will receive each week or month.

▷ *Overtime pay* This is pay for working more than normal hours. It might be paid at a higher rate than you would get for your normal working hours.

▷ *Bonus* This is extra pay, and can be given for a number of reasons. You may have been able to produce more, and be given a **productivity bonus**. You may receive a bonus at Christmas or before your holiday.

▶ **2 Deductions**

These are all the sums of money that will be taken out of your gross pay before you get it. Money is deducted for various reasons:

▷ *Income tax* This money is used by the government to provide services like education and defence.

▷ *National Insurance contributions* This money is used by the government mainly to make payments to workers who are out of work for any reason, for example because they are ill, unemployed or retired.

▷ *Superannuation and private pension scheme contributions* You may have to make payments for a pension scheme run by the organisation you work for, as well as a payment for a state pension.

▷ *Other deductions* Money may also be taken out of your pay packet for things like trade union subscriptions, saving schemes, and private health insurance.

▶ **3 Net pay**

This is your gross pay minus deductions. It is your **take-home pay**. It is sometimes called your **disposable income**, because it is what you have available to spend on goods and services.

### Different ways of getting paid

In most jobs people are paid on a **time rate**. This means that they are paid for the length of time that they work, rather than the amount they produce. For example, in an engineering firm, John is a shopfloor worker who is paid an hourly rate. Ann, who works in one of the offices, is paid a monthly salary. Both of them are paid a time rate.

In some jobs, people are paid on a **piece rate**. This means that they are paid for the amount they produce, no matter how many hours they work. For example, in another engineering firm, Ted is paid so much for each valve he produces. This is a piece rate. Ted likes piece work because he can earn a lot when the job is going smoothly, but if he has a problem with one of the valves, then his wage goes down as he takes time to sort it out.

There are wide differences in wages for different jobs. The reasons for these are explained in Unit 7.3.

**Figure 4.1b**
What information is shown on a pay slip?

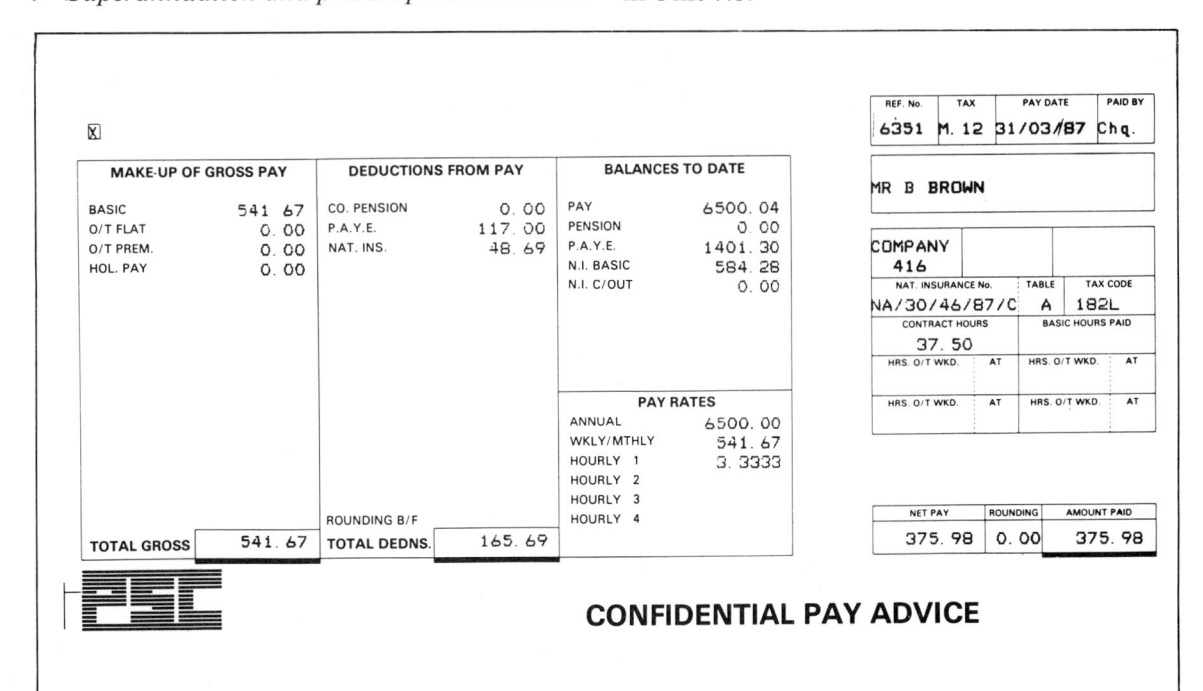

**Figure 4.1c**
What is the name given to a reward for working other than pay, such as a company car?

### Other rewards for working

Sometimes employees are given **perks** or **fringe benefits** instead of extra pay in their pay packets. Some organisations give their workers luncheon vouchers, or provide cheap canteen food. Some people get free private medical insurance. A company car is a particularly valuable fringe benefit.

### Real and money income

We have already seen that the value of money is what you can buy with it. When Liz started work she earned £100 a week. This sum was her **money income**. Liz used this money to buy goods and services to the value of £100. The amount of goods and services that she could buy is called her **real income**. At the end of her first year Liz didn't get a pay rise, but prices had risen during the year. Her money income was the same (£100 a week), but her real income had fallen because she could buy less with it. At the end of her second year Liz did get a pay rise, but it was less than the rise in prices, so although her money income had now risen, her real income was still falling.

Unit 4.1 *Getting paid*

## DATABASE

# Methods of wage/salary payment

|  | 1976 | 1981 | 1983 |
|---|---|---|---|
|  |  | per cent |  |
| Proportion of employees paid in cash | 59 | 44 | 41 |
| Proportion paid by bank methods | 39 | 53 | 56 |
| Other | 2 | 3 | 3 |
| Total | 100 | 100 | 100 |

Source: *Inter-Bank Research Organisation*

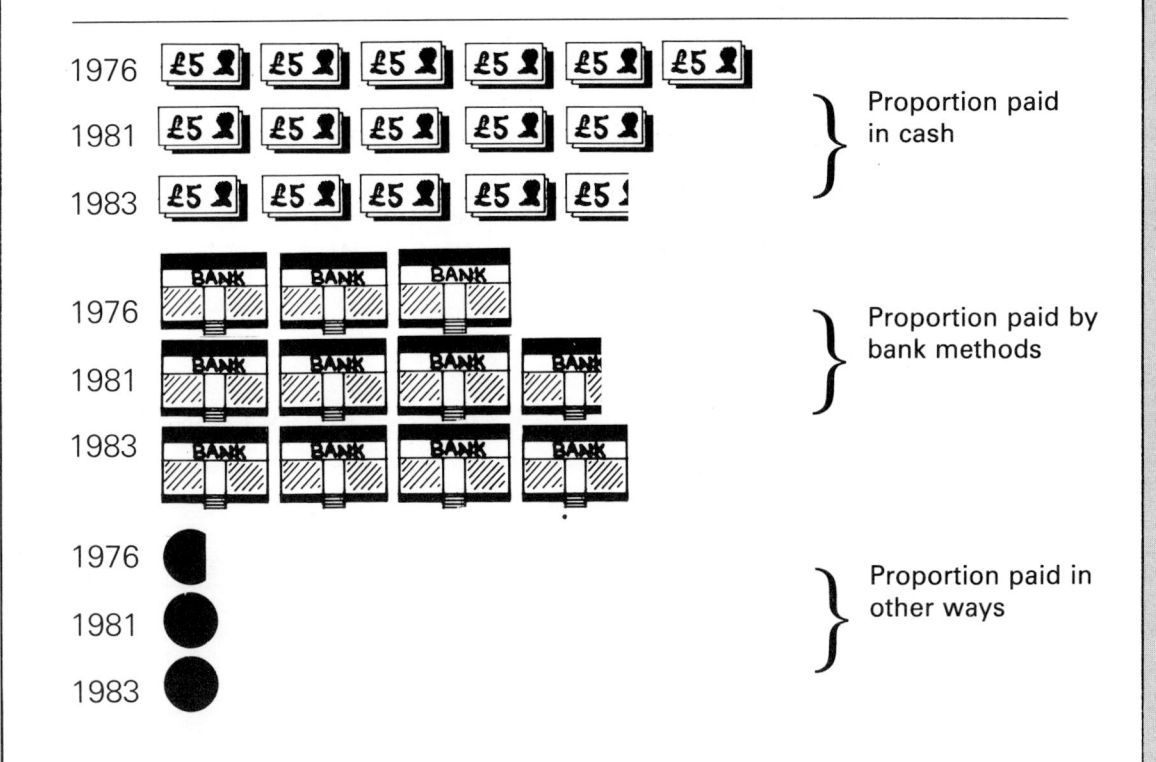

Proportion paid in cash:
- 1976
- 1981
- 1983

Proportion paid by bank methods:
- 1976
- 1981
- 1983

Proportion paid in other ways:
- 1976
- 1981
- 1983

(Source: *A Guide to the British Financial System*, Banking Information Service, 1984)

## ACTIVITIES

### SECTION A: FOCUS ON UNIT 4.1

Go back and answer the questions raised in the Focus.

### SECTION B: STEPPED QUESTIONS

1 a ▷ Describe the items that are included in 'gross pay'.
    ▷ Describe the items that are deducted from gross pay to give net pay.
  b Explain the factors that might cause the following to change:
    ▷ gross pay
    ▷ deductions
    ▷ real income.
2 a What is meant by:
    ▷ a piece rate
    ▷ a time rate?
  b Explain why factory workers are often paid on a piece-work basis whereas teachers are paid time rates.
  c What are the benefits and drawbacks for an employer of paying someone on a time-rate basis?

### SECTION C: DATA RESPONSE QUESTIONS

1

**Mark, the car worker**

Mark's minimum wage in any five-day week is £100. He works an eight-hour day. If he and the other workers manage to produce more cars than usual, he receives up to a £30 bonus when business is good. Mark can work five hours overtime which pays time-and-a-half. Sometimes the employer may add £10 on top of the other payments. Last year was unfortunately a bad year for Mark; although his earnings rose, his real income fell.

  a ▷ What is Mark's basic pay?
    ▷ What kind of bonus is the £30 called?
    ▷ Name one fringe benefit that Mark could receive.
  b What is the maximum amount Mark can be paid in a week for overtime?
  c What is Mark's maximum weekly earnings?
  d Explain why Mark's real income fell, even though his earnings rose.

Unit 4.1 *Getting paid*

**2** *Household income in the UK*

| Income (percentages) | 1978 | 1980 | 1982 |
|---|---|---|---|
| Wages and salaries | 67 | 65 | 62 |
| Income from self-employment | 8 | 7 | 7 |
| Rent, dividends, interest | 6 | 8 | 8 |
| Private pensions etc. | 5 | 6 | 7 |
| Social security benefits | 12 | 12 | 13 |
| Other current transfers | 2 | 2 | 3 |
| Total household income (£s billion) | 128.0 | 181.1 | 218.1 |
| Total household disposable income (£s billion) | 102.7 | 146.7 | 173.8 |
| Real household disposable income per head (index numbers, 1980 = 100) | 94 | 100 | 99 |

(Source: *Social Trends 1984*)

**a** What was the approximate value of:
▷ wages and salaries in 1980
▷ deductions in 1982?
**b** ▷ What does 'real household disposable income per head' mean?
▷ Assuming the population was constant, did money disposable income rise faster than inflation between 1980 and 1982?
Explain your answer.
**c** Describe the trends shown in the data.
**d** Suggest some reasons for the trends you found.

# UNIT 4.2 Planning your spending

**FOCUS**

▶ What is meant by **budgeting**?

▶ What are the major items of expenditure involved in owning a house?

▶ How can different methods of transport impose costs and benefits on both the individual and on society as a whole?

▶ What economic considerations affect an individual's choice of holidays?

## Budgeting

Are you the kind of person who gets to the end of a week and finds that you have no money left? If you are, does it annoy you that other people who seem to receive the same amount of income as you manage to save some of their money and never get into debt? A possible reason why some people appear to manage their money better than other people is that they **budget**: this means that they plan their spending carefully. As people get older and their commitments increase it becomes increasingly more important to budget. If you have to run a home, for example, you will have a great number of expenses and if you do not plan carefully you could quickly run into debt. It may be sensible to start budgeting when you are young to get into good habits for when your financial situation becomes more complicated.

### Recording your income and expenditure

A budget can cover any period of time you wish, although for personal budgeting a week is a sensible period to take. A budget consists of two sections: income and expenditure. The income section shows all the money you have received from whatever source. For example, if you find a £1 coin down the back of the sofa (and you decide to keep it!) you should put '£1 found' on the budget. The usual sources of income for young people are pocket money, wages, interest on savings, presents etc. The expenditure section shows all the ways in which the income has been used, for example spending on clothes, going out, savings etc. The income and expenditure sections must be equal, as shown in *Peter's Weekly Budget* in Fig 4.2a.

You will notice from Peter's budget that his expenditure has exceeded the amount of income he earned from his wages and from interest on savings. He had to borrow from his parents to make up the difference. At some future date his expenditure will have to show '£ 7 repaid loan to parents'.

The rest of this Unit will look at three major areas of expenditure that require careful budgeting: running a home, transport and holidays.

## Running a home

Are you sometimes amazed that adults seem to earn so much yet they are grumbling constantly about money? The problem could be the tremendous costs involved in running a home. Once these costs have been met there may be little surplus for 'luxuries' such as entertainment and holidays.

### The costs of running a home

There are basically two types of costs involved in running a home. The first type of costs are called **fixed costs**, and these costs basically stay the same no matter how much the facilities of the home are used. Rents and mortgage

Figure 4.2a

**Peter's weekly budget**

| Income | | Expenditure | |
|---|---|---|---|
| Wages | £50 | To parent(s) for keep | £20 |
| Interest on savings | £ 5 | Clothes | £15 |
| Borrowed from parents | £ 7 | Record | £ 7 |
| | | Bus fares | £ 5 |
| | | Lunches | £ 5 |
| | | Wedding present for brother | £10 |
| | £62 | | £62 |

repayments are examples of fixed costs. Other costs rise with the increasing use of the home; these costs are called **variable costs** and include payments for services like electricity. Figure 4.2b shows some of the costs of running a home. In addition to the costs shown in the figure there are other costs which can be considerable, for example maintenance and repairs. There are also the costs associated with decorating and furnishing the home, and buying items like washing machines and fridges.

### Consumer durables

Certain items which have a relatively long life and can be used many times over are called **consumer durables**. These are things like washing machines and fridges. There are an increasing number of consumer durables found in modern homes, recent additions being computers, videos and dishwashers. Consumer durables can involve consumers in considerable expense which requires careful budgeting. There are fixed costs and variable costs associated with buying and using consumer durables. For example, Bill bought a washing machine on hire purchase. The payments he makes to the hire purchase company each month are fixed costs. Julie bought her dishwasher out of her savings, but she now puts a fixed amount into her savings account each month for when she has to buy her next one. These payments too are fixed costs; they are to cover the wearing out of the dishwasher and are payments for **depreciation**.

When Bill's washing machine broke down he had to call an engineer to repair it. This was a variable cost. Julie, however, took out a service agreement when she bought her dishwasher. She makes a regular payment to a service company each year and they agree to maintain the dishwasher for no extra cost. So Julie has organised her maintenance as a fixed cost.

### Budgeting for running a home

You should realise by now that it can be very expensive to run a home, and that payments for the home may have to take precedence over payments for other goods and services. Unless you plan very carefully you could easily run into financial difficulties, and if these became really serious you could even find your home being repossessed by a landlord or by the institution that has lent you money to buy your home.

## The choice of transport

Over recent years transport has become an increasingly important part of consumer expenditure. In 1982, for example, £26,332 million was spent on transport and communication, and this category of consumer spending represented about 16 per cent of total consumer spending. Figure 4.2c shows how methods of transport to work changed in the ten-year period from 1971 to 1981. You can see how important the car has become as the main means of transport to work.

The choice of transport made by the individual for his or her journey to work has important implications for the individual and for the community as a whole. The costs and benefits to an individual of choosing a particular method of transport are called **private costs and benefits**. These costs and benefits may be measured partly but not wholly in money terms. For example, Dave walks to work rather than drives in his car because he saves money and improves his health. On the other hand, he has less time when he gets home to spend with his family or on his hobbies. Each method of transport has its financial and non-financial private costs and benefits.

The choice of transport you make also affects the rest of society. For example, by driving to

**Figure 4.2b**

**The basic costs of running a three-bedroomed terraced house in Greater London: 1986**

| Property Payments: | Local rates | £168 per half-year (paid in April & October) | | |
|---|---|---|---|---|
| Insurance: | Mortgage | £500 per month* | | |
| | Buildings | £ 72 per year (paid in April) | | |
| | Contents | £ 60 per year (paid in April) | | |
| | Mortgage protection | £ 10 per month | | |
| **Basic Services:** | | | | |
| Period covered | Gas | Electricity | Phone | Water |
| Jan–March | £80 | £70 | £45 | |
| April–June | £50 | £60 | £45 | } £36 |
| July–Sept | £40 | £50 | £45 | |
| Oct–Dec | £70 | £60 | £45 | } £36 |

*assumes a mortgage of approximately £50,000

**Figure 4.2c**
Principal means of transport to work: 1971–1981 (% of total)

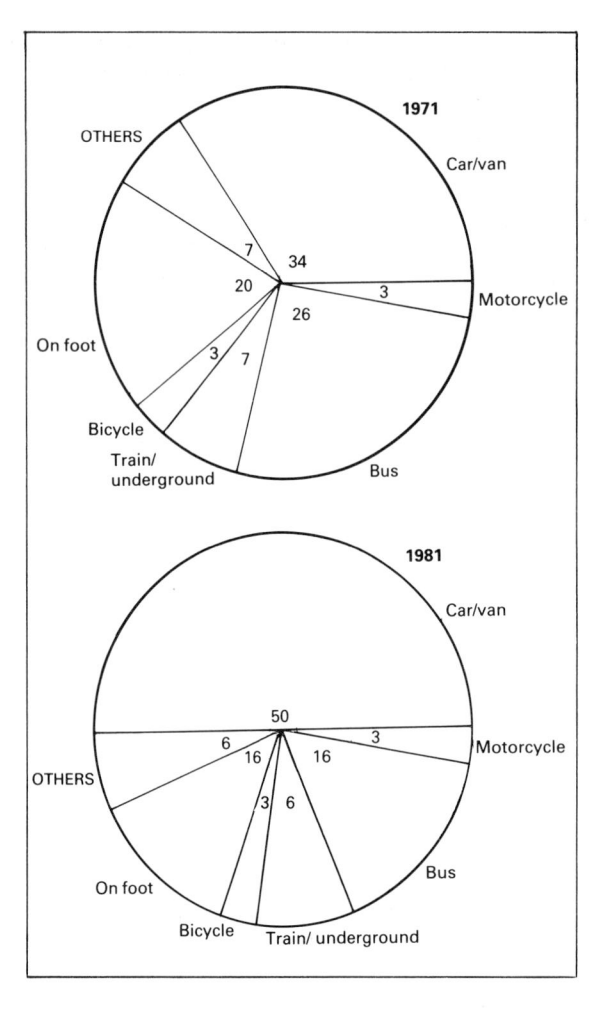

[Pie chart 1971: Car/van 34, Motorcycle 3, Bus 26, Train/underground 7, Bicycle 3, On foot 20, Others 7]

[Pie chart 1981: Car/van 50, Motorcycle 3, Bus 16, Train/underground 6, Bicycle 3, On foot 16, Others 6]

## The choice of holiday

There are three main questions to ask yourself when thinking about a holiday, and each has important implications for your budget. The questions are: when should you go?; where should you go?; and how should you travel?

### ▶ 1 When should you go?

Have a look at Fig 4.2d which shows the prices of holidays at different times of the year and think about how the time of the year could influence your choice of holiday.

### ▶ 2 Where should you go?

There is an enormous variety of locations where people can spend their holidays. Much will depend on the type of holiday that you are looking for. If you want to spend a lot of time on the beach you will obviously look for somewhere hot and dry. If, on the other hand, you want an 'activity' holiday where you can spend your time mountaineering or walking, then you may choose somewhere inland that is relatively cool and remote.

Another important factor in deciding where to spend your holiday is whether to travel abroad or stay in the UK. In recent years more and more holidays have been taken abroad as incomes have risen, the cost of travelling has fallen, and the cost of staying in foreign countries is often lower than the cost of staying in the UK.

### ▶ 3 How should you travel?

The cost of getting to your holiday location can be one of the major expenses for which you will need to budget. Nowadays many people choose to buy a package holiday where the travel costs are included in with the cost of accommodation and other costs like food. If you do not go on a package holiday you will need to compare the alternative methods of transport available. Figure 4.2e shows the cost of various methods of travelling to Athens.

work you will add to pollution and congestion by emitting noise and fumes and by further clogging up already crowded roads. On the other hand you may be benefiting society because when you buy a car you create jobs and income. The costs and benefits that fall on society as a whole as a result of an economic decision are called **external costs and benefits**. The total costs and benefits (i.e. the private costs and benefits plus the external costs and benefits) of an economic decision, such as the decision about how to travel to work, are called **social costs and benefits**.

## Holidays

Budgeting helps make you think carefully about the economic choices that you have to make when planning your spending. Some items of expenditure are particularly large and they must be thought about especially carefully. Holidays, for example, account for £4 out of every £100 spent by the average family. The decision to take a holiday will mean the sacrifice of other items of expenditure and it is important that spending on a holiday is carefully planned.

**Figure 4.2e**

**The cost of travelling to Athens**
**(Return prices, August 1986)**

| | |
|---|---|
| Coach | £ 73 |
| Rail (full-price) | £227.40 |
| (Interrail card) | £119.00 (exc. Lon–Dover) |
| Plane (full-price scheduled) | £564 |
| (standby) | £214 |
| (APEX – booked two weeks in advance) | £159 |
| ('bucket shop') | £109 |

### The 'hidden costs' of a holiday

Even if you decide to go on a package holiday the cost of the holiday may greatly exceed the basic cost of travel and accommodation. Figure 4.2f shows the kind of statement included in many travel brochures. It shows that the price of a holiday does not necessarily include all the expenses of taking a holiday. Some holiday firms, unlike the one shown, will put a surcharge (extra payment) on to the price of the holiday if, for example, the price of oil and therefore aviation fuel suddenly increased.

## Budgeting for your holiday

Once you have decided on your holiday you will need to plan how you are going to pay for the holiday. You could either save for your holiday or you could pay for the holiday on credit, i.e. borrow the money. The advantages and disadvantages of saving and borrowing are described in later Units, as are the different methods of payment (for example cash, credit card, cheque etc.) that you could use to pay for the holiday and to make payments while you are away.

Figure 4.2d

| The price of Splendide Holidays (all prices in £s sterling) | | | |
|---|---|---|---|
| Departure Dates (Fridays) | **Camp Delight** | **Apartments** | **Hotel Del Sol** |
| Apr 25th–May 9th | 130 | 150 | 180 |
| May 16th–Jun 6th | 190 | 210 | 250 |
| Jun 13th–Aug 22nd | 200 | 230 | 270 |
| Aug 29th–Sept 5th | 190 | 210 | 250 |
| Sept 12th–Oct 3rd | 160 | 180 | 220 |

Figure 4.2f

**Extract from the brochure of Splendide Holidays**

What the price of your holiday includes:
★ Travel to and from your holiday resort from the point of departure
★ All motorway tolls, port fees etc. payable on the journey
★ All accommodation charges for your camping, self-catering or hotel holiday
★ Courier services and sightseeing tours as specified in the brochure

What the price of your holiday does not include:
★ Holiday insurance
★ The cost of travel to the point of departure
★ Refreshments on the journey to the holiday resort

★★★★★★★★**NO SURCHARGE GUARANTEE**★★★★★★★★

**There will be no hidden or late additions to the prices quoted in the brochure providing that you book before 31st January.**

# DATABASE

## Holiday accommodation used by adults resident in Great Britain, 1971 and 1982

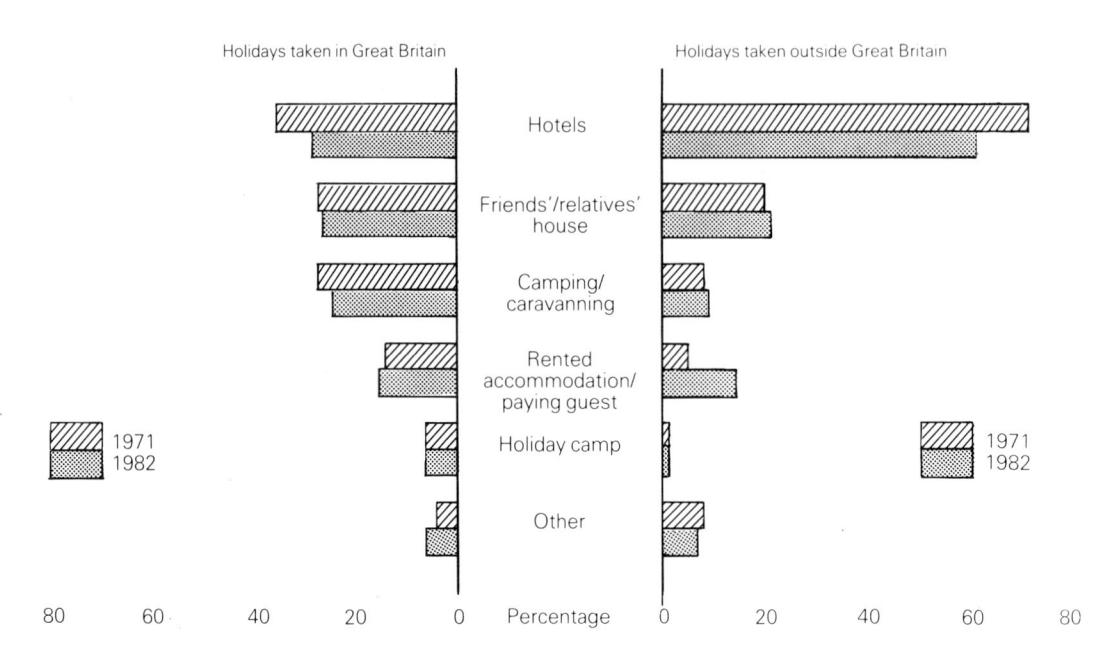

Holidays taken in Great Britain | Holidays taken outside Great Britain

- Hotels
- Friends'/relatives' house
- Camping/caravanning
- Rented accommodation/paying guest
- Holiday camp
- Other

1971
1982

Percentage: 80 60 40 20 0 — 0 20 40 60 80

1971
1982

(Source: *Social Trends 1984*)

Unit 4.2 *Planning your spending*

## ACTIVITIES

### SECTION A: FOCUS ON UNIT 4.2

Go back and answer the questions raised in the Focus.

### SECTION B: STEPPED QUESTIONS

1. **a** Describe the items that you would include in your weekly income and expenditure.
   **b** Explain why keeping a written record of income and expenditure can help people to manage their money more successfully.
   **c** Draw a grid to show how a home owner would plan for his or her annual spending on their home. Use the figures in Fig 4.2b or use figures obtained from your parents. Across the top of the grid you should have the months of the year and down the side you should have the various items of expenditure shown in Fig 4.2b. Fill in the appropriate figures in the appropriate boxes, noting that bills for services tend to come in the month after the period they refer to.
   **d** Calculate the cost of running the home each month and show the information in a bar chart.
   **e** Explain how having a service agreement on a washing machine can turn a variable cost into a fixed cost.

2. **a** List the different ways by which someone could make a one-mile journey to work each day.
   **b** Draw four columns headed 'Private Costs', 'Private Benefits', 'External Costs' and 'External Benefits'. List the various costs and benefits associated with using a bus to travel to work.

3. **a** Why is it so much more expensive to take a holiday at some times of the year than at others?
   **b** Explain what economic idea is described by the sentence: 'The decision to take a holiday will mean the sacrifice of other items of expenditure.'
   **c** Explain how changes in the transport industry have affected people's choice of a holiday.

## SECTION C: DATA RESPONSE QUESTION

| Ownership of consumer durables, 1984 | |
|---|---|
| % of homes | with: |
| 0–20 | Dishwasher<br>Microwave oven |
| 21–40 | Video recorder<br>Home computer<br>Separate freezer |
| 41–60 | Clothes dryer<br>Power lawn mower |
| 61–80 | Central heating<br>Car<br>Telephone |
| 81–100 | Washing machine<br>Cooker<br>Cassette player<br>Record playing equipment<br>Colour television<br>Refrigerator<br>Vacuum cleaner<br>Radio |

(Source: *Midland Bank Review* 1986)

a Name *three* consumer durables found in less than half of all homes in 1984.

b ▷ Name *three* goods that may have been considered 'luxuries' in the past which may be considered 'necessities' nowadays.
▷ Give reasons for your answer.

c Explain why most households possess an increasing number of consumer durables in spite of the expense associated with owning and running them.

d ▷ Which consumer durables are sometimes rented rather than bought?
▷ Explain why this may happen.

# UNIT 4.3  Saving

## FOCUS

▶ For what reasons might a person save?

▶ Why are people paid interest on savings?

▶ What different methods of saving are available?

▶ Why do different methods pay different rates of interest?

▶ What is an **index-linked** savings scheme?

## Why people save

People save for many reasons. These are just some of them:

▶ 1 They save up to buy something that they cannot afford at the present time, like a car or the deposit on a house.

▶ 2 People save 'for a rainy day'. They like to have some money put aside for emergencies. For example, they might have an unexpected expensive repair bill on their car.

▶ 3 People save for their old age. Putting money into a pension scheme so you will have some money when you retire is a way of saving.

▶ 4 People save for their children. Some people put money aside regularly in a savings account for their children, and give the children the money when they have grown up.

## One person's saving is another person's borrowing

Although we might not realise it, sometimes when we save we are in fact lending our money to someone else. If we save in a building society we are lending the money to people who borrow it to buy houses. If we save with the National Savings Bank we are in fact lending to the government. Of course, if we put our money in a piggy bank at home, no one else gets the benefit of borrowing it.

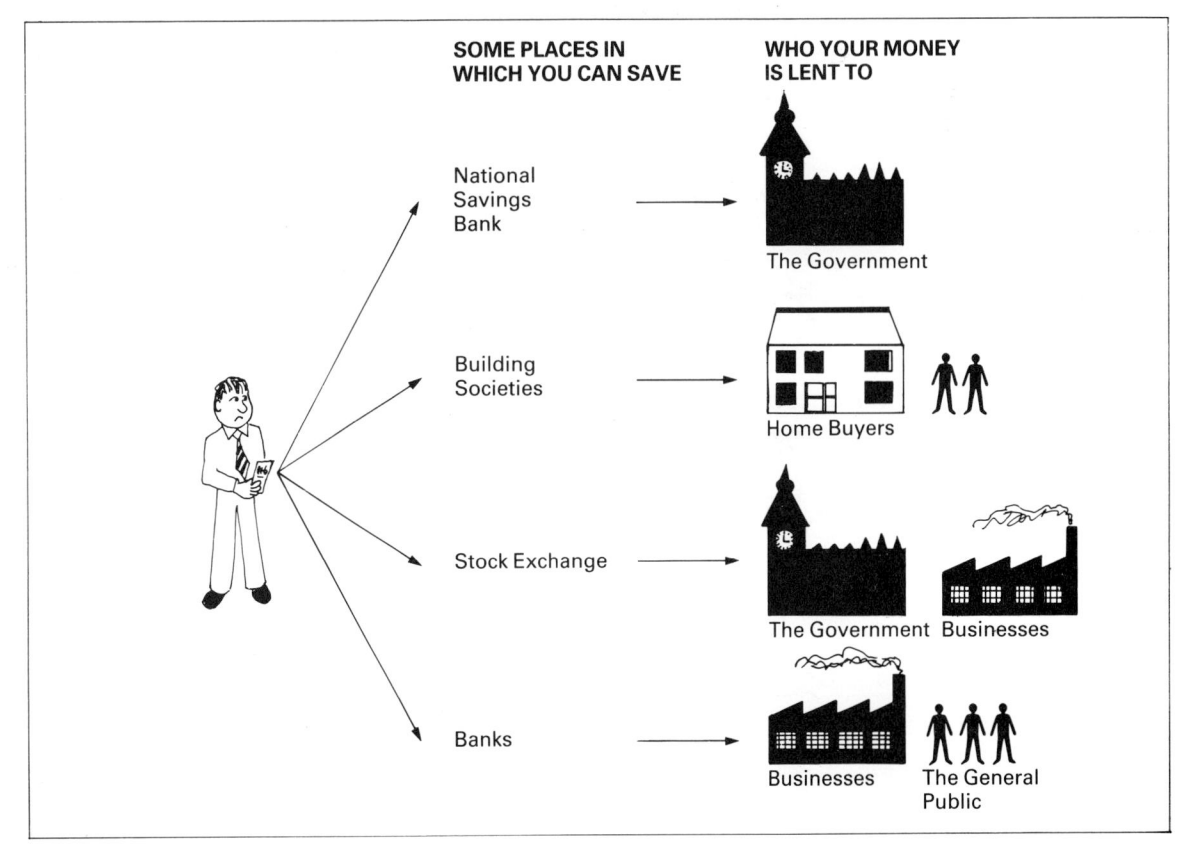

**Figure 4.3a**
How may one person's lending be another person's borrowing?

| SOME PLACES IN WHICH YOU CAN SAVE | WHO YOUR MONEY IS LENT TO |
|---|---|
| National Savings Bank | The Government |
| Building Societies | Home Buyers |
| Stock Exchange | The Government, Businesses |
| Banks | Businesses, The General Public |

## Earning interest on savings

If we save, and lend our money to someone else, they will pay us for the privilege of borrowing our money. The extra amount that they pay is the **interest**. It follows that if we borrow someone else's money, say by taking out a bank loan, we have to pay interest ourselves. This is because savers are giving up the opportunity to spend their money now, in order to spend it later.

Look at this example: John and Liz both have £100. John took his and put it in his piggy bank, pleased with the idea that it will be there when he needs it. Liz took her money and opened a building society account with it. The society paid 5 per cent interest on the account, so at the end of a year Liz had £100 × 5% = £5 interest, plus of course the £100 she started with. At the end of a year John still had £100.

Liz left her money, now £105, in the building society for another year, and they paid her 5% interest on that sum: £105 × 5% = £5.25, so now she had £110.25. At the end of two years John still had his £100.

If Liz left her money in the building society for ten years she would have a grand total of £162.89. If the rate of interest was as high as 10 per cent a year Liz would have had £259.37 at the end of ten years. John would still have had his £100! It does not pay to leave your money in a piggy bank!

**Figure 4.3b**
What is the amount you pay someone for the service of lending you money called?

*"You borrowed 10p at 10% per annum for 1 month – that comes to 10.08333p you owe me!"*

## Interest and income tax

Once you have more than a certain amount of money coming in each year (your **income**), you will have to pay **income tax** on it. Interest on savings counts as part of your income, and when you go to work your income may be high enough for you to have to pay tax on any interest you receive from savings. Tax can affect the way you receive interest, and interest can be paid in the following ways:

▶ **1 Gross of tax**

This means you get all the interest without any tax taken off. If you are a taxpayer you must tell the government about your interest, as they will want a percentage of it for tax. Most interest on National Savings is paid gross of tax.

▶ **2 Net of tax**

This means that tax has already been taken off. If you do not have to pay tax, you cannot reclaim the tax. People who do not pay tax therefore might be best advised to put their money in savings schemes which pay interest gross of tax. Building societies and banks usually pay interest net of tax.

▶ **3 Free of all tax**

Some savings schemes pay interest that no one has to pay tax on. Much of the interest paid out if you have a National Savings Bank ordinary account is free of all tax.

## Why some savings schemes pay more interest than others

If you have looked in the window of, for example, a building society, you will have seen that they advertise many different savings schemes all with different rates of interest. This is because savers have to be paid more to persuade them to give up more of their money, or to give their money up for a longer time. For example, some savings schemes tend to pay lower rates of interest because:

▶ **1** You need only have a small amount, often as low as £1, to open the savings account.

▶ **2** You can get your money out quickly, possibly without giving any **notice**, without losing any interest.

▶ **3** It is very easy to pay in and take out money whenever you like.

Other schemes tend to pay higher rates of interest because:

▶ **1** You have to start off with a large sum to open an account, often £500 or more, or you have to put money into the savings account on a regular monthly basis.

▶ **2** You may have to say one week, one month or more in advance that you want your money out (this is called **giving notice**), or you may take out your money more quickly, but with a great loss of interest.

▶ 3 You may have to leave your money in the savings account for some minimum period of time, often a year, before you earn the highest rates of interest.

## Where you can save your money

There are many places you can go to open a savings account. This section looks at just a few of them.

▶ **1 Building societies**
▷ *Share accounts* This is a very popular way of saving. Harry opened his account with £1. He gets a pass book which lets him put money in and take it out whenever he likes.
▷ *Regular savings accounts* Alma saves £20 a month with her account. It pays her a higher rate of interest than an ordinary share account.
▷ *Accounts for saving large sums* Ken has one of these accounts. It pays him a high rate of interest, but he had to open it with £500, and he must give 28 days' notice to take it out without loss of interest. Some of these accounts have a 'stepped' interest rate. This means that they pay you more interest as you save more money. You can usually take your money out without losing interest.

▶ **2 Banks**
Banks, including the 'Big Four' of Barclays, Lloyds, Midland and National Westminster as well as the Trustee Savings Bank (TSB), offer savings schemes in addition to a range of banking services.

▷ *Deposit accounts* Richard has a deposit account, and this pays him interest, unlike his current account. He can put money in and take it out whenever he likes, but he might lose interest on it. He gets a regular statement telling him how much he has in his deposit account.
▷ *Savings accounts* June uses this account to save regularly. It pays her a higher rate of interest than a deposit account. Many banks are also competing with building societies by offering higher interest accounts for large sums.

▶ **3 The Post Office**
The Post Office operates the National Savings Scheme. These are some of the savings schemes which you can join through the Post Office.
▷ *National Savings Bank ordinary account* Theresa opened her account with £1, and she can take out up to £100 at a time. Some of the interest she earns will be tax free.
▷ *National Savings Bank investment account* Terry opened his account with £5, but he must give one month's notice before he can take his money out. The account pays him a higher rate of interest than the ordinary account.
▷ *National Savings Certificates* Ray buys these in units of £25. He is paid a fixed rate of interest which increases each year for five years. These are very popular with taxpayers because the interest is free of tax.
▷ *National Savings Certificates (index-linked)* These are a type of National Savings Certificate which can be bought in £25 units. Martin bought some, and if he keeps them for a year, the repayment value of them will be linked to the Retail Prices Index. This means that the

**Figure 4.3c**
Why does the National Savings Bank offer so many different savings schemes?

government has agreed to keep the value of the certificates in line with inflation. If Martin keeps his certificates for five years he will get a bonus.

▷ *Yearly plan* Shelley joined this plan. She agreed to make a regular payment for a year. At the end of the year she gets a Yearly Plan Certificate. This certificate will earn interest for Shelley for another four years, and all of the interest is tax free.

▷ *Premium bonds* Joy decided to take a chance. She bought some premium bonds. She had to buy £5 worth (5 units) to start with. A computer randomly selects premium bond numbers. The lucky people who hold the bonds with these numbers receive all of the interest in the form of cash prizes. Prizes vary from £50 to £250,000, but Joy is still waiting for her win!

▷ *Income bonds* Savita has over £2,000 to save, so she can buy income bonds. She can buy further bonds in units of £1,000 and will be paid interest in the form of a regular monthly income.

### ▶ 4 Other ways of saving

The organisations listed offer other schemes of saving in addition to those outlined here.

They are constantly offering new schemes, and changing the conditions of the existing ones. If you want to know more, it is best to go along to the organisations themselves and ask for information.

You can use life insurance as a savings scheme too. The section on insurance further on tells you how life assurance can be used for savings.

You can save money by investing on the Stock Exchange. The Stock Exchange is looked at more closely in Unit 6.4. If you buy stocks and shares on the Stock Exchange you are investing your money in business and in the government. There is more risk in this type of saving if the businesses fail, but possibly more return if they do well. You will usually need a large amount of money to make investment in stocks and shares worthwhile.

## DATABASE

1

## Interest rates on savings in August, 1986

### YOUR SAVINGS

|  | % Interest net | % gross equiv. for basic rate taxpayer | Tax | £ Min |
|---|---|---|---|---|
| **BANKS** | | | | |
| Deposit | 4.3-4.375 | 6.05-6.16 | paid | 1 |
| Regular savings | 5.5-6.625 | 7.75-9.33 | paid | 10/month |
| Lump sum 1 month | 6.75 | 9.51 | paid | 2,500 |
| Lump sum 3 months | 6.625 | 9.33 | paid | 2,000 |
| High interest savings account | 6.4-7.125 | 9.01-10.04 | paid | 1,000+ |
| High interest cheque account | 7-7.2 | 9.86-10.14 | paid | 2,500 |
| **BUILDING SOCIETIES** | | | | |
| Share account | 5.25 | 7.39 | paid | 1 |
| Instant access | 7.00 | 9.86 | paid | 500+ |
|  | 7.5 | 10.56 | paid | 5,000+ |
|  | 7.75 | 10.92 | paid | 10,000+ |
| 90 day | 8.00 | 11.26 | paid | 500+ |
| High interest term | 8.45 | 11.9 | paid | 500+ |
| **TRUSTEE SAVINGS BANK** | | | | |
| Deposit | 4.25 | 5.99 | paid | 1 |
| Premium deposit | 7.00 | 9.86 | paid | 1,000 |
| Marketlink | 6.75 | 9.51 | paid | 10,000 |
|  | net of 29% tax | % interest gross | tax | £ min. |
| **NATIONAL SAVINGS** | | | | |
| Ordinary account | 3 | 3 | 1st £70 free | 1 |
| *Ordinary account | 6 | 6 | 1st £70 free | 500 |
| Investment account | 7.63 | 10.75 | to pay | 5 |
| Deposit bond | 7.99 | 11.25 | to pay | 100 |
| Monthly income bond | 7.99 | 11.25 | to pay | 2,000 |

* Per calendar month if £100 min. held over 1986.

| | | | | |
|---|---|---|---|---|
| **NATIONAL SAVINGS CERTIFICATES (31st issue)** | | | | |
| 1-5 years | 7.85 | 11.06 | free | 25 |
| General extension rate | 8.01 | 11.28 | free | — |
| **INDEX-LINKED CERTIFICATES (4th issue)** | | | | |
|  | RPI linked + 4.04 p.a. compound | — | free | 25 |
| **YEARLY PLAN** | 8.19 | 11.54 | free | 20/month |
| **LOCAL AUTHORITIES** | | | | |
| 1 year | 7.1 | 10 | paid | 500 |
| 10 years | 6.2 | 8.7 | paid | 1,000 |

(Source: *The Guardian* 17.8.86.)

## DATABASE

2

# SHORT TERM FINANCIAL ASSETS OF THE PERSONAL SECTOR.

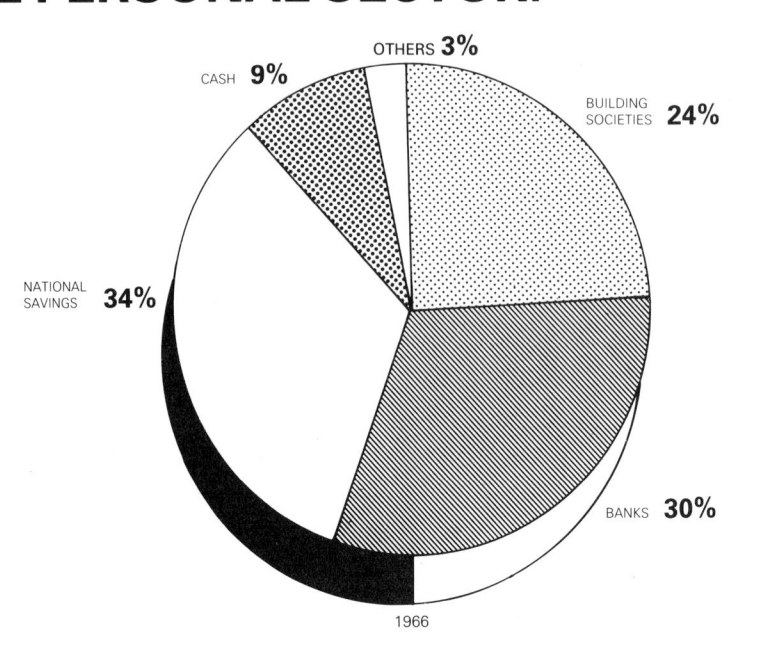

OTHERS **3%**
CASH **9%**
BUILDING SOCIETIES **24%**
NATIONAL SAVINGS **34%**
BANKS **30%**

1966

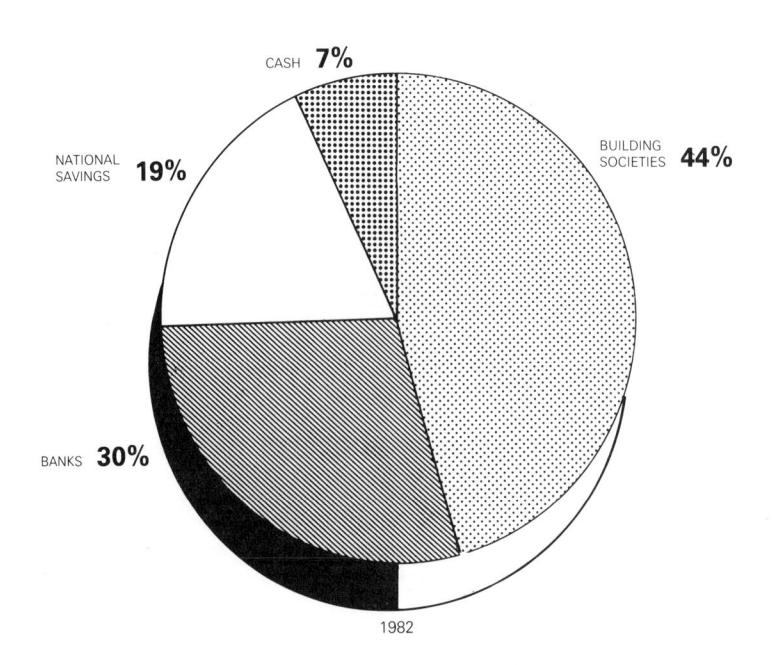

CASH **7%**
BUILDING SOCIETIES **44%**
NATIONAL SAVINGS **19%**
BANKS **30%**

1982

**(Source: *Understanding Building Societies* The Building Societies Association)**

**ACTIVITIES**

## SECTION A: FOCUS ON UNIT 4.3

Go back and answer the questions raised in the Focus.

## SECTION B: STEPPED QUESTIONS

1. **a** Using Database 2, find the percentages of total household savings in 1982 for the following methods of saving:
   ▷ banks
   ▷ National Savings
   ▷ building societies.
   **b** Describe the advantages of the following methods of saving:
   ▷ NSB ordinary account
   ▷ Index-linked National Savings Certificates
   ▷ building societies.
   (Use Database 1 to help you.)
   **c** ▷ What is the opportunity cost of saving?
   ▷ How does opportunity cost apply to the decision whether to save money with a high interest or low interest method of saving?

2. **a** Give one savings scheme you would recommend in each of the following cases:
   ▷ A college student wants to put money in and take money out whenever its needed, particularly on Saturdays.
   ▷ A young worker wants to save £50 a month for at least one year.
   ▷ A pensioner who does not pay tax wants to put away £2,000, and he will not want to withdraw the savings in a hurry.
   **b** Explain the reasons for your choices of schemes in **a**.
   **c** How would the real rate of interest affect a saver's decision about whether or not to save?

## SECTION C: DATA RESPONSE QUESTION

### National Savings Income Bonds

If you need regular income from capital the Income Bond should suit you. It offers:

- Income paid monthly
- Competitive interest
- Access to capital at any time on three months' notice
- No risk to capital

**What is the income?**
The interest rate is 12.75% p.a. from 2 September 1984 (until 2 September 10% p.a.). The rate of interest will vary from time to time but will be kept competitive. Any change in the rate will be widely publicised giving six weeks' notice.

Here are some examples of the income you would receive with interest paid at 12.75% p.a. quoted above:

| HOLDING | ANNUAL INCOME (AT 12.75%) | MONTHLY* INCOME (AVERAGE) |
|---|---|---|
| £2,000 | £255.00 | £21.25 |
| £5,000 | £637.50 | £53.13 |
| £10,000 | £1,275.00 | £106.25 |
| £25,000 | £3,187.50 | £265.63 |
| £50,000 | £6,375.00 | £531.25 |

Each additional investment of £1,000 adds an average of £10.63 to the monthly income, equivalent to £127.50 additional annual income. (Maximum holding £50,000.)

*The precise amount payable will depend on the number of days in each month.

**How much can you invest?**
Your first investment must be at least £2,000. Larger purchases and additions to existing holdings are in multiples of £1,000. The maximum holding is £50,000.

**When is income paid?**
Monthly, on the fifth of each month. The first interest payment on a new Bond will be made on the next interest date after you have held the Bond for 6 weeks and will include all interest due from the date of purchase.

**How is income paid?**
You have the choice of income being paid:

- directly into your bank account or National Savings Bank account.
- by warrant (like a crossed cheque) sent to you by post.

**How is interest calculated?**
Interest is calculated on a day-to-day basis from the date your payment is received at the Bonds and Stock Office.

**What about tax?**
Interest is taxable but is paid in full without deduction of tax at source. Income Bonds are therefore especially attractive to individuals or organisations not subject to Income Tax.

**How much notice for repayment?**
The terms for repayment are being improved. All Income Bond holders can benefit. Under the new terms, any repayment for which notice is given on or after 1 October 1984 will be at three months' notice. (If repayment is required before the end of 1984 the repayment terms of the original prospectus apply.)

(Source: *The Department for National Savings.*)

**a** ▷ Why might savers choose National Income Bonds as opposed to other savings schemes?
  ▷ What is the monthly income on a holding of income bonds of £10,000?
  ▷ What is the minimum amount someone can invest in this scheme?
**b** How is interest paid?
**c** Why is it so attractive to people who do not pay tax?
**d** How long do you have to wait if you want to withdraw money from the scheme?
**e** What other savings schemes would you consider to be similar to Income Bonds?

# UNIT 4.4 Borrowing money

**FOCUS**

▶ Why does the cost of borrowing vary?

▶ What different methods of buying goods on credit and borrowing are available?

## Borrowing money and buying on credit

More and more these days people are buying goods without having the money available at the time to pay for them. They are using other people's money to make the purchases. If you borrow money from someone else in order to buy something, you are said to be buying **on credit** or buying by means of **deferred** (put off) **payments**.

When you buy on credit or by means of deferred payments you are purchasing goods with borrowed money which will need to be paid back at some future date. Consumer durables (e.g. cars and washing machines) are often bought on credit, because it spreads the large cost of these items over a longer period.

### Interest on borrowed money

When you save money, you receive interest for lending your money to someone else. When you buy on credit you need to pay interest on the money you have borrowed. The amount of interest you pay depends on a number of things. These are just some of them:

▶ **1 The amount you borrow**
You may have to pay more for borrowing larger amounts, but this is not always the case.

▶ **2 The length of time you borrow**
It will often cost more to borrow for longer periods of time, but once again, this is not always the case.

▶ **3 The security you can offer**
Sometimes people are unable to repay a loan, and the person or organisation who lends the money will therefore lose it. If you can offer something of value which can be sold to pay for the loan if you cannot repay it for any reason, this could make it easier and possibly cheaper to borrow the money. If someone owns a house, for example, they can offer this as security against a large bank loan.

▶ **4 Your credit rating or creditworthiness**
The more likely you are to pay back a loan without any problems, the easier and cheaper it is likely to be to get the loan. For example, if you have a steady job and you have successfully paid back loans in the past, you will be considered creditworthy with a good credit rating.

## Ways of buying goods on credit

There are many ways you can 'buy now, pay later'. This section looks at some examples of the more popular ones.

▶ **1 Personal loans from banks, and bank overdrafts**
You read about these in the section on banking. They are very popular ways of borrowing because the interest you pay is usually lower than with, for example, hire purchase or credit cards.

▶ **2 Hire purchase**
Consumer durable goods like cars, fridges and washing machines are often bought by means of HP. Hire purchase works like this:

▷ **a** You go to the shop, choose the goods you want, and sign a hire purchase agreement with a finance company who will pay the shop on your behalf.

▷ **b** You pay a deposit when you sign the agreement. This means that you have to pay part of the cost of the good before you can take it away.

▷ **c** From then on you hire the goods from the finance company by paying them instalments (regular weekly or monthly payments). The goods become legally yours only when the last payment has been made.

▷ **d** If you fail to keep up repayments the finance company can repossess the goods. If you have paid one third of the amount you owe, however, they will need a court order to take the goods back.

▷ **e** Because you are hiring the goods, you can return them before the final instalment. If you have not paid half the instalments, however, you might be made to pay them, and you might also be required to pay for any damage.

▶ **3 Credit sale agreements**
These are similar to hire purchase sales, except that you become the legal owner of the goods as soon as you take them out of the shop. You cannot therefore take the goods back if you cannot keep up with the payments.

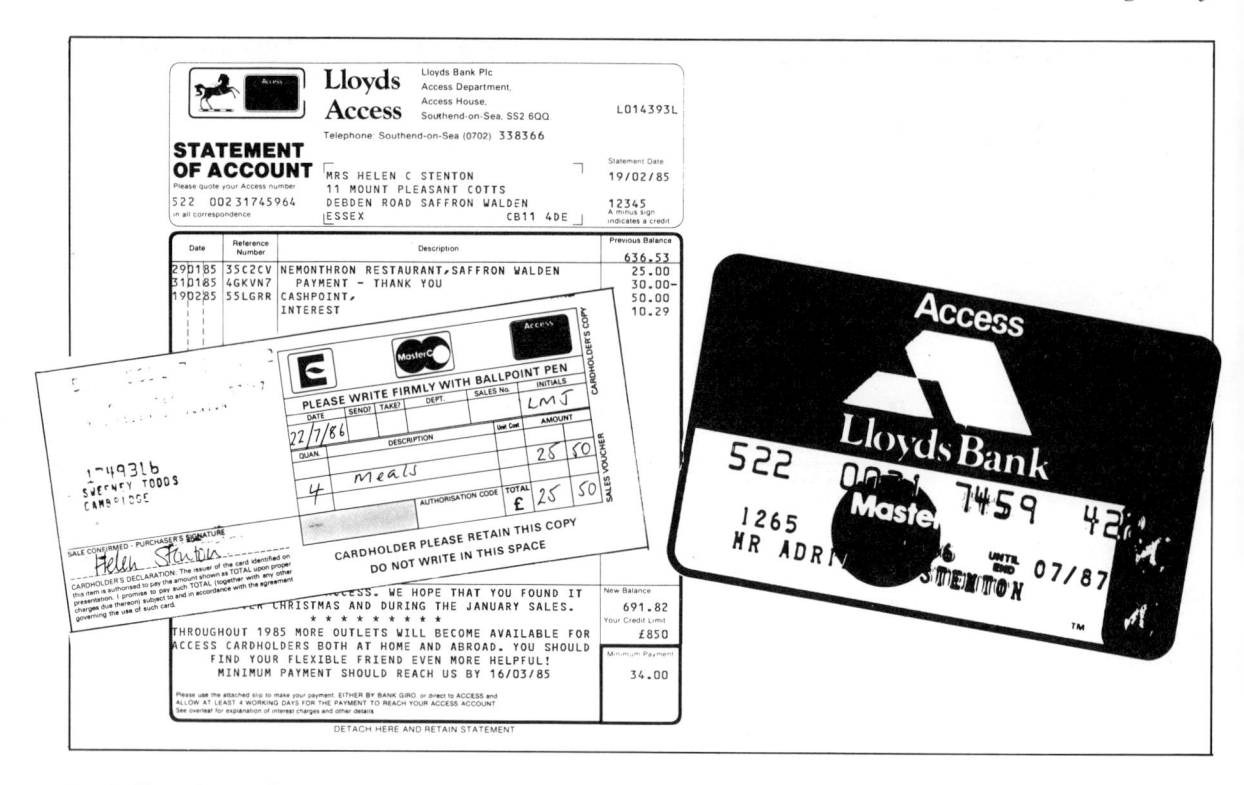

**Figure 4.4a**
How is a credit card used to pay for goods and services?

### ▶ 4 Credit cards

You can apply to your bank, or write directly to a credit card company, if you would like a credit card. A credit card is a small piece of plastic that allows you to buy goods by borrowing from a credit card company. The two most well known credit cards in use in the UK are Access and Visa. Some shops, like Marks and Spencer, now offer their own credit cards. Credit cards work like this:

▷ **a** You will be given a **credit limit**, which is the most you can spend with the card.

▷ **b** You go to a shop, choose the goods you want, and hand over your card.

▷ **c** A copy of the details on the card is made on two vouchers, one of which you keep, and the other of which is sent to the credit card company so that they can pay the shop.

▷ **d** Each month the credit card company sends you a statement saying how much you owe them as a result of using the card. If you pay the full amount straight away or in a short time, you pay no interest. If you pay less than the full amount (you can choose to pay any amount from a certain minimum printed on the statement) you will need to pay interest on the amount left over.

### ▶ 5 Charge cards

American Express and Diners Club are charge cards. They work in a similar way to credit cards except that you have to pay the full amount that you owe when you are sent the statement each month. You may also have to pay to get the card in the first place, whereas you do not need to pay for credit cards.

### ▶ 6 Budget accounts with shops

If you open a budget account with a shop you will agree to pay them a certain fixed sum each month. You will be allowed to spend up to several times the amount that you put away each month, but you will of course be charged interest if you have spent more than you have in your account.

### The advantages of buying on credit

Many years ago people tended to think that it was better to save for something rather than to borrow in order to get it. Now attitudes have changed. Some of the advantages of buying on credit are as follows:

### ▶ 1 You have the use of the goods you want at once

Many people would prefer to have the use of a video now, for example, and pay it off over two years, rather than save up for two years without having the use of the video in the meantime.

### ▶ 2 In times of inflation prices are constantly rising

If you save up for a video it could rise in price while you are saving for it. If you buy on credit, and there is high inflation, even though you have to pay interest, you may buy the good at a lower price.

### ▶ 3 Credit cards can give you interest-free borrowing

If you pay all you owe when you receive your statement each month, you pay no interest.

Unit 4.4 *Borrowing money*

**Figure 4.4b**
Should this washing machine be bought on credit or would it be better to save up for it?

## The disadvantages of buying on credit

Although buying on credit can be very useful, there are certain problems to watch out for. These are a few of the problems or disadvantages of buying on credit:

▶ **1 It can be very expensive to buy on credit**

You should always look at the APR (Annual Percentage Rate of charge) before you borrow. This figure must be shown when credit is offered. The lower the figure, the cheaper it will be to borrow. It should be remembered, however, that you will sometimes get a discount (money off) something bought on credit, and this could make up for a high APR

▶ **2 You can be tempted to overspend**

It is often extremely easy to buy on credit – you might just have to show a card or sign a piece of paper. You may be tempted to 'impulse buy', to see something you like and go in and buy it without thinking carefully about whether you can afford it.

▶ **3 Your circumstances might change after you have bought goods on credit**

There is no telling when you might lose your job, or have a serious accident or some other serious personal disaster. A heavy burden of outstanding debt can only add to your difficulties.

## Protecting the consumer

The Consumer Credit Act helps to protect consumers buying on credit. It is explained in more detail in Unit 6.8.

## DATABASE

# 1. Repayment tables for flat rate loans at 10% per annum

| REPAYMENT OVER 24 MONTHS | | | |
|---|---|---|---|
| Amount of Loan (£p) | Amount of Interest (£p) | Loan plus Interest (£p) | Monthly Repayment (£p) |
| 10 | 2.00 | 12.00 | 0.50 |
| 20 | 4.00 | 24.00 | 1.00 |
| 30 | 6.00 | 36.00 | 1.50 |
| 40 | 8.00 | 48.00 | 2.00 |
| 50 | 10.00 | 60.00 | 2.50 |
| 100 | 20.00 | 120.00 | 5.00 |
| 200 | 40.00 | 240.00 | 10.00 |
| 300 | 60.00 | 360.00 | 14.00 |
| 400 | 80.00 | 480.00 | 20.00 |
| 500 | 100.00 | 600.00 | 25.00 |
| 600 | 120.00 | 720.00 | 30.00 |
| 700 | 140.00 | 840.00 | 35.00 |
| 800 | 160.00 | 960.00 | 40.00 |
| 900 | 180.00 | 1080.00 | 45.00 |
| 1000 | 200.00 | 1200.00 | 50.00 |
| 2000 | 400.00 | 2400.00 | 100.00 |
| 3000 | 600.00 | 3600.00 | 150.00 |
| 4000 | 800.00 | 4800.00 | 200.00 |
| 5000 | 1000.00 | 6000.00 | 250.00 |

(Source: *Banking Information Service*)

## DATABASE

## 2. The true cost of credit

### Examples of APR
The following examples show how a camping tent, cash price £375, might be bought from the same store, using different types of credit.

### Hire purchase arranged through the store
Cash price £375 to be repaid by 24 equal monthly instalments of £20.93
Total amount payable = £502.32
APR = 34.2%

### Personal loan from a bank
Loan £375 to be repaid by 24 equal monthly instalments of £18.61
Total amount payable = £446.64
APR = 18.8%

### The store's own budget account
The method of charging interest under a budget account varies. The most common method is to charge a certain percentage on the outstanding balance at the end of each month, and add it to the account.

In this example, the monthly rate of charge is 2.2%. The credit limit is 24 times the customer's chosen monthly payment (subject to a certain minimum). The cash price of the goods is £375.

This is a 'period rate' transaction, so the APR = 29.8% — that is, 2.2% compounded 12 times throughout the year. But, because the customer chooses how much he will pay each month, the length of the agreement and hence the total amount payable will vary depending on the level of the monthly payment. For example:

**Customer chooses to pay £20 a month** (which gives a credit limit of £480)
APR = 29.8% as stated
To clear the account will require 24 payments of £20 plus £8.88 from the 25th payment
Total amount payable = £488.88

**Customer chooses to pay £16 a month** (which gives a credit limit of £384)
APR = 29.8% as stated
To clear the account will require 33 payments of £16 plus £5.04 from the 34th payment
Total amount payable = £533.04

### Please note
The examples were realistic at time of going to press, but APRs can change at any time to reflect different interest rates and terms.

(Source: *Office of Fair Trading* 1983)

## ACTIVITIES

## SECTION A: FOCUS ON UNIT 4.4

Go back and answer the questions raised in the Focus.

## SECTION B: STEPPED QUESTIONS

1 a Explain the benefits and drawbacks of purchases on credit for the consumer.
  b How do firms benefit from credit purchases?
  c How might a large amount of credit purchases affect the economy?
2 a What kinds of goods are bought on credit, and why?
  b What factors should a consumer take into account when deciding:
    ▷ whether or not to buy on credit
    ▷ which methods of buying on credit to choose?
  c How will the real rate of interest affect a consumer's decision about whether or not to buy on credit?

## SECTION C: DATA RESPONSE QUESTION

### Finance company personal loan

Shops, car dealers, gas and electricity boards sometimes offer to arrange a finance company personal loan when you're buying a big item. If you pay this way, the APR *could* be quite high. A loan which you could get yourself from another finance company could be cheaper, as terms vary from company to company. You often see personal loans advertised in newspapers. The minimum is around £100 or £200, and usually you pay back over three years. It's important to choose a reputable firm. You may be asked for security.

A finance company loan is useful if you want to borrow a large sum, and can't find a cheaper way to get money.

These loans can be expensive. And some companies ask for your house as security. KEEP CLEAR of such a deal, unless you're looking for a second mortgage.

### Moneylenders

For some people moneylenders are convenient. They can arrange many types of loan. Some will lend to almost anyone – often when no-one else will! So it's obvious they're going to charge very dearly for their risks. With security, charges may be less than without security. Either way they can be extremely high. In fact they can be *more* than you're actually borrowing.

A moneylender may take payments weekly – helpful if money's inclined to slip through your fingers!

There are moneylenders and moneylenders! If you use one make sure he's licensed. And NEVER part with a child allowance or pension book as security.

Source: There's More to Credit than Just H.P. Office of Fair Trading July 1981

a What is the main disadvantage that both finance company loans and moneylender loans have over a personal loan from a bank?
b What does it mean when it says 'there are moneylenders and moneylenders'?
c The passages advise you against offering three things as security for a loan. What are they?
d What is it that most people who use moneylenders are likely to have in common?

# UNIT 4.5  Insurance

103

**FOCUS**

▶ What is the **pooling of risk**?

▶ What are the basic principles of insurance?

▶ What kinds of insurance are available?

▶ How can an insurance policy be taken out?

▶ In what ways can you insure your life?

▶ What is involved in taking out motor insurance?

## Insurance

During your life you, or those close to you, may suffer sudden and unexpected events which can prove very expensive for everyone involved. If you are married, for example, your wife or husband might die suddenly and you may be left not only with grief and suffering, but also with a loss of all or some of your income. Insurance involves putting aside sums of money to cover you and those close to you against serious financial problems if something unfortunate happens to you.

## The pooling of risk

Insurance is based on the 'pooling of risk'. This is where a large number of people each pay a sum of money into a common fund. If any one of them suffers a loss, he or she will be compensated with money from the fund.

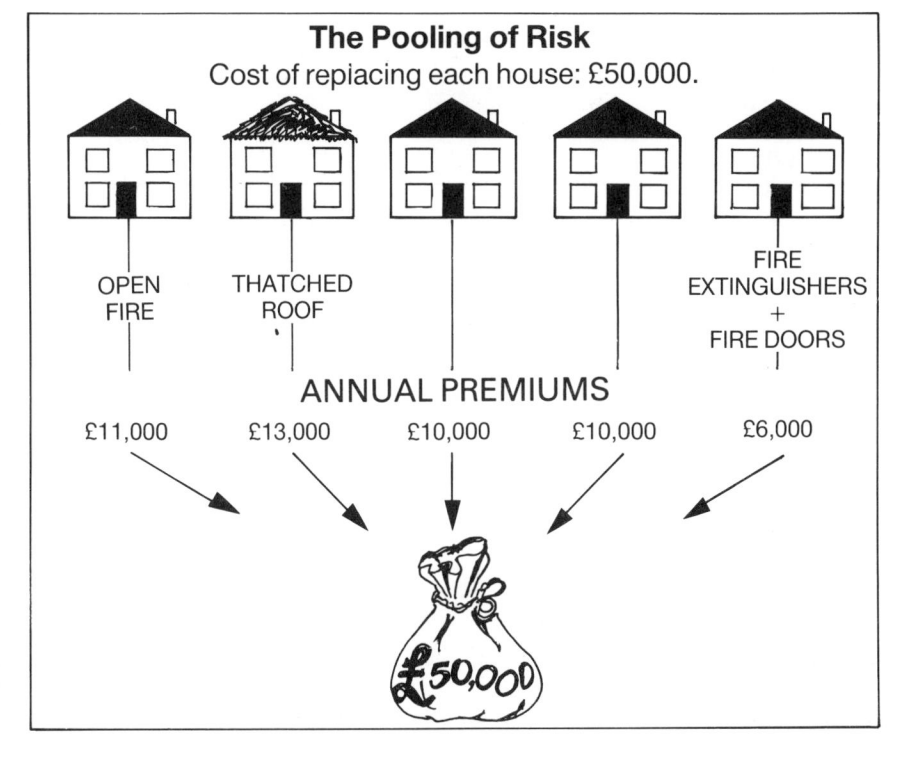

## The principles of insurance

Insurance is based on certain basic principles. Here are three of them:

▶ **1 Utmost good faith**
Both the company and the insured person must act in utmost good faith. This means that the insured person must tell the company everything it needs to know in order to insure him or her. It also means that the company must keep its promises if the person claims on the insurance.

▶ **2 Insurable interest**
If you have an insurable interest in something, you either own it or are responsible for it, and you will suffer financially if something unfortunate happens to it.

▶ **3 Indemnity**
In some forms of insurance, like term life assurance, a specific sum will be promised if the unfortunate event (e.g. your death) happens. In other types of insurance, like house contents insurance however, the insurance company undertakes to restore you to the same financial position after the unfortunate event as you were before it. This is called **indemnity**.

## What can be covered by insurance

During their lives most people will have some form of motor insurance to cover them against accidents in cars and on motor cycles. Many people will also pay to insure a house against fire, and the contents of a house against fire, robbery and other damage. Many people will also insure themselves against dying unexpectedly. All workers have to be insured through National Insurance against being away from work through unemployment and sickness, and for other reasons.

**Figure 4.5a**
The amount paid into the fund varies according to the risk. Obviously the group will usually be much larger than 5, so the premiums will be lower.

### The Pooling of Risk
Cost of replacing each house: £50,000.

| OPEN FIRE | THATCHED ROOF | | FIRE EXTINGUISHERS + FIRE DOORS |
|---|---|---|---|

ANNUAL PREMIUMS

£11,000   £13,000   £10,000   £10,000   £6,000

→ £50,000

**Figure 4.5b**
Why should you check the 'small print' on an insurance policy very carefully?

In practice you can insure nearly anything, including parts of your body on which your living might depend. For example a surgeon or a musician might insure her hands.

### How to find out about insurance
There are many ways you can find out about insurance, and take out an insurance policy. These are a few of them:

▶ **1 You can visit an insurance broker**
Brokers can be found in most high streets. They can show you insurance information from several different insurance companies. They will be able to advise you which insurance policy will be best for you. Brokers do not charge for their services because they are paid by the insurance companies when they sell insurance policies.

▶ **2 You can write directly to an insurance company, or call in at one of their offices**
If you know someone who has been very pleased with one particular insurance company, you can go directly to that company. They may even send an agent round to your home to tell you about their policies. Remember, however, that they will always tell you that their policies are best, even when other companies may in fact offer policies better suited to your needs. It pays to shop around.

▶ **3 You might be able to arrange insurance through your employer or trade union**
They could have a special arrangement with a company offering particularly good policies on particularly generous terms.

### Taking out insurance
The following example shows the various things you need to do to take out an insurance policy. Julie has just bought a second-hand Mini:

▶ **1 The proposal form**
This form is really a request by Julie to the insurance company to insure the car on her behalf. She had to write down the following:
▷ **a** Her name, address, telephone number, and other personal information.
▷ **b** Details about the thing to be insured. She had to write down the car's make, model, year of manufacture, and so on.

She then had to sign the form. Her signature gives an undertaking that, to the best of her knowledge, all the information she has provided is correct, and that she hasn't left anything out.

Julie was very careful to fill in the form honestly, as she knew that if she gave false information any claim she made might be delayed or even refused.

▶ **2 The premium**
Julie has to pay a sum of money each year for her insurance cover. The amount she pays – her **premium** – depends on the details she filled in on her proposal form. Because she is only 19, and this is her first car, her premiums are quite high. They are not as high as her brother Dave's though.

Dave is 17 and has a 750cc Honda motorcycle. He belongs to a group of drivers who statistically have a very high chance of making a claim on their insurance – their **degree of risk** is very high as far as the insurance company is concerned. Dave has already had several accidents, so his insurance cover costs even more again.

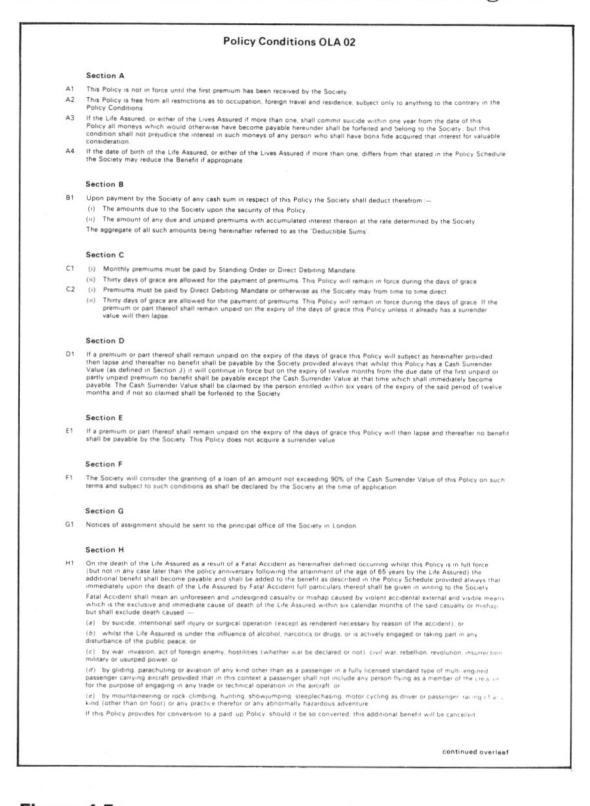

**Figure 4.5c**
Why are insurance policies so detailed?

### ▶ 3 The policy
Several days later Julie received her policy. This is a document that sets out exactly what is covered by her insurance, and the circumstances in which she can make a claim for payment.

### ▶ 4 The certificate
This is the piece of paper that shows that Julie has insurance cover. She uses it when she wants to tax the car, and if she gets stopped by the police.

### ▶ 5 The renewal notice
Each year this arrives to tell Julie how much she has to pay for her next year's insurance cover. The premium tends to go up every year.

### ▶ 6 The claims form
On the way to work one morning Julie slid off the road on the ice and crashed into a wall. She had to fill in a claims form giving the insurance company details of what happened, and the names and addresses of any witnesses. Julie's comprehensive cover insures her for the damage to the wall, and for the damage to her car.

You need to avoid being 'under insured'. If you insure something for less than its full value, you will not be entitled to full compensation. For example, if your motorbike is insured for £600 when it's really worth £1,200, and you totally destroy it (**write it off**) in an accident, you will get only a portion of the £1,200, not the full value.

## Motor insurance
If you drive a motor vehicle you must by law insure yourself against any injury you cause in an accident to other people, including any passengers in your own vehicle. There are four main types of motor insurance:

**Figure 4.5d**
What types of risk should you be covered against if you own a car?

### ▶ 1 Road Traffic Act only
This is the least amount of insurance cover you are allowed to have. David has this because it is also the cheapest. It covers him for injuries to other people in an accident, but not for damage to property. When David ran into the back of someone's car, his insurance covered him for the whiplash injury to the other driver, but he had to pay for the repairs to the other person's car out of his own pocket.

### ▶ 2 Third party
Faye decided to go for the slightly more expensive third party cover. This covers her for injuries to other people and for damage to property, but does not cover any damage to her own car.

### ▶ 3 Third party, fire and theft
Barbara decided that she needed the added cover of third party, fire and theft. This covers her car if it is stolen, or if it is burnt.

### ▶ 4 Fully comprehensive
Denis decided to go for comprehensive cover. This covers him for damage to his own car, as well as everything else shown above. He chose this because his car is quite new and is worth a lot of money, but the insurance premiums are the most expensive for this kind of cover.

## The amount of motor insurance premium
Below are some of the reasons why some people seem to pay so much more for motor insurance than other people:

### ▶ 1 They are young
Generally you will pay less if you are over 25 years old.

### ▶ 2 They have had several accidents and made several claims
Insurance companies deduct money from the premium for each year you do not make a claim. Your annual premium can be reduced by as much as 65 per cent if you do not claim for several years. The amount by which the premium is reduced is called a **no-claims bonus**.

### ▶ 3 They work in a job which makes much use of their car
A travelling representative for example, would need to pay more for insurance than a teacher.

### ▶ 4 They live in an area with a bad record for car thefts

### ▶ 5 They keep the car on the road rather than in a garage

### ▶ 6 They own a sports car of a foreign make, and the car is worth a great deal of money

## Life assurance
Insurance against death can be called either **insurance** or **assurance**. There are four basic types of life assurance policy:

### ▶ 1 Whole life policies
Daley has a whole life policy. He pays an annual premium until he dies. When he dies the insurance company will pay out the amount that he insured himself for – the **sum assured** – to his next of kin.

### ▶ 2 Term policies

Pam has a term policy. She pays premiums for a fixed period, in her case 20 years. If she dies within this period, her next of kin receive the sum assured. If she lives for the full term, she doesn't get anything. Term policies are usually quite cheap, and are popular with young people like Pam.

### ▶ 3 Endowment policies

Jenny has an endowment policy. She pays a premium for a fixed period, like Pam, but if Jenny lives for the full term she gets a lump-sum payment at the end of the period. Jenny is using her policy as a form of saving, but it is quite expensive.

### ▶ 4 Annuities

Arif had quite a large sum of money available, so he decided to invest it in an annuity. He gave the money to an insurance company who then pays him a regular sum of money until he dies. They then keep the money. Obviously, Arif is hoping to live longer than the insurance company expects him to, so that he can get the full benefit from his annuity!

# DATABASE

## Working out your premium points.

### Basis of Rating
The premium payable is fixed by the total number of points allocated to the various Rating Factors described below.

| Rating Factors | Table of Points | Enter points below |
|---|---|---|
| **Rating District** in which the car is usually kept – see ©. In certain districts higher premiums are required for cars left in the road overnight. | ▶ Rating District<br>If left in road overnight in<br><br>\| A \| B \| C \| D \| E \| F \|<br>\| 2 \| 3 \| 4 \| 5 \| 7 \| 9 \|<br><br>Districts D, E or F **add 1 point** (except Third Party Only policies). | |
| **Car Group.** Cars are classified into groups. Some examples are given in ⓓ. | ▶ Car Group<br><br>\| 1 \| 2 \| 3 \| 4 \| 5 \| 6 \| 7 \|<br>\| 0 \| 3 \| 5 \| 8 \| 12 \| 15 \| 18 \| | |
| **Age of Car.** Subtract the year first registered from the year in which the insurance becomes operative | ▶ Age of car<br><br>\| 0–3 \| 4–5 \| 6 \| 7–8 \| 9–11 \| 12 or over \|<br>\| 5 \| 4 \| 3 \| 2 \| 1 \| 0 \| | |
| **Age of Proposer** and whether there are any drivers, other than the proposer, under 25 years of age.<br>For limited companies use age 35 to 49. | ▶ Age of Proposer<br>Other drivers under 25<br>–None<br>–One or more<br><br>\| 17 \| 18 \| 19 \| 20 \| 21 \| 22 \| 23 \| 24 \| 25 to 34 \| 35 to 49 \| 50 to 64 \| 65 or over \|<br>\| 14 \| 13 \| 12 \| 11 \| 9 \| 8 \| 7 \| 5 \| 3 \| 2 \| 1 \| 0 \|<br>\| 15 \| 14 \| 14 \| 13 \| 11 \| 10 \| 9 \| 7 \| 6 \| 6 \| 5 \| 4 \| | |
| **Class of Use** – see Ⓔ. | ▶ Class of Use<br><br>\| Farmers \| 1 or 2 \| 3 \| 4 \|<br>\| 0 \| 2 \| 7 \| 10 \| | |
| **Cover and Driving Restrictions** – Higher premiums are required for cars valued at more than £15,000 (except Third party Only policies). | ▶ Cover<br>Voluntary Excess<br>Any Driver<br>Restricted Driving<br><br>\| \| Comprehensive \| \| \| TPFT \| TP \|<br>\| \| Nil \| £25 \| £50 \| £100 \| – \| – \|<br>\| \| 15 \| 14 \| 13 \| 12 \| 4 \| 2 \|<br>\| \| 13 \| 12 \| 11 \| 10 \| 2 \| 0 \| | |
| **Optional Extension – Personal Accident Benefits –** | ▶ Personal Accident Benefits<br><br>\| Comprehensive Policies \| Other Policies \| Not Required \|<br>\| 1 \| 2 \| 0 \| | |
| **Abnormal or Special Risks –** the standard rates do not necessarily apply to risks which require special underwriting consideration because of occupation, claims or conviction record, type or value of car, etc. | ▶ Add for Abnormal or Special Risks | |
| **Total Points** – see Schedule of Premiums | ▶ Total Points | |

*Continued*

# DATABASE

**Ⓒ Rating Districts (examples)**
A: Cheshire, Somerset, North Yorkshire, Wirral
B: Bristol, Brighton, Norfolk, Newcastle
C: Luton, Bolton, Wirral, Leeds
D: Watford, Birmingham, Edinburgh
E: Greater London, Manchester, Liverpool, Glasgow
F: Inner London (Postal Districts)

**Ⓓ Car groups (examples)**
1: Austin Metro 1.0
2: Ford Escort 1100
3: Ford Sierra 1.6
4: Nissan Sunny
   Rover 216
5, 6, 7, 8: Sports cars
            Luxury cars

**Ⓔ Class of Use**
Farmers  — Farmers' cars
Class 1  — Vehicles used for social, domestic and pleasure purposes only
Class 2  — Vehicles owned by individuals, and used for their own business only
Class 3  — Cars owned by limited companies or business partnerships
Class 4  — Cars used for commercial travelling, driving tuition or motor trade purposes

**Ⓑ Schedule of premiums**
(excluding no-claims discount)
Where exceeded the proposal must be submitted for special quotation.

| Total Points | Basic Premium £ | Total Points | Basic Premium £ |
|---|---|---|---|
| 0 | 56.20 | 25 | 241.30 |
| 1 | 59.60 | 26 | 255.70 |
| 2 | 63.20 | 27 | 271.10 |
| 3 | 66.90 | 28 | 287.30 |
| 4 | 71.00 | 29 | 304.60 |
| 5 | 75.20 | 30 | 322.80 |
| 6 | 79.70 | 31 | 342.20 |
| 7 | 84.50 | 32 | 362.80 |
| 8 | 89.60 | 33 | 384.50 |
| 9 | 95.00 | 34 | 407.60 |
| 10 | 100.70 | 35 | 432.00 |
| 11 | 106.70 | 36 | 458.00 |
| 12 | 113.10 | 37 | 485.40 |
| 13 | 119.90 | 38 | 514.60 |
| 14 | 127.10 | 39 | 545.40 |
| 15 | 134.70 | 40 | 578.20 |
| 16 | 142.80 | 41 | 612.90 |
| 17 | 151.40 | 42 | 649.60 |
| 18 | 160.40 | 43 | 688.60 |
| 19 | 170.10 | 44 | 729.90 |
| 20 | 180.30 | | |
| 21 | 191.10 | | |
| 22 | 202.60 | | |
| 23 | 214.70 | | |
| 24 | 227.60 | | |

**Short Period Rates** for period (months) not exceeding

| 1 | 2 | 3 | 4 | 5 | 6 | 7 | 8 | 9 | over 9 |
|---|---|---|---|---|---|---|---|---|---|
| 10% | 20% | 30% | 40% | 50% | 60% | 70% | 80% | 90% | 100% |

Percentage of annual premium payable

(Source: *CIS Motor Car Insurance Prospectus*)

*Unit 4.5 Insurance*

## SECTION A: FOCUS ON UNIT 4.5

Go back and answer the questions raised in the Focus.

## SECTION B: STEPPED QUESTIONS

1. **a** Describe the kinds of insurance that would be required by a couple with three children, a house, and a car.
   **b** Explain the factors that would have to be taken into account in choosing a policy for each of the kinds of insurance described in (a).

2. **a** Why does car insurance usually cost more than house insurance?
   **b** Explain the circumstances under which a person is likely to have to pay very high motor insurance premiums.
   **c** Explain how the principle of indemnity would affect the compensation for:
   ▷ the loss of a car bought new five years ago for £5,000
   ▷ the loss of a vintage car bought ten years ago for £5,000.

# SECTION C: DATA RESPONSE QUESTION

## Term assurance

### When Life is Cheap

The very cheapest form of life cover which British life companies sell is temporary (for term) assurance. The companies themselves tend to describe the cost of this as 'dirt' or 'ridiculously' cheap, and they are not guilty of gross exaggeration.

Temporary assurance provides protection for families, not savings nest-eggs. You buy life assurance cover for a period of time (the 'term' of the policy). If you die during this time, the life company will pay an agreed sum ('the sum assured') to your dependants. If you survive, no cash is paid out. It works, in other words, rather like household or motor insurance: no claim, no cash. So there's no savings value.

The cost of temporary assurance depends on your age; your health (many companies now offer discounts for non-smokers, for instance); the amount of cover you want; and the length of time you wish to be protected. A woman is always rated as if she was three or four years younger than a man. You probably won't be asked for a medical examination if you're under 50.

All life companies have their own tariff of premium rates. A man of 29, however, wanting to cover his life for £25,000 for a period of 15 years, will be able to find a dozen or so companies prepared to sell him such a policy at a cost of 50p to 65p a week. If the man was 44, the cover could still cost only £2.20 to £2.70 a week. If he was 54 he should be able to buy the protection for less than £7.40 a week.

We seem to score in this country, too, in the range of different types of temporary assurance which are available. These include:

- **Ordinary level term assurance.**
This is the cheapest type. The amount of cover stays the same throughout the term of the policy.
- **Family Income Benefit policies.**
These policies do not pay out a lump sum if the policyholder dies. Instead regular annual tax-free income is paid which continues until the end of the policy term.
- **Convertible term assurance.**
These policies contain an option to convert to another type of policy during the term. The advantage of this is that you can convert to the new policy, at the premium rates applicable for someone who is in good health, whatever the state of your own health may happen to be at that time.
- **Decreasing term assurance.**
Here the amount the policy will pay out if you die goes down during the policy term. Such policies are usually used by those buying a house on a mortgage.
- **Increasing term assurance.**
With these policies, in contrast, the amount that will be paid out on your death increases each year during the policy term.

(Source: *Observer Magazine Money Extra* 3/10/82)

a Why is term assurance 'dirt cheap' compared to other life assurance policies?
b What four things will the assurance company take into account when deciding on the premium someone should pay for term cover?.
c ▷ What are two possible advantages of taking out term assurance when you are under 50?
▷ Why do women pay lower premiums than men?
d How are Family Income Benefit policies different from other types of term assurance?
e Which of the policies listed might be best for someone who was worried about rising inflation, and why?

# UNIT 4.6 Buying and renting a home

### FOCUS

▶ What are the different types of housing in the UK?

▶ Why do some people choose to buy their own homes and what problems can be caused by home ownership?

▶ What is a **mortgage**?

▶ Where does someone go to borrow money to buy a home, and what types of loan are available?

▶ What benefits are there in renting a home and what problems can be involved?

Buying or renting a home is one of the most expensive things that people have to pay for during their lives. Most people live in houses or flats that they rent from either a private landlord (private rented dwellings) or from a housing association or local council (public rented dwellings). Many people live in homes that they are buying themselves (owner-occupied dwellings).

### Housing associations

There are about 2,600 housing associations in Britain. They are financed mainly by the Housing Corporation, an organisation which lends housing associations money which it obtains mainly from the government. Housing associations build new homes and restore older buildings. The majority of these are then rented out, but some are made available for sale. Housing associations own about half a million properties in Britain.

### The advantages of buying your own home

This section will look at some of the reasons why people often choose to buy their own homes rather than live in homes rented from someone else.

▶ 1 Most people borrow the money to buy their own home (this is called getting a **mortgage**). If you don't move, the mortgage will eventually be paid off, and you will not have to pay out any more for your home. You will then own something of great value. If you rent, however, you will be paying out all your life.

▶ 2 Although the amount you pay on your mortgage will go up and down as interest rates change, the actual amount of money you pay out each month for your mortgage will not change very much from year to year. If the amount you earn goes up as you get older, the proportion of your income spent on the mortgage will decrease, and the difficulty of paying the mortgage will get less and less each year. Rents, however, are likely to keep going up and up.

▶ 3 Providing that you keep within planning and other laws, you can make more or less whatever changes you feel like to your property. In addition, you know that any home improvements will put up the value of your property, benefiting you and not a landlord.

▶ 4 It is often easier to move if you own your own home. If you get a new job a long way from where you live, you could find it very difficult to change council houses or find suitable private rented accommodation.

▶ 5 You get tax relief on the interest on your mortgage payments. This means that the government helps you pay for your mortgage by cutting down the income tax you have to pay.

### The disadvantages of buying your own home

Although more and more people are buying their own home, there are some problems involved. These are some of them:

▶ 1 It can be very expensive to buy a home, especially for the first time. You will probably need a mortgage, and in order to get one you may be asked to put down a deposit. This is a sum of money, usually several thousand pounds, that you have to have before you will be given the loan. In addition you may need money to pay a solicitor to look after the legal problems involved with buying a home and a surveyor to check for any faults.

▶ 2 It is very expensive to move from one home to another, and it can be very complicated. In addition to legal fees, you may need to pay for an estate agent to sell your home, and a removal firm to transport your belongings. It may take many months to find a new home, find someone to buy your own home, and complete all the legal steps that have to be taken. Sometimes the move can fall through at the last moment, and this is often very upsetting.

▶ 3 You will be responsible for all the maintenance and repairs of your property. In rented

**Figure 4.6a**
How does someone work out how much money he or she can borrow to buy a home?

accommodation much of this could be the responsibility of the landlord.

### Mortgages
If you do decide to buy your own home, you will almost certainly need a mortgage. This is a loan for buying or improving property.

### Where to go for a mortgage
▶ **1 Building societies**
If you have saved for many years with a building society this could be the best place to go for a mortgage. Building societies account for about 80 per cent of all mortgages, and these are usually **repayment** mortgages. If demand for mortgages is not very high, a building society may give you a mortgage even if you have not saved with them.
▶ **2 Insurance companies**
Insurance companies will offer mortgages linked to life assurance policies. These are called **endowment mortgages**.
▶ **3 Banks**
Some banks now offer mortgages on similar terms to building societies. Mortgages are only a part of a bank's business, and the amount that they lend for house purchase changes considerably from year to year.
▶ **4 Local authorities**
Sometimes local authorities will provide a mortgage, or arrange for one with a building society. They are most likely to do this for people who work for them.

### Types of mortgage
Mortgages are given usually for periods of between 15 and 30 years. The amount of deposit you will need to put down varies, but sometimes you can obtain a 100 per cent mortgage. This means that you do not need a deposit. You will usually be able to borrow between two and three times your annual salary, and if you are married you might also be able to borrow an amount equal to your partner's salary. There are two main types of mortgage:
▶ **1 Repayment mortgages**
Ben borrowed £30,000 to buy a flat. He decided to take out a **repayment mortgage**. His repayments consist of two parts. He has to pay back the money he borrowed – the £30,000 – and this is called the **principal**. And he has to pay interest on the £30,000. The interest payments are very large: at 10% he would have to pay back £250 a month. So at first his repayments are nearly all interest. But, over the years, as he gradually pays back some of the principal, the interest gets less, and he can afford to pay back more of the principal each month.

As Ben gets tax relief on the interest payments but not on the principal payments, this means that he gets most tax relief in the early years, and less in the later years. This should suit him as he expects his salary to rise over the years and so he should be better able to afford the repayments.
▶ **2 Endowment mortgages**
Chrissie decided to take out an **endowment mortgage**. This means that she takes out a life assurance policy for the amount she needs to borrow, and for the period of the policy she has to pay life assurance premiums, and interest on the loan. At the end of the period the insurance policy matures and there is a lump sum payment which is used to pay off the principal.

Chrissie decided to pay more for her policy so that there was also a lump sum for her when the policy matured. Chrissie's policy also gave her life assurance, so that if she died the mortgage would be paid off, whereas Ben had to pay extra for life assurance cover during the period of his repayment mortgage.

### The advantages of renting your home
People who have the choice nowadays may prefer to buy their own home, but there are reasons why some people prefer to rent. Here are some of them:
▶ 1 You do not need to put down a very large deposit (you may be asked for some deposit, however), and you will not need to pay for legal fees before you move in.
▶ 2 Rent can be cheaper than a mortgage for young people.
▶ 3 Moving is cheaper and often quicker than if you own your own home.
▶ 4 You may be protected by the Rent Acts against unfair eviction (being thrown out by your landlord) providing you have kept within the law. Also you may be protected against unfairly high rents.
▶ 5 The landlord may be responsible for maintenance and repairs of the property.

### The disadvantages of renting your home
These are some of the reasons why many people choose to buy rather than rent, given the choice:
▶ 1 When you pay rent you are paying for something that you will never own. Rents keep going up, and you may have to keep paying until you die.
▶ 2 Any money you spend on your rented accommodation will benefit you while you live there, but not when you move.
▶ 3 There may be restrictions on the changes you can make to your accommodation.
▶ 4 Changing where you live can be very difficult, especially if you live in a council house. Most councils have a long waiting list for homes. In many big towns there is also a great shortage of privately rented accommodation.

## DATABASE

### 1. The ownership of homes 1971–1981

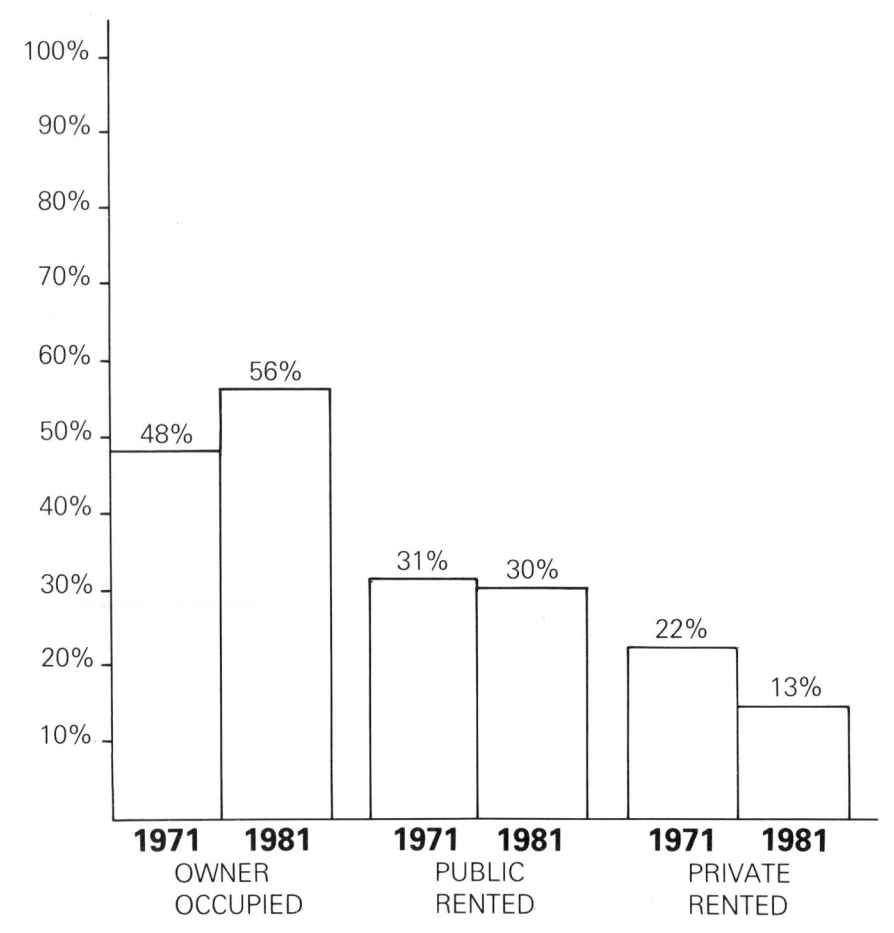

| | 1971 | 1981 |
|---|---|---|
| OWNER OCCUPIED | 48% | 56% |
| PUBLIC RENTED | 31% | 30% |
| PRIVATE RENTED | 22% | 13% |

(Source: *Office of Population Surveys*)

## DATABASE

### 2. Sources of home loans (end 1982)

| | Lending outstanding (£ million) | Percent of total |
|---|---|---|
| Building societies | 56,894 | 75.2 |
| Banks (and other institutions in the monetary sector) | 10,714 | 14.2 |
| Other financial institutions | 2,147 | 2.8 |
| Public sector | 5,941 | 7.8 |
| Total | 75,696 | 100.0 |

(Source: *A Guide to the British Financial System*, Banking Information Service, 1984)

# ACTIVITIES

## SECTION A: FOCUS ON UNIT 4.6

Go back and answer the questions raised in the Focus.

## SECTION B: STEPPED QUESTIONS

1  a  What is the meaning of:
      ▷ owner-occupied dwellings
      ▷ public rented dwellings
      ▷ private rented dwellings?
   b  What are the benefits and drawbacks of renting a home?
   c  Most people would like to own their own homes. Why, then do 44 per cent of people live in rented accommodation?
2  a  What is meant by:
      ▷ a repayment mortgage
      ▷ an endowment mortgage?
   b  What factors should be taken into account when deciding which method of borrowing money to use when buying a home?

## SECTION C: DATA RESPONSE QUESTION

### Building societies' fortunes blossom
**By Margaret Dibben, Money Editor**

Building societies had their best year for savers and borrowers in 1983. But because the demand for mortgages is still running at an unseasonally high level the societies feel no pressure to cut their interest rates just yet.

The boost to the societies' fortunes came only in the second half of the year after interest rates were raised in July.

The popularity of the higher rates lasted right through December. Despite a record degree of Christmas spending, net receipts in December were higher than during the previous month.

Total net new savings last year were £600 million more than in 1982, which itself was a record year. In 1983 they totalled just over £7 billion. In the first six months the net income averaged £375 million a month, this rose to £800 million a month in the second half of the year.

Building societies lent 26 per cent more in 1983 as the value of home loans approached £20 billion. More than 100,000 extra house buyers were granted mortgages last year, making a total in the 12 months of 962,000.

(Source: *Guardian* 14/1/84)

a  What was special, as far as the building societies were concerned, about 1983?
b  What happened in July 1983 to explain the answer to (a)?
c  How many home buyers were lent money by building societies in 1983?
d  What would need to happen for building societies to cut their interest rates?
e  If building societies lent about 70 per cent of all the money lent to home buyers in 1983, roughly how many people in total borrowed money to buy homes in 1983?
f  What effect do you think the rise in the number of home loans had on house prices? Explain your answer.

## PART 4: COURSEWORK SUGGESTION

### SAVINGS SCHEMES FOR YOUNG PEOPLE

1. Collect information from savings institutions on the savings schemes that are available specifically for young people.
2. Analyse each savings scheme under the same group of headings for example by interest rates offered, minimum amount to start on account, etc.
3. Write a report for a consumer magazine on savings schemes for young people. Part of the report should include information shown in the form of grid. Another part of the report should include your own opinions on the schemes possibly with stars or blobs used to rank the different schemes, or different features of each scheme.
4. Design an advertising campaign to encourage young people to use at least one of the savings schemes you have studied.

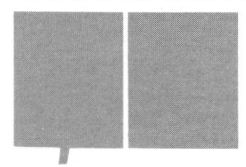

---

Here are some more words and phrases for your Dictionary of Economic Terms. Remember to look for each word or phrase in the text and then write your own definition for it.

Annual Percentage Rate of Charge (APR)
budgeting
consumer durable
credit
depreciation
disposable income
endowment assurance
endowment mortgage
gross pay
indemnity
index-linking
insurance
interest
life assurance
money income
mortgage
net pay
real income
repayment mortgage
saving
term assurance
whole life assurance

# Part 5
Population

# UNIT 5.1 Population size and why it changes

## FOCUS

▶ Why are economists interested in population, and how do they find out information about it?

▶ What factors affect the total size of a population?

▶ When does a natural increase in the population occur?

▶ What has happened in recent years to the population size of the UK?

### People as consumers and producers

When people buy goods and services, they are consumers. Economists are interested in population changes because it helps them to predict what might happen to the demand for goods and services in future. It is important to know, for example, whether the number of old people is growing, because this will mean that the government has to plan to provide extra services such as hospital beds.

When people form their own businesses, or work for someone else, they are producers. If economists know what population changes are about to happen, they may be able to predict what changes there will be in the workforce. If they know, for example, that not many babies were born in 1970 compared with earlier years, then they can predict that there will not be as many young workers joining the workforce in 1986 as there have been in earlier years.

### The census

The **Census of Population** is a count of the population. It takes place every ten years, and the next one will be in 1991. The census is an enquiry based on large forms sent to every household, which ask many questions about the people in the household on census day. The form has questions not only about people's ages and occupations, but also about the type of facilities available for the people in the household.

In addition to census information the government provides a lot of detailed information each year about births, deaths, marriages and migration. There is therefore plenty of information for economists to use to work out population changes.

### The total size of the population

Economists are interested in three main sets of figures when they are studying changes in the total size of the population. These are **birth rate**, **death rate** and **external migration**.

### Birth and death rates

The birth rate is the number of live births for every 1000 people in the country in a given year. The death rate is the number of deaths for every 1000 people in the country in a given year. You should be careful not to confuse 'birth rate' with the actual number of births. Birth rate is found by the formula:

$$\frac{\text{Number of live births} \times 1{,}000}{\text{Total population}}$$

For example, if there are 60 million people in the country and 600,000 babies are born, the birth rate is 600,000 × 1,000 divided by 60 million, i.e. 10 per thousand.

### The relationship between birth rate and death rate

If a country has the same number of people entering it as leaving it, then the following are true:

▶ 1 If birth rate is above death rate, the population will rise. If birth rate is above death rate there is a **natural increase in the population**.

▶ 2 If birth rate and death rate are the same, there will be no change in population size.

▶ 3 If death rate is above birth rate, the total size of the population will fall. If death rate is above birth rate there is a **natural decrease in population**.

### External migration

Migration means the movement of people. Migration can be **internal**, meaning the movement of people within a country, or **external**, meaning the movement of people between countries. **Immigration** means that people are coming into the country, and **emigration** means that they are leaving it.

Only external migration can affect the total size of the population. If more people are immigrating (coming in) than emigrating (going out) then the population size will rise (assuming no natural change in the population

**Unit 5.1** *Population size and why it changes*

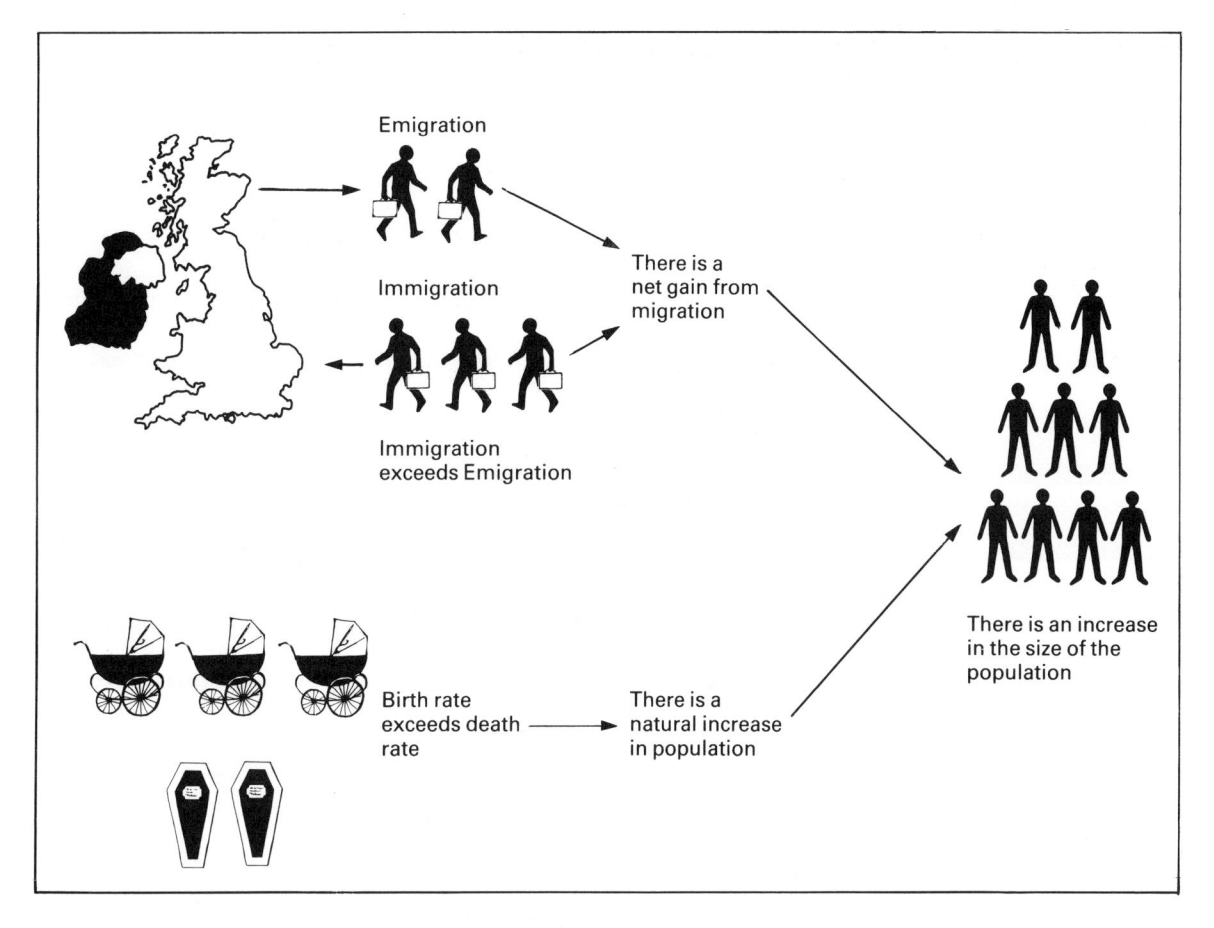

**Figure 5.1a**
How can a country's population increase in size?

**Figure 5.1b**

size). If the reverse is true, then the total size of the population will fall. If immigration is greater than emigration, then there is a **net gain from migration** or **positive net migration**, but if emigration is greater than immigration there is said to be a **net loss from migration** or **negative net migration**.

## Changes in the size of the UK population

| | | | |
|---|---|---|---|
| 1801 | 12,500 (est.) | 1951 | 50,225 |
| 1851 | 22,259 | 1961 | 52,709 |
| 1901 | 38,287 | 1971 | 55,515 |
| 1911 | 42,082 | 1981 | 55,776 |
| 1921 | 44,027 | 1991 | 57,912 (est.) |
| 1931 | 46,038 | 2001 | 57,968 (est.) |
| | | 2011 | 58,403 (est.) |

(est.) means "estimated"
All figures are 000s

(Source: *Annual Abstract of Statistics 1984* (HMSO))

Figure 5.1b shows that the UK population has grown since the first Census of Population in 1801. However, you can see that there has been very little change in the size of the UK population since 1971, and the population is expected to rise only very slowly until the end of the century. The main reason for this has been the change in the birth rate.

### Changes in the UK birth rate

The trend in the UK birth rate has been downwards since about 1881. The main exceptions to the trend have been sudden rises in the birth rate called **baby booms**.

### Baby booms

The baby boom in the early 1920s happened because people put off having children in the First World War between 1914 and 1918. The baby boom in the 1940s followed the end of the Second World War in 1945. The baby boom from the second half of the 1950s was during a period of full employment when most people felt very well off and confident about the future. The rise in the number of babies in the late 1970s came about when the babies born in the late 1950s became old enough to have children themselves.

### The reasons for the general downward trend in the birth rate

Baby booms are exceptions to the trend. Here are some of the possible reasons why there has been a general downward trend in the birth rate since 1881:

▶ 1 Up to about the middle of the last century children worked from a very early age. They earned money for their parents. When laws were passed to limit the amount of work children could do (and to make sure that children had at least some education), the birth rate started to fall.

▶ 2 In the last century infant mortality was very high. This meant that many children died in the early years of life. People often had larger families in the expectation that some of their children would die.

▶ 3 Children used to look after their parents when their parents were old. Nowadays older people have pensions, and they can get help from social security and the social services. It is no longer so necessary to have lots of children to look after you when you get old.

▶ 4 Women are more able to follow a career. Many women work for a long time before starting a family. Some women have one or two children and then return to work. All these things lead to a fall in the birth rate.

▶ 5 Many people choose to have children later, so that they can achieve various things while they are still young and possibly both earning a wage, for example they may want to save up for their own home. The birth rate goes down if people put off having children.

▶ 6 When unemployment is high and wages are not increasing much the birth rate seems to fall. This happened in the UK in the 1930s and again in the 1970s. In an economic depression children are regarded as an economic burden.

▶ 7 Nowadays people seem pessimistic about the future. This means that they think things are going to get worse. They do not want to have children who will grow up in a world with high unemployment and the possibility of a nuclear war.

▶ 8 In recent years contraception (birth control) has become more common. People can choose when to have babies. Families can be planned.

▶ 9 There seem to be fashions in family size. In the last century in the time of Queen Victoria it was fashionable to have a very large family. Nowadays small families seem to be more fashionable.

▶ 10 Housing is expensive in some parts of the country. Most young couples live in small flats or houses, where there is simply not enough room to have lots of children.

### Changes in the UK death rate

The trend in the UK death rate has been downwards, although in recent years it has hardly changed at all.

### Reasons for the general downward trend in the death rate

▶ 1 People understand more about the connection between cleanliness and health. For example, when babies are delivered and cared for everything is kept spotlessly clean. Feeding bottles are sterilised. Great care is taken to make sure that no germs get into a baby's food. All this has led to a fall in the **infant mortality rate**, the main cause of a high death rate in the past.

▶ 2 Medical treatment has become more effective, and it is easier and cheaper for people to get medical help. This means that many diseases like smallpox, which used to kill millions, have now almost disappeared.

▶ 3 People eat much better than they used to. Most people receive the vitamins and minerals they need for good health.

▶ 4 Housing has improved. In the past many people lived in houses which were damp and did not have proper drainage. In those conditions illness and disease were very common.

### Changes in UK external migration

Between 1931 and 1951 more people came into the UK than left it. This was because of people from Europe fleeing from the Nazis. The net gain from migration between 1955 and 1961 was because there were many job opportunities in the UK and immigration was encouraged. At the present time more people are leaving the UK than are coming into it. But in 1984 total emigration was 164,000 and total immigration was 201,000. There was therefore a net gain from migration of 37,000, making 1984 an unusual year.

Some of the possible reasons why people leave one country to go and live in another are as follows:

▶ 1 People are oppressed because of their race, political beliefs or religious beliefs. This means that they are treated badly because they are different from the majority of people in their country, or they hold different opinions from them. In the 1930s, when Hitler came to power, many Jewish people emigrated from Germany. In the 1970s, following their defeat in the Vietnam war, many people emigrated from South Vietnam.

▶ 2 People go in search of better job opportunities. In the 1950s the UK had more jobs available than people to do them. The government encouraged immigration from many countries, including India, Pakistan, the West Indies and Ireland. From 1962 immigration has been strictly controlled. In recent years the government has been very worried about the number of highly trained British people who have gone to work abroad. These include doctors, scientists and engineers. These people find that they can earn more money, pay lower taxes, and enjoy greater status in countries like the USA, Canada and Australia.

Unit 5.1 *Population size and why it changes*

## DATABASE

### 1. Birth and death rates in the UK 1881–1985

Rates per 1000 of the population (y-axis, 5 to 35)

BIRTH RATE
DEATH RATE

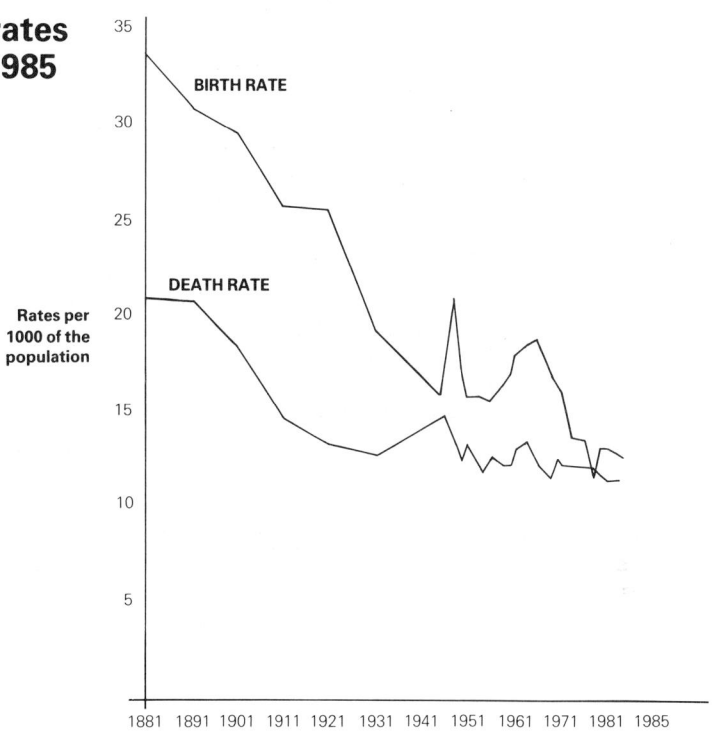

x-axis: 1881 1891 1901 1911 1921 1931 1941 1951 1961 1971 1981 1985

Birth & death rates given for 10 year periods only until 1945

## DATABASE

### 2. Immigration and emigration 1983

| Countries of Immigration into UK | (in 000s) | Countries of Emigration from UK | |
|---|---|---|---|
| **Commonwealth Countries** | | | |
| 1 Australia, New Zealand & Canada | 32 | 1 | 41 |
| 2 India, Bangladesh, Sri Lanka | 13 | 2 | 4 |
| 3 Caribbean | 5 | 3 | 3 |
| 4 Other | 35 | 4 | 25 |
| **Non-Commonwealth Countries** | | | |
| 5 EEC | 31 | 5 | 29 |
| 6 USA | 26 | 6 | 32 |
| 7 South Africa | 6 | 7 | 9 |
| 8 Pakistan | 12 | 8 | 1 |
| 9 Middle East | 13 | 9 | 20 |
| 10 Other | 29 | 10 | 21 |
| Total inflow | 202 | Total outflow | 185 |

(Source: Population Trends 40, Summer 85)

**ACTIVITIES**

## SECTION A: FOCUS ON UNIT 5.1

Go back and answer the questions raised in the Focus.

## SECTION B: STEPPED QUESTIONS

1. **a** What information is collected in the census?
   **b** Local authorities provide services like primary and secondary schools:
   ▷ What population information do you think they would need in order to provide the right number of school places in the future?
   ▷ Explain how such information would affect their plans.
2. **a** What has been the trend in the UK birth rate this century?
   **b** What factors affect the birth rate?
   **c** What do you think will be the trend in the birth rate over the next twenty years? Give reasons for your answers.

## SECTION C: DATA RESPONSE QUESTION

Changes in population size

| YEAR | BIRTH RATE | DEATH RATE | NET GAIN/LOSS THROUGH MIGRATION |
|------|------------|------------|-------------------------------|
| 0    | 30         | 30         | +100,000                      |
| 100  | 30         | 25         | +100,000                      |
| 200  | 25         | 25         | 0                             |
| 300  | 25         | 20         | 0                             |
| 400  | 20         | 20         | −100,000                      |

**a** In which year or years did the following happen?
▷ There was a natural increase in the population.
▷ The total size of the population increased.
▷ The total size of the population remained unchanged.
▷ The total size of the population fell.

**b** Give possible reasons for the changes in, or stability of, birth rate and death rate between the following years:
▷ year 100 and year 200
▷ year 200 and year 300.

**c** What do you think is happening to the economic development of the country in this example? Give reasons for your answer.

Unit 5.1 *Population size and why it changes*

**EXTENSION MATERIAL 7**

## Theories of population

Economists have been concerned with the effects of changes in population size since the beginning of the nineteenth century. This section will look at two ideas concerned with the growth in the size of populations.

### The theory of Thomas Malthus

Thomas Malthus was an economist who wrote an important essay about population in 1798. In it he put forward the theory that population would double every 25 years, but the amount of food would grow by only the same fixed amount every 25 years.

Malthus believed that the growth in population would eventually slow down as a result of famine and disease caused by a shortage of food. He hoped that before things got that bad, people would find other ways of limiting the growth in population, for example, by getting married later. Fortunately Malthus' fears about population and food growth have not come to pass in the UK although, as we shall see in Unit 8.5, they may seem to be relevant for some other countries. The reasons why the UK has not fulfilled Malthus' gloomy predictions are as follows:

▶ Food production increased in the UK much faster than Malthus thought it would. This is because of greater use of machinery, the increased use of fertilisers, and the introduction of new crops and new ways of farming.
▶ Population has grown more slowly than Malthus thought that it would. The birth rate has actually fallen.

### An optimum population

A country has a certain amount of land space, and a certain quantity of natural resources like coal, iron ore, timber and good farmland. If the population is too small to make the best use of its natural resources it is said to be **underpopulated**. If its population is so large that there are not enough resources to go round, it is said to be **overpopulated**. If the country has just about the right size population for its resources, it is said to have an **optimum population**.

Figure 5.1c
What did Malthus' theory predict?

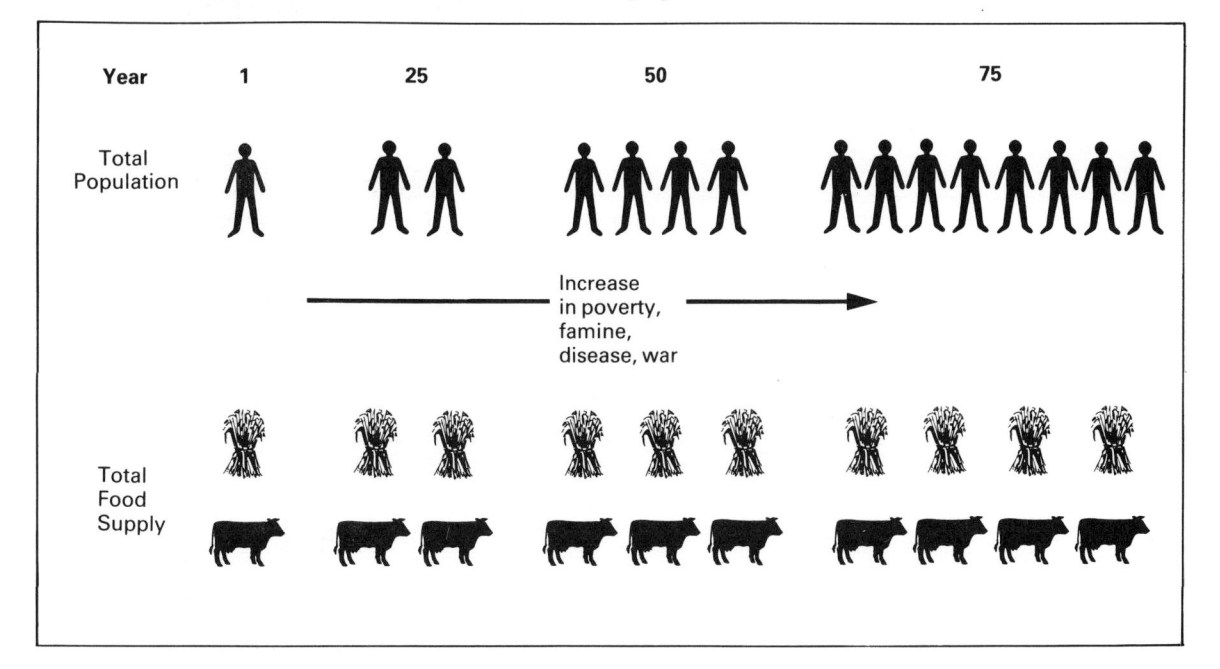

**Questions**
1. There are still many starving people in the world. Is this evidence that Malthus' theories are correct? Explain your answer.
2. 'The idea of an optimum population is not a useful idea because the optimum population of a country can never be measured.' Do you agree with this statement? Give reasons for your answer.

# UNIT 5.2 The structure of the population

**FOCUS**

▶ What are the effects of an aging population?

▶ Why has there been an increase in the size of the UK workforce in recent years?

▶ What changes have there been in where people live in the UK in recent years?

▶ What changes have there been in people's occupations?

## The structure of the population

A population is **structured** just like anything else: it is made up of people of different ages and sexes; it is made up of people in different jobs, and people who do not work at all; and it is made up of people who live in different parts of the country (see Fig 5.2a opposite).

### People in different age groups

This section looks at the **age distribution** of the population. This is the number of people found in each age group. An age group can be whatever economists want it to be. For example, a four-year-old child could be put in an age group called 'Children under Five Years of Age', and also in an age group called 'Children Aged Four to Five'.

Figure 5.2b shows what is called an **age–sex pyramid**. It shows how many people there are in each age group. Age–sex pyramids are different for different countries, and even for the same country at different times.

### An increase in the number of very old people

The age–sex pyramid shows one of the main changes that will be happening over the next few years. You can see that there is a large number of people between 65 and 75 years of age. There will therefore be an increase in the number of people over the age of 75 from about 3.3 million in 1981 to about 4.2 million by the year 2001. Most of these will be women, partly because women live longer than men, and partly because many of the men who would have been in this age group were killed in the First World War from 1914 to 1918.

Some possible consequences of the increase in the number of very old people are:

▶ **1** More hospital and nursing home places will be needed for those old people who cannot cope at home.

▶ **2** More help will be needed for very old people who stay at home but find difficulty with things like cleaning and shopping.

▶ **3** More public spending will be needed to

**Figure 5.2b**
What does an age-sex pyramid show?

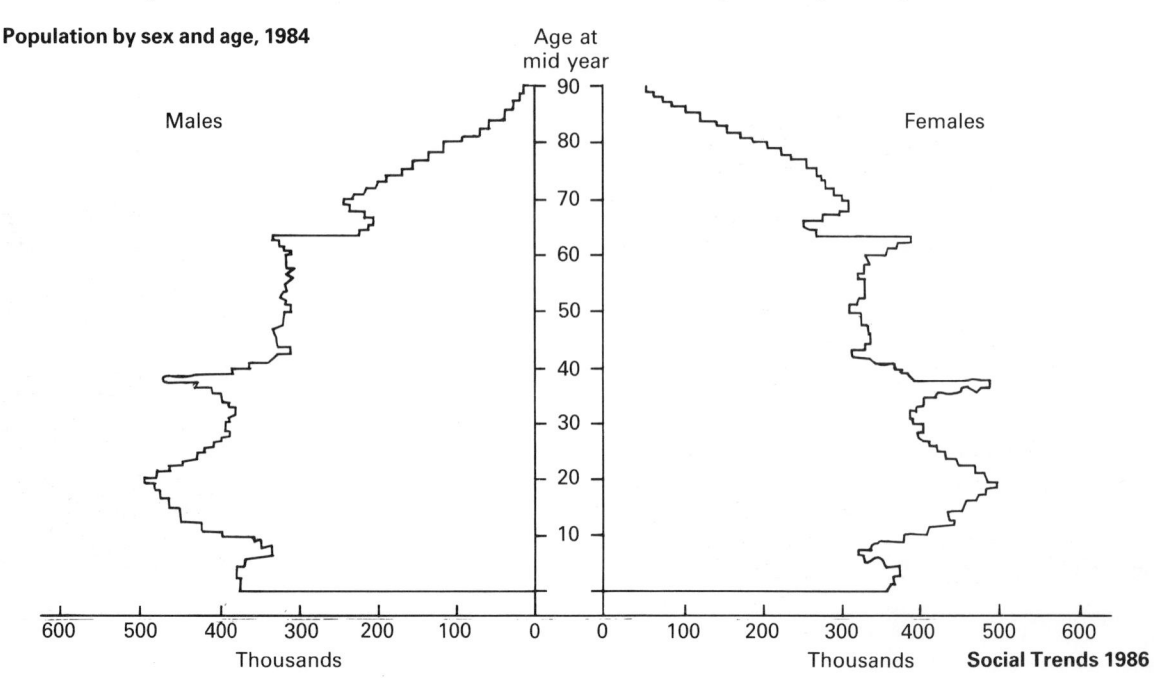

**Population by sex and age, 1984**

**Social Trends 1986**

*Unit 5.2* *The structure of the population*

**Figure 5.2a**
The structure of the population

The working population and the dependant population

Geographical or regional distribution

The total population

Age distribution

Sex distribution

Occupational distribution

Unit 5.2 *The structure of the population*

provide these extra services and extra pensions, and this could mean higher taxation.

### The working population and the dependent population

The age distribution of the population is important because it helps economists to find out how many potential workers there will be in the future. People who do not work and who are not trying to get work are called the **dependent population**. Most of the dependent population are found in the under 16 and over 60/65 age groups. Anyone who works or is trying to get work is part of the **working population**. The working population therefore includes those people who are registered as unemployed, as well as those in work. The working population of the UK in 1985 was 27.5 million. Most of the working population is found in the 16–64 age group.

Of course many people between the ages of 16 and 65 are not counted as part of the working population. These include housewives and full-time students. Also many people go on working after the age of 65. This means that the age distribution of the population can only be a rough guide to the size of the working population.

### Changes in the working population

The working population can increase in size for two reasons. Firstly, there could be a change in the size of the population of working age: an increase in the number of people between 16 and 64 will increase the working population. Secondly, there could be an increase in the proportion of people who want to work. For example, if more married women decide to work there will be an increase in the working population. Since about 1983 the working population has risen sharply because the population of working age has increased, and the proportion seeking work has also increased. The growth of the working population is expected to slow from about 200,000 a year in 1984 to about 65,000 a year in 1990. Part of the reason for this fall will be a decrease in the number of young workers as a result of a fall in the birth rate in the 1970s. This trend was being offset by the mid-1980s, however, by a steep rise in part-time female employment.

A fall in the number of young workers could help to bring down unemployment. On the other hand, it could mean a generally older workforce who will be less willing to change jobs and try new ways of working. As there will be fewer younger workers, there could be less demand for the goods and services that young people buy. This fall in demand for things like clothing, cars and entertainment could be bad for industry.

### The number of males and females in the population

This section is about the **sex distribution** of the population.

For every 100 girls that are born, there are about 106 boys. After birth, however, more boys die. Also, women live longer, and there are more old women than old men.

| Age | Males | Females |
|---|---|---|
| 0–4 | 1,606 | 1,527 |
| 5–44 | 14,220 | 13,784 |
| 45–74 | 7,368 | 8,090 |
| 75 + | 1,049 | 2,118 |

(Source: *Population Trends 40* Summer 85)

**Figure 5.2c**
The number of males and females in England and Wales 1987 (Mid Year)

### People in different jobs

This section looks at the jobs people do, and how things have changed from the past. The way in which people are divided into different jobs is called the **occupational distribution of the population**.

Figure 5.2d shows how the distributions of jobs between primary, secondary and tertiary work has changed over the last 150 years.

|  | 1841 | 1901 | 1971 | 1984 |
|---|---|---|---|---|
| **Primary** | 25.8 | 14.8 | 3.3 | 3.0 |
| **Secondary** | 41.5 | 40.7 | 42.3 | 30.7 |
| **Tertiary** | 32.7 | 44.5 | 54.4 | 66.3 |

NOTE In this table construction has been included in secondary industries, and gas, electricity and water in tertiary industries.

**Figure 5.2d**
The occupational distribution of the working population – the percentages in each type of industry

Some of the reasons for the changes shown in Fig. 5.2d are as follows:

▶ 1 Farming and mining have become much more mechanised. This means that these industries now use machinery far more than they used to, and so they employ fewer workers. This explains the fall in the percentage of workers employed in the primary sector.

▶ 2 The recent fall in the percentage employed in the secondary sector (manufacturing industries) is also because of more mechanisation. Industrial robots are increasingly taking over routine jobs in, for example, the car industry. Another reason for the fall was the general economic depression and lack of demand in the early 1980s. A third reason is the level of foreign imports of many products like cars, other consumer durables and office machinery.

Although the percentage employed in the secondary industries remained unchanged for 130 years, there were great changes within the secondary sector. Up to the First World War (1914–1918), the most important manufacturing

**Unit 5.2** *The structure of the population*

industries were iron and steel, textiles, ship-building and heavy engineering (the industry that made large items of heavy machinery for the other industries).

After 1918 demand for the products produced by these industries fell, partly because of cheaper foreign imports, and partly because of new products. For example, the British cotton and wool industries found it very difficult to compete with cheaper clothing made with cheap labour in countries like India. Also many clothes were being made with artificial fibres like nylon.

As the old manufacturing industries declined, so new ones grew up. Between 1918 and 1939 (the beginning of the Second World War) the car industry became increasingly important. Other industries which grew in importance were chemicals, light engineering (producing goods like fridges, washing machines, and office machinery) and aircraft manufacture.

In recent years cheap imports have threatened employment in most British manufacturing industry. There is some growth in jobs in areas like electronics, but new industries tend to to be **capital-intensive**. This means that they use relatively little labour and lots of machinery, so they do not create many new jobs.

▶ 3 Tertiary (service) industries are the only type of industry that is growing in terms of employment. Before 1914 most tertiary workers were in domestic service. This meant that they worked as housekeepers, maids, butlers and other types of servant in the homes of rich people. Now this area of employment is of much less importance. In the 1980s many tertiary workers help to provide social services like teaching, medicine and social work. Other tertiary workers are found in the rapidly growing fields of insurance, banking and other financial services. Many tertiary workers are found in wholesaling, retailing and transport, all industries which are responsible for getting goods and services to the public.

**Where people live**
This section is about where people live, and why they live there. It is about the **geographical** or **regional distribution** of the population.
**Internal migration**
The geographical distribution of the population is closely linked to the occupational distribution. This means that over a long period of time people move towards where jobs are found. The movement of people is very slow because of **immobility**. The causes of immobility are explained in Unit 7.5.

Some of the main movements of people (**internal migration**) in the UK have been as follows:
▶ 1 After 1750 people moved out of the countryside into towns built on the coalfields. These towns offered jobs in the new industries of the Industrial Revolution like iron and steel, textiles and shipbuilding.
▶ 2 Between 1918 and 1939 people moved to the new industries like cars and consumer electrical goods (fridges, vacuum cleaners, radios etc.) which were found mainly around Birmingham and London. The new industries depended on electricity, and they were set up near to large centres of population where the goods could be sold.
▶ 3 Since 1945 one of the main movements in population has been out of the big cities, and into the suburbs, into smaller towns near the big cities or into new towns. Many people are willing to travel a long way to work (they are willing to **commute**) rather than live in big towns. For example, many people who live in Brighton travel in to central London each day to work.

Many new industries are growing up outside the larger towns. For example, many new businesses have been set up near the M4 motorway between London and Bristol. These new businesses are in the countryside, or in smaller towns like Swindon, Slough and Reading.
▶ 4 There is a growth in the size of the population in certain coastal towns like Clacton. This is because people are choosing to go and live by the sea when they retire.

**Figure 5.2e**
Which industry:
▶became very important after 1919 and has been employing fewer people since the 1970s?
▶has had falling employment for over fifty years?
▶is one of the few manufacturing industries that could offer more jobs in the future?

## DATABASE

### 1. The percentage of the population found in each region of the UK 1983

- SCOTLAND **9.1%**
- NORTHERN IRELAND **2.8%**
- NORTH **5.5%**
- YORKSHIRE & HUMBERSIDE **8.7%**
- NORTH WEST **11.4%**
- EAST MIDLANDS **6.8%**
- WEST MIDLANDS **9.2%**
- EAST ANGLIA **3.4%**
- WALES **5%**
- SOUTH EAST **30%**
- SOUTH WEST **7.8%**

(Source: *Regional Trends*)

Unit 5.2 *The structure of the population*

## DATABASE

## 2. Population change: the inner cities

**The downhill run:** population change, 1961 = 100.

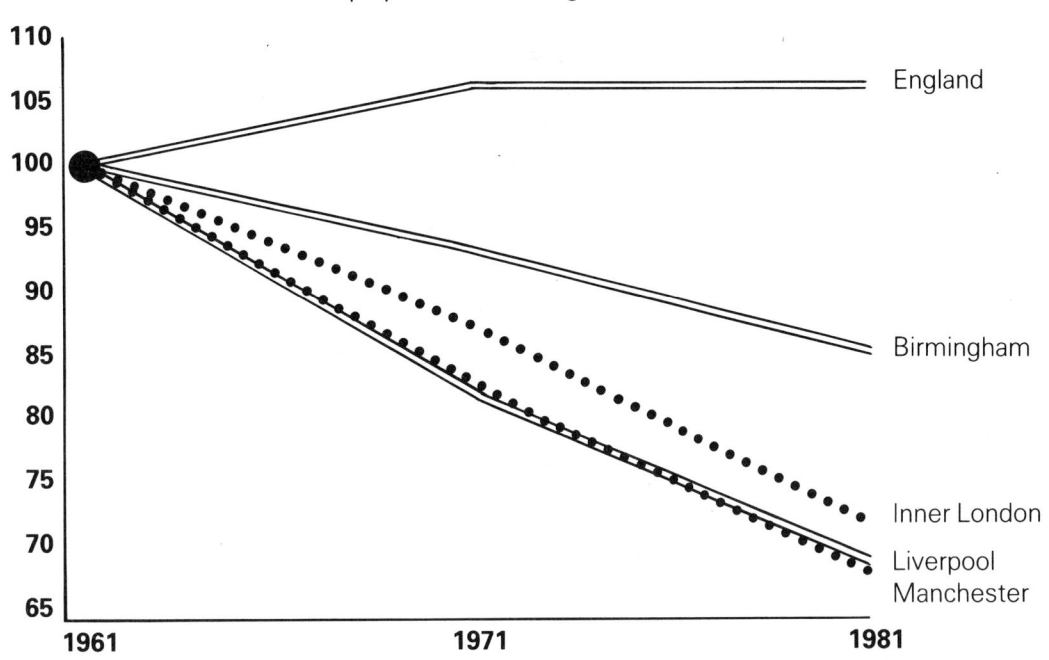

```
                                                    England
                                                    
                                                    Birmingham
                                                    
                                                    Inner London
                                                    Liverpool
                                                    Manchester
1961              1971              1981
```

(Source: *The Economist* April 10, 1982)

## ACTIVITIES

### SECTION A: FOCUS ON UNIT 5.2

Go back and answer the questions raised in the Focus.

### SECTION B: STEPPED QUESTIONS

1. **a** What is meant by the terms 'working population' and 'dependent population'?
   **b** Giving reasons, say how you think the following changes would affect the size of the working and dependent populations now and in the future:
   ▷ a rise in unemployment
   ▷ a rise in birth rate
   ▷ a rise in the number of women choosing to work.
2. **a** What is the 'occupational distribution of the population'?
   **b** What changes do you expect in it over the next twenty years, and why do you think they will happen?
3. The questions that follow are about the age–sex pyramid for Great Britain (see Figure 5.2b).
   **a** How many children roughly were there under the age of sixteen years in the UK in 1984?
   **b** Was the birth rate higher or lower in 1965 than in 1975? How can you tell?
   **c** Why were there so many people aged between fifteen years and twenty-five years old?
   **d** Why are there sharp sections sticking out from the pyramid for people in their mid sixties and for people in their middle to late thirties?

## SECTION C: DATA RESPONSE QUESTIONS

**1 The distribution of the total working population in the UK 1971–1981 (000s)**

|  | 1971 | 1981 |
|---|---|---|
| Agriculture, forestry, fishing | 434 | 343 |
| Mining and quarrying | 396 | 336 |
| **Manufacturing** | | |
| Food, drink and tobacco | 770 | 627 |
| Coal and petroleum products | 44 | 29 |
| Chemicals and allied industries | 438 | 403 |
| Metal manufacture | 557 | 322 |
| Mechanical engineering | 1,051 | 772 |
| Instrument engineering | 166 | 133 |
| Electrical engineering | 812 | 680 |
| Shipbuilding and marine engineering | 193 | 140 |
| Vehicles | 816 | 608 |
| Metal goods not elsewhere specified | 576 | 446 |
| Textiles | 622 | 318 |
| Leather, leather goods and fur | 47 | 30 |
| Clothing and footwear | 455 | 272 |
| Bricks, pottery, glass, cement, etc. | 307 | 216 |
| Timber, furniture, etc. | 270 | 218 |
| Paper, printing and publishing | 596 | 510 |
| Other manufacturing industries | 339 | 252 |
| Construction | 1,262 | 1,139 |
| Gas, electricity and water | 377 | 338 |
| Transport and communication | 1,568 | 1,422 |
| Distributive trades | 2,610 | 2,715 |
| Financial, business, professional and scientific services | 3,964 | 4,944 |
| Miscellaneous services (excluding catering, hotels, etc.) | 1,946 | 2,522 |
| National government service | 596 | 589 |
| Local government service | 914 | 931 |

(Source: *CSO - Annual Abstract of Statistics*)

**a** How many fewer people worked in agriculture, forestry and fishing in 1981 than in 1971?

**b** Explain what happened to employment in textiles, and give three reasons why it happened.

**c** Which type of service employment created the most new jobs from 1971 to 1981?

**d** Using the terms 'primary industries', 'secondary industries' and 'tertiary industries', explain the trends that are shown in the table.

## 2 Women at work

**How many women work? – 1981**

|  | % of all ages | % rise since 1970 |
|---|---|---|
| Denmark | 44.4 | 7.5 |
| USA | 38.4 | 8.3 |
| Japan | 36.7 | 1.3 |
| UK | 35.8 | 4.5 |
| France | 32.3 | 3.4 |
| Germany | 31.1 | 0.8 |
| Italy | 25.4 | 3.5 |
| Netherlands | 21.9 | 3.1 |
| Spain | 20.7 | 3.4 |
| Ireland | 18.0 | −1.4 |

Men and women compared – December 1981 – UK
% share of each sex in each category

|  | Men | Women |
|---|---|---|
| Total labour force | 61 | 39 |
| Full-time employees | 68 | 32 |
| Part-time employees | 15 | 85 |
| Production employees | 76 | 24 |
| Service employees | 46 | 54 |

(Source: *Lloyds Bank Economic Bulletin* **June 1982**)

a What percentage of women of all ages in the UK worked in 1981?
b Name two countries in which less than a quarter of women work.
c In 1981, what percentage of the total labour force in the UK was women?
d Has the percentage of women who work risen or fallen in the UK? Give some possible reasons for your answer.
e ▷ What seem to be the major differences between male and female employment in the UK as shown in the second set of figures?
  ▷ What possible reasons are there for these?

## COURSE WORK

### PART 5: COURSEWORK SUGGESTION

**The age distribution of the local area**
1. Visit a local main library and find copies of the Census of Population for the UK and for your local area. Find out the numbers of people in different age groups at the time of the census both nationally and for your local area.
2. Use the information to construct age–sex pyramids for the UK and for your local area.
3. Use the age–sex pyramids to write an account of the similarities and differences between the UK and your local area in terms of the age distribution of the population.
4. Write a report for the local authority which brings to their attention the economic implications of changes in the age distribution of the local population over the twenty years after the census. Your report should concentrate on possible changes in the pattern of demand for local services, and changes in the size and composition of the workforce and how this might affect local employment. Use a variety of methods of presentation for your results, for example bar charts, graphs, tables etc.

## DICTIONARY

Here are some more words and phrases for your Dictionary of Economic Terms. Remember to look for each word or phrase in the text and then write your own definition for it.

age distribution
birth rate
census
death rate
dependent population
geographical distribution
internal migration
net migration
occupational distribution
sex distribution
working population

EXTENSION

optimum population

# Part 6
## Production

# UNIT 6.1 Production and costs

**FOCUS**
- ▶ How are the different stages in the production process linked?
- ▶ What costs are associated with the production of goods and services?
- ▶ How is the profit of a firm worked out?

## The chain of production

Production involves combining factors of production (**inputs**) to produce goods and services (**output**) as shown in Fig. 6.1a.

The chain of production refers to the links between different industries (primary, secondary and tertiary). The chain starts with the collection of raw materials and ends with the consumer receiving the product.

### Different types of output

Economists divide output into two basic groups. Goods and services used to make other goods are called **capital goods**, or **producer goods**, and goods and services wanted by the general public are called **consumer goods**. These two groups can be divided further, as shown in Fig. 6.1c.

Factories, machinery, steel and timber are all examples of capital goods. Cars, televisions, food and clothing are all usually examples of consumer goods. Sometimes it is difficult to decide. For example, are company cars and factory canteen food examples of capital or consumer goods?

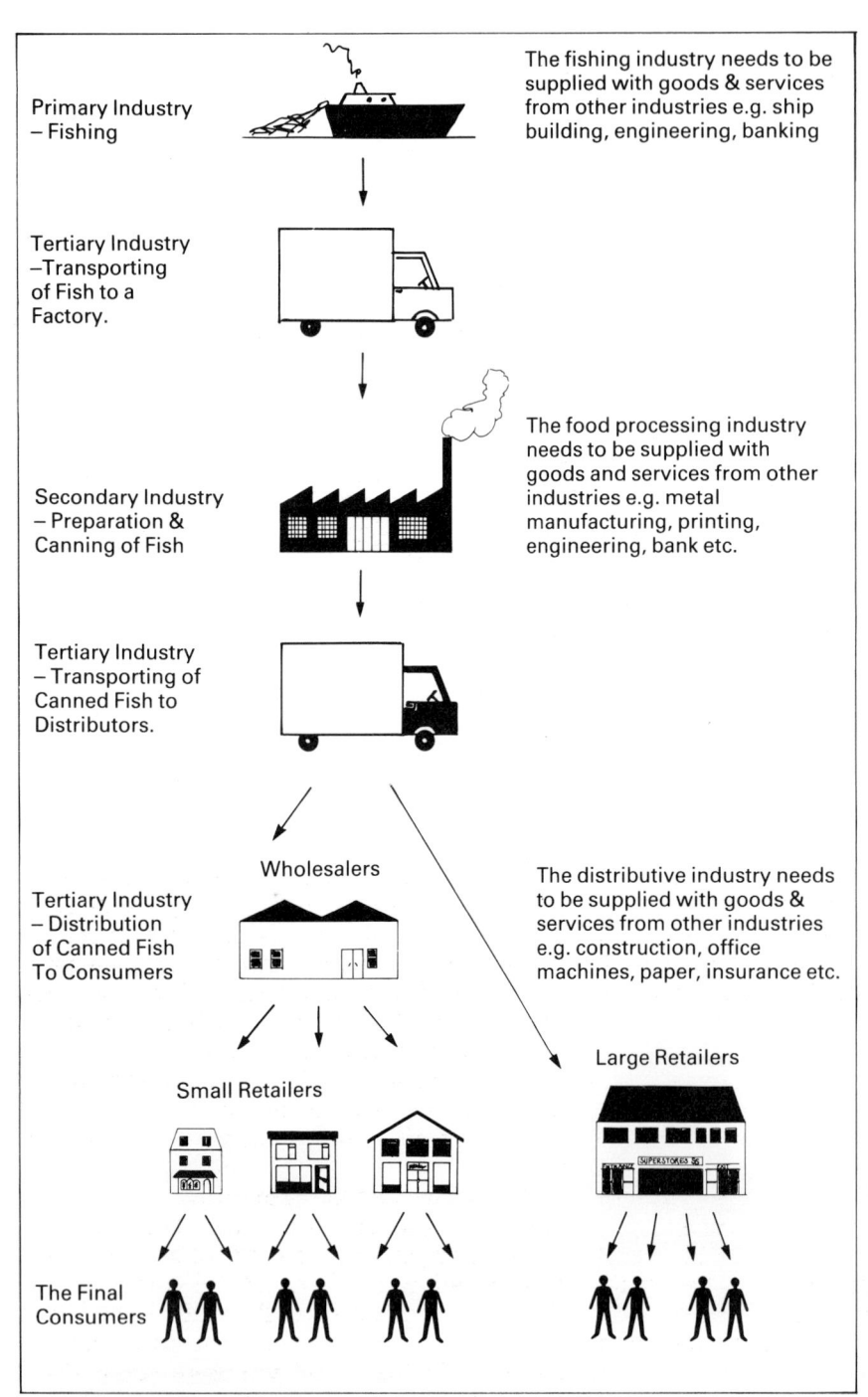

**Figure 6.1b**
What do economists call the process represented here?

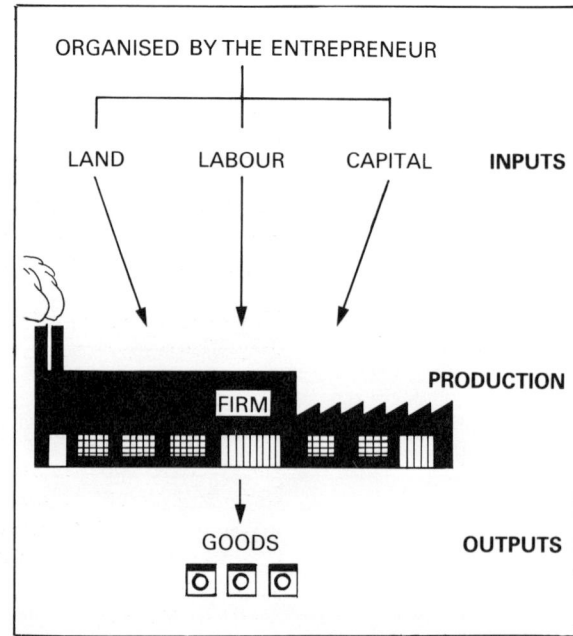

**Figure 6.1a**
Production involves combining factors of production (inputs) to produce an output.

Unit 6.1 *Production and costs*

**Figure 6.1c**
The outputs of production

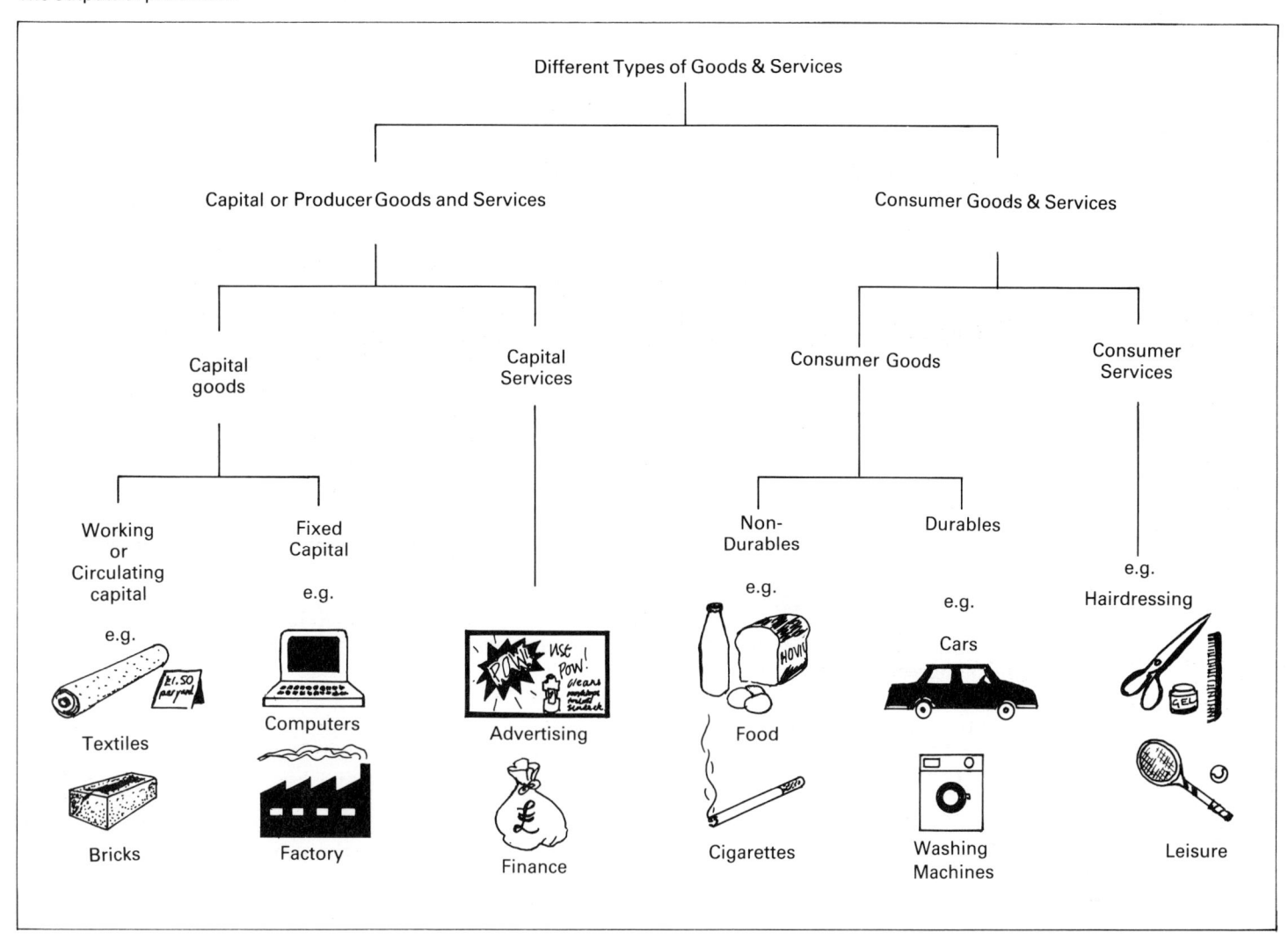

```
                        Different Types of Goods & Services
                       /                                    \
      Capital or Producer Goods and Services        Consumer Goods & Services
         /              \                              /              \
    Capital          Capital                      Consumer         Consumer
    goods            Services                     Goods            Services
      /    \                                       /    \
 Working   Fixed                                Non-     Durables       e.g.
   or      Capital                              Durables                Hairdressing
 Circulating  e.g.                                e.g.       e.g.
 capital                                                     Cars
   e.g.     Computers    Advertising             Food
 Textiles                                                 Washing         Leisure
 Bricks     Factory      Finance                 Cigarettes  Machines
```

## The costs and benefits of production

When a business decides to produce goods and services there are various types of cost involved. There will also be benefits following any decision to produce goods and services.

**Types of costs and benefits**

▶ 1 **Private costs and benefits**

These are the costs and benefits to anyone directly involved in a particular production decision. For example, if you own a toy factory the private costs to you will be the money you have to pay out to buy and hire the factors of production needed to make the toys. The private benefits will be the satisfaction or **utility** given to the children who buy the toys, and the profit made by the firm.

▶ 2 **Externalities**

When a firm produces goods and services it will be most concerned with its own private financial costs and the revenues it will receive from selling its output. Production may create some costs and benefits, however, which affect the whole community, and which cannot necessarily be measured in money terms. These costs and benefits are called **external costs and benefits**, or just **externalities**. They can include, for example, the noise and smells created by a new factory, or an improvement in the environment in a village after the building of a new by-pass road.

▶ 3 **Social costs and benefits**

These are the total costs and benefits, both private and external, of a production decision.

▶ 4 **Fixed, variable and total costs**

Private financial costs will now be looked at in more detail. Private financial costs can be divided into **fixed** and **variable** costs. Fixed costs are the costs of production which stay the same however much the firm produces. If you owned a toy factory, for example, you might have to pay out each week a certain amount for things like rent, rates, lighting, heating, basic wages and interest on any loans, no matter how many toys you produced. You might need to find £1,000 per week to cover these items whether you produced just one toy or one thousand toys a week. However, the more toys that you produced, the lower would be the fixed cost per toy. For example, if only 250 toys a week are produced then the fixed cost per toy would be £1,000 ÷ 250 = £4 per toy. If production was increased to 500 toys per week then the fixed cost per toy would fall to £1,000 ÷ 500 = £2 per toy. Businessmen and women sometimes refer to fixed costs as **overheads**, and they like to spread their overheads over as large an output as possible to reduce costs per unit. If you can reduce the costs per unit you can either sell for a lower price, or increase your profit.

Variable costs of production are the costs which rise as output rises, and fall as output falls. As the production of toys rises more may need to be spent on things like textiles, power to work machines, and overtime pay. These costs vary directly with the amount produced, and are in addition to fixed costs.

**Total costs** are the sum of the fixed and variable costs of production. If you look at Fig. 6.1d you can see that the total cost of producing 500 toys a week would be £1,000 in fixed costs plus £2,500 in variable costs which gives a total cost of production of £3,500.

**Figure 6.1d**
What happens to fixed costs, variable costs and total costs as output rises?

**The Cost of Production**

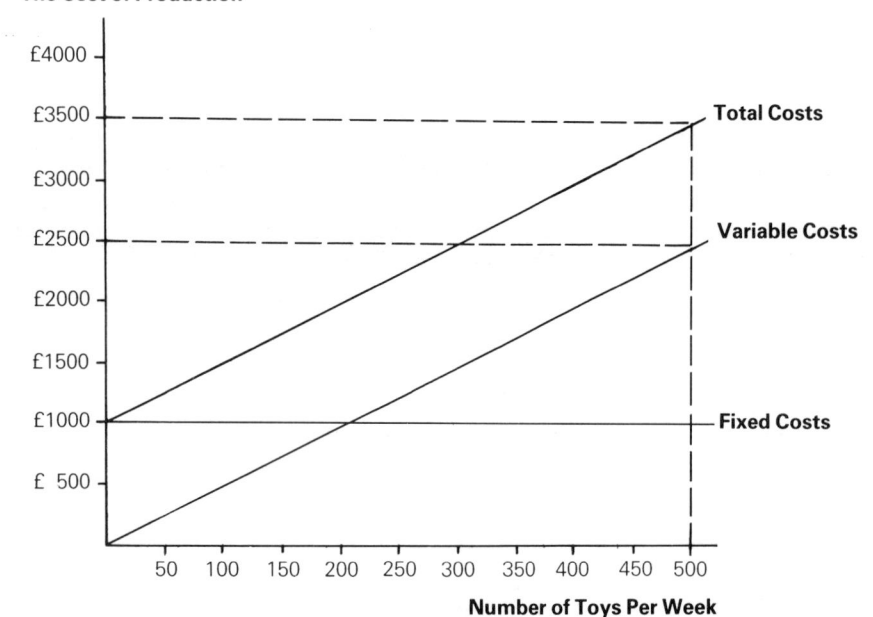

▶ **5 Marginal cost**
Marginal cost is the additional cost of increasing output by a single unit. For example, if output in the toy factory is increased by one unit, and total costs rise from £2,500 to £2,507, then the marginal cost of the last toy is £2,507 − £2,500 = £7.

The lowest total cost does not necessarily mean the highest profit for the producer, who must also take into account the demand for the product. This will affect the price he or she is able to charge. Once an appropriate price has been decided on, one where consumers will buy the product, the producer can then work out the total revenue from selling the product like this:

Total revenue = price × quantity sold

The producer must also take into account the difference between total revenue and total costs. This difference is the profit or loss, and is worked out like this:

Profit = total revenue − total cost

Figure 6.1e shows how all of this is worked out, when the price of each toy is £10

| Quantity sold per week | Total Revenue (£) | Total Cost (£) | Profit or Loss |
|---|---|---|---|
| 100 | 1000 | 1500 | −500 |
| 200 | 2000 | 2000 | 0 |
| 300 | 3000 | 2500 | +500 |
| 400 | 4000 | 3000 | +1000 |
| 500 | 5000 | 3500 | +1500 |

Notice that the producer needs to sell more than 200 toys to make a profit, and that he or she will only take into account the private cost of production, not the social cost.

**Short-run costs and long-run costs**
A producer could reduce his or her costs of production in two quite different ways. Firstly, he or she could make a product more cheaply per unit by making better use of existing fixed factors. For example, if a manager reorganised the inside of the factory so that workers could produce more output in the same time, production could rise for no increase in costs. This would lead to a fall in the cost per unit or average cost of production. A cut in costs achieved by making more efficient use of existing fixed factors is called a **short-run** fall in average costs. This Unit has been about short-run costs because only in the short-run are any factors fixed.

Another way to reduce costs is by increasing all factors of production, for example by building a factory extension. If this leads to a cut in average costs then costs are said to have fallen in the **long-run** and the firm is said to be experiencing **economies of scale**. Economies of scale are described in more detail in Unit 6.5.

## DATABASE

## Costs of a pop record

**Price of a full-price pop LP – £6.49 in 1986**
Where the money goes:

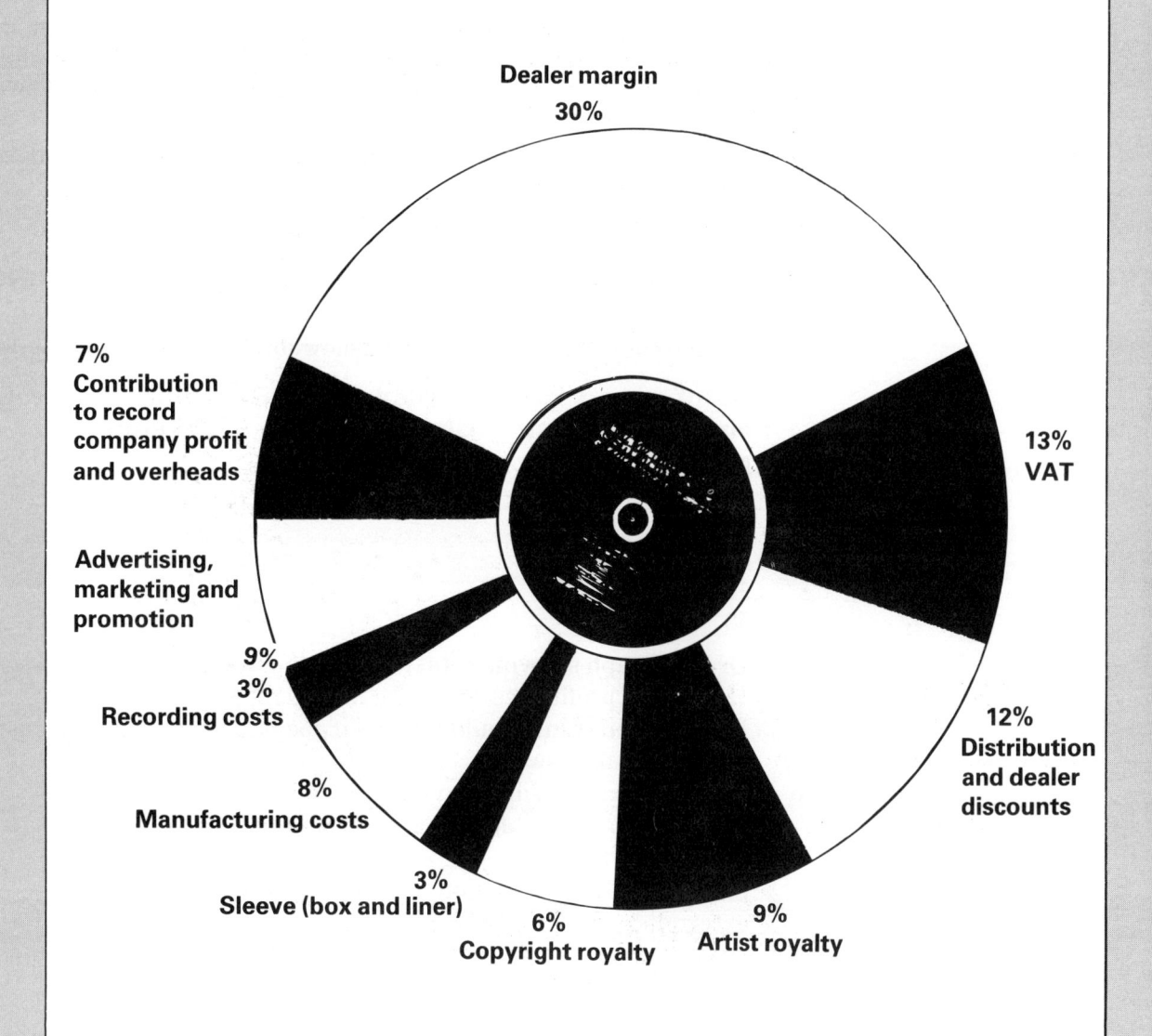

- Dealer margin 30%
- 13% VAT
- 12% Distribution and dealer discounts
- 9% Artist royalty
- 6% Copyright royalty
- 3% Sleeve (box and liner)
- 8% Manufacturing costs
- 3% Recording costs
- 9% Advertising, marketing and promotion
- 7% Contribution to record company profit and overheads

## ACTIVITIES

### SECTION A: FOCUS ON UNIT 6.1

Go back and answer the questions raised in the Focus.

### SECTION B: STEPPED QUESTIONS

1. Joe Peters owns his own small garage. He pays out about £200 in fixed expenses each week and, on average, £30 per customer on materials and other variable costs. He charges, on average, £50 per customer, and usually gets around 30 customers per week.
   a. Draw two columns, headed 'fixed costs' and 'variable costs' and list *five* of each type of cost for Joe's business.
   b. How much would Joe have to pay in:
      ▷ fixed costs
      ▷ variable costs
      if he had 40 customers per week?
   c. Copy and complete the costs table below for Joe's business:

   | No. of customers per week | Fixed Cost (£) | Variable Cost (£) | Total Cost (£) | Total Revenue (£) | Profit (£) |
   |---|---|---|---|---|---|
   | 10 | 200 | 300 | 500 | 500 | 0 |
   | 20 | | | | | |
   | 30 | | | | | |
   | 40 | | | | | |
   | 50 | | | | | |

   d. ▷ Draw a graph showing total revenue and total costs. Shade in the area of profits.
      ▷ How much profit does Joe make in an average week?
      ▷ What do you think would happen if Joe had fewer than ten customers per week? Explain your answer.
   e. ▷ Suggest some possible ways Joe could increase his profits.
      ▷ Suggest some possible effects of Joe increasing his profits.

2. a. What is meant by:
      ▷ private costs of production
      ▷ external costs of production?
   b. Give *three* examples of each of the types of costs in **a**.
   c. ▷ Explain why firms do not take external costs into account.
      ▷ Why are external costs very difficult to measure?

3. a. Draw a chain of production for a loaf of bread. The stages you should show are: growing the wheat, milling the flour, baking the bread, and distribution to customers.
   b. ▷ Write down three fixed costs and three variable costs that would have to be paid by Sally Sharp, a small baker, who bakes and sells bread on the same premises.
      ▷ What possible reasons could there be for Sally NOT to aim to make as much profit as possible?
   c. Explain how a loaf of bread could be a capital good to the owner of a restaurant, but a consumer good to a person buying a loaf.

# SECTION C: DATA RESPONSE QUESTION

The line between success and bankruptcy

> In strictly financial terms, soccer is on the brink of wholesale bankruptcy and badly in need of restructuring. There are obvious parallels between British Leyland or British Steel of a few years ago and the game which attracts over 20 million a year to its stadiums and pulls in television audiences of millions each week.
>
> Attendances have fallen steadily in the past three decades. In 1950–51 for example, around 40 million people watched the game live. Last season the number had sunk below 22 million and a further drop in the current indifferent, weather-beaten season is probable.
>
> Most clubs, even the rich ones like Liverpool, have felt the pinch and turned increasingly to sponsorship and lotteries to make up for the income lost from paying customers.
>
> But running costs, especially players' wages, have risen even faster and the cost of borrowing money for a game traditionally overdrawn at the bank has been calamitous.
>
> Mr John Quinton of Barclays Bank estimated only last week that the 92 clubs owed between £25 and £30 million to their friendly bank managers.
>
> By the end of last season, the 92 clubs were probably paying out at least £3 million in interest on their bank loans and that figure has certainly grown in the current season.

(Source: *Guardian* 4.2.82)

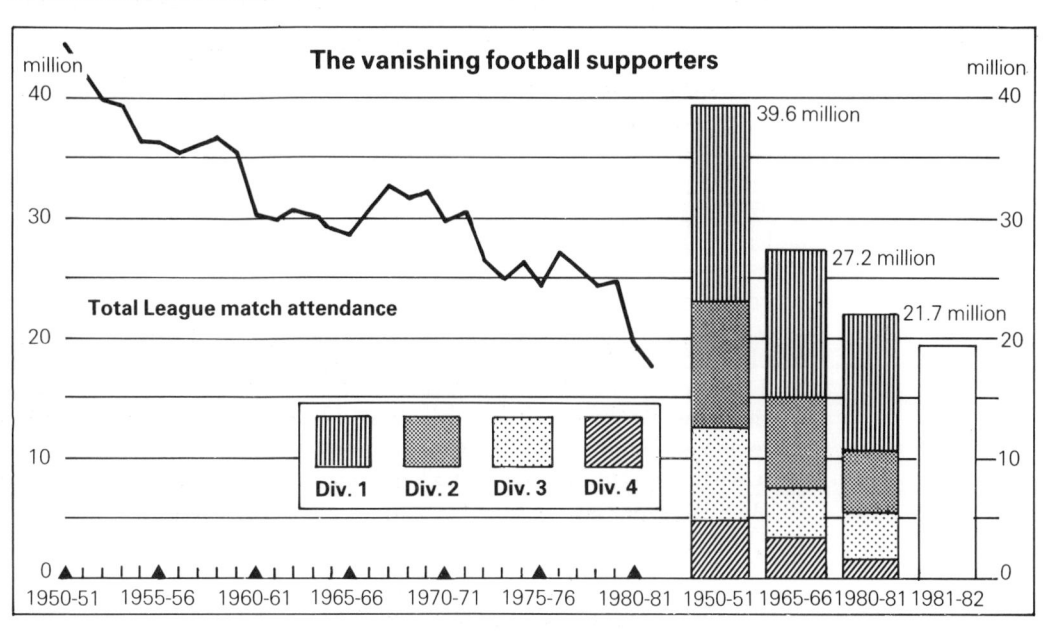

**The vanishing football supporters**

Total League match attendance — 1950-51: 39.6 million; 1965-66: 27.2 million; 1980-81: 21.7 million; 1981-82: (approx 20 million). Divisions: Div. 1, Div. 2, Div. 3, Div. 4.

a What is the major cause of soccer's problems? Give some figures to back up your answer.

b ▷ Which cost of running a football club has risen particularly fast in recent years?
▷ How much was being paid out in interest on loans at the end of the 1980–1981 season?

c Name two ways described in the article in which clubs are trying to boost revenue.

d Give *two* examples of:
▷ fixed costs
▷ variable costs
involved in running a football club.

e What other ways can you think of to save soccer clubs from bankruptcy? You should suggest ideas to reduce costs and/or increase revenue.

# UNIT 6.2 Private sector firms

**FOCUS**

▶ What different aims may a firm have?

▶ What different types of firm are there in the private sector?

▶ How are large companies organised?

▶ What are co-operatives and how are they organised?

▶ How do multi-nationals operate?

## The aims of firms

A firm can be just one person in business on his or her own, or it can be a huge company employing several hundred thousand people throughout the whole world. This section is all about the aims of firms – the basic things they try to achieve. Here are some of the possible aims of firms:

▶ **1 To make maximum profit**
Firms may try to make the biggest possible profit. The calculation of a firm's profit is explained in Unit 6.1.

▶ **2 To make satisfactory profit**
Firms may aim to make a satisfactory level of profit. If a firm aims to make the largest possible profit it will need to work very aggressively to sell as much as it can, to reduce costs to the lowest possible level, and to produce a constant stream of new, attractive products. Some firms may settle for a quieter life and some reasonable level of profit.

▶ **3 To sell as much as possible**
Firms may aim to sell as much as possible and have as big a share of the market as possible. A firm with this aim may be involved constantly in takeover bids for other firms.

▶ **4 To provide a good, cheap public service**
Firms may aim to provide the best possible service to the public at the lowest possible price, for example nationalised postal services to rural areas.

## How firms are organised

People can organise themselves in several different ways if they wish to run a business. This section looks at how privately-owned firms are organised.

### Sole proprietor or sole trader

This type of business has the following features:
▶ 1 One person owns and controls the business, even though he or she may employ other people.

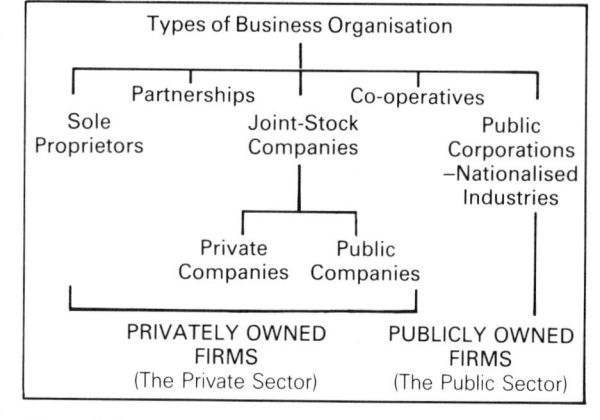

**Figure 6.2a**
This diagram shows the main types of business organisation in Britain.

*Types of Business Organisation*

- Sole Proprietors
- Partnerships
- Joint-Stock Companies
  - Private Companies
  - Public Companies
- Co-operatives
- Public Corporations – Nationalised Industries

PRIVATELY OWNED FIRMS (The Private Sector) | PUBLICLY OWNED FIRMS (The Public Sector)

▶ 2 The owner of the business (the sole proprietor) has **unlimited liability**. This means that if he or she goes bankrupt, he or she could have to give up their personal possessions to pay off any outstanding debts of the business. If a plumber goes bankrupt, for example, the court could order the plumber to sell his or her house to help pay anyone who is owed money.

**Figure 6.2b**
Why might unlimited liability worry this sole proprietor?

# Unit 6.2 Private sector firms

▶ 3 Sole proprietorships are small businesses. They are very common in services like shops, plumbing and electrical repairs.

Some advantages and disadvantages of small businesses like sole proprietors are looked at in Unit 6.5.

## Partnerships

This type of firm has the following features:
▶ 1 Partnerships are owned by at least two partners, with an upper limit on the number of partners of twenty in some cases. The partners run the business unless they are **sleeping partners**, as described below.
▶ 1 At least one partner must have unlimited liability. A partner who just wishes to invest money in the partnership but take no part in running the business, is called a sleeping partner. Sleeping partners have limited liability.
▶ 3 Partnerships are very common in professional services like doctors, lawyers and architects.

## Companies

This type of firm has the following features:
▶ 1 People buy shares in the ownership of a company and become the owners of it. These people are called **shareholders**. At least two shareholders are needed to start a company.
▶ 2 The shareholders elect a board of directors to run the business for them. In large companies the directors are not necessarily shareholders. In small (private) companies the directors tend to be the main shareholders.
▶ 3 All shareholders have **limited liability**. This means that they cannot lose more money than the amount that they have invested in the company if it becomes bankrupt.
▶ 4 Shareholders can sell their shares so that the company can continue in business even though the owners change.

There are two types of company, private limited companies and public limited companies. Here are the differences between them:

| Private Limited Companies | Public limited Companies |
|---|---|
| They must have 'limited' (Ltd.) in the name e.g. Bloggs & Son Ltd. | They must have plc after the name, e.g. Lloyds Bank plc. |
| They are usually small family businesses | They are usually larger businesses employing a large number of people. |
| Shares cannot be offered to the general public. | Shares can be sold to the general public, and then sold again on the Stock Exchange without permission of the other shareholders. |

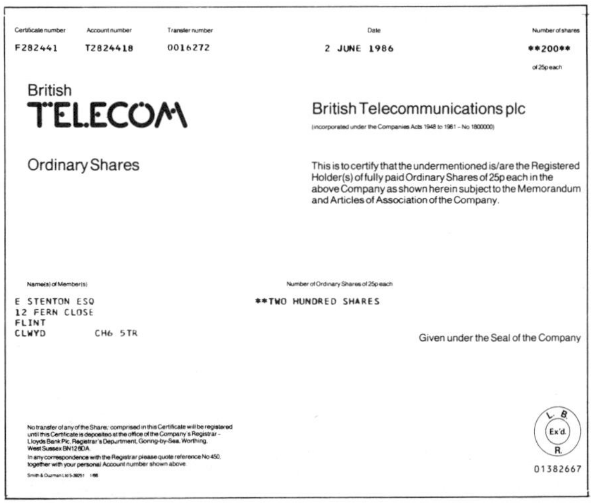

### Different types of share

There are many different types of shares in companies. People who own shares will receive a share of the profits of the company if profits are made. When profits are paid out to shareholders they are called **dividends**.

There are two main types of shares in a company. They are called **ordinary shares** and **preference shares**. Here are some of the differences between them:

| Ordinary Shares | Preference Shares |
|---|---|
| Ordinary shareholders can usually vote in all a company's affairs where a vote is needed, e.g. at the annual general meeting (AGM). Shareholders have one vote for each share they own. | Preference shareholders can usually vote only if their dividend has not been paid. Shareholders have one vote for each share they own. |
| The dividend payable to ordinary shareholders is not a fixed amount of money each year. The board of directors decides how much to pay ordinary shareholders, and this depends on the amount of the company's profits. | The dividend payable to preference shareholders is a fixed amount each year. It is only paid if profits are made. |
| Ordinary shareholders are paid dividends only when loan interest has been paid and preference shareholders have been paid. | Preference shareholders must be paid their dividend before ordinary shareholders receive theirs. |

The buying and selling of shares is dealt with in Unit 6.4.

**Figure 6.2c** A share certificate

**Figure 6.2d**
The organisation of a typical company

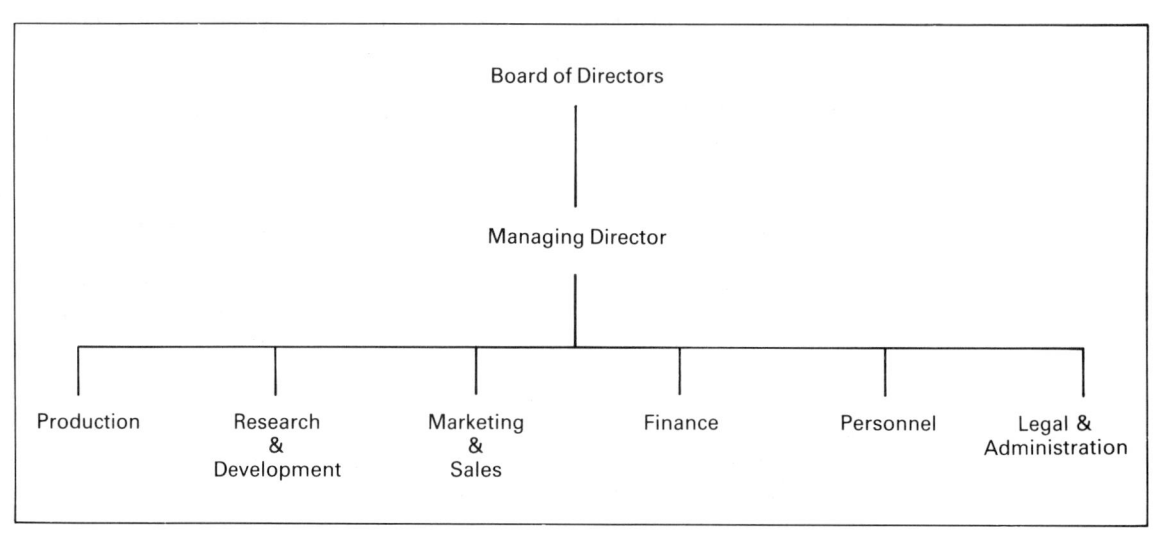

```
                    Board of Directors
                            |
                    Managing Director
                            |
   ┌──────────┬──────────┬──────────┬──────────┬──────────┐
Production  Research   Marketing   Finance   Personnel   Legal &
              &           &                              Administration
           Development   Sales
```

**Figure 6.2e**
Who do shareholders elect to run a company?

### How large companies are organised

A large company might be divided up into several departments. Figure 6.2d shows how a typical large company could be organised.

▶ **1 The board of directors and managing director**

The board of directors and managing director will make the most important decisions that affect the company. They will decide, for example, whether a new product should be produced, whether a factory should be expanded or closed down and who to appoint for the day-to-day running of the firm. The managing director will try to make sure that the whole business runs smoothly.

▶ **2 Production**

This department makes the products that the board of directors have decided should be produced. Production involves careful planning. At every stage of production quality must be checked. Care must be taken that there are enough raw materials and parts in store at any given time. Machinery and equipment must be carefully serviced to avoid breakdowns. Production involves many people working together in a team.

▶ **3 Research and development**

This department looks at ways of improving the firm's products. They try to find ways of cutting costs without reducing quality. They try to come up with new products that will sell well and keep the firm ahead of its rivals.

▶ **4 Marketing and sales**
This department is concerned with finding out what people think of existing products, and what new products people might buy in future. They are also responsible for seeing that products are offered for sale in a way that will attract customers.

▶ **5 Finance**
This department makes sure that the company earns enough money from sales to pay its debts and to make a reasonable profit. They look at whether new products are likely to be profitable.

▶ **6 Personnel**
This department looks after all matters to do with hiring, training and looking after the welfare of staff.

▶ **7 Legal and administration**
This department looks after services used by the other departments. It makes sure that other departments keep to laws concerned with, for example, safety and working conditions. It looks after the lighting, heating and maintenance of the place of work. It may provide computer facilities and other services used by other departments.

## Multi-nationals

These are companies which produce goods or provide services in several different countries. There is usually a head office in one developed country which receives the profit. General Motors and Ford are USA-based multi-nationals who produce cars in the UK. ICI is a UK-based multi-national. Unilever is based in the UK and Holland.

Multi-nationals are often controversial because they are able to move their production around to countries with the cheapest labour, or in order to avoid import controls. They can also be very powerful, and make it difficult for governments to control their activities. However, Japanese firms have built factories and created jobs in the UK, for example car and electronics factories in the north-east of England and in Wales.

## Co-operatives

There are two types of co-operatives, **producer co-operatives** and **retail co-operatives**.
**Producer co-operatives or worker co-operatives**
This type of firm has the following features:
▶ 1 It is owned by all the workers who produce the goods or services.
▶ 2 It is run by all the workers who make decisions at meetings, or through a group of workers chosen for this purpose.
▶ 3 Each worker will have put some of their own money into the business. Shares are not sold to the general public.
▶ 4 Producer co-ops are usually found in very small businesses involving only a few people, like printing and making leather goods.

**Retail co-operatives**
This type of business organisation is very common in the co-op shops found up and down the country. Retail co-ops have the following features:
▶ 1 They are owned by the customers who can buy shares in (and become members of) their local co-op shop.
▶ 2 Members have one vote in the affairs of the co-op, no matter how many shares they own.
▶ 3 Members choose a management committee to run the co-op, and the management committee appoints shop staff.
▶ 4 Any profit made is paid to customers in the form of a dividend, often given as stamps.
▶ 5 Co-op shops are provided with their goods by the Co-operative Wholesale Society (CWS). The CWS also runs a bank and insurance business.
▶ 6 In recent years smaller co-ops have been closing down and being replaced by larger and larger stores. These larger shops are better able to compete with rivals like Sainsburys and Tesco.

**Unit 6.2** *Private sector firms*

## DATABASE

### 1. Who owns the shares?

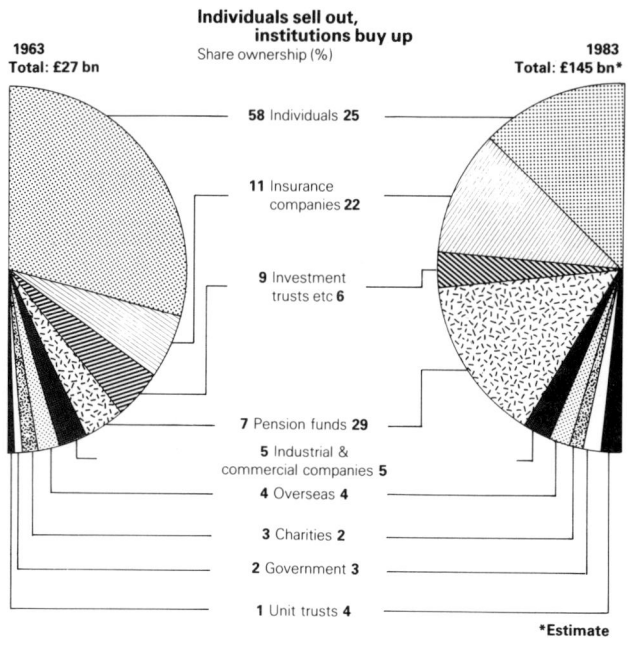

**Individuals sell out, institutions buy up**
Share ownership (%)

1963 Total: £27 bn
1983 Total: £145 bn*

| 1963 | | 1983 |
|---|---|---|
| 58 | Individuals | 25 |
| 11 | Insurance companies | 22 |
| 9 | Investment trusts etc | 6 |
| 7 | Pension funds | 29 |
| 5 | Industrial & commercial companies | 5 |
| 4 | Overseas | 4 |
| 3 | Charities | 2 |
| 2 | Government | 3 |
| 1 | Unit trusts | 4 |

*Estimate

(Source: *The Economist* 14.7.84)

## DATABASE

### 2. Foreign-controlled share of Britain's manufacturing, 1981

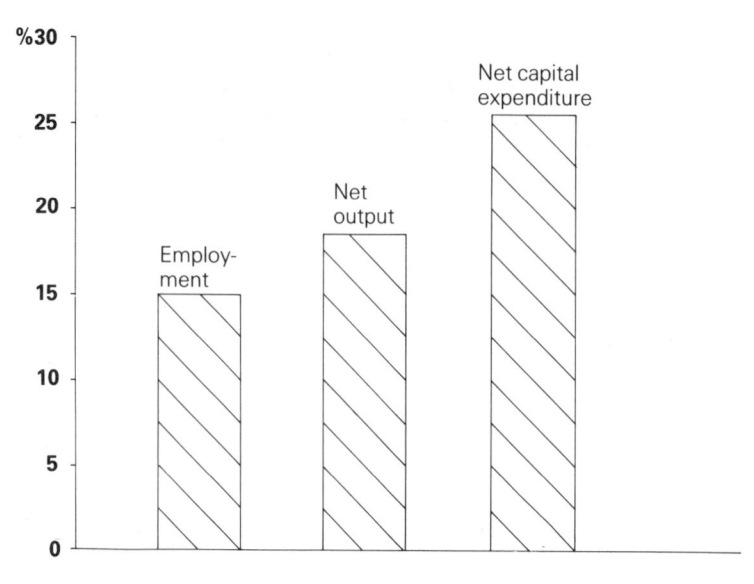

Employment: ~15%
Net output: ~18%
Net capital expenditure: ~25%

Source: *The Economist*, 7.12.85

**ACTIVITIES**

## SECTION A: FOCUS ON UNIT 6.2

Go back and answer the questions raised in the Focus.

## SECTION B: STEPPED QUESTIONS

**1 a** Which types of firms in the private sector usually have unlimited liability for the owner(s)?

**b** What is meant by:
▷ limited liability
▷ a public limited company?

**c** Which types of business organisations do the following statements refer to?
▷ They are privately owned businesses often employing thousands of people throughout the country, e.g. Marks & Spencer.
▷ They issue shares which can be sold on the Stock Exchange.
▷ Members have only one vote in the running of the business no matter how many shares they own.
▷ They are the usual form of business organisation for lawyers and accountants.
▷ Shareholders have one vote per share in the business, and shares cannot be offered to the general public.
▷ At least one of the owners of the business must have unlimited liability.

**d** Below are listed five types of private firm. Explain the features of EACH of them under the following headings:
▷ ownership
▷ control
▷ distribution of profits.

sole proprietor
partnership
private limited company
public limited company
co-operative

**2 a** ▷ What is a 'multi-national company'?
▷ Give *two* examples of USA-based multi-nationals operating in the UK.

**b** Explain why multi-nationals are sometimes controversial.

**c** What are the possible costs and benefits of a Japanese firm setting up a new car factory in Liverpool?

## SECTION C: DATA RESPONSE QUESTION

## Analysis of shareholders in United Biscuits plc

### at 28th December 1985

**Table 1**

|  | No. of holders | No. of shares 000's | % of shares |
|---|---|---|---|
| Individuals | 16,671 | 58,226 | 14.3 |
| Trustee and joint holders | 576 | 7,507 | 1.8 |
| Banks and nominee companies | 1,573 | 178,539 | 44.0 |
| Insurance companies | 201 | 58,211 | 14.3 |
| Investment companies | 80 | 10,525 | 2.6 |
| Pension funds | 108 | 27,250 | 6.7 |
| Other companies | 457 | 25,100 | 6.2 |
| Others | 244 | 41,100 | 10.1 |
|  | 19,910 | 406,458 | 100.0 |

### Analysis of individual shareholders

**Table 2**

| Shares held | No. of holders | % of all holders | No. of shares 000's | % of share capital |
|---|---|---|---|---|
| 1 – 1,000 | 6,256 | 31.4 | 3,645 | 0.9 |
| 1,001 – 5,000 | 8,880 | 44.6 | 19,755 | 4.9 |
| 5,001 – 20,000 | 1,336 | 6.7 | 11,536 | 2.8 |
| 20,001 – 50,000 | 126 | 0.6 | 3,717 | 0.9 |
| Over 50,000 | 73 | 0.3 | 19,573 | 4.8 |
|  | 16,671 | 83.6 | 58,226 | 14.3 |

**a** What is meant by plc?

**b** Look at Table 1. What kinds of organisation own the largest proportion of shares in United Biscuits?

**c** What advantages do the owners of a plc have over a sole proprietor if the firm goes bankrupt?

**d** ▷ Using Table 2, what percentage of shareholders held 5,000 shares or less?
   ▷ How much say do you think these shareholders have in the running of the firm?

**e** Explain why banks, insurance companies and investment companies might want to buy shares in United Biscuits.

**f** ▷ Is the pattern of ownership of United Biscuits similar to the pattern of ownership of shares in the UK as a whole? Use Database 1 to help, and explain your answer.
   ▷ What are the possible economic effects of this pattern of ownership?

# UNIT 6.3 Nationalised industries and privatisation

**FOCUS**

▶ How are nationalised industries organised and run?

▶ What is **privatisation**?

▶ Should nationalised industries remain in public ownership or should they be sold off as public companies?

## Nationalised industries

In a mixed economy many goods and services are provided through state-owned industries. Some goods and services like coal and electricity, are provided through the price system like privately-owned businesses. They are called **nationalised industries**. Other goods and services are not sold for a price, and these will be looked at later in the book. Figure 6.3a shows the ways in which the government is involved in the production of goods and services.

Here are some of the main features of nationalised industries:

▶ 1 They are run as public corporations, and they are owned by the state and controlled by the government.

▶ 2 A minister of the government decides overall policy for the industry and appoints a board to be responsible for the day-to-day running of the industry.

▶ 3 Parliament chooses a group of Members of Parliament who form a Select Committee on Nationalised Industries. The committee watches

**Figure 6.3a**
How the government is involved in the production of goods and services

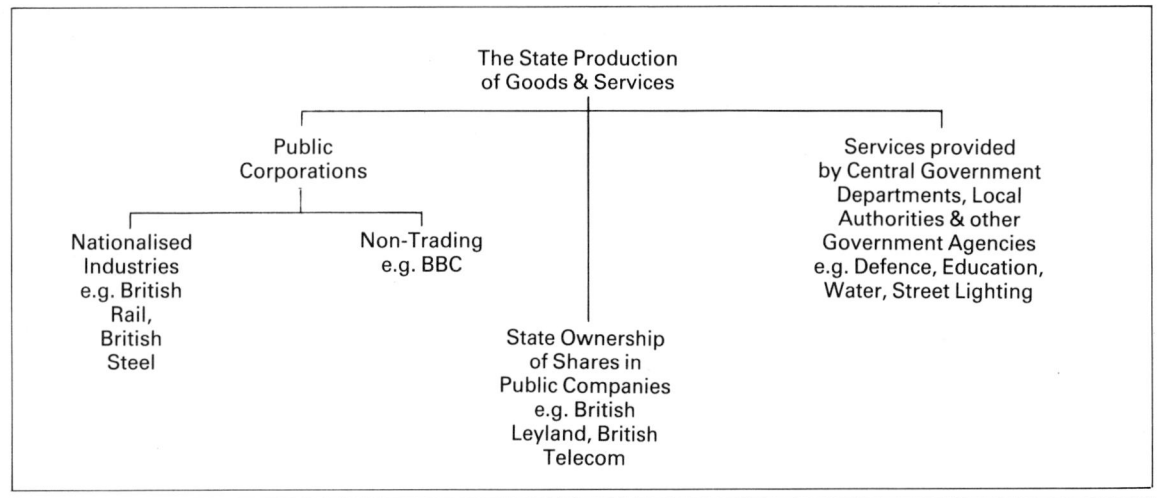

```
                    The State Production
                    of Goods & Services
         ┌──────────────┼──────────────────────┐
     Public                                Services provided
     Corporations                          by Central Government
   ┌─────┴─────┐                           Departments, Local
Nationalised   Non-Trading                 Authorities & other
Industries     e.g. BBC                    Government Agencies
e.g. British                               e.g. Defence, Education,
Rail,              State Ownership         Water, Street Lighting
British            of Shares in
Steel              Public Companies
                   e.g. British
                   Leyland, British
                   Telecom
```

**Figure 6.3b**
The main nationalised industries in 1986

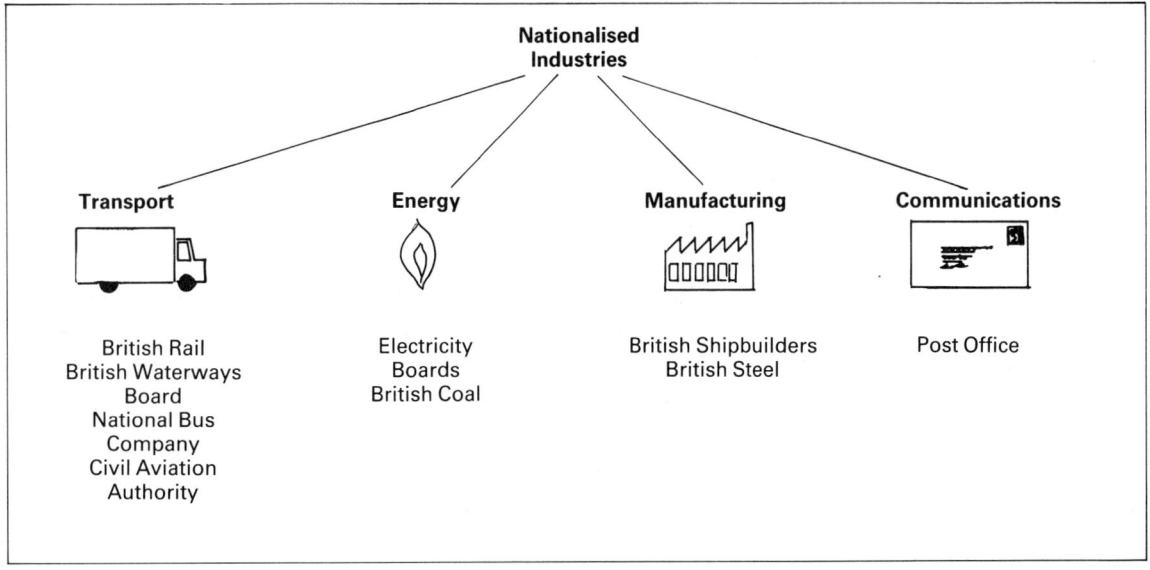

```
                      Nationalised
                       Industries
        ┌──────────┬──────┴──────┬──────────────┐
    Transport    Energy     Manufacturing   Communications

  British Rail   Electricity   British Shipbuilders   Post Office
  British Waterways  Boards    British Steel
  Board          British Coal
  National Bus
  Company
  Civil Aviation
  Authority
```

over the industry on behalf of parliament.

▶ 4 Each nationalised industry has a consumer council to look after the interests of customers. They give the views of customers to the minister and the board, and they deal with the complaints of customers about the service given by a nationalised industry.

▶ 5 Nationalised industries are financed by government grants and the government may also give the industry permission to borrow from the private sector.

**Figure 6.3c**
How nationalised industries are organised.

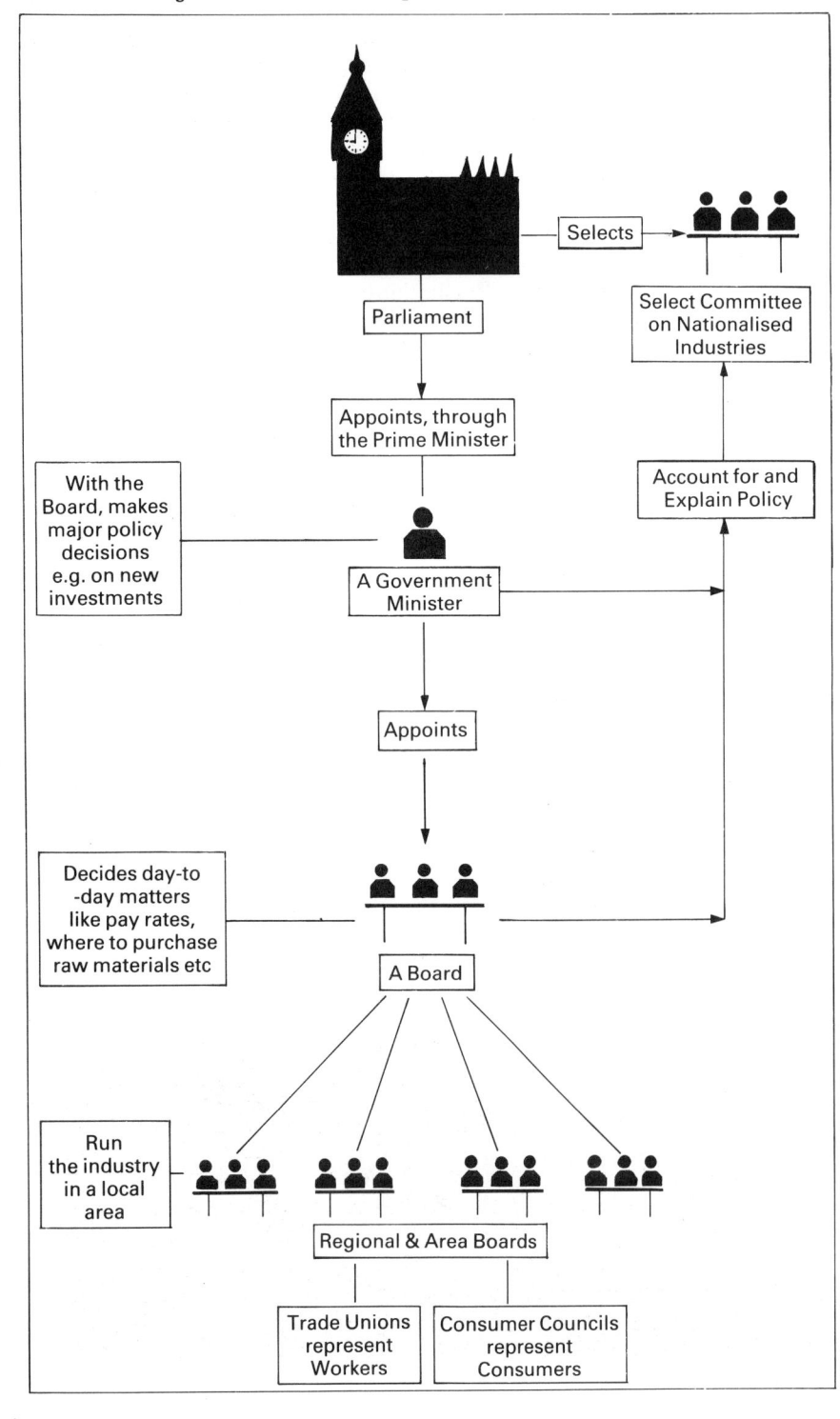

## The arguments in favour of nationalisation

Politicians spend a great deal of time arguing about whether nationalisation is good or bad for the country. Here are some of the arguments that are made in favour of the state owning and the government controlling a business:

▶ **1 Some industries are natural monopolies**

Some industries are **natural monopolies**. This means that it would be very wasteful to have more than one firm in the industry because everything would have to be duplicated.

Electricity is a natural monopoly. If there was to be proper competition in electricity then power stations, cables and electricity fittings in homes would need to be duplicated.

Some natural monopolies like electricity and railways are nationalised because if the industry was privately owned, companies might take advantage of consumers' lack of choice to charge high prices and provide poor services.

▶ **2 Some industries need very large capital investment**

Some industries need enormous sums of money spent on them to modernise them and improve their efficiency, and to take advantage of what economists call economies of scale. If demand for the products of these industries is falling, private business may not be willing to spend the money. This is one of the reasons why the government nationalised the coal industry in 1947 and the steel industry in 1967.

▶ **3 Nationalised industries can be used for managing the economy**

The government can use industries to manage the whole economy if they are nationalised. If unemployment is very high in the country, for

**Figure 6.3d**
How does this illustrate the advantage of nationalising a natural monopoly?

*Unit 6.3 Nationalised industries and privatisation*

example, the government could employ more workers in the nationalised industries. If inflation is high, they could tell nationalised industries to hold down their prices.

▶ **4 Nationalised industries can provide cheap and efficient public services where they may not otherwise be provided**

Nationalised industries aim to provide a public service efficiently and cheaply. This means that they may provide services which a privately owned firm out to make profits would not provide. For example, if the postal service was privately owned, there may be no postal services in the north of Scotland because it may not be profitable to provide them there.

▶ **5 Nationalised industries can take account of externalities**

People sometimes argue that nationalised industries will take more account than privately owned firms of externalities and social costs when planning production. This is because they are not concerned mainly with producing at high profits. For example, if a nationalised industry builds a nuclear power station they may take account of all the consequences of the decision. They could plan to make the power station look attractive and blend in with the environment. They can take the most elaborate and expensive safety measures, and they can try to make sure that dangerous waste materials are safely discarded. Private firms could try to cut corners on safety to reduce financial costs, and this could have disastrous results.

### The arguments in favour of privatisation

The Conservative Government that came to power in 1979 believed in **privatisation**. This means that they wanted to let private business produce many of the goods produced in the past by the nationalised industries.

In recent years the government has sold off shares it held in public companies like British Sugar and British Petroleum. Some local authority services like refuse disposal have been privatised. Shares have been sold in nationalised industries like British Aerospace and British Telecom, turning them from public corporations into public companies.

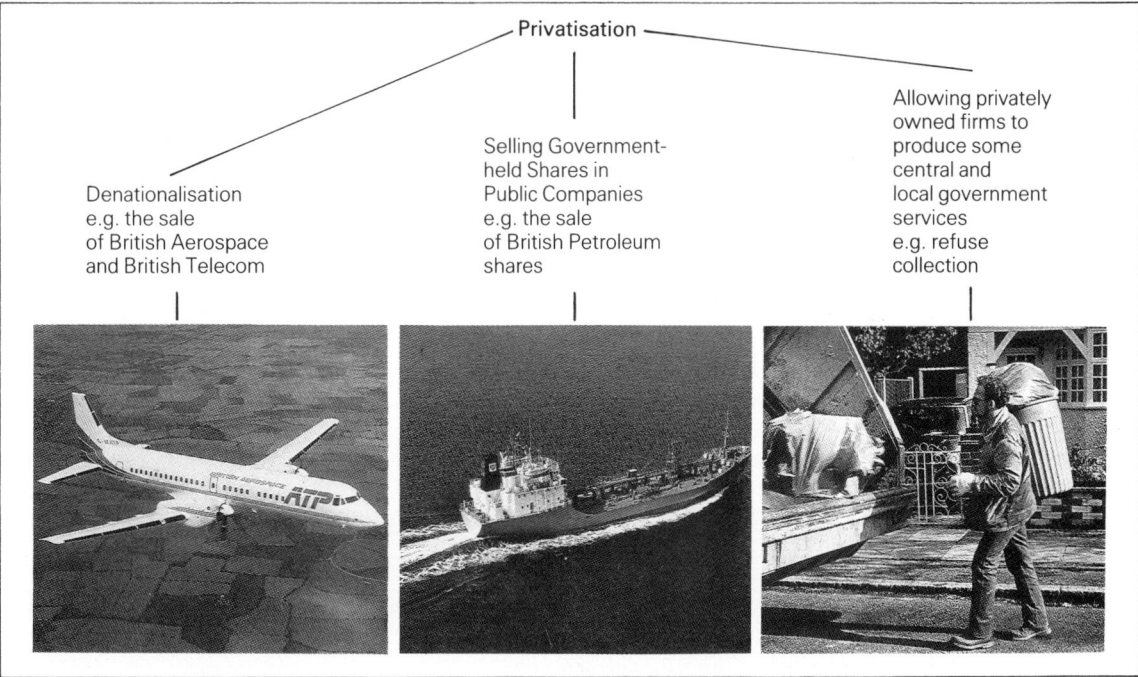

**Figure 6.3e**
Why might this homeowner be worried about the privatisation of the Post Office?

**Figure 6.3f**
This diagram shows that privatisation can be achieved by the government in three different ways.

Here are some of the reasons why it may be decided to privatise an industry:

### ▶ 1 Nationalised industries often make losses

Nationalised industries have not always made profits. This may be because it has sometimes been unclear whether the main aim of the industry has been to run a public service, even at a loss, or to run only services that can cover their costs and pay their way. If nationalised industries were in the private sector they would have to make profits to survive.

### ▶ 2 Nationalised industries may be poorly managed

Management may be better in a privatised industry. The management would know that if the firm did not make a profit it would not be rescued by the government, and this would provide an incentive for the firm to run efficiently, particularly if the firm is faced with a number of competitors. Management would also be free from interference from politicians, who may make decisions affecting the business that reflect political aims rather than the efficiency of the business.

### ▶ 3 Selling nationalised industries raises revenue for the government

When the government sells shares in nationalised industries it raises a great deal of money. For example, the sale of British Gas shares from December, 1986, was expected to raise over £8bn over a period of four years. This may allow the government to cut taxes or increase government spending elsewhere.

### ▶ 4 Nationalised industries may provide limited choice and poor quality

If the privatised industry is open to competition there can be a wider choice and lower prices for the consumer, and an improvement in the quality of goods and services.

### ▶ 5 Privatisation involves wider share ownership

The selling of shares in large businesses such as British Telecom and British Gas enables more individuals to own shares and share in the profits of successful companies.

## DATABASE

# 1. Privatisation: some major sales

|  |  | Amount (£m) |
|---|---|---|
| **1979/80:** | 5% of B.P. | 276 |
| **1980/81:** | North Sea Oil Licences | 195 |
|  | 51% of British Aerospace | 43 |
| **1981/82:** | 55% of Cable & Wireless | 224 |
| **1982/83:** | 51% of Britoil | 627 |
| **1983/84** | 7% of B.P. | 565 |
|  | 25% of Cable & Wireless | 260 |
| **1984/85** | 100% of Enterprise Oil | 392 |
|  | 50% of British Gas Onshore Oil | 215 |
|  | 100% of Jaguar | 297 |
|  | British Telecom | 3916 |
| **1985/86** | 48% of British Aerospace | 346 |
|  | British Shipbuilders |  |
|  |    Warship Yards | 200(est) |
|  | British Airports Authority | 400(est) |
| **1986–1990/91** | British Gas (over four years) | 8000–10000 |
| **1987** | British Airways | 900 |

**Other possible sales**
National Bus Company, Rolls Royce, Unipart, parts of the electricity industry, British Nuclear Fuels.

## DATABASE

## 2. Working out social costs ('cost/benefit analysis')

### Travel time and delays

In appraising road projects, each hour of time saved or lost is given a cash value in the calculations:

- Working time, because time spent travelling has to be paid for by an employer, and could instead be used more productively.

- Leisure time, because this has a benefit to travellers themselves, as has been found in a large number of empirical investigations.

- Walking and waiting time, because the extra effort and stress involved puts a premium value on such time savings.

The Department of Transport recommends values for these categories. The most recent recommendations were provided for 1979 and extracts are shown below. Advice is also given on how the user should bring them up to date (basically in proportion to the growth or decline in national income) so that the figures at the time of writing taking account of inflation are 40%-45% higher, e.g., nearly 80p/hour for in-vehicle leisure time and up to £6/hour for work time.

(Source: *The Future of the Bus* Bus and Coach Council, 1982)

### Official advice on how to value time savings in road projects

| Working time: | (£1 per hour) |
|---|---|
| Car driver | 4.11 |
| Bus passenger | 2.73 |
| Bus driver | 2.77 |
| All workers | 3.93 |
| *Non-working time:* | |
| In-vehicle | .55 |
| Walking or waiting | 1.11 |

### Official advice on how to value road accidents

| | £ per accident |
|---|---|
| Fatal accidents | 149,200 |
| Serious accidents | 7,900 |
| Slight accidents | 1,080 |
| Damage-only accident | 460 |

### Economic effect of an increase in London Transport fares

| | Value (£ million) |
|---|---|
| Increase in accidents | 25 |
| Time losses due to increased congestion | 40 |
| Increased consumption of petrol and other resources | 10 |
| Value of lost trips to travellers | 25 |
| Expenditure on other resources | 50 |
| Total resource cost | 150 |
| Money gain to ratepayers | −200 |
| Money loss to passengers | 200 |

Unit 6.3 *Nationalised industries and privatisation*

**ACTIVITIES**

## SECTION A: FOCUS ON UNIT 6.3

Go back and answer the questions raised in the Focus.

## SECTION B: STEPPED QUESTIONS

1. **a** Give *five* examples of nationalised industries.
   **b** Explain how ministers, boards, area boards, consumer councils and select committees are involved in the running of nationalised industries.
   **c** Under what circumstances could nationalised industries be criticised for:
   ▷ making a loss
   ▷ making a profit?
   Explain your answer.
2. **a** Give *four* examples of industries or firms that have been privatised since 1979.
   **b** Explain the possible costs and benefits of privatisation to:
   ▷ the firm or industry concerned
   ▷ workers
   ▷ consumers
   ▷ the government.

## SECTION C: DATA RESPONSE QUESTION

# Feeling blue but still in the red

**Mrs Thatcher, privatisation and the start on dismantling monopolies have done nothing to change the basic arithmetic of Britain's nationalised industries. This year, they will cost the treasury about the same cash figure of £2.7 billion that the Conservatives inherited in 1979-80. They had hoped for a net surplus of £700m. The treasury's plans, year by year, have been blown to pieces by recession and old-fashioned rigidities in old-fashioned industries. Coal, steel and the railways form the financially crippled alliance that drains the profits from the electricity and gas monopolies.**

(Source: *The Economist* 14.5.83)

  **a** What is meant by 'privatisation'?
  **b** How much did the Treasury have to pay out in 1983 to keep the nationalised industries as a whole in business?
  **c** What is meant by the phrase that the Conservative Government had 'hoped for a net surplus of £700m' by 1983?
  **d** Name two nationalised industries that made a loss in 1983, and two that made a profit.
  **e** Why are electricity and gas called 'monopolies'?
  **f** ▷ Explain why the steel industry has been so unprofitable in recent years.
  ▷ What would be the likely economic effects of requiring the steel industry to make a profit?

# UNIT 6.4  The financing of firms

**FOCUS**

▶ Why do firms need finance?

▶ In what ways can firms raise finance?

▶ How does the Stock Exchange help provide business finance?

▶ What factors can cause share prices to rise and fall?

▶ What is meant by the **yield** on a share?

## How firms raise finance

Firms need finance to pay their fixed and variable costs, including materials, stocks, labour and investment in capital goods. This section looks at some of the ways in which firms can raise finance. These are called **sources of finance**.

### ▶ 1 Retained profit
Firms often keep some of the profit they make to pay for new investment. The profit that they keep is called **retained profit**, and it is the most important source of a firm's finance.

### ▶ 2 Borrowing from commercial banks
Bank loans and overdrafts from banks like the Midland are another important way in which firms obtain finance. Many firms have almost permanent overdrafts. Bank loans usually last for periods of up to five years.

### ▶ 3 Borrowing from special banks
Some organisations exist specially for the purpose of lending money to industry. Investors In Industry (3i), for example, lends mainly for large projects in relation to the size of business, and often takes risks that commercial banks would not take.

### ▶ 4 Trade credit
Firms often borrow from each other. They usually do not pay other firms for the goods they receive from them at the time the goods are delivered. A firm may, for example, give another firm several weeks to pay for a piece of equipment that they have sold to them.

### ▶ 5 Hire Purchase (HP)
A firm can buy a piece of equipment on HP in the manner described in Unit 4.4. When the firms uses HP, it is borrowing from a finance company.

### ▶ 6 Leasing
A firm is leasing a piece of equipment when it

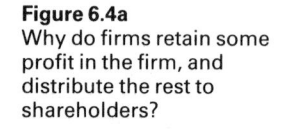

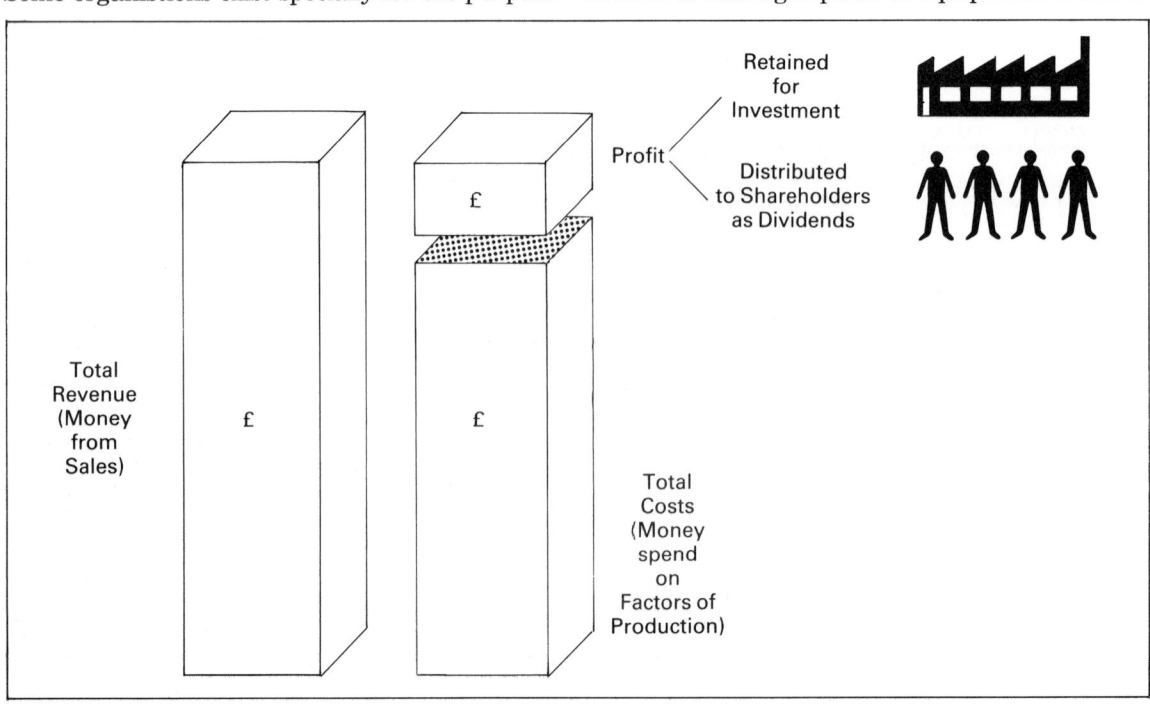

**Figure 6.4a**
Why do firms retain some profit in the firm, and distribute the rest to shareholders?

rents it from a bank or other financial organisation. Computers and company cars are often leased.

▶ **7 Selling securities**

Companies sell securities (stocks and shares) when they start up business, and they can sell securities at other times to raise finance. A security is a piece of paper which shows that someone has lent or given money to a firm. In return the person (a shareholder) will receive a dividend or interest from the firm. Securities can be sold to other people. The government also sells securities when it wishes to borrow money.

▷ **a** *Stocks* Large firms borrow funds for long periods of time by issuing pieces of paper called **stocks**. The person who buys the stock receives a fixed amount of interest each year in return for making the loan. After a certain number of years the firm repays the loan. Some long-term loans are called **debentures**.

**Figure 6.4b**
Different types of security

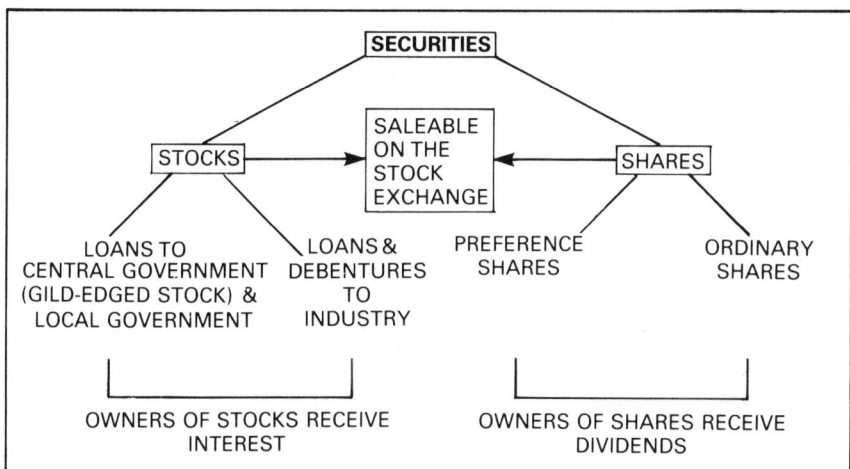

**Figure 6.4c**
The different ways of selling shares

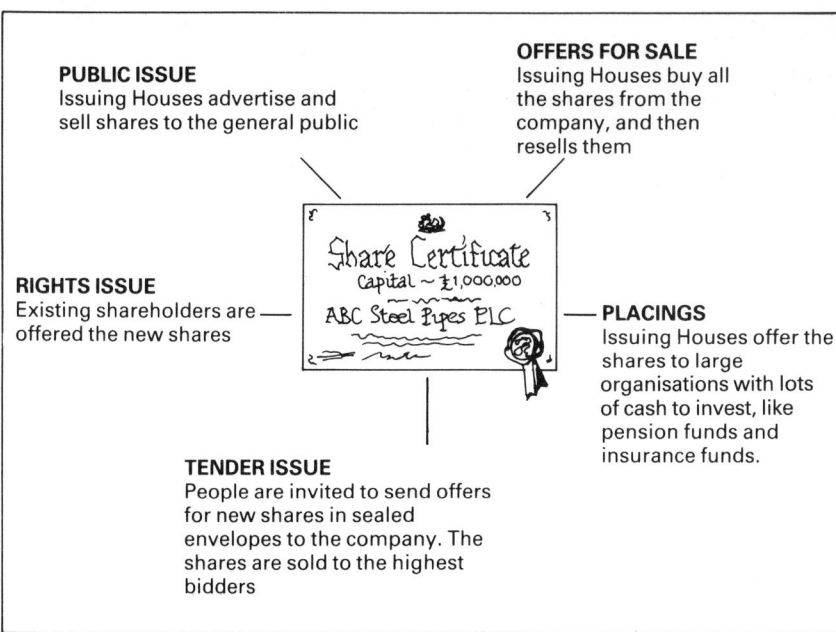

▷ **b** *Shares* People who buy shares in a firm take part in the ownership of the firm. Most shares will never be repaid by the firm. Shareholders receive **dividends** (a share of the company's profits) rather than interest. The different types of shares were described earlier in the chapter. Figure 6.4d shows the different ways in which shares can be issued.

Most securities are bought by large organisations whose businesses involve them receiving large sums of money from the general public. Insurance companies and pensions funds, for example, invest much of the money that they receive from the general public in the shares of firms.

▶ **8 The government**

Here are some of the ways in which the government helps firms financially:

▷ **a** *Regional policy* The government gives grants and other types of help to firms moving into areas with particularly serious unemployment problems. There is more about regional policy in Unit 6.6.

▷ **b** *The Loan Guarantee Scheme* Under this scheme, the government guarantees 80 per cent of some loans made by banks to small businesses. This means, for example, that if a bank lends £40,000 to a small firm, and the firm goes bankrupt, the government will pay the bank £32,000 of the loan. The scheme makes it easier for small firms to borrow money.

▷ **c** *The Business Expansion Scheme* This scheme is designed to help people invest in the shares of new companies. The government will give income tax relief on the money used to buy the shares provided that the money is left in the business for at least five years. The aim of this scheme is to make it easier for people to obtain finance to start a new business.

## Deciding which source of finance to use

Generally speaking, the smaller the firm, the fewer the ways it will have of raising finance. Someone starting out in business as a self-employed plumber may need to use his or her own savings, and borrow from relatives and the bank. Partnerships and small companies will also rely heavily on these sources, but they may use some of the other methods of raising money, like Investors In Industry, or leasing. Larger companies will be able to choose from most of the sources listed above, and they will need expert advice before deciding, for example, whether to go for a bank loan or to issue shares.

## The Stock Exchange

People will only buy securities if they can easily sell them again. The Stock Exchange is a market for people who want to trade in securities. Most share dealings on the Stock Exchange are in ordinary shares that have already been issued. If an individual wants to buy or sell shares, something like the following process is usually involved:

Mary has about £6,500 which she wants to use to buy ICI shares. She first contacts a **broker/dealer** (a member of the Stock Exchange) to obtain the shares for her. (She could have asked a bank to act for her, but the bank would still buy the shares through a broker/dealer.) The broker/dealer then consults a **SEAQ** screen which is linked to a computer. SEAQ stands for Stock Exchange Automated Quotations. The broker/dealer calls up the appropriate page for ICI shares (see Fig 6.4d) and buys the shares from the **market maker** offering the lowest selling price. In this case one of three market makers could be chosen and we will assume that the broker/dealer buys 1,000 shares from Kleinwort Grieveson (KGLE) for £6,340. The broker/dealer will then send details of the transactions to Mary, adding a commission (of e.g. 2%) for his/her services. The total cost of the transaction to Mary would in this case be £6,340 + £126.80 = £6,466.80.

### Recent changes in the stock market

There were significant changes in the operation of the stock market in October, 1986. These were known popularly as the **Big Bang**. Three main changes took place:

▶ 1 Single firms are now able to both buy shares from companies and buy and sell shares from clients.

▶ 2 The SEAQ computerised system was introduced. This enables dealers to compare many different share prices and make instant decisions to buy and sell.

▶ 3 The fixed commission payable to share dealers for buying and selling stocks and shares has disappeared. Different firms may charge different commissions, for example lower commissions for customers who buy very large amounts of shares, such as insurance companies.

Apart from the 'Big Bang' changes there were two other important changes in recent years:

▶ 1 The Stock Exchange has allowed outside businesses to own share dealing firms, or to become members of the Stock Exchange themselves as Nomura of Japan and Merrill Lynch of the USA have done.

**Figure 6.4d**
A SEAQ screen

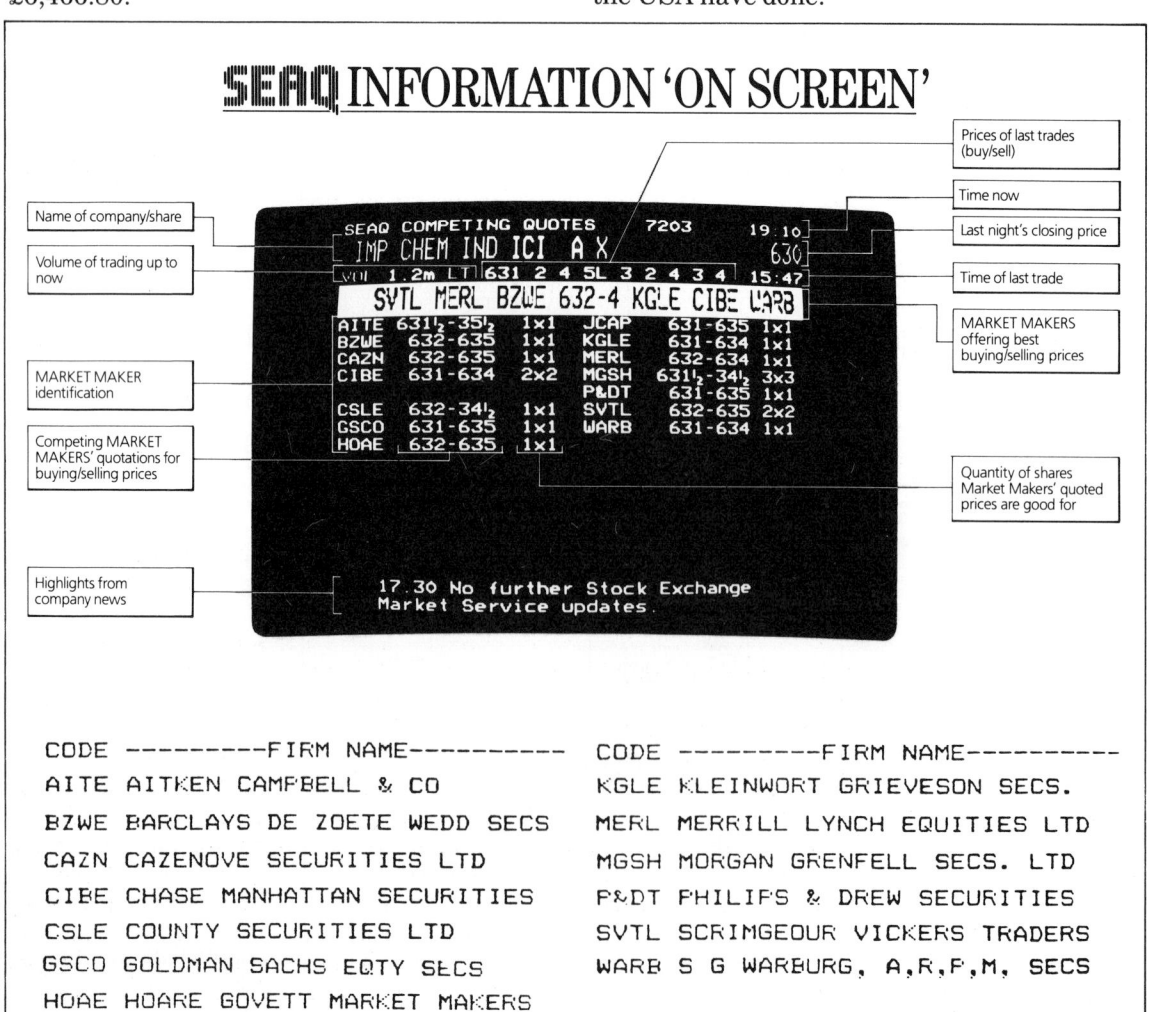

(Source: *Spectrum, Autumn/Winter 1986,* published by the Stock Exchange)

**BULLS**
These are speculators who buy shares expecting they will rise in price and can be resold at a profit

**STAGS**
These are speculators who buy new shares, hoping that the price will rise as soon as trading begins on the Stock Exchange.

**BEARS**
These are speculators who sell shares, believing that they are about to fall in price.

**Figure 6.4e**
The different types of speculator found on the Stock Exchange

▶ **2** There is a growing concentration of financial services in the hands of fewer and fewer large firms. Mergers have led to the growth of large conglomerates offering a full range of financial services including the sale and purchase of stocks and shares on a national and international basis. The appearance of large Japanese and American firms on the stock market reflects this.

### The Unlisted Securities Market
In the past it was very expensive for smaller firms to sell shares to raise finance. The introduction in November, 1980 of the Unlisted Securities Market on the Stock Exchange has allowed smaller companies to sell shares at a lower cost than a full Stock Exchange listing. This is because less detailed accounts and prospectuses, for example, are needed. Some well-known companies quoted on the USM in 1986 were Fuller's Breweries, Acorn Computers, and TV-AM.

### The purpose of the Stock Exchange
Very little of the money that changes hands on the Stock Exchange finds its way directly back to businesses. Firms receive money only when they sell securities in the first place. Nevertheless the Stock Exchange helps businesses in several ways:

▶ **1** People may not be willing to buy securities in the first place if they could not sell them again. Shareholders know that shares can always be resold on the Stock Exchange and this makes them willing to buy new shares.

▶ **2** People buy securities because they believe that the securities might rise in value. The Stock Exchange publishes figures each day showing what is happening to security prices. This gives the public some idea of the profitability of individual firms and industry as a whole. Without such information people may not be willing to invest in securities.

### Why shares rise and fall in value
Shares rise and fall in value because there is a change in either the demand or supply of them. Here are some of the reasons why the demand or supply for shares might change:

▶ **1 Changes in company profits**
If a company's profits rise it will mean that they can afford to pay larger dividends to shareholders. This will increase demand for the company's shares and push up their price.

▶ **2 Changes in interest rates**
If interest rates rise, share prices tend to fall, and vice versa. If interest rates rise it could mean less borrowing, less spending, and poor prospects for company profits in future. This would cause share prices to fall.

▶ **3 Interference in the supply of goods and services**
Anything that is likely to interfere with the supply of goods and services to industry or the public will cause share prices to fall. Strikes, wars, and natural disasters like earthquakes could, for example, affect the supply of raw materials to factories, and this would cause share prices to fall.

▶ **4 Rumours**
Share prices often rise because of rumours. For example, if one firm is rumoured to be about to try and take over another firm, the price of shares in the firm that might be taken over will rise.

▶ **5 Government policy**
Government policy affects share prices. For example, if the government decides to increase taxes this could cause a fall in share prices. Higher taxes could mean less spending, lower profits and lower company profits and dividends.

### How changes in share prices are measured
Changes in share prices are measured by a variety of different indexes, most of them published by the Financial Times (FT). The most commonly used indexes are the FT 30 Share Index, which measures the average of thirty of the leading industrial and commercial share prices, and the FTSE 100, which measures the average of 100 leading UK share prices.

### Different types of speculator
Speculators are people who buy and sell securities in the hope of making a profit. Speculators do not buy securities as long-term investments. At any one time some speculators will be buying securities, thinking prices will rise in future, while others will be selling, expecting prices to fall in future.

### The yield on a share
Dividends are declared on the **nominal** or **par value** of a share. This is the value written on the share. For example, if someone has a £1 share, and the dividend is declared as 5 per cent, the shareholder will receive a 5p dividend that year.

The yield or real return on the share depends on the market price of the share. If the share is being quoted at £2 on the Stock Exchange, the yield is 5p expressed as a percentage of £2, i.e. 2.5 per cent. If a security pays a fixed sum every year, the yield will vary inversely with the price of the security on the Stock Exchange. As the market price of the security rises the yield will fall, and vice versa.

## DATABASE

## 1. Sources of funds for industrial and commercial companies, 1984

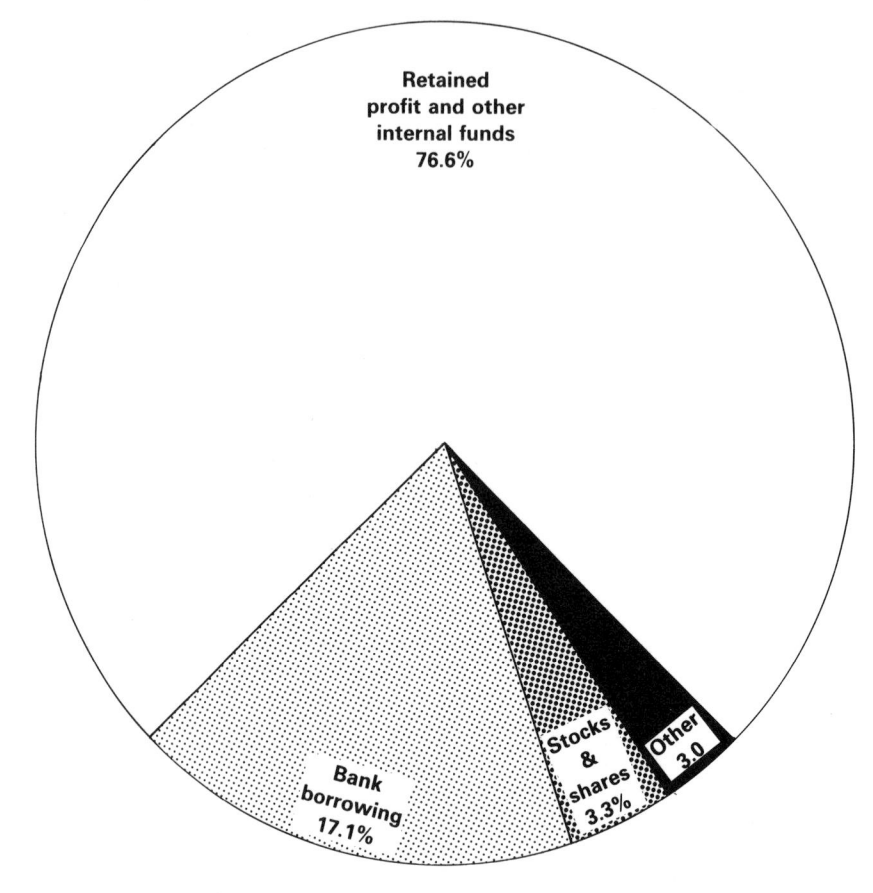

Retained profit and other internal funds 76.6%

Bank borrowing 17.1%

Stocks & shares 3.3%

Other 3.0

(Source: *Lloyds Economic Bulletin* 6.6.85 No. 78)

Unit 6.4 *The financing of firms*

## ACTIVITIES

### SECTION A: FOCUS ON UNIT 6.4

Go back and answer the questions raised in the Focus.

### SECTION B: STEPPED QUESTIONS

1  a  For what purposes might the following need finance:
      ▷ a plumber with his or her own business?
      ▷ a large multiple retailer which is a public limited company?
    b  What methods of finance are available to EACH of the businesses in **a**?
    c  What factors would affect the price of the retailer's shares?
    d  ▷ What kinds of people and organisations might own shares in a large multiple retailer?
      ▷ Explain why they might want to own shares in such a company.
2  a  What is 'the Stock Exchange'?
    b  What is the purpose of the Stock Exchange?
    c  ▷ Describe some recent changes in the stock market.
      ▷ What are the likely economic effects of these changes?
    d  What benefits and drawbacks might the activities of the Stock Exchange have for:
      ▷ firms
      ▷ consumers?

### SECTION C: DATA RESPONSE QUESTIONS

1  How companies raise finance by selling securities

|  | STOCKS Loan Stock (Debt) | | SHARES Preference Shares | | SHARES Ordinary Shares | | Total Issues |
|---|---|---|---|---|---|---|---|
|  | Total debt £m | Percentage of total issues | £m | Percentage of total issues | £m | Percentage of total issues | £m |
| 1978 | 8.8 | 1.3 | 41.3 | 6.2 | 612.5 | 92.5 | 662.5 |
| 1979 | 61.4 | 6.9 | 34.6 | 3.9 | 780.2 | 89.2 | 885.1 |
| 1980 | 217.2 | 19.6 | 37.1 | 3.3 | 853.6 | 77.1 | 1,107.9 |
| 1981 | 440.4 | 16.5 | 113.1 | 4.2 | 2,110.8 | 79.2 | 2,664.3 |
| 1982 | 1,116.1 | 48.2 | 32.5 | 1.4 | 1,165.3 | 50.4 | 2,313.9 |
| 1983 | 758.9 | 23.6 | 80.7 | 2.5 | 2,370.1 | 73.9 | 3,209.7 |

Adapted from the Midland Bank Review Spring, 1984.

a How much finance did companies raise by selling securities in
  ▷ 1978
  ▷ 1983?
b What percentage of the finance raised by selling securities came from selling ordinary shares in
  ▷ 1978
  ▷ 1983?
c What two advantages are there for a company in raising finance by selling ordinary shares as opposed to borrowing money?
d Give two possible reasons why investors spent over twice as much on ordinary shares in 1983 compared to 1982.
e Explain why it is better to be an ordinary shareholder than a preference shareholder if a company makes unexpectedly large profits.

2 Share Prices

> The surprise cut in US interest rates yesterday caused considerable rises in share prices early on, but when the Bank of England indicated that UK interest rates should not be reduced, share prices fell again.
>
> There were still some firm pockets of activity, however. The rise in oil companies' share prices continued due to the expectation that crude oil prices will rise. Construction industry shares also rose in price on hopes that mortgage rates will be lowered again.
>
> There was less enthusiasm for breweries, following a gloomy report on Scottish and Newcastle's current profit position. S and N shares dipped 6p to 180p.

(Source: *The Guardian* 21.8.86)

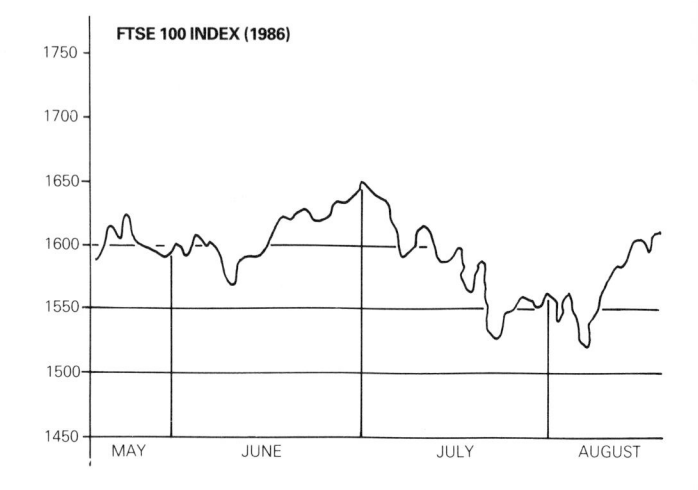

a ▷ What caused a rise in share prices early on 20th August?
  ▷ What is the FTSE 100 Index?
b ▷ What was the overall change in share prices over the whole day?
  ▷ According to the graph, what was the general trend in share prices in August 1986?
c In what kind of share was there
  ▷ a bull market?
  ▷ a bear market?
d Explain the reasons for the changes in EACH of the share prices you found in c.
e Do you think the 'hopes that mortgage rates will be lowered' were fulfilled? (Look again at the first sentence.) Explain your answer.

# UNIT 6.5 Large and small firms

**FOCUS**

▶ Why are economies of scale important in explaining the existence of large firms?

▶ What types of economies of scale can firms benefit from?

▶ What other reasons are there for the growing size of firms?

▶ In what ways do firms grow larger?

▶ Why are there still a large number of smaller firms operating in the UK economy?

## Large firms

In Britain there are firms of all sizes, ranging from sole proprietors, like many local shopkeepers, to giant public corporations like the Post Office. The largest companies are found in many different industries including engineering, chemicals, banking and retailing. One of the major reasons why production of many goods and services is dominated by large firms is that they can produce goods more cheaply in the long run: the reductions in costs per unit (increases in efficiency) from which large firms specifically can benefit are called **internal economies of scale**.

## Internal economies of scale

In some industries the cost of producing each unit of output falls as the industry increases its size or **scale**. Figure 6.5a shows the example of a firm which has built a factory extension. With the extension, twice as many chairs are produced. Although the total cost of producing chairs has risen, the long-run average cost, or cost per chair, has fallen with the increase in the scale of production. This firm is benefiting from internal economies of scale.

**Figure 6.5a**
Why has this firm's long-run average cost fallen?

|  | UNEXTENDED FACTORY | EXTENDED FACTORY |
|---|---|---|
| NUMBER OF CHAIRS PRODUCED EACH WEEK | 1000 | 2000 |
| TOTAL COST OF PRODUCTION EACH WEEK | £3000 | £5000 |
| COST PER CHAIR (AVERAGE COST) | £3.00 | £2.50 |

Here are some of the internal economies of scale that a firm can gain as it grows larger.

▶ **1 Technical economies**
Large firms are more able to buy larger and more efficient machinery and equipment. For example, a large clothing manufacturer may be able to employ a machine to cut material, whereas a very small firm may have to cut material by hand. This enables the large firm to produce more at a lower average cost. Large firms may also be able to afford research and development facilities which enable them to find more advanced methods of production. Large firms with production lines are more able to take advantage of the division of labour. Storage and transport may be relatively cheaper for a large firm. In Fig. 6.5b Massive plc's warehouse and lorry will hold twice as much as Minor Ltd's but they will not cost twice as much to buy and run for the firm.

▶ **2 Financial economies**
Large firms have more assets that they can use as security for loans and this may enable them to obtain larger loans at lower rates of interest.

▶ **3 Managerial economies**
Large firms are able to employ specialised staff to manage different departments, for example personnel, finance, marketing. In a small business managers may have to do all these tasks themselves, and they may be unable to carry out any of these tasks as efficiently as specialists.

▶ **4 Marketing economies**
Large firms may be more able to afford effective advertising. They can spread the cost of the advertising over a large number of products so that the average cost of advertising each product can be lower than for the smaller firm, even for a big advertising campaign.

▶ **5 Buying economies**
Large firms can buy in very large quantities. This is called **bulk buying**. Suppliers are usually

willing to supply larger amounts at lower prices or at a **discount**.

▶ **6 Risk-bearing economies**
Larger firms usually sell a wider range of products in more areas than smaller firms. They will suffer less if there is a drop in demand for one of their products.

### Internal diseconomies of scale
It is possible for a firm to grow so large that long-run average costs may actually rise as output rises. This could occur, for example, when communication problems between departments delay decisions and raise costs.

### How firms grow large
Firms can grow large by constantly expanding on their own, or they can increase in size by joining together with other firms. When two or more firms join together it is called **integration**. The firms can join together on a more or less equal basis in which case we say that they have **merged**, or one firm can take over ownership and control of another firm, in which case we say that there has been a **takeover**.

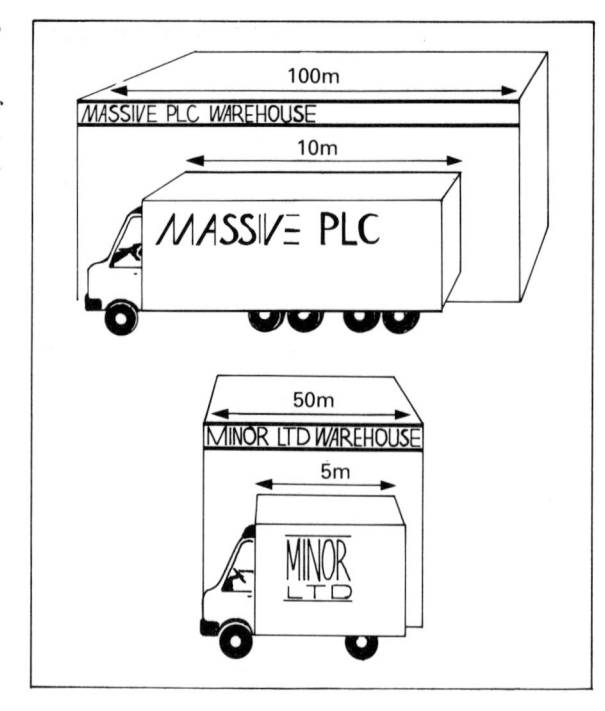

**Figure 6.5b**
The costs of transport and storage will be cheaper per unit for a larger firm.

**Figure 6.5c**
This diagram shows some of the different types of integration, using the example of the paper industry.

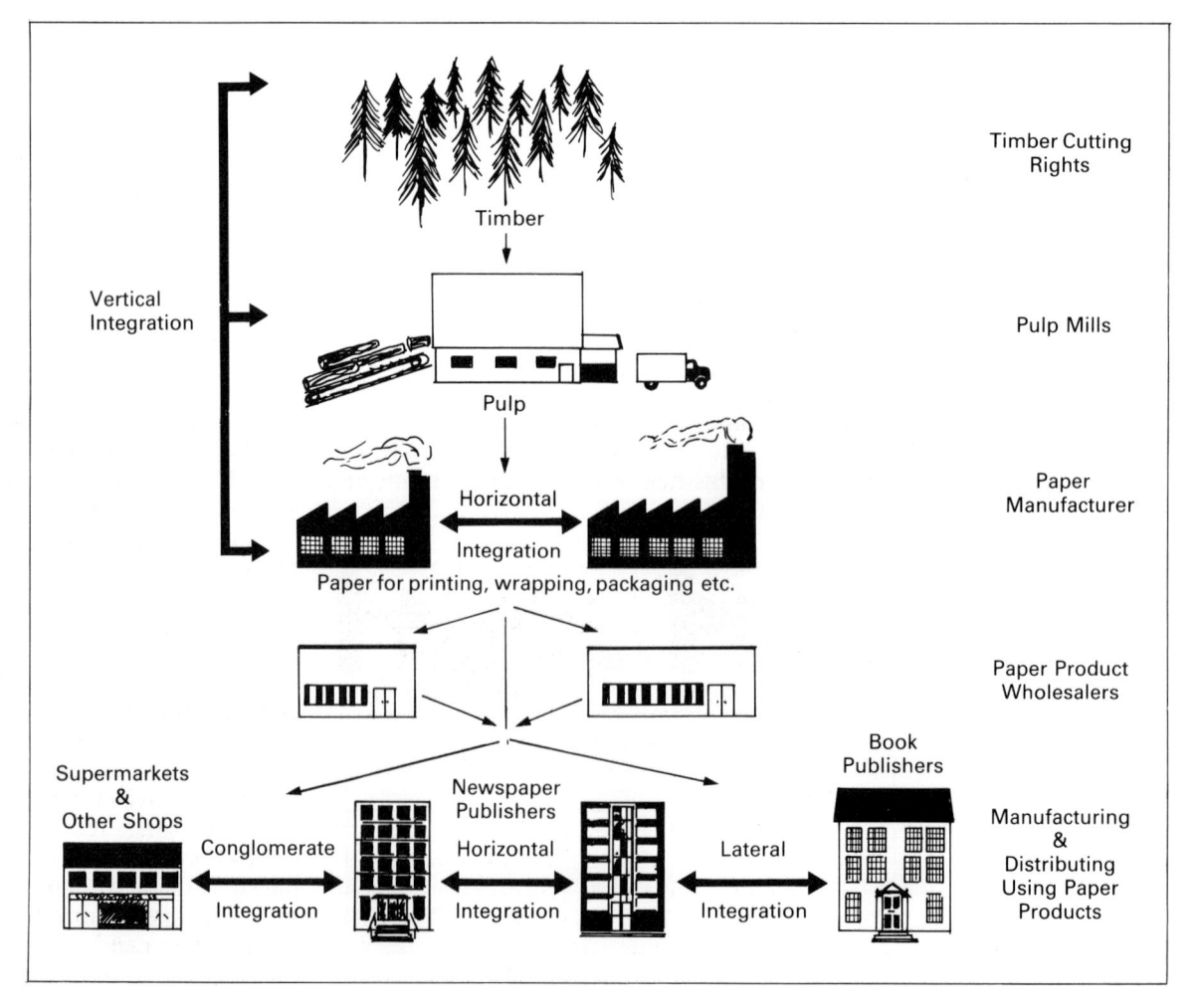

## Types of integration

There are four main types of integration:

### ▶ 1 Vertical integration
This is where the firms involved are concerned with the production of the same good or service, but they operate at different stages in the chain of production. In 1980, for example, the beer producer, Allied Breweries, bought over 200 pubs.

### ▶ 2 Horizontal integration
This is where the firms involved in the merger or takeover are in competition with each other. This means that they produce more or less the same good or service. Rowntree-Mackintosh, the sweet manufacturers, was formed from the two companies which make up the name.

### ▶ 3 Lateral integration
This is where the firms involved in the merger or takeover are in a similar line of business but they are not in direct competition. In 1983 Habitat, a firm which owns shops selling furniture and household goods, took over Mothercare, which sells goods required by people expecting or having children.

### ▶ 4 Conglomerate integration
This is where the firms involved in the takeover or merger are in quite different lines of business. British American Tobacco have bought businesses involved in paper production and food retailing.

## Reasons for integration

There are many reasons why firms integrate. Here are just some of them:

### ▶ 1 Internal economies of scale
When firms are involved in mergers or takeovers, they create a much larger business which can enjoy economies of scale.

### ▶ 2 Rationalisation
A successful firm may buy up a less successful firm because its share price is low, and then close down the inefficient parts of the business and concentrate on the efficient parts. This is called rationalisation. For example, if a brewer takes over another brewer's pubs, the least profitable ones could be shut, and the rest redecorated and fitted with new furniture.

### ▶ 3 Increasing market power
When a firm takes over one of its competitors it increases its power in the market by reducing competition. It may be able to raise prices while spending less on improving its services to the customer. This can lead to increased profits.

### ▶ 4 Control of supplies and the sale of goods
A takeover may allow a producer to take control of its raw material supplies, or supplies of machinery and equipment it uses. The firm can then be more sure of its supplies, and it may be able to keep supplies from its competitors. Several paper manufacturers, for example, have bought the pulp mills which supply them. A takeover or merger may allow a producer to control the sale of its products; for example, a brewery can make sure that the pubs it owns sell only the beers it brews.

### ▶ 5 Financial reasons
A larger firm will have more assets that can be used as security for loans, or sold off to provide more funds.

### ▶ 6 Diversification
Integration may increase the number of goods and services sold by a firm. This is called diversification, and it means that the firm will be in less trouble if there happens to be a fall in demand for one of its products. Cigarette companies are buying firms making other products because they fear a long-term fall in demand for cigarettes.

## Small firms

In spite of all the advantages that economies of scale bring to large firms, small firms continue to be very important in the British economy. Here are some of the areas in which small firms are common:

### ▶ 1 Where personal services are provided
Small firms provide many personal services. Many builders, decorators and plumbers, for example, are sole proprietors.

### ▶ 2 Where goods and services are provided for a local area
Goods and services for just one small area may be provided by small firms. A hairdresser has to be near its customers for convenience. Small local shops are convenient for extra items needed in a hurry (see Unit 6.7).

### ▶ 3 Where luxury goods and services are provided
Luxury or 'top end of the market' goods are often provided by small firms. Jewellery and leather handbags, for example, are often made by small firms employing specialist craftspersons.

### ▶ 4 Where specialist engineering goods are provided
Engineering goods are often wanted on a one-off basis. A car firm, for example, may go to a small engineering firm to be provided with a special drill that will never be asked for again.

### ▶ 5 Where small firms can group together
Small independent shops sometimes join together in groups (like Spar and Mace) to buy from one supplier. The supplier can buy goods in bulk, sell cheaply to the shops in the group, and allow the shops to compete with large supermarkets.

Small firms often benefit from grouping together in a particular area. The benefits they gain are called **external economies of scale** and are explained in Unit 6.6 on the location of industry.

### The advantages of small firms

You can see that small firms are common where economies of scale are not very important and where demand is limited. Here are some advantages that small firms have over larger ones:

▶ **1 Easier management**

Small firms are much easier to manage and control. In a large company or corporation, communication between workers and management, the different departments, and the company and the customer, may be very difficult. The sales department, for example, may work hard to win a big order, only to find that the production department cannot provide the goods. This kind of communication problem is less of a problem in a firm which employs just a few workers.

▶ **2 People may work harder**

People may work harder in a small business. Small businesses are more likely to go bankrupt, and every worker knows how important their own contribution is to the survival of the business. In large firms workers can feel that they are just small cogs in large wheels, and that what they do does not really matter.

▶ **3 Fewer strikes**

Small firms have very few strikes. Most strikes in Britain are in large organisations. In small firms the manager is much closer to the other workers, and problems can be sorted out as soon as they happen.

▶ **4 High employment**

Small firms tend to be labour-intensive. This means that they use relatively little machinery and a relatively large number of workers compared to larger firms. It is hoped that small firms will create most of the new jobs that appear in the future.

▶ **5 Quick responses to changes in demand**

Small firms can change production very quickly if there is a change in demand. A large car firm, for example, will take many years to bring out a new model, whereas a small clothing manufacturer may be able to change its production within a few days to meet a change in fashion.

### Help for small firms

In recent years the government and other organisations have given increasing support to smaller firms. Here are some of the ways in which the support has been given:

▶ **1 The Loan Guarantee and Business Start-Up Schemes**

These were described in Unit 6.4 about the finance of industry.

▶ **2 The Unlisted Securities Market**

In the past it was very expensive for firms to sell shares to raise finance. The introduction in recent years of the Unlisted Securities Market on the Stock Exchange has allowed smaller companies to sell shares at a lower cost (see Unit 6.4).

▶ **3 Tax changes**

In recent years the amount of Corporation Tax paid by small firms has been reduced. The government has given tax advantages to business managers who build small factories and workshops under a scheme called the 'Small Workshop Scheme'.

▶ **4 Enterprise Zones**

These are areas, usually inside large towns, in which businesses can start production more cheaply and with fewer administrative hold-ups than elsewhere. They are described in more detail in Unit 6.6 on the location of industry.

▶ **5 Changes in employment regulations**

The government has changed employment regulations to make it easier for small firms to employ workers and make workers redundant, so that they can respond to changing demand conditions.

## DATABASE

## 1. Britain's 30 largest companies in 1985

|  | Market Value (£m) |
|---|---|
| 1 British Telecom (-) | 12,720.0 |
| 2 British Petroleum (1) | 9,513.9 |
| 3 Shell Transport & Trading (2) | 7,733.8 |
| 4 Imperial Chemical Industries (4) | 4,727.2 |
| 5 BAT Industries (6) | 4,635.5 |
| 6 Glaxo (7) | 4,441.1 |
| 7 General Electric (3) | 4,437.3 |
| 8 BTR (8) | 3,681.1 |
| 9 Marks & Spencer (5) | 3,431.7 |
| 10 Barclays (13) | 2,550.6 |
| 11 Hanson (Tst) (26) | 2,545.4 |
| 12 Beecham Group (9) | 2,375.1 |
| 13 National Westminster (17) | 2,347.6 |
| 14 Cable & Wireless (21) | 2,347.2 |
| 15 Grand Metropolitan (10) | 2,153.6 |
| 16 Sainsbury (J) (15) | 2,090.2 |
| 17 Prudential Corp (18) | 1,923.1 |
| 18 Great Universal Strs (16) | 1,868.1 |
| 19 Unilever (14) | 1,738.8 |
| 20 Bass (30) | 1,710.6 |
| 21 Rio Tinto-Zinc (11) | 1,700.8 |
| 22 Associated Dairies (31) | 1,585.0 |
| 23 Royal Insurance (35) | 1,517.2 |
| 24 Allied-Lyons (38) | 1,459.1 |
| 25 Imperial Group (27) | 1,361.0 |
| 26 Lloyds Bank (28) | 1,356.9 |
| 27 Land Securities (19) | 1,328.8 |
| 28 Sears Holdings (25) | 1,314.1 |
| 29 Boots (20) | 1,312.8 |
| 30 BOC Group (22) | 1,164.2 |

Figures in brackets show 1984 positions

(Source: *Observer* July 1985)

## DATABASE

## 2. Outcome of references to Monopolies Commission 1980–84

| | No. of references | No. abandoned during investigation | Blocked | Cleared Failed takeover | Cleared Successful takeover | |
|---|---|---|---|---|---|---|
| 1980 | 5 | 1 | 1 | 0 | 3 | 1. Blue Circle Industries/ Armitage Shanks<br>2. S&W Berisford/British Sugar Corporation<br>3. Compagnie Internationale Europcar/Godfrey Davies |
| 1981 | 8 | 1 | 5 | 0 | 2 | 1. BTR/Serck<br>2. British Rail Hovercraft/ Hoverlloyd |
| 1982 | 10 | 2 | 4 | 2 | 2 | 1. Nabisco Brands/ Huntley & Palmer Foods<br>2. ICI/Arthur Holden |
| 1983 | 9 | 2 | 4 | 3 | 0 | |
| 1984 | 4 | 1 | 0 | 2 | 1 | 1. British Electric Traction/ Initial |

(Source: *The Economist* 25.1.86)

## ACTIVITIES

### SECTION A: FOCUS ON UNIT 6.5

Go back and answer the questions raised in the Focus.

### SECTION B: STEPPED QUESTIONS

1 The owner of one of two small bakery shops selling bread, sandwiches and cakes buys another similar shop in the locality:
   a What type of integration is involved?
   b How could the new organisation benefit from:
      ▷ internal economies of scale?
      ▷ reduced competition?
      ▷ rationalisation?
   c Are large firms always more efficient than small firms? Explain your answer.

2 a What is meant by:
      ▷ vertical integration?
      ▷ horizontal integration?
      ▷ conglomerate integration?
   b Give examples of vertical, horizontal and conglomerate integration as they might involve a brewery.
   c How can the following types of integration result in control over a market for a firm:
      ▷ horizontal integration?
      ▷ vertical integration?
   d What are the possible economic effects of the concentration of production in the hands of a smaller number of large firms?

## SECTION C: DATA RESPONSE QUESTION

### Gallaher to Take Over Prestige

The Prestige Group, one of the world's leading manufacturers of housewares, is being taken over by the giant American-owned cigarette and tobacco company, Gallaher, in a £49 million deal announced yesterday.

Gallaher, which already earns one third of its profits from non-tobacco interests, has made no secret of its desire to continue to diversify, and the Prestige acquisition fits in well with its stated intention of focusing on branded consumer products.

Prestige is one of the largest houseware manufacturers outside the United States, producing a wide range of products such as cookware, kitchen tools, pressure cookers and cutlery. The company employs almost 1,500 people in the UK, where it has big factories in Derby, Burnley and Blackburn. It has a further 780 employees overseas. Last year it made a profit of £6.7 million on sales of £63 million.

Gallaher's tobacco business – taking in leading brands such as Benson and Hedges, Silk Cut and Hamlet – enjoyed strong growth last year when its UK market share rose from around 29.7 per cent to 32.4 per cent on the back of a 10 per cent volume gain. But while the group continues to have faith in the future of the tobacco business, and is indeed investing heavily in the sector, it is also keen to branch out into other sectors to enhance its overall growth prospects.

(Source: *The Guardian* 27.3.84)

**a** ▷ Name two brands of cigarette produced by Gallaher.
  ▷ Name three products made by Prestige.
**b** How much was the takeover deal worth?
**c** What type of integration was involved?
**d** What percentage of Gallaher's business was involved with non-tobacco products before the takeover of Prestige?
**c** Why was Gallaher so keen to take over businesses unconnected with tobacco?

**Unit 6.5** *Large and small firms*

**EXTENSION MATERIAL**

## Competition and monopoly

There will be more competition in a market, the greater the number of firms there are in the market, and the greater the similarity of the products produced by the firms. Competition is reduced where firms either on their own, or working together with other firms, gain a degree of **monopoly power**. Firms have monopoly power when they have a considerable amount of influence on prices in the market and over the conditions of sale of goods and services. This will be more possible when a firm or group of firms can stop other firms coming into the market. A firm will tend to have increased monopoly power in a market which is highly **concentrated** – where there are a small number of large firms. The concentration of industry has been increasing throughout the twentieth century, particularly in the 1960s and 1980s when there have been 'merger booms'.

### The disadvantages of monopoly power

▶ 1 Firms with monopoly power may charge higher prices than would be the case if there was competition in the market. Firms facing considerable competition are forced to keep prices low. Economists call this situation **consumer sovereignty** because if one firm puts up prices there are many other cheaper firms in the market from which consumers can buy.
▶ 2 Firms facing little competition may become complacent and inefficient. They may not strive to cut costs and develop new products.
▶ 3 Once established, firms with monopoly power may find ways of keeping new firms from entering the market. They may engage in expensive advertising, for example, which a new firm could not hope to match.

### The law and competition

In the UK, firms with 25 per cent market share, locally or nationally, are considered to be 'monopolies'. Smaller firms that act together to give themselves 25 per cent of a local or national market are also considered to be monopolies. Monopolies are not considered illegal in the UK, but some of the actions they take (called **monopolistic** or **restrictive practices**) may be considered against the public interest.

The three main laws governing monopolies and competition are the 1973 Fair Trading Act, the 1976 Restrictive Practices Act, and the 1980 Competition Act. The laws are enforced mainly by the Secretary of State for Trade and Industry, the Director-General of Fair Trading, the Monopolies and Mergers Commission, and the Restrictive Practices Court.

### Monopolies and mergers

The Director-General of Fair Trading has certain powers to look into areas where competition is threatened by monopoly power. He or she also keeps a close watch on mergers which could create a monopoly, or a new very large firm. If concerned about a certain monopoly, or a proposed merger, or a specific anti-competitive practice, he or she can attempt to resolve the matter. If this fails, the matter can be referred to the Monopolies and Mergers Commission (MMC). The MMC carries out investigations and makes a report to the Secretary of State. Only the Secretary of State for Trade and Industry, has the power to act on an MMC report.

### Restrictive practices

Firms sometimes act together to cut down competition. They may agree, for example, to fix prices and outputs, to divide the market up geographically, or to put pressure on suppliers to sell only their goods. Most of these restrictive practices must be registered with the Director-General of Fair Trading. They are considered generally against the public interest, but it is up to the Director-General to decide whether to take further action. He or she may do nothing, or may contact the firms involved asking them to change or abandon the restrictive practice. He or she may also refer the restrictive practice to the Restrictive Practices Court. The Restrictive Practices Court is a court of law. It is up to the firms involved to prove that a restrictive practice is in the public interest. They might show, for example, that without the restrictive practice unemployment would rise, or after-sales service would suffer, or retail outlets would disappear. If the court accepts the firm's arguments, the agreement will remain in force. If not, it will have to be abandoned.

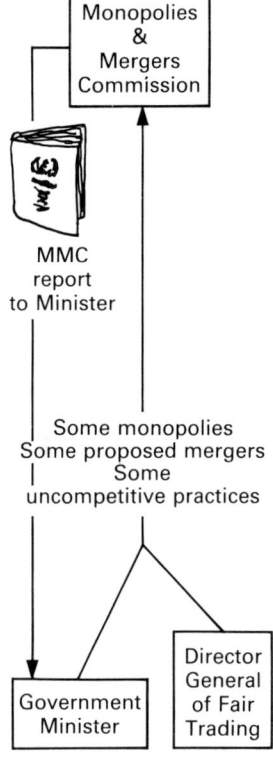

**Figure 6.5d**
This diagram shows how the MMC works.

**EXTENSION QUESTION 7**

Questions

a What is meant by 'monopoly power'?
b In what ways could a firm or group of firms gain monopoly power?
c What are the possible economic effects of monopoly power?
d How are monopolies and restrictive practices controlled in the UK?

# UNIT 6.6  The location of firms

## FOCUS

▶ What considerations will a firm take into account when deciding where to locate its place of work?

▶ Why is unemployment higher in some areas of the UK than others?

▶ How does the government assist in the location of firms?

This Unit looks at why industries are found in certain locations throughout the country, and why a firm may decide to open up a new place of work in one area rather than another. A firm that wishes to make the largest possible profit will set up its business where the difference between the benefits and costs of a particular location is greatest. A firm may set up near London, for example, if it sells most of its goods in London and it wants to keep the cost of transporting its goods to its market as low as possible, even though rent and rates may be high.

### The factors that affect the location of industry

▶ **1 Personal preference and historical factors**

Many businesses are found in particular places for reasons that are no longer important. For example, in 1893 William Morris opened a cycle repair shop in Cowley near Oxford because that is where he happened to be living at the time. He went on to service, sell, and then make Morris cars on the same site. British Leyland still make cars in Cowley just because William Morris happened to start his business there.

Some industries started in a particular area because there used to be a local supply of raw materials. The industries often remain in the area long after the raw materials have been used up. This is called **industrial inertia**. The clay used by the pottery industry in Stoke, for example, is now brought in from outside the area.

▶ **2 Transport costs**

Firms may try to find a site which keeps down the cost of transporting raw materials to the factory, or keeps down the cost of transporting finished goods to the market.

▷ **a** *The source of raw materials* Some industries are called **bulk-decreasing industries**. This means that the finished product is cheaper and easier to transport than the raw materials used to make it. These industries try to get as near as possible to the place from which they get their raw materials. The Port Talbot steel works, for example, is in a good position because imported iron ore arrives directly at the docks near the steelworks from overseas countries. It is easier and cheaper to transport finished steel than iron ore because iron ore contains much waste.

▷ **b** *The market* Some industries are called **bulk-increasing industries**. This means that the finished product is more expensive and difficult to transport than the factors of production used to make it. Bulk-increasing industries try to get as near as possible to their market. The furniture industry is situated mainly in and around London because furniture is bulky and expensive to move, and London is the main market.

▷ **c** *Footloose industries* Transport costs are fairly unimportant to many industries, and these industries are called **footloose industries**. A food-processing firm, for example, which produces packaged food like yoghurt, cheese and butter, might receive its raw materials from farms spread over a large area, and it may sell its goods throughout much of the country. It could locate its factories in several different areas without making much difference to its transport costs.

▶ **3 The cost and skills of the labour force**

Labour is usually the firm's largest cost of production, and firms may move to where wages

**Figure 6.6a**
Why are bulk-decreasing industries like steelworks often located near the coast?

Unit 6.6 *The location of firms*

**Figure 6.6b**
Why are bulk-increasing industries like furniture often located near the market?

are lowest. Areas where wages are low, however, may be expensive areas in other ways. They might be far from the market, for example. Firms might be more interested in the skills of the labour force than in their wages. If a car firm set up a new factory in the Midlands, for example, it might find many of the skilled workers it needed already in the area. This would cut down training time and training costs.

▶ **4 The cost of renting land**
Compared to other costs, rents tend to be a fairly small cost for most firms. Only in inner cities are rents and rates likely to be so high that they might put a firm off building a factory or other place of work.

▶ **5 The nearness of power supplies**
Until the beginning of this century most industries relied on coal for power. This made nearly all of them bulk-decreasing, and they had to be located on the coalfields. Now most businesses use electricity, gas and oil for power, and power supplies make little difference to where they locate.

▶ **6 The nearness of water supplies**
Some industries use huge amounts of water, particularly for cooling purposes. This is why some factories like nuclear power stations have to be near the coast.

▶ **7 Good infrastructure**
Infrastructure refers to the facilities which enable industry to work efficiently for example roads, railways, housing, schools, hospitals and water-mains. Many expanding firms have set up factories and offices along the M4 motorway between London and Bristol in towns like Swindon, Reading and Slough. Computer firms like Digital and Hewlett Packard have set up in

Are transport costs important, and do I want to be near my suppliers or my markets?

Do I need many unskilled workers, or certain highly-skilled workers?

Where can I find a site with reasonable rents and rates?

Do I need to be near special power supplies or water supplies?

Do I need to be near a motorway, railway, port or airport?

Should I find an area offering Government help to industry?

Should I look for area where there are many firms in my industry?

**Figure 6.6c**
Why might this business manager locate a business in an area even though the rent and rates are high?

this area. Poor or outdated infrastructure may deter a firm from locating in an area.

▶ **8 The nearness of other firms working in the same industry**

Many industries are **localised**. This means that firms in the industry tend to be found concentrated together in certain areas of the country. Industries that are localised can benefit from external economies of scale, sometimes known as **economies of concentration**. These are cost savings gained by a firm by being in an area with other firms in the same line of business.

Here are some of the **external economies of scale** that could be gained by an insurance company locating in central London, an area which specialises in the industry:

▷ **a** *Specialist workers* Many workers in London specialise in areas of work important to an insurance company, like secretarial work, accountancy, and computer programming.

▷ **b** *Specialist training courses* Colleges in London provide many training courses to help people gain the kind of skills needed in the insurance industry like office practice.

▷ **c** *Supporting firms* There are many firms in London providing specialist services to help the insurance industry. Banks and advertising agencies, for example, learn to deal with the needs of the insurance business. There are many firms selling office equipment, computers and stationery in London.

▷ **d** *A good reputation* If an insurance firm has a London address it may help it to attract customers especially from overseas.

There are external economies of scale other than those mentioned. Furniture firms in High Wycombe, for example, finance a research and development unit which carries out research on timber development. Transport firms in the area are specially equipped to deal with needs of the furniture industry.

▶ **9 Government regional policy**

For over fifty years the government has tried to persuade firms to move to areas of particularly high unemployment. This policy is called **regional policy**, and it affects where some industries locate their places of work.

The areas of particularly high unemployment are mainly those with industries generally in decline. They include areas which used to specialise in iron and steel manufacture, textiles, shipbuilding, coal mining and heavy engineering. In recent years any area which specialises in manufacturing has tended to suffer when compared to areas in which tertiary industries are more important.

### Assisted areas

In order to carry out its regional policy the government names certain areas as **assisted areas**. In order of seriousness of their unemployment problems they are called Development Areas and Intermediate Areas. Northern Ireland, which has particular problems, is treated as a special case and it receives special help.

### Help for firms in assisted areas

Firms in assisted areas can get the following help:

▶ 1 Cash grants of money for new buildings and machinery and equipment are automatically available in Development Areas only. These are called Regional Development Grants. They cover 15 per cent of capital costs.

▶ 2 Extra cash help for particular projects designed to save jobs may be available. This is called Regional Selective Assistance.

▶ 3 The government builds factories which firms can rent on very good terms.

▶ 4 Financial help from the European Economic Community for projects that can help to create jobs is available. For example, new roads have been built in assisted areas with funds from the Regional Fund of the European Economic Community.

▶ 5 The government might place orders for things it needs with firms in assisted areas, and it might spend money to improve infrastructure facilities like roads and railways to make the area more attractive to new firms.

### Enterprise Zones

These are smaller areas, mainly in the middle of large cities like Newcastle and Glasgow and towns where large factories or businesses have closed down (e.g. Corby). Firms moving into Enterprise Zones are given financial help through tax cuts and not having to pay rates for a certain period. It is very easy for them to obtain planning permission to build factories, and they do not have to give much information to the government. Firms in Enterprise Zones can start business very cheaply and easily, hopefully creating new jobs in some particularly depressed areas.

### Changes in regional policy

In 1984 the government introduced some changes to its regional policy. It said that in future it wanted to make sure that money spent on regional policy actually created plenty of new jobs. Any project throughout the country that created jobs should possibly be able to receive government help. Service industries should receive more help than in the past. Spending on regional policy has been reduced significantly in recent years. For example, Regional Development Grants were cut from £659 million in 1982–83 to £177 million in 1985–86.

Unit 6.6 *The location of firms*

## DATABASE

### 1. The percentage of the workforce unemployed in different regions of the UK – 1st quarter, 1986

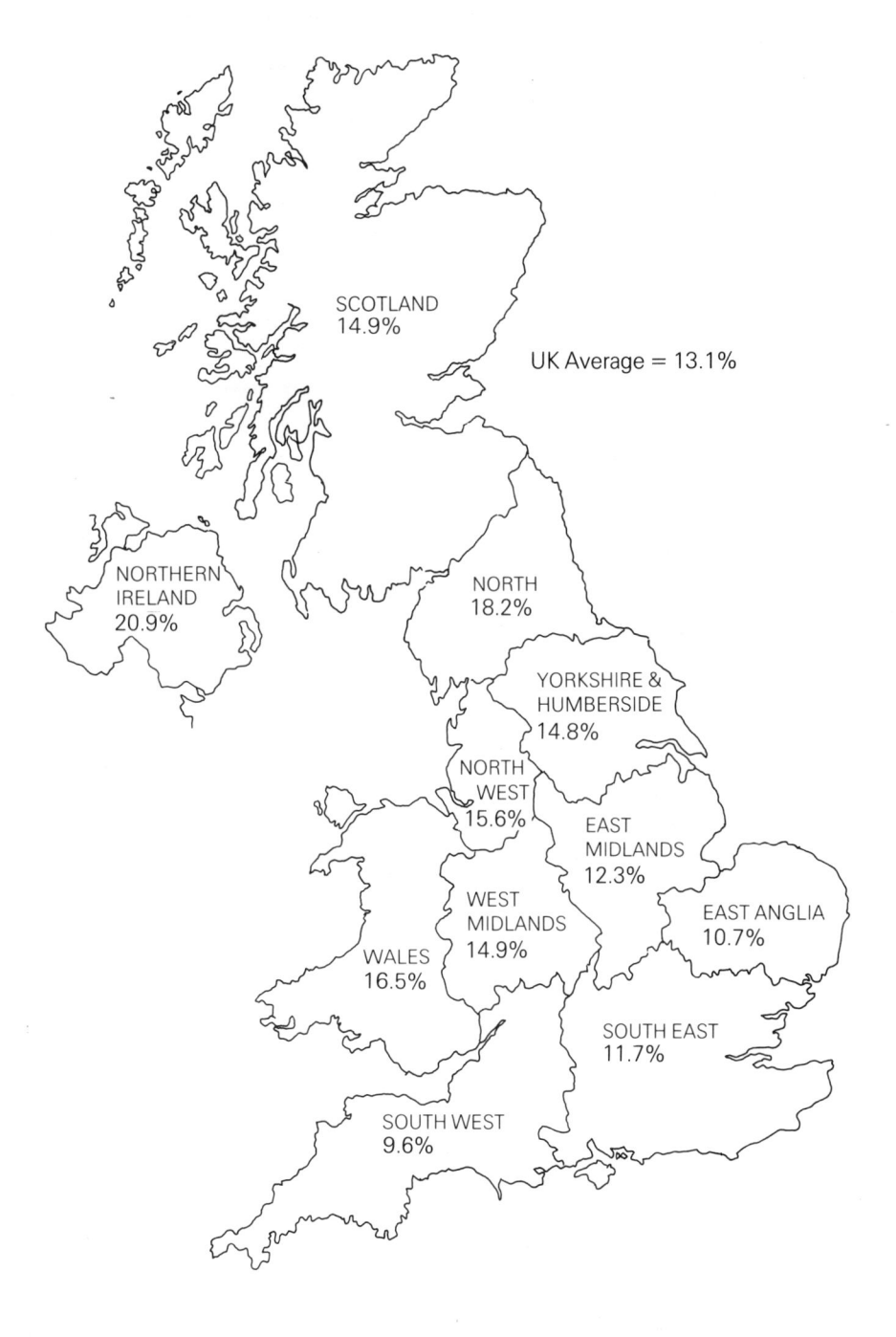

- SCOTLAND 14.9%
- UK Average = 13.1%
- NORTHERN IRELAND 20.9%
- NORTH 18.2%
- YORKSHIRE & HUMBERSIDE 14.8%
- NORTH WEST 15.6%
- EAST MIDLANDS 12.3%
- WEST MIDLANDS 14.9%
- EAST ANGLIA 10.7%
- WALES 16.5%
- SOUTH EAST 11.7%
- SOUTH WEST 9.6%

(Source: *Economic Trends*)

## DATABASE

## 2. The assisted areas

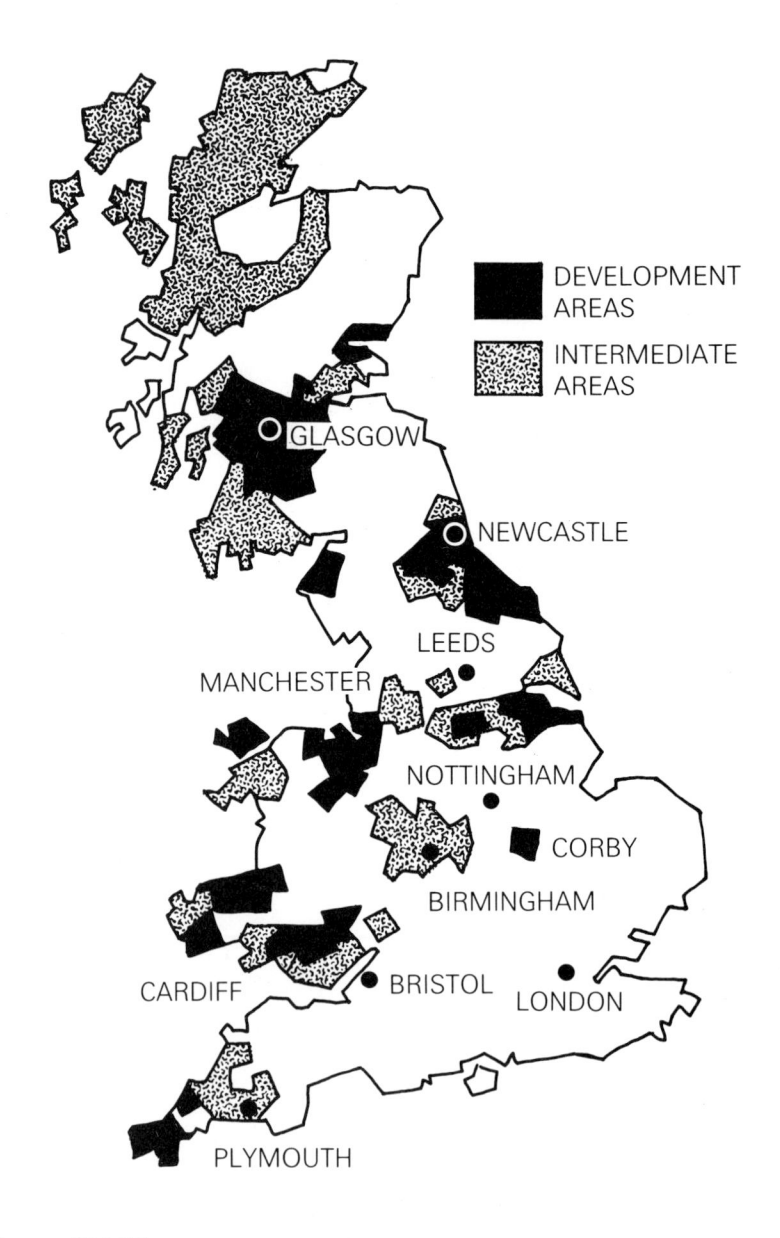

DEVELOPMENT AREAS

INTERMEDIATE AREAS

GLASGOW
NEWCASTLE
LEEDS
MANCHESTER
NOTTINGHAM
CORBY
BIRMINGHAM
CARDIFF
BRISTOL
LONDON
PLYMOUTH

(Source: *Observer* 25.9.85)

Unit 6.6 *The location of firms*

**ACTIVITIES**

## SECTION A: FOCUS on 6.6

Go back and answer the questions raised in the Focus.

## SECTION B: STEPPED QUESTIONS

1 A Japanese electronics manufacturer is considering setting up a factory in the UK:
  a Name two Japanese electronics firms.
  b Explain the factors the manufacturer would be likely to take into account in deciding where to locate the factory.
  c Would you describe computer manufacturing as a 'footloose' industry? Explain your answer.
  d What would be the likely economic effects of a decision to build the factory near Heathrow Airport?
2 a Give *two* examples of declining industries.
  b Use Database 1 to find:
    ▷ the three areas with the highest unemployment
    ▷ the area with the lowest unemployment.
3 a What is meant by 'regional policy'?
  b Give *three* examples of incentives available to firms as part of regional policy.
  c Why may firms choose to ignore regional incentives and set up in unassisted areas?
  d What are the possible economic effects of cuts in spending on regional policy?

## SECTION C: DATA RESPONSE QUESTIONS

Look at the map on the next page.

1 a ▷ List two benefits available for firms that move into Corby that exist because Corby is a Development Area.
    ▷ List two benefits available for firms that move into Corby that exist because Corby is an Enterprise Zone.
  b How does Corby try to attract firms that want easy access to large markets?
  c ▷ Corby has a high unemployment rate because a major industry has closed down in the town. The industry is mentioned in the advertisement. Which industry is it?
    ▷ Explain why this industry is declining.
  d Explain why the areas shown on the map are called 'Development Areas'.

# Development areas: nowhere else comes within miles of Corby

If you're planning to develop your business you need look no further than Corby.

Corby is a **Development Area** so your business gets the help of Development Area benefits. For most companies this means the better deal for them of either 15% grants on plant, machinery and equipment or £3000 per job created. There is also selective assistance for some job creating projects.

Corby is also a **Steel Opportunity Area**, and this means even more incentives

Corby is **England's first Enterprise Zone**. There are factories off the peg, from 500 sq.ft. to 50,000 sq.ft., some of which are rates free until 1991. You can also choose from offices, warehouses, and high tech buildings.

Corby has **EEC aid for small businesses**. £1m is now available to aid efficiency.

Above all, Corby is right in the heart of England. Within 80 miles of London. 50 miles from Birmingham. Strategically placed for any business that needs fast, inexpensive, easy access to the big South East and Midland population centres.

However far you look, you will find that, as a total package for the success of your business, nowhere else comes within miles of Corby.

Development Areas

as defined by
The Department of
Trade and Industry
to take effect from 29.11.84

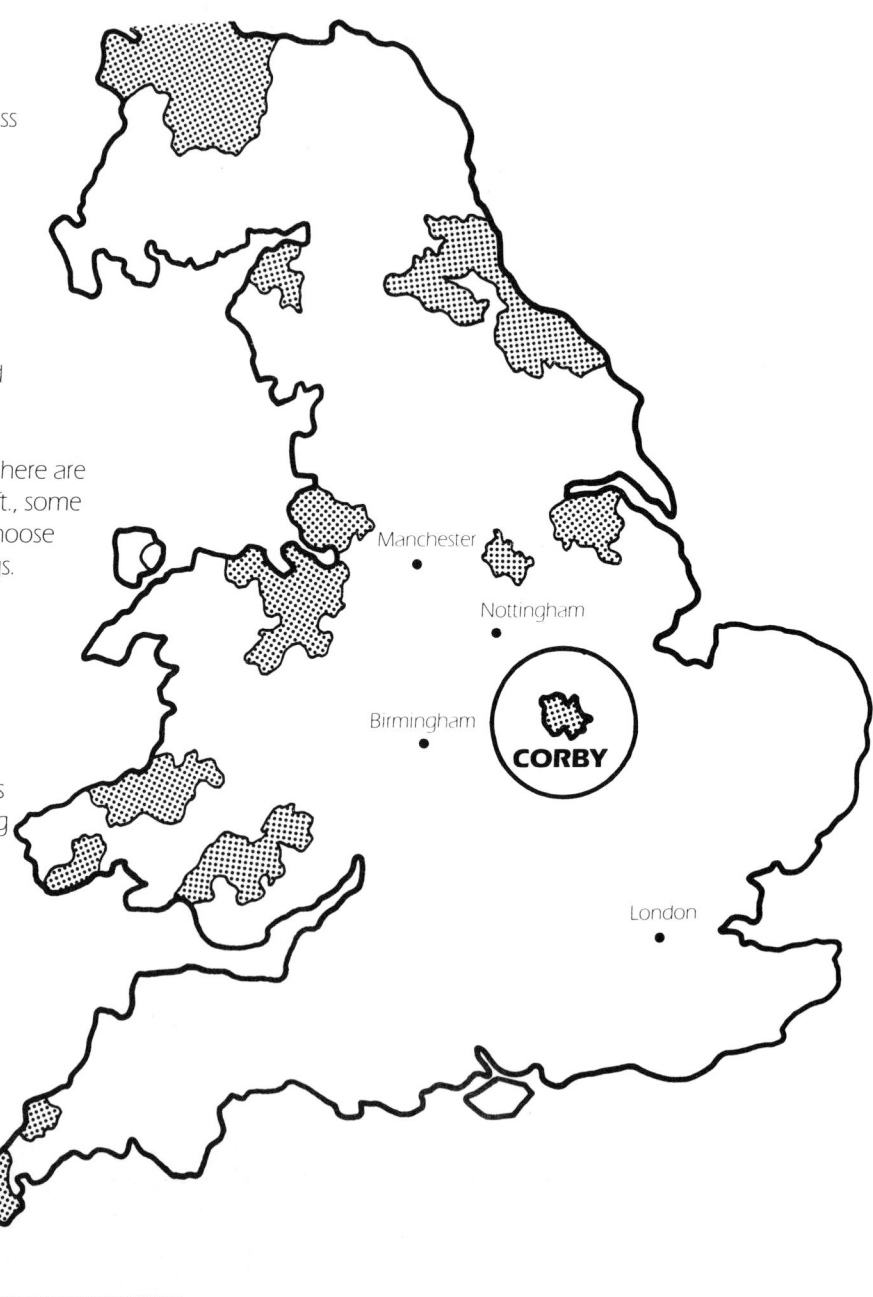

Name: ..................................................................................
Company: ............................................................................
Position: ..............................................................................
Address: ..............................................................................
..............................................................................................

# UNIT 6.7 Retailing, wholesaling and advertising

**FOCUS**
▶ What is the difference between **wholesaling** and **retailing**?

▶ What have been the major changes in the pattern of retailing in the UK in recent years?

▶ What are the purposes of **advertising**?

▶ What methods or media can advertisers use?

## The distribution of goods

This Unit looks at how goods reach the consumers from the manufacturers that produce them. There are several ways that this can happen. Figure 6.7a shows two of them.

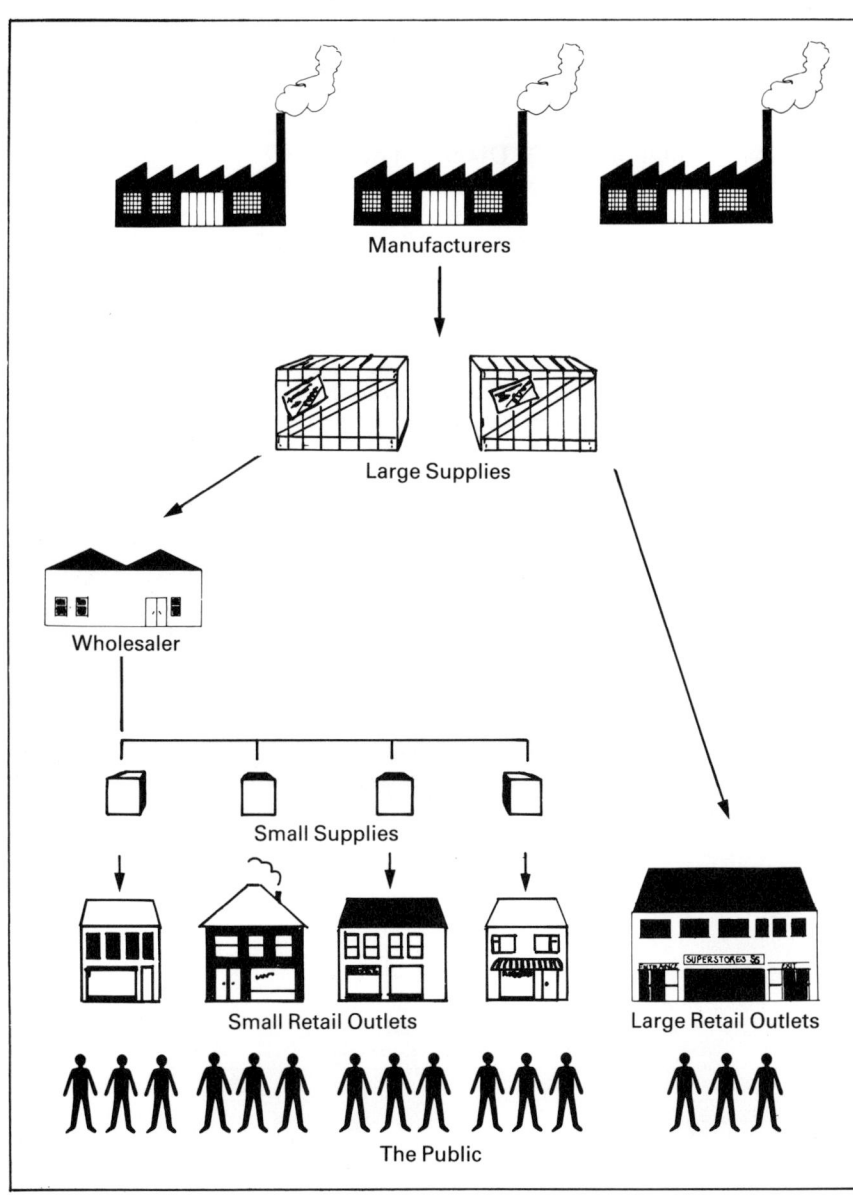

**Figure 6.7a** What are the roles of wholesalers and retailers in the distribution of goods?

## Wholesalers

Wholesalers are businesses that buy goods in very large quantities from manufacturers, and sell them in smaller amounts to the retailers that deal directly with the consumers.

### The services provided by wholesalers

▶ 1 Wholesalers repack goods in small amounts for the owners of small shops. Without wholesalers, retailers might be forced to take very large deliveries straight from the manufacturers.

▶ 2 Wholesalers can sell mixed batches of goods to retailers, providing exactly what they need, and no more.

▶ 3 Wholesalers can 'shop around', filling their warehouses with goods from the cheapest manufacturers. The retailers and their customers benefit from lower prices.

▶ 4 The wholesaler can keep manufacturers informed about changes in demand. They deal with large numbers of shops, and they get to know what customers want to buy.

▶ 5 Wholesalers give retailers advice about new products and special offers from manufacturers.

▶ 6 Wholesalers provide retailers with credit. Small shops may not be able to pay for goods instantly, and the credit given by wholesalers may help them to survive.

## Retailers

Retailers are the last link in the chain of production. They buy goods from wholesalers and manufacturers and sell them direct to consumers.

### Different types of retail outlet
▶ 1 Independent retailers

These are small shops usually owned by a sole proprietor. They are often found near large areas of housing. People often use independent retailers when they just 'pop around the corner' for something that they forgot to buy during their weekly shop. Independent retailers sometimes get together in groups like VG and Spar to buy cheaply from a single wholesaler. Co-op shops work in a similar way.

**Figure 6.7b**
What problems would be faced by small retailers if they had to deal directly with large manufacturers?

### ▶ 2 Multiple or chain stores

These are groups of shops owned by the same company. Each shop in a chain tends to have the same design inside and outside. Some multiples specialise in certain products, for example Mothercare, while others sell a wide range of goods, like Woolworths. Those that sell a wide range of goods are called **variety chains**.

### ▶ 3 Supermarkets

These are large self-service food shops. In a self-service shop the customers help themselves to what they want, and then they pay at a cash till. Most supermarkets are also multiples, like Sainsburys.

### ▶ 4 Department stores

These are very large shops with several floors. Often each floor sells different goods and services. The ground floor, for example, may sell mens' clothing, food and stationery, while the second floor sells women's clothing and bedding. Department stores often offer services like banks, hairdressers, and restaurants. They are usually found in large town centres.

### ▶ 5 Discount stores

These retail outlets sell consumer durable goods like music systems, washing machines and furniture. Do-it-yourself products like paint and timber are often sold in discount stores. Discount stores are often found in huge warehouses on industrial estates, where there is plenty of parking available. Comet is a discount store that specialises in electrical goods. MFI specialises in furniture. B & Q specialises in DIY products.

### ▶ 6 Hypermarkets

These are massive shops, usually on one floor,

**Figure 6.7c**
Why are most high streets dominated by chain stores?

selling a wide range of products. They have different sections for most household goods, and they are mainly self-service. They are found mainly on the outskirts of large towns, and they have hundreds of parking spaces. Carrefour and Asda are two companies which operate hypermarkets.

▶ 7 **Mail order**

Several companies sell products through the post. Customers choose what they want to buy from a large, glossy catalogue, and send away for it. Mail order companies usually offer customers credit, but customers may have to pay postage. Littlewoods is a large mail order company.

▶ 8 **Vending machines**

In places like train stations it is very common to find machines selling things like hot and cold drinks and crisps.

▶ 9 **Market stalls**

Market stalls are perhaps the oldest type of retail outlet. Goods are often cheaper because the stall holder does not have to pay for expensive shop premises. Stallholders sometimes move from town to town.

▶ 10 **Convenience stores**

These are a fairly recent development in the UK. They are chains of shops, still open when others are closed, selling goods such as food, drink, newspapers and snacks. Layout of the shop and packaging are designed to be particularly attractive for the customer, particularly for **impulse buying**. Examples are '7–11' and Sperrings.

▶ 11 **Direct sales**

Some goods and services are sold on people's doorsteps, or as a result of a telephone call. Many people have had their homes double-glazed as a result of a visit from a representative of a double-glazing firm. Milk deliveries are the most well known examples of door-to-door selling.

### Recent changes in retailing

▶ 1 **Shopping for the car owner, and the increasing size of retailers**

An increasing number of goods and services are being sold through very large retail outlets like giant supermarkets and discount stores. These retailers can often provide good parking which is a great attraction for car owners. They can sell at low prices because they benefit from internal economies of scale.

▶ 2 **Cheaper prices**

Large retailers employ relatively few staff and they get a discount for buying in bulk. In this way they can charge lower prices. Goods are becoming available to customers in larger and larger packs because they can take them away in cars. Frozen foods and washing powder, for example, can be bought in large amounts.

▶ 3 **The spread of self-service**

Self-service started in supermarkets, but it is becoming more common in all types of retail outlet. Even small, local newsagents are now often self-service. Self-service means lower staff costs for the shops and a quicker service for the customers.

## Advertising

It is no good producing goods and services unless the consumers know about them. The public are told about goods and services through advertising.

### The advantages of advertising

Here are some of the benefits of advertising for producers and consumers:

▶ 1 **Advertising lets consumers know about new products**

Advertising may contain a lot of information about products, and it can help consumers compare products before they actually spend their money.

▶ 2 **Advertising helps one firm increase its sales compared to its rivals**

Advertising is very important to firms that produce very similar goods or services. This is one reason why banks advertise so much.

▶ 3 **Advertising helps to pay for the production of other goods and services**

Many top sporting events are sponsored by big firms in return for having their name used in connection with the event.

### The disadvantages of advertising

▶ 1 **Advertising is expensive**

Millions of pounds are spent each year on advertising. Some people feel that this is a waste of resources that could be used, for example, on improving products.

▶ 2 **Advertisements can mislead**

Some advertisements mislead people. An advert for an aftershave, for example, may suggest that it helps men attract women when in fact it makes no difference.

▶ 3 **Advertisements may be for harmful products**

Advertising may try to persuade people to buy goods and services that are bad for them, like cigarettes.

▶ 4 **Advertising may cause overspending**

Advertising may tempt people to buy things that they cannot really afford.

▶ 5 **Advertising may lead to dissatisfaction**

Advertising may make people dissatisfied with what they have got. Advertisements for holidays in exotic places, for example, may make people on lower incomes even more upset that they cannot afford a holiday.

## Types of advertising

▶ **1 Informative advertising**

Some advertisements give a great deal of information about a product to try and convince people to buy. The advertisements themselves may not be particularly attractive.

▶ **2 Persuasive advertising**

Some advertisements try to catch the eye, and they may give little information. Here are some of the ways in which advertisements try to persuade us to buy a product:

▷ **1** They hint that a product will make us more attractive to the opposite sex. Cosmetics adverts may be of this type.

▷ **2** They suggest that all caring housewives and mothers should use the product. Advertisements for washing powder are frequently of this type.

▷ **3** They tell us that the product has been produced as a result of the use of the most modern technology, and are therefore of a very high standard. Advertisements for hi-fi equipment may be of this type.

▷ **4** They tell us that the product is used by the rich and famous, and suggest that it would be very sophisticated for us to use it. Advertisements for alcoholic drink frequently make this sort of appeal.

## Advertising media

This refers to the methods that advertisers use to sell their products, for example local and national newspapers, television, posters, leaflets through the door, advertising in the shop (called **point of sale**) and in specialist magazines.

The choice of method depends on the cost, and on the size and type of market, for example local, national, specialist, luxury etc. For example, a peak time national television advertisement will not be justified for the opening of a small local shop.

**Figure 6.7d**
What type of advertisements are these?

Unit 6.7 *Retailing, wholesaling and advertising*

## DATABASE

### 1. Changing shares of the total retail trade – by type of store

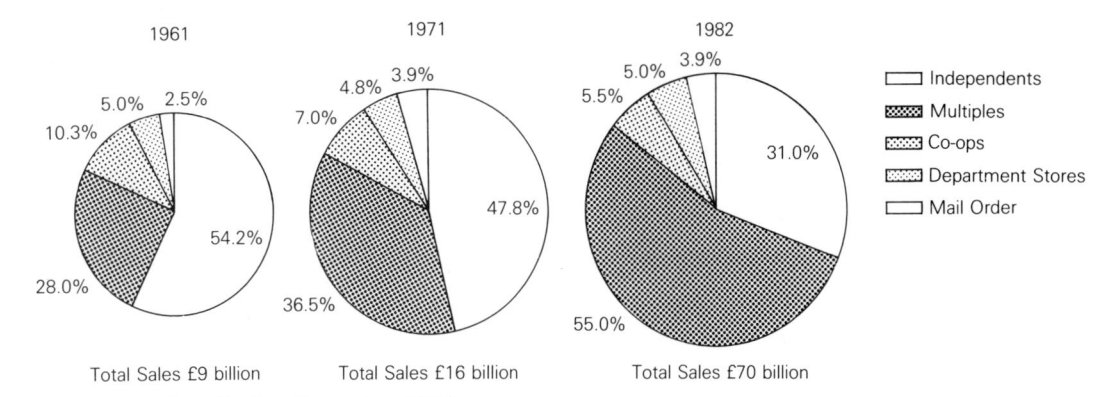

**1961** (Total Sales £9 billion)
- Independents: 54.2%
- Multiples: 28.0%
- Co-ops: 10.3%
- Department Stores: 5.0%
- Mail Order: 2.5%

**1971** (Total Sales £16 billion)
- Independents: 47.8%
- Multiples: 36.5%
- Co-ops: 7.0%
- Department Stores: 4.8%
- Mail Order: 3.9%

**1982** (Total Sales £70 billion)
- Independents: 31.0%
- Multiples: 55.0%
- Co-ops: 5.5%
- Department Stores: 5.0%
- Mail Order: 3.9%

(Source: *Barclays Review* November 1985)

## DATABASE

### 2. Still mostly print

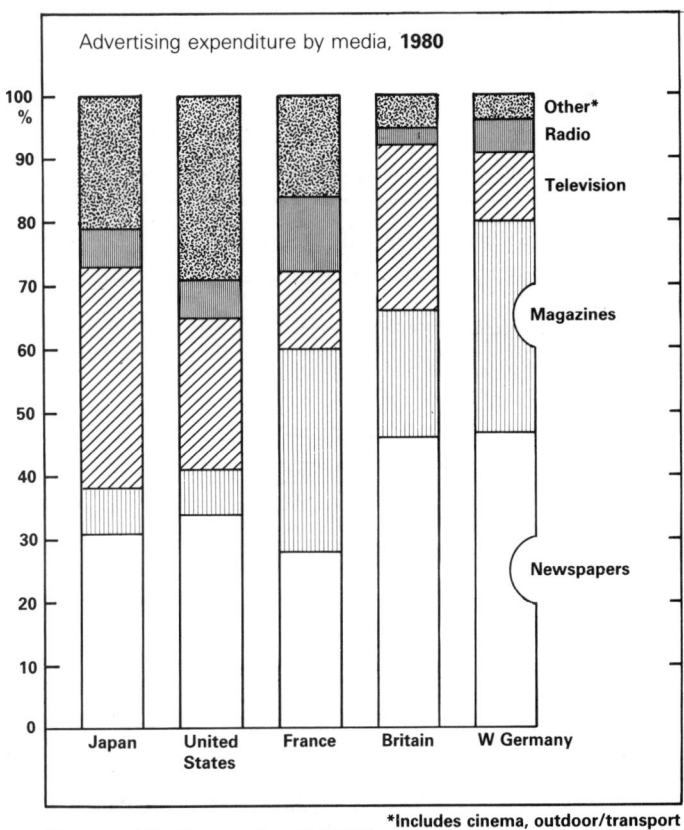

Advertising expenditure by media, **1980**

Categories (bottom to top): Newspapers, Magazines, Television, Radio, Other*

Countries: Japan, United States, France, Britain, W Germany

*Includes cinema, outdoor/transport

(Source: *The Economist* 14.11.81)

## ACTIVITIES

### SECTION A: FOCUS ON UNIT 6.7

Go back and answer the questions raised in the Focus.

### SECTION B: STEPPED QUESTIONS

1  **a**  Copy and complete the following table, using *two* examples for *each* type of retailer in your local area:

| TYPE OF RETAILER | EXAMPLES |
|---|---|
| Independents | |
| Specialist Multiples | |
| Variety Chains | |
| Supermarkets | |
| Department Stores | |
| Discount Stores | |

   **b**  Using Database 1, describe the changes in shares of the retail trade taken by different types of retailer.
   **c**  Explain why these changes have taken place.
   **d**  What are the possible economic effects of these changes?

2  **a**  What methods or media can firms use to advertise their products?
   **b**  Explain, using examples of suitable goods and services, how an advertiser would decide which method to use.
   **c**  What are the possible economic effects of advertising?
   **d**  Economists say that producers always respond to consumer demand. Does advertising make consumers respond to producers' demands? Explain your answer.

# SECTION C: DATA RESPONSE QUESTIONS

## 1. A retailing check-list

Five of the most significant recent tie-ups among retailers in Britain are:

**Burton/Debenhams.** If it succeeds, Burton's £480m bid for the department-stores group Debenhams will give it an extra 4.5m square feet of selling space. It badly needs it. Through its Top Man and Top Shop outlets, Burton's has a big share of the fashion market for 15- to 25-year-olds. Together with Sir Terence Conran's Habitat Mothercare group, Burton wants to chase the lucrative market for 30-plus buyers. Habitat has an option to take up to 20% of the enlarged group, if the bid succeeds.

**MFI/Associated Dairies.** In making an agreed bid in April for the furniture group MFI, Associated Dairies (Asda) found a solution to several of its problems. It found (a) a home for its cash pile, (b) a successor (in MFI's chairman, Mr Derek Hunt) to its own 64-year-old chairman, Mr Noel Stockdale and (c) a way to expand beyond its customary foods. Asda got big by selling own-label groceries on the edges of towns in the north of England; MFI by selling self-assembly furniture on similar sites in the wealthier south. Together, they will be Britain's fourth biggest retailer, with annual sales of £2 billion.

**Dixons/Currys.** Currys, a lacklustre electrical retailer, had a big chunk of the market for white goods (ie, fridges, washing machines, etc) whereas Dixons was known as one of the busiest retailers of cameras and computers. Put the two together and what have you got? A 20% share of the brown-goods market, and room to grab a bigger share of the white goods one by applying Dixons' go-go marketing skills to Currys.

**Sears/Foster Bros.** Until March this year Sears Holdings sold most things except men's clothing. It plugged the gap by spending £114m on the purchase of Foster Bros, the high-street chain that (at the time) was fighting off an unwelcome bid from the mini-conglomerate Ward White. Foster Bros was added to a list of businesses that included Selfridges department store; the Freeman Hardy & Willis shoe chain; Olympus sportswear shops and Lewis' department stores.

**Woolworth/Comet.** Tugged free of its American parent by a consortium buyout in 1982, Britain's Woolworth Holdings has since been in search of a new identity. By buying Comet for £117m last year, it got a 10% share of the electrical-goods market and pre-tax profits of £14.9m in 1984. Add to that the £28.6m Woolworth made from B&Q, its edge-of-town do-it-yourself retailer, and Woolies can afford to wait awhile to get its dowdy stores back into profit.

(Source: *The Economist* 1.6.85)

    **a** What kinds of retailer are:
       ▷ Burtons
       ▷ Debenhams?
    **b** ▷ Only one of the 'recent tie-ups' mentioned is between *two* specialist multiples. Which two?
       ▷ Which three retailers make up Woolworth Holdings?
    **c** How did ASDA and MFI get big?
    **d** Explain the advantages of the following takeovers or mergers for the firms named in brackets:
       ▷ Burton/Debenhams (Burton)
       ▷ Dixons/Currys (Dixons and Currys)
       ▷ Sears/Foster Bros (Sears)
       ▷ Woolworth/Comet (Woolworth).

2

## Detergent Advertising

DETERGENT manufacturer Proctor & Gamble is on one of the biggest binges in British advertising history, putting it securely on course to remain the top single advertiser this year with a budget of well over £50 million.

The astronomical rise of P&G's spending – part of an unsuccessful rearguard action against Lever Brothers – raises the question whether the consumer pays dearly for the stranglehold the two companies have on the market. Latest figures up to last month show the advertising expenditure is still rocketing.

Figures based on Audits of Great Britain data, show that last year P&G and Lever held a total of 89 per cent of the washing powder market worth £298 million a year.

What P&G is attempting to do is end Lever's dominance in the automatic powders market which was cornered after its competitor's launch of Persil Automatic in 1968. Last year, according to figures from Media Expenditure Analysis, over £7 million was spent on promoting P&G's rival, Ariel. Nearly £5 million has been spent so far this year.

P&G refuses to discuss its marketing. But it is estimated that its advertising expenditure in soaps and detergents grew five-fold between 1978 and last year when it was £32 million, or almost £20 million more than Lever's comparable expenditure on higher sales. Its market share increased by just 2 per cent over that period to 32 per cent.

(Source: *Observer* 26.6.83)

a How much did Proctor & Gamble spend on advertising in 1983, and how did that compare to 1978?
b What is the name of Proctor & Gamble's main competitor?
c What percentage of the total washing powder market was held by the two firms together in 1982?
d How successful has Proctor & Gamble's advertising been in winning customers from their competitor?
e Do you think that the amount spent on advertising washing powders is justified?

# UNIT 6.8    Protecting the consumer

**FOCUS**

▶ Why is it necessary for people to be protected when they buy goods and services?

▶ What are the main laws that protect consumers?

▶ What are the main organisations which exist to protect consumers?

## Protecting consumers' interests

It would be good to think that people who manufactured and sold goods and services always had their customers' best interests at heart. Unfortunately this is not always the case, as some firms may try to cut their costs at the expense of the consumer, in order to increase their profit. Figure 6.8a shows some of the ways in which consumers could be wrongly treated if there were no laws to protect them.

**Figure 6.8a**
In what ways could consumers be taken advantage of if there were no laws to protect them?

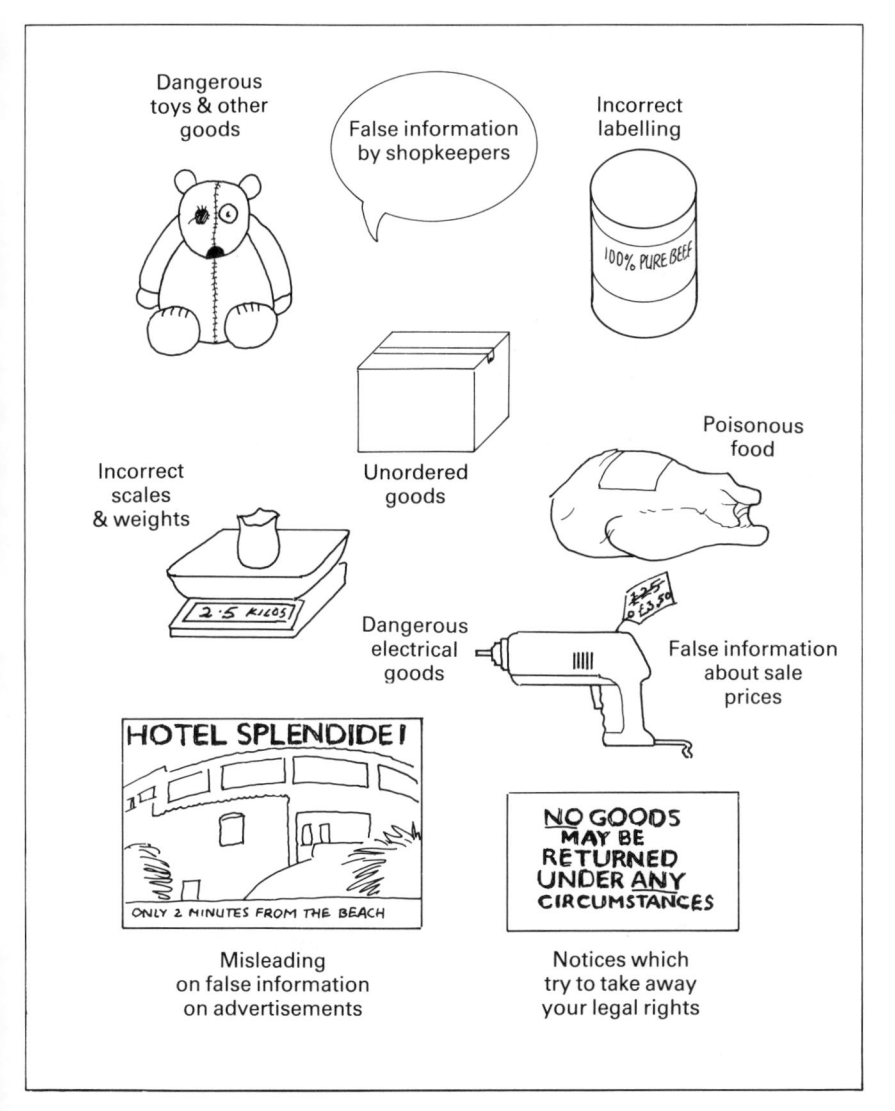

- Dangerous toys & other goods
- False information by shopkeepers
- Incorrect labelling
- Incorrect scales & weights
- Unordered goods
- Poisonous food
- Dangerous electrical goods
- False information about sale prices
- Misleading on false information on advertisements
- Notices which try to take away your legal rights

## Protection by the law

The consumer is protected by **civil laws** and **criminal laws**. If a person or organisation is found guilty of breaking a civil law, the person who has suffered may receive a sum of money as **compensation** from the guilty person. If a person or organisation is found guilty of breaking criminal law the punishment will be a fine or imprisonment. The injured party could receive **damages** under criminal law at the discretion of the judge.

## Some of the laws that protect consumers

Here are some of the Acts of Parliament that have been passed to protect consumers:

▶ **1 The Sale of Goods Act**
This Act says that when you buy goods:
▷ **a** They must be of **merchantable quality**. This means they must be fit to be sold. A teapot, for example, must not be sold with a crack in it.
▷ **b** They must be **fit for the purpose** for which they are intended. The bristles of a toothbrush, for example, should not fall out when you clean your teeth with it.
▷ **c** They must **meet the description** applied to them. If a pair of trousers is labelled as having a 30″ waist, then it must fit someone of that size.

**Figure 6.8b**
What Act of Parliament could entitle this man to ask for his money back?

**Figure 6.8c**
If this woman bought the trousers she probably could not return them and ask for her money back. Why not?

If any of these things do not apply to something that you have bought, you can ask for your money back. The shop cannot blame the manufacturer and refuse to give you a refund.

The law does not cover you in some circumstances, for example:
▷ **a** If you could have seen the fault when you bought the goods.
▷ **b** If you have bought the goods from someone who does not normally sell them. If you buy a shirt from a garage, for example, the Act may not cover you.

**Figure 6.8d**
Which Act of Parliament protects us if an advertisement claims wrongly that a beach is "only a five-minute cycle ride from the hotel"?

### ▶ 2 The Supply of Goods and Services Act
This Act applies the conditions of the Sale of Goods Act to goods supplied to you as part of a service (e.g. taps fitted by a plumber), goods supplied on hire, or supplied in part-exchange. The Act also says that people who provide a service to you must provide the service:
▷ **a** with reasonable skill and care
▷ **b** within a reasonable time
▷ **c** for a reasonable charge.

### ▶ 3 The Consumer Credit Act
This Act protects consumers against some of the problems they can face when borrowing money. Here are some of the things it covers:
▷ **a** It sets out how organisations offering credit must obtain a licence from the Office of Fair Trading.
▷ **b** It explains how the Annual Percentage Rate of Charge (APR) must be displayed on advertisements.
▷ **c** It makes it illegal for people to visit homes uninvited to try and sell goods on credit.
▷ **d** It tells you what to do if you have changed your mind about a credit agreement you have signed at home after being visited by a salesperson.
▷ **e** It requires that the firm offering credit shows the cash price, total credit price and instalments on the agreement.

### ▶ 4 The Trade Descriptions Act
This Act makes it illegal to describe goods and services inaccurately in advertisements and other places. It also makes it illegal to advertise something at a sale price, unless it was sold at the higher price mentioned for at least 28 consecutive days within the last six months.

### ▶ 5 The Weights and Measures Act
This Act makes sure that manufacturers put a weight on many products, for example, canned food.

### ▶ 6 Food and Drugs Act
This Act protects consumers against the sale of unfit food, or food inaccurately described. It says, for example, how much meat there should be in a sausage, and how food sold in packages should be labelled with their contents.

### ▶ 7 Consumer Protection Act
This Act gives a government minister the power to make regulations for any type of goods to prevent or reduce the risk of death or injury. In 1984, for example, the government banned the sale of erasers that smell or look like food. There are also regulations about things like the flammability of children's nightdresses.

There are many other Acts of Parliament which protect consumers, and this section has given only the briefest outline of some of the most important laws.

Unit 6.8 *Protecting the consumer*

**Figure 6.8e**
Which organisation publishes these leaflets?

## Organisations that help consumers

There are many organisations that help to protect your interests as a consumer. Here are brief descriptions of just some of them:

▶ **1 The Office of Fair Trading**

Here are some of the ways in which the OFT helps consumers:

▷ **a** It encourages trade organisations to prepare and publish codes of practice. Shops that sell electrical goods, for example, can look up a code of practice telling them how to mark goods with prices, how long repairs should take, and what spare parts they should keep.

▷ **b** It publishes information leaflets on all kinds of consumer matters. This information is available at places like Citizens' Advice Bureaux and local libraries.

▷ **c** It chases up organisations that keep breaking consumer protection laws.

▷ **d** It licences and watches over organisations that deal in credit.

▷ **e** It watches over the activities of firms that might lead to a loss in competition in an industry and higher prices and poorer services for consumers.

▶ **2 Local Authority Trading Standards and Environmental Health Departments**

Your local council is responsible for enforcing some of the laws protecting consumers. These include the Trade Descriptions Act, the Weights and Measures Act, and the Consumer Safety Act.

▶ **3 Local Authority Consumer Advice Centres**

These give information about consumers' rights. They employ expert staff to deal with consumer problems, and they publish leaflets and other written information on consumer matters.

▶ **4 Citizens' Advice Bureaux**

These provide a free consumer advice service. They are found in most local areas, and they may be the best place to start if you have an unsolved problem to do with buying goods and services.

▶ **5 Nationalised Industries' Consumer Councils**

These deal with complaints from consumers about services like electricity and they try to make sure the nationalised industries act in consumers' best interests.

▶ **6 Trade Associations**

Many manufacturers and retailers of goods belong to groups called trade associations. These organisations publish codes of practice that their members are supposed to follow. The Motor Agents' Association and the Association of British Travel Agents are both well-known trade associations.

▶ **7 Organisations that test goods for quality and safety**

▷ **a** *The British Standards Institution* This

organisation tests goods mainly for safety like crash helmets and pressure cookers. Goods that pass the tests receive a BSI kitemark.

▷ **b** *The British Electrotechnical Approvals Board* This organisation tests goods like electric fires and electric hairdriers, and awards a special kitemark to safe electrical goods.

▷ **c** *The Design Centre* This organisation awards labels to products that it believes to be both good to look at and efficient to use.

▷ **d** *The Consumers' Association* This is a private organisation which people pay to join. It publishes the results of tests on different goods and services in a magazine called *Which?* which it sends out to its members.

**Figure 6.8f**
Which organisations issue these labels?

## DATABASE

# Making your complaint

**To make a complaint:**
- stop using the item
- tell the shop at once
- take it back (if you can)
- take a receipt or proof of purchase (if you can)
- ask for the manager or owner
- keep calm!
- If it is a tricky problem it may be better to write. To be on the safe side you could use recorded delivery. Keep copies of all letters. Do not send receipts or other proof of purchase – give reference numbers or send photocopies.

**If you phone:**
- first, make a note of what you want to say
- have receipts and useful facts handy
- get the name of the person you speak to
- jot down the date and time and what is said
- keep calm!

If the local shop or office cannot help, contact the managing director at the head office. Find out if the firm belongs to a trade association. Some associations will intervene in disputes. Those with Codes of Practice have a special system for dealing with complaints.

**If you see a notice like this you can do two things:**

1 Ignore it. 2 Tell your Trading Standards Department. Such notices are illegal, even for sale goods. A trader *cannot* wriggle out of his responsibility if he sells you faulty goods.

(Source: OFT Leaflet, *How to put things right*)

**ACTIVITIES**

## SECTION A: FOCUS ON UNIT 6.8

Go back and answer the questions raised in the Focus.

## SECTION B: STEPPED QUESTIONS

1   a   List the laws which apply to the protection of the consumer when buying goods and services.
    b   Match up the following with the consumer protection laws that they might break:
        ▷ A customer is charged for 1lb of cheese, even though he is actually given 12oz.
        ▷ A car is driven away from the garage but when the customer arrives home he is unable to engage reverse gear.
        ▷ A brochure claims that a hotel looks out onto the beach, when the beach can be seen only from the toilet.
        ▷ A car is advertised as having done 25,000 miles, which is shown on the mileometer, although it has actually done 80,000 miles.
        ▷ A customer asks for a drill for brickwork, which works on wood but breaks when it is used on a brick.
        ▷ A soup tin contains no label stating ingredients.
    c   Explain the possible effects of a removal of all consumer protection laws.

2   a   What labels or symbols should consumers look out for when buying:
        ▷ electrical equipment
        ▷ car safety seats for children
        ▷ holidays?
    b   Explain when it would be appropriate for a consumer to get help from EACH of the following organisations:
        ▷ Trading Standards Departments
        ▷ Citizens' Advice Bureaux
        ▷ The Consumers' Association.

## SECTION C: DATA RESPONSE QUESTIONS

### "I'LL SUE YOU"

Unfortunately, problems are not always solved on the trader's premises or in the CAB. Sometimes, it is necessary to take the matter to court to enforce your rights. Never be afraid of going to court for a small claim. It's a simple matter these days and your CAB will help you with all the procedures necessary to take the matter further. However, before you do take the matter to court, always get professional advice as to the validity of your case.

Here's a little story to show you what it's all about. "I'll sue," said Mandy. Unfortunately, the shop manager did not take her at her word, and was probably most surprised to receive a summons to court a short time later.

Mandy did not want to sue, but, after repeated visits to the shop, and a letter to the managing director of the firm, she had still received no satisfaction. Her £14.50 shoes were not, in her opinion, of 'merchantable quality'. Her local CAB agreed with her and advised her that, under the Sale of Goods Act, she should return the shoes to the shop and ask for a cash refund. However, the shop had so steadfastly refused, that, reluctantly, she decided to take legal action.

**(Source: Office of Fair Trading booklet *Get Smart*)**

a  What do the letters CAB stand for?
b  What is meant by the underlined sentence?
c  ▷ What are the *three* conditions that must apply to any goods offered for sale under the Sale of Goods Act?
   ▷ Describe *three* circumstances in which you could take faulty goods back but the shopkeeper could refuse to change them.
   ▷ "The Sale of Goods Act in theory gives adequate protection for the consumer but it may do little to help the most vulnerable groups in society." Who are 'the most vulnerable groups' and why may the existence of strong consumer laws fail to protect them?

## COURSE WORK

### PART 6: COURSEWORK SUGGESTION

A STUDY OF A SMALL LOCAL FIRM

1. Make a study of a small local firm by using interviews, collecting written information, visiting the premises, etc.
2. Analyse your data under suitable headings, e.g. range of products, location of the firm, prices, costs, etc.
3. Write an account of the firm that the firm would be happy to present to prospective customers. Include your information in as attractive a form as possible, using pie charts, graphs, etc. to show information.

### EXTENSION COURSEWORK

4. Imagine that you work for a firm of business consultants who have been called in to investigate the firm and make recommendations for improvements that could lead to increases in profits. Write a confidential report for the owner(s) of the firm explaining the changes that you think should occur, giving reasons for your suggestions. Use various methods of presentation for your report including graphs, tables, charts, etc.

## DICTIONARY

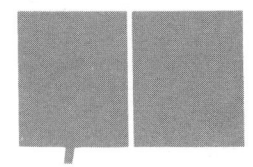

Here are some more words and phrases for your Dictionary of Economic Terms. Remember to look for each word or phrase in the text and then write your own definition for it.

bear
bull
consumer protection
co-operative
costs
Development Area
diversification
dividend
economies of scale
Enterprise Zone
external economies of scale
externalities
fixed costs
footloose industry
infrastructure
integration
internal economies of scale
limited liability
localised industry
long-run costs
marginal costs
multinational
nationalised industry
natural monopoly
Office of Fair Trading (OFT)
ordinary share
partnership
preference share

private costs and benefits
private limited company
privatisation
producer co-operative
profit
public limited company (plc)
rationalisation
regional policy
retail co-operative
retailing
short-run costs
social costs and benefits
speculator
stag
Stock Exchange
total costs
total revenue
unlimited liability
variable costs
wholesaling
yield

**Extension material**
concentration
Monopolies and Mergers Commission (MMC)
monopoly
restrictive practices

# Part 7
## The government & the economy

# UNIT 7.1 The public sector and government spending

## FOCUS

▶ What is **the public sector**?

▶ What are the main items of government spending?

▶ How has government spending grown in recent years and why do some people wish to see it reduced?

▶ What benefits are available to the individual through the **social security** system?

A **mixed economy** consists of a **private sector** and a **public sector**. The private sector is owned and run by individuals aiming to make a profit. The public sector is the part of the economy owned and run by the state. It exists mainly because some things such as defence, welfare services and roads could not be adequately provided if there was only a private sector. It can also give the government some degree of control over the economy.

The public sector includes public services provided by central and local government and nationalised industries. Figure 7.1a shows how central and local government planned to spend the money collected in taxes and from other sources in 1986–87. Note that spending on the **welfare state** is the largest category.

Local government (such as county, borough, and district councils) is responsible for a particular range of services. Figure 7.1b shows how one local council, the London Borough of Harrow, spent its income in 1984–85. Smaller district councils are not responsible for some of these activities, for example education.

### The growth of government spending

Government spending as a percentage of the value of all the goods and services produced in the country (the **Gross Domestic Product** of the country) tended to go up year by year until 1981–82. Since that time it has stayed at about 42 per cent of Gross Domestic Product.

The Conservative government that came to power in 1979 stated that it would try to stop the growth in public spending, and then reduce it. Here are some of the reasons why government spending may be cut:

### The case for cutting public spending

▶ **1** If the government cuts spending, it will be able to cut taxes. It will mean that people can keep more of their income to spend on the extra goods and services produced and may mean that they have an incentive to be more productive, as they will take home more of any increases in pay that they earn. Businesses will have more incentive to invest if spending increases. All these benefits of tax cuts could lead to a fall in unemployment.

▶ **2** If the government cuts spending, it may need to borrow less from the public. If the government borrows a great deal, it may need to put up interest rates to get people to lend it money. High interest rates put up the costs of production for business, which can mean less investment in new machinery and equipment. The government may prefer to borrow less and keep interest rates down, so helping industry to invest more and produce more cheaply.

▶ **3** Some people believe that the government does not provide goods and services very efficiently. They believe that wherever possible goods and services should be provided by pri-

**Figure 7.1a**
Government spending 1986–87

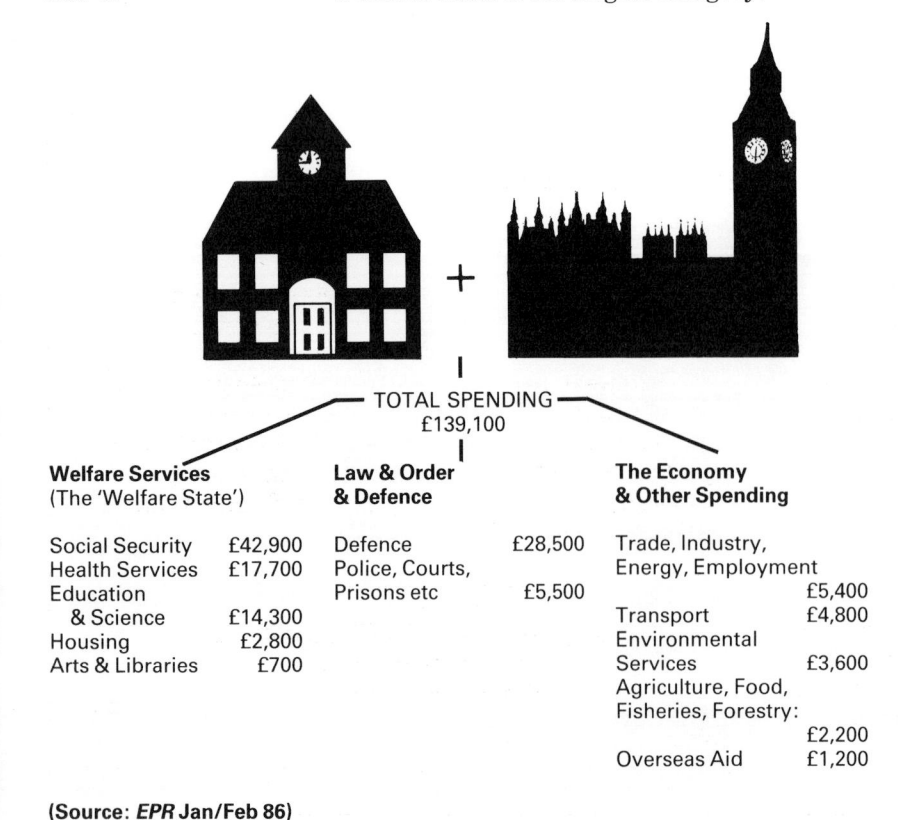

TOTAL SPENDING
£139,100

**Welfare Services**
(The 'Welfare State')

| | |
|---|---|
| Social Security | £42,900 |
| Health Services | £17,700 |
| Education & Science | £14,300 |
| Housing | £2,800 |
| Arts & Libraries | £700 |

**Law & Order & Defence**

| | |
|---|---|
| Defence | £28,500 |
| Police, Courts, Prisons etc | £5,500 |

**The Economy & Other Spending**

| | |
|---|---|
| Trade, Industry, Energy, Employment | £5,400 |
| Transport | £4,800 |
| Environmental Services | £3,600 |
| Agriculture, Food, Fisheries, Forestry: | £2,200 |
| Overseas Aid | £1,200 |

(Source: *EPR* Jan/Feb 86)

*Unit 7.1* *The public sector and government spending*

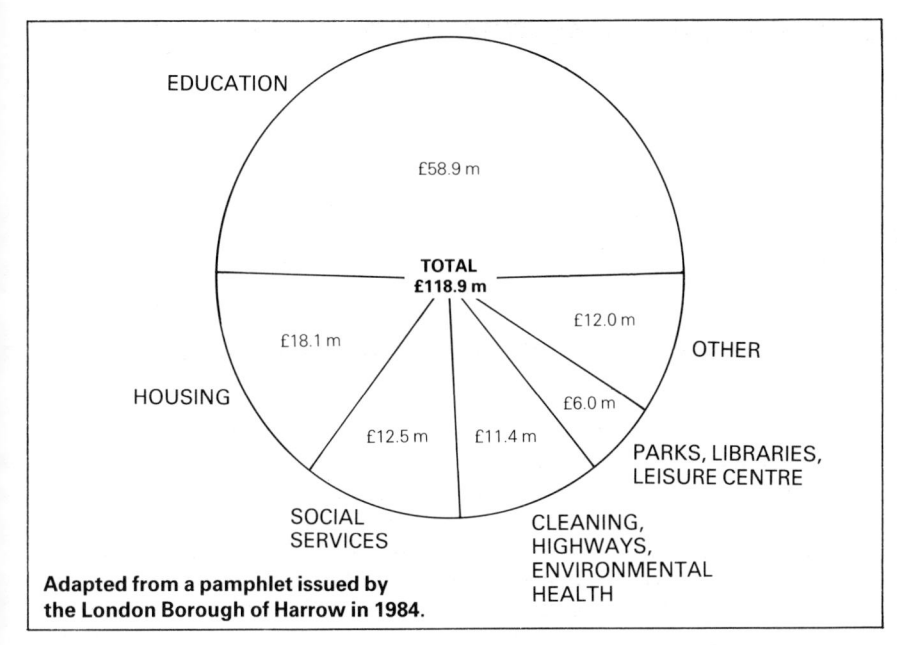

**Figure 7.1b**
How the London borough of Harrow spent its income in 1984–85

Pie chart: TOTAL £118.9 m
- EDUCATION £58.9 m
- HOUSING £18.1 m
- SOCIAL SERVICES £12.5 m
- CLEANING, HIGHWAYS, ENVIRONMENTAL HEALTH £11.4 m
- PARKS, LIBRARIES, LEISURE CENTRE £6.0 m
- OTHER £12.0 m

Adapted from a pamphlet issued by the London Borough of Harrow in 1984.

vately owned businesses which have to be efficient to survive.

### The case against cutting public spending

▶ 1  Much government spending helps poorer people. If social security, health services, education and council house building are cut, poorer people suffer more than richer people.

▶ 2  The government is storing up trouble for the future if it cuts capital spending. This is basically investment spending on renewing and replacing things like housing, roads, school buildings and sewerage systems. Sooner or later these things will have to be replaced, and then it will cost much more to replace them.

▶ 3  A cut in government spending can lead to more unemployment. Cuts in spending can mean fewer people working in schools, hospitals, local council offices and so on.

▶ 4  For every government worker laid off, the government will have to pay more unemployment benefit and it will collect fewer taxes. This could lead to more borrowing by the government rather than less borrowing. Reducing borrowing is one of the reasons for cutting spending in the first place.

▶ 5  The government can reduce external costs through its spending programme. For example it can pass and enforce laws to reduce pollution and preserve the countryside, and it can spend money on new roads to relieve congestion.

## The social security system

Figure 7.1a shows that social security spending accounts for more government money than anything else. The idea of social security is to give people help in times of financial need, and to make sure that nobody needs to fall below a certain basic standard of living.

Most social security payments are given in the form of cash payments, for example child benefit, but some are given in the form of goods and services, for example free school meals.

### The three types of social security benefit

Figure 7.1c shows that there are three types of social security benefit. Here is a brief description

**Figure 7.1c**
Different types of social security benefit

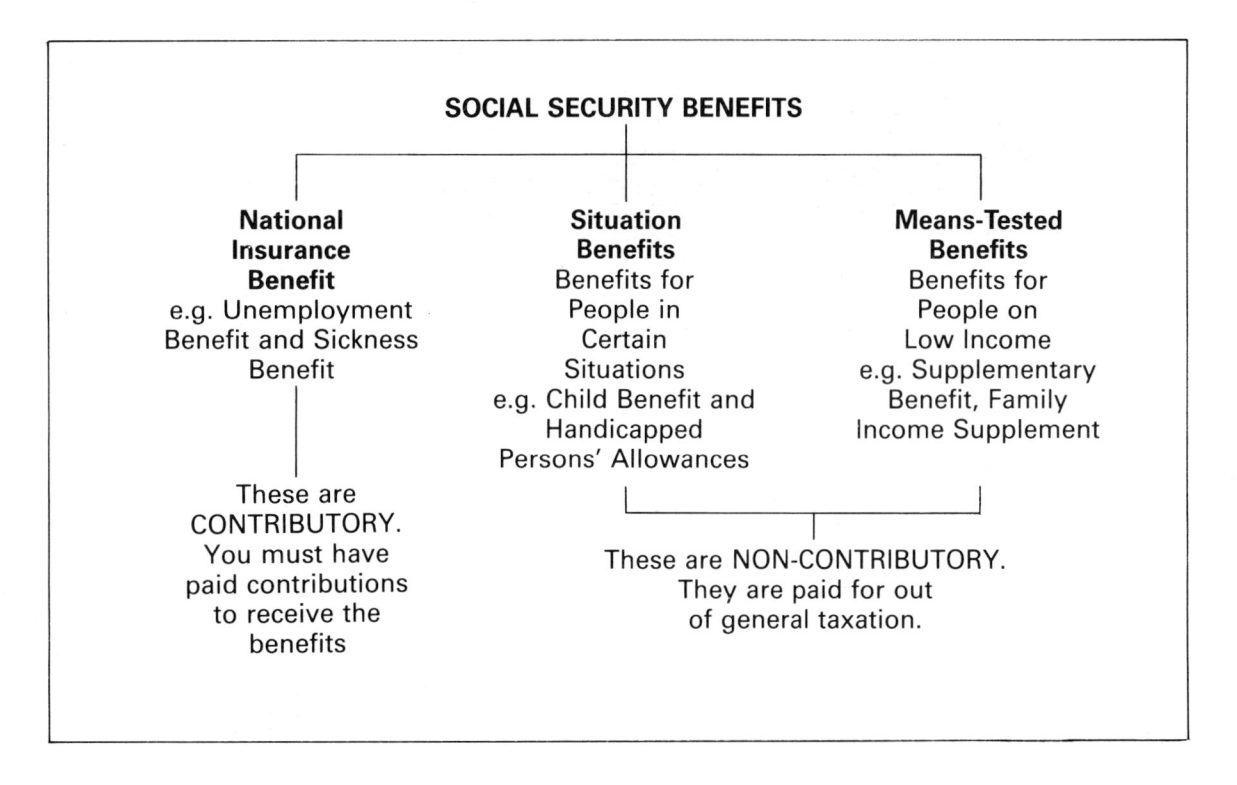

**SOCIAL SECURITY BENEFITS**

| **National Insurance Benefit** | **Situation Benefits** | **Means-Tested Benefits** |
|---|---|---|
| e.g. Unemployment Benefit and Sickness Benefit | Benefits for People in Certain Situations e.g. Child Benefit and Handicapped Persons' Allowances | Benefits for People on Low Income e.g. Supplementary Benefit, Family Income Supplement |

These are CONTRIBUTORY. You must have paid contributions to receive the benefits

These are NON-CONTRIBUTORY. They are paid for out of general taxation.

### ▶ 1 National Insurance benefits

In order to get National Insurance benefits you must pay National Insurance contributions. Most people between the ages of 16 and 65 who are working have to pay contributions. People can even volunteer to pay when they are out of work, or when their earnings are very low. There are four different types or classes of contribution, and these are shown in Fig. 7.1d.

| | |
|---|---|
| Class 1 | This is paid by employees who earn above a certain amount. Contributions rise as earnings rise. |
| Class 2 & 4 | Class 2 contributions are paid at a flat rate by self-employed people. If a self-employed person earns more than a certain amount, they will pay extra contributions called Class 4 contributions. |
| Class 3 | These are flat-rate contributions paid by people out of work, or on low incomes, because they wish to keep the right to claim some benefits. Payment of these contributions is voluntary. |

**Figure 7.1d** The different classes of National Insurance contribution

There are various benefits you can claim according to which class of contribution you have made, and how many contributions you have made. Here are just some of them:

▷ **a** *Unemployment benefit* This is paid for up to a year, and you get more if you have dependents.

▷ **b** *Sickness pay and benefits* For the first 28 weeks of sickness you receive sick pay and benefits, and after that time you may be able to claim invalidity benefits.

▷ **c** *Maternity allowance and maternity leave* Women can claim this benefit for eleven weeks before they have a baby, and for a further six weeks after that.

▷ **d** *Retirement pension* This is available to women over 60 and men over 65 who have retired. Women over 65 and men over 70 still get the pension even if they go on working. The law is likely to be changed so that the retirement age of men and women is the same.

▷ **d** *Widow's benefits* A woman whose husband dies can claim various benefits, including a pension if the woman is over 40.

### ▶ 2 Benefits for people in certain situations

Some benefits can be claimed by anyone in a particular situation, however rich or poor. No contributions have to be made, and the benefits are paid for out of general taxation. Here are some of them:

▷ **a** *Child benefit* This is paid at a flat rate to mothers for each child under the age of sixteen. Single parents can claim at a higher rate.

▷ **b** *Benefits for people injured at work, and for people suffering from an industrial disease* People who are injured at work, or who suffer a disease caused by their work, can receive benefits even if they have not paid National Insurance contributions. Benefits are also payable to a widow whose husband dies as a result of an accident at work.

▷ **c** *Guardian's allowance* This is payable to someone who takes in an orphaned child.

▷ **d** *Allowances for people who are handicapped* There are allowances for people who are severely handicapped, or for people who have to look after severely handicapped children and adults.

There are many other benefits, especially for expectant mothers, children and pensioners. These include not only cash help, but also free services such as free prescriptions and free milk and vitamins.

Total £33,752 m

Pensions £14,791 m

Supplementary Benefit £5,693 m

Child Benefit £4,011 m

Rent & Rate Benefits £278 m

Invalidity Benefits £2,798 m

Unemployment Benefit £1,528 m

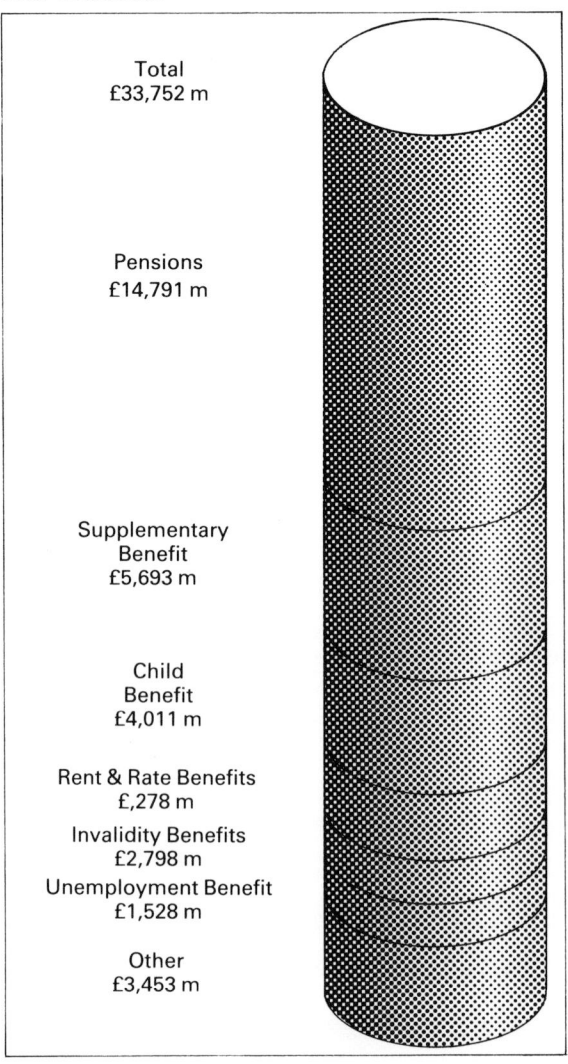

Other £3,453 m

**Figure 7.1e** Government spending on social security benefits 1983–84

### 3 Benefits for people on low incomes

Some benefits are 'means-tested'. This means that you have to show that you earn below a certain amount to qualify for the benefit. No contributions have to be made for these benefits, which are paid for out of general taxation. Here are some of the benefits:

▷ **a** *Supplementary benefit* This is a benefit for people who do not have enough money to live on. It can be claimed by people who are *not* working full-time. It can be paid on top of other benefits, part-time earnings, or pensions.

▷ **b** *Family income supplement* This is for families bringing up children on a low wage. The benefit can be claimed by two-parent families where the man works full-time, and by people who are bringing up children alone. The family must contain at least one child. Families that receive this benefit are also entitled to free schools meals, free dental treatment, and other free goods and services.

**Where to go for advice** There are very many benefits in addition to those listed here, and the rates for each benefit are changed usually every year. The Department of Health and Social Security (DHSS) publishes many leaflets which explain the benefits in more detail. You can obtain leaflets from many libraries, from social security offices, and directly from the DHSS.

**Figure 7.1f**
Some social security rates (per week) 1985–1986

| | | |
|---|---|---|
| Pensions: | Single person | £38.30 |
| | Married couple | £61.30 |
| Child benefit: | Each child | £7.00 |
| | One-parent benefit | £4.55 |
| Unemployment benefit: | Single person | £30.45 |
| | Adult dependent | £18.80 |
| Sickness benefit: | Single person | £29.15 |
| | Adult dependent | £18.00 |
| Family Income Supplement: | Income below which FIS is payable to family with one child aged 11–15 | £98.50 |
| | Maximum weekly amount paid to one-child family where the child is 11–15 | £25.50 |
| | Addition for each extra child aged 11–15 | £3.00 |
| Supplementary benefit: | Ordinary weekly rate | Long-term* weekly rate |
| Couple | £47.85 | £60.00 |
| Person living alone | £29.50 | £37.50 |
| Non-householder over | | |
| 18 years | £23.60 | £30.00 |
| 16–17 | £18.20 | £23.00 |

*For people over pension age, or who have been getting supplementary benefit continuously for a year or more.

## DATABASE

## 1. Changes in government spending in real terms (after removing inflation effects)

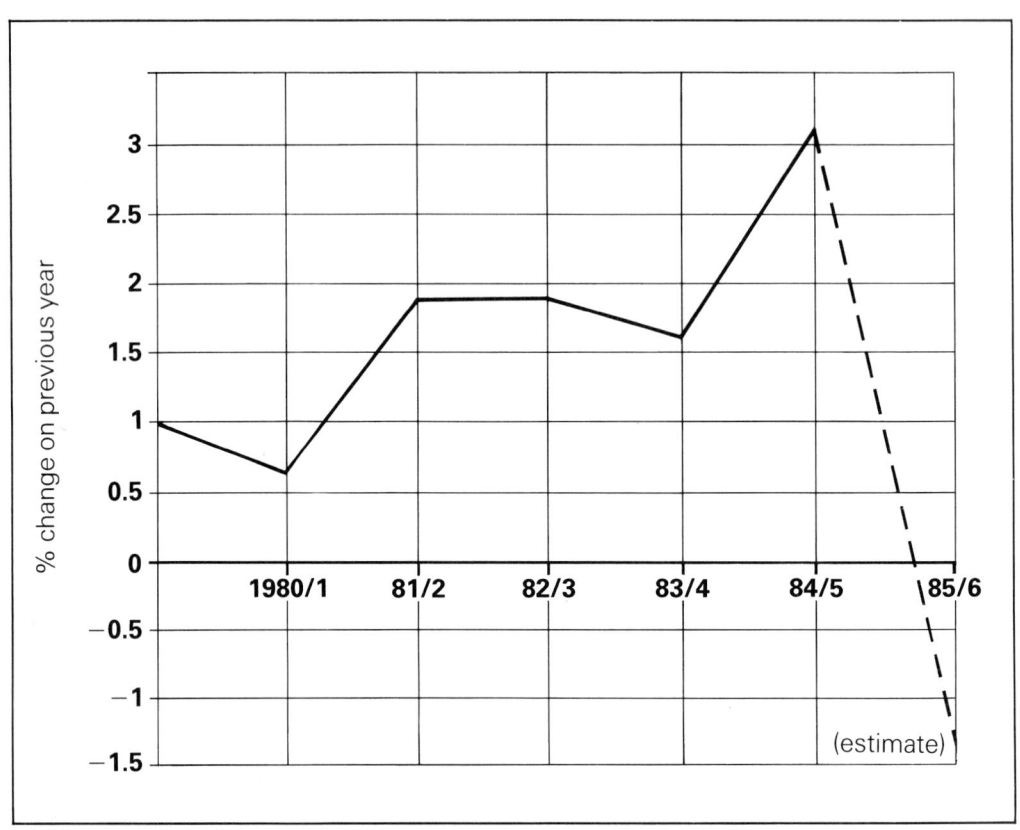

[Line graph: % change on previous year, from 1980/1 to 85/6. Values approximately: 1980/1: 1.0; 81/2: 0.65; 82/3: 1.9; 83/4: 1.9; 84/5: 1.6; 85/6: 3.1; then dashed line dropping to about -1 (estimate).]

(Drawn from Government Spending Plans, published 9.1.86, re-printed in *The Guardian* 10.1.86)

# DATABASE

## 2. Government spending in seven countries

(Capital and current spending as percentage of output in the economy)

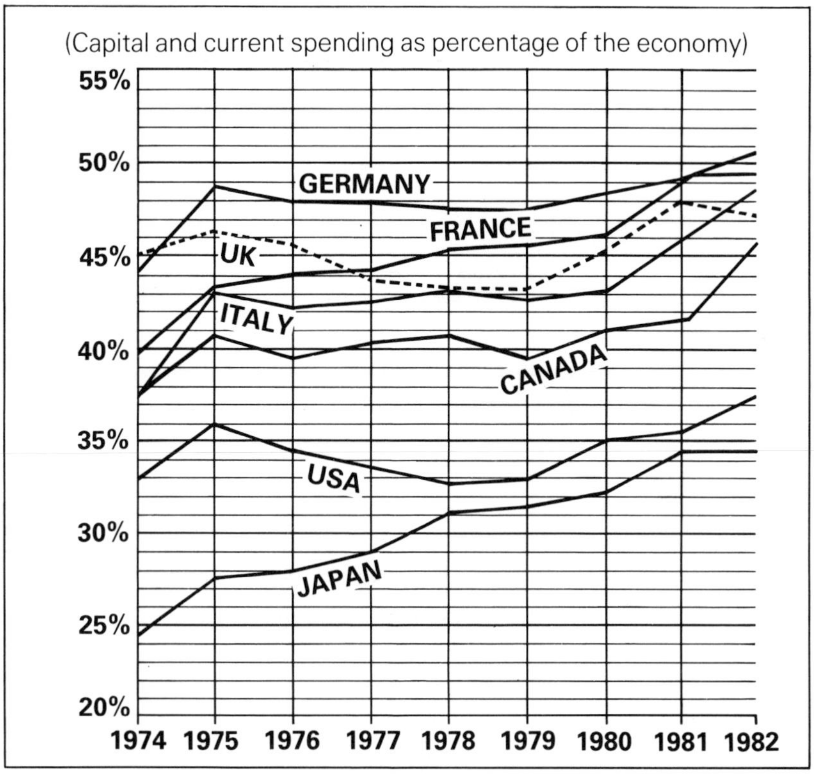
(Capital and current spending as percentage of the economy)
55%
50%
45%
40%
35%
30%
25%
20%
1974 1975 1976 1977 1978 1979 1980 1981 1982
GERMANY
FRANCE
UK
ITALY
CANADA
USA
JAPAN

A graph comparing Britain's public spending against that of other nations. The share of public spending in national income is lower in Britain than in most other European countries, according to figures from the Organisation for Economic Co-operation and Development

**(Source: *The Guardian* 23.1.85)**

## ACTIVITIES

### SECTION A: FOCUS ON UNIT 7.1

Go back and answer the questions raised in the Focus.

### SECTION B: STEPPED QUESTIONS

1  **a**  List *four* items of *local* government spending. (Use Figure 7.1c to help you.)
   **b**  Draw three columns headed 'Welfare State', 'Law and Order and Defence', and 'The Economy and Other Spending', and put each of the following items into the appropriate column: (Use Fig. 7.1a to help you.)
   - ▷ hospitals
   - ▷ schools
   - ▷ roads
   - ▷ riot shields
   - ▷ social security benefits
   - ▷ police cars
   - ▷ railway carriages
   - ▷ nuclear submarines
   - ▷ farmers' subsidies
   - ▷ council houses
   - ▷ Harrier fighter jets
   - ▷ training schemes

   **c**  ▷ Explain how opportunity cost is involved in government spending decisions.
   ▷ List the twelve items in Fig. 7.1a in order of spending (the highest first). Do you think this order of spending is appropriate? Explain your answer.

2  **a**  Which of the following are part of the 'public sector'?
   - ▷ the Post Office
   - ▷ the National Health Service
   - ▷ Marks and Spencer
   - ▷ British Telecom
   - ▷ the army.

   **b**  All families benefit from the 'welfare state'. In what ways do you and your family benefit?
   **c**  What factors affect the level of unemployment benefit received by a claimant?
   **d**  What are the possible economic effects of the abolition of the 'welfare state'?

## SECTION C: DATA RESPONSE QUESTIONS

### 1. Public spending and inflation

**Public expenditure planning totals 1978–1979 to 1986–1987**

| | (£ million) | |
| --- | --- | --- |
| | Cash | With the Effects of Inflation Removed (Base Year = 1984/85) |
| 1978/79 | 65,800 | 117,401 |
| 1979/80 | 76,900 | 118,532 |
| 1980/81 | 92,700 | 119,196 |
| 1981/82 | 104,600 | 121,471 |
| 1982/83 | 113,400 | 123,757 |
| 1983/84 | 120,300 | 125,735 |
| 1984/85 | 129,600 | 129,638 |
| 1985/86(est.) | 134,200 | 127,812 |
| 1986/87(est.) | 139,100 | 126,735 |

(Source: adapted from *The Economic Progress Report Supplement* Dec 1983, and *The Guardian* 10.1.86)

**a** How much more did the government spend in cash terms in 1984–85 than in 1978–79?

**b** After the effect of inflation has been removed, how much more was spent in 1984–85 than in 1978–79?

**c** ▷ Give *two* reasons why a government may wish to cut down government spending.
▷ Give *two* arguments against cutting public spending.

**d** In 1984–85 the government borrowed about £10,200 million. How much did they collect in taxes, fees and charges?

**e** Why do the government publish figures for public spending that take out the effect of inflation?

## 2. Housing benefits

**Housing Benefit (means tested)**
You may be able to get help from your local council, whether you are working or not, if you find it hard to pay your full rent or rates. If you are a council tenant you can apply for rent rebate, or if a private tenant, a rent allowance. You can apply for rate rebate whether you are a council or a private tenant or an owner occupier. The amount of help you get depends on how much money you have got coming in, the size of your family, and how much rent and rates you have to pay.

(Source: *Which Benefit?* DHSS/CSO Nov 84)

a ▷ Where should people apply for housing benefit?
   ▷ Under what circumstances should people apply for housing benefit?
b Which people may be entitled to a rent rebate and which people may be entitled to a rent allowance?
c ▷ List *three* things that will help to decide how much people may be paid in housing benefit.
   ▷ List *three* other social security benefits available only to people on low incomes.
d What is the difference between a means-tested benefit and social security benefits that are not means-tested?
e How might the UK social security system be criticised?

# UNIT 7.2　Government income

**FOCUS**

▶ What is a **direct tax**?

▶ What is an **indirect tax**?

▶ What are the major direct and indirect taxes that the government uses to raise revenue?

▶ What are the qualities of a 'good' tax?

## Taxation

The government spends roughly £140,000 million of our money each year. Most of the money to finance this comes from taxation, with smaller amounts being raised from sources such as rents and interest. The government fails to raise all the finance it needs to cover its spending, so it has to borrow the difference.

A tax is a sum of money that someone has to pay to the government. In this section we will be looking more carefully at taxation.

## Direct taxes

Direct taxes are taxes on money received, i.e. on income. They are paid straight to the Inland Revenue (a department of the government) by the taxpayer, or, if you are an employee paying income tax, they are paid through your employer. Here are some of the main direct taxes:

▶ **1 Income tax**

This is a tax on income you receive in various ways. You are taxed on income from your employment, income earned on investment (for example interest on a savings account), income from pensions, and income from various other sources. Income tax is worked out and paid in the following way:

▷ **a** Taxpayers pay income tax on their **taxable income**. Taxable income is a person's total or **gross income** minus any allowances. Allowances are amounts of income a person can earn without paying any tax on them.

**Figure 7.2a**
The main allowances 1986–87

| Allowance | Amount | Comment |
|---|---|---|
| Single person | £2,335 | You can claim this as soon as you start work, providing you are single. |
| Married man | £3,655 | This can be claimed by a married man being taxed jointly with his wife. |
| Wife's earned income | £2,335 | If husband and wife are taxed together, the wife can earn this amount before paying tax. |
| Additional personal | £1,320 | This is added to a person's single person's allowance in certain circumstances e.g. if a single person is looking after a child. |
| Expenses | | Certain expenses related to a person's work can be claimed as a sort of allowance. These could include any special tools or clothing used in the work. |

There are other allowances, including allowances for blind people, keeping a housekeeper etc.

▷ **b** Most taxpayers in 1986–87 paid tax at the basic or standard rate of 29% of taxable income. Figure 7.2b shows that if you earned taxable income over £17,200 in 1986–87 you had to pay extra tax. For example, if someone earning £41,200 worth of taxable income gets a £1,000 pay rise, they will have to pay 60 per cent of the extra £1,000 in income tax.

**Figure 7.2b**
Higher rates of income tax 1986–87

| Amount of taxable income | Tax Payable |
|---|---|
| £17,201 – £20,200 | 40% |
| £20,201 – £25,400 | 45% |
| £25,401 – £33,300 | 50% |
| £33,301 – £41,200 | 55% |
| £41,201 and over | 60% |

Here is an example which shows how the tax is worked out for a single person earning £5,000 per year.

| | |
|---|---|
| Gross income | £5,000 |
| − Allowances | £2,335 |
| = Taxable Income | £2,665 |
| Tax at 29% of taxable income | £772.85 |

This person has to pay about 15.5 per cent of gross income in tax.

▷ **c** Employees pay tax by the **Pay As You Earn** (PAYE) method. This means that the employer takes the tax from the wages or salaries of his or her workers before paying the salaries.

▷ **d** Each year the Inland Revenue sends employees a 'Notice of Coding' slip. This shows the employee's PAYE Code. This code is three numbers followed by a letter, for example 223L. The three numbers are the amount of the employee's allowances, minus the last number. The letter shows what type of taxpayer the employee is. For example, a code of 233L means allowances of £2,335 per year, and the taxpayer is a single person. Employees are asked to check their Notice of Coding to make sure that they are not going to pay too much tax.

▷ **e** Self-employed people, and people with more complicated tax positions, have to fill in an income tax return each year showing their total income and allowances.

▶ **2 Corporation tax**

This is a tax on company profits. This tax has been reduced gradually over recent years, becoming by 1986–87 35 per cent of taxable profits. At the same time certain allowances that could be claimed against corporation tax are being reduced or ended. These are mainly allowances for erecting industrial buildings and putting in capital equipment.

▶ **3 Capital gains tax**

This is a tax on profits or gains made when people sell certain things, like property or shares. Some things are let off or exempt, and these include profits made from selling your own home or car. In 1986–87 the first £6,300 of capital gains made were not liable for capital gains tax.

▶ **4 Inheritance tax (capital transfer tax up to 1986)**

This is a tax payable mainly on gifts made at death. Any gifts made within seven years of death are taxable on a sliding scale. In 1986 gifts up to £71,000 made at death were not subject to this tax, but gifts over that amount were taxable at rates from 30 per cent, up to 60 per cent for gifts worth over £317,000.

▶ **5 North Sea oil taxes**

Companies that extract oil from the North Sea have to pay extra tax on the profits that they make.

▶ **6 National Insurance contributions**

Employees, employers and the government pay into the National Insurance Fund. Payments are compulsory, and therefore National Insurance is a kind of tax. The payments or contributions go towards paying benefits for workers when they are off work. These are described in more detail in Unit 7.1 on the social security system.

**Figure 7.2c**
What is the name given to the tax on gifts made in a will?

▶ **7 Rates**

Rates are a tax paid to local authorities by people who own property. Rates are one of three basic ways in which local authorities raise finance, and the importance of the different ways are shown in Fig. 7.2d. **Rate Support Grant** is money paid to local authorities from the central government out of general taxation, and fees and charges include things like council house rents and swimming pool charges. Rates are worked out as follows:

▷ **a** Each property is given a **rateable value**, which is supposed to be what the property could be rented out for.

# Unit 7.2 Government income

▷ **b** The rates paid on a property are worked out by multiplying the rateable value of the property by **the rate** which is set by the local authority. For example, if the rateable value of a property is £300, and the rate is announced as being '80p in the pound', then the rates payable would be 300 × 80p = £240 for the year. Rates can be over a pound in the pound. A rate of £2.20 in the pound means that the rate payable would be 300 × £2.20 = £660 for the year.

In recent years central government has been trying to gain more control over local government spending. It has attempted to reduce the percentage of local government finance coming from the Rate Support Grant. It has tried to limit rate rises, by using **rate-capping** to keep down rate increases in some authorities.

**Figure 7.2d**
How local government raised revenue in 1983–84

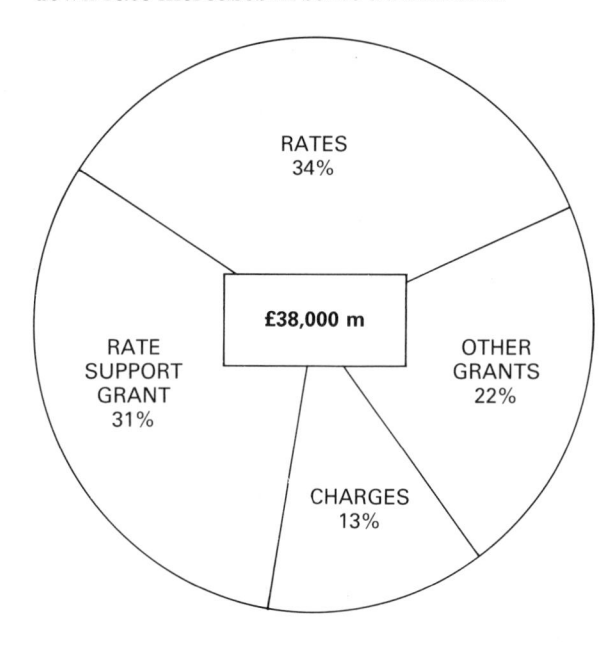

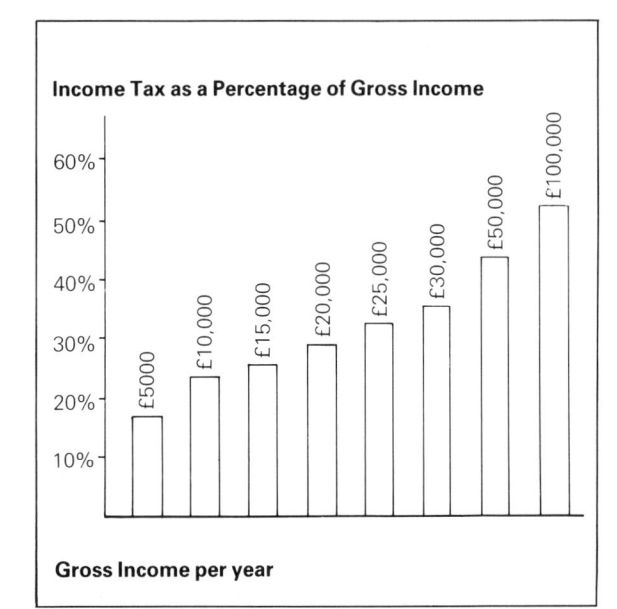

**Figure 7.2e**
The income tax paid by a single person (with no other allowances) at different income levels

## Indirect taxes

Indirect taxes are taxes on money spent, i.e. on **expenditure**. Indirect taxes are paid to the Customs and Excise Department.

▶ **1 Value-Added Tax (VAT)**

This is a tax paid by final consumers at 15 per cent of the price of most things they buy. Value-added tax is not paid on some goods like children's clothing and newspapers.

VAT is also paid by producers of goods and services on the factors of production that they use. Producers, however, can claim back any VAT they have paid, so the tax is paid only by the final consumer.

▶ **2 Customs and Excise duties**

**Customs duties** are paid on some goods entering Britain from other countries. **Excise duties** are indirect taxes on goods sold in the country. The main excise duties are placed on the sale of cigarettes, alcoholic drink, petrol, and on betting.

## Other taxes

There are several other types of taxes. These include various licences such as TV and car licences, and stamp duty on certain legal documents.

## The principles of taxation

It has been said that a government should bear certain things in mind when deciding what makes a good tax. These things are called the principles of taxation, and they include:

▶ **1 Taxes should be fair**

This sounds simple enough, but fairness can mean different things to different people. Here are three different ways in which a tax could be said to be fair:

▷ **a** The tax takes an increasing proportion of a person's income as he or she gets richer. This kind of tax is called a **progressive tax**. Income tax is progressive. If you earn about £5,000 a year you will probably pay no more than 17 per cent of your income in income tax. If you earn £50,000 a year, you may well pay over 40 per cent of your income in income tax.

▷ **b** The tax takes the same amount of money from everyone. This kind of tax is called a **regressive tax**. Indirect taxes are regressive. If a rich man buys a packet of cigarettes he pays exactly the same amount of tax as a poor man. The tax is a far smaller percentage of the richer person's income than of the poorer person's income, however, and this makes the tax regressive.

▷ **c** The tax takes the same proportion of everyone's income. This kind of tax is called a **proportional tax**. For most workers National Insurance contributions are proportional to their incomes.

▶ **2 Taxes should be easy to understand**

If a tax is a good tax, people will understand how

to pay it, when they have to pay it, and how much they have to pay.

▶ **3 Taxes should be easy and cheap to collect**

A good tax will collect a great deal of money for the government compared to the cost of collecting it.

▶ **4 Taxes should preserve incentives**

A good tax will not put people off work because of the amount of tax they have to pay. Some people say that the higher rates of income tax act as a disincentive to people to work really hard and become rich.

### Direct or indirect taxes?

Economists and politicians have often talked about whether direct taxes on our incomes are better than indirect taxes on our spending. There are advantages to both types of tax, and here are some of the possible advantages of each:

▶ **1 The advantages of direct taxes**

▷ **a** They can be made progressive, and many people think that this is fairer on poorer people. In a country with progressive taxes, incomes are likely to be more evenly spread than in a country without progressive taxes.

▷ **b** They can be increased to raise more money for the government without raising prices. Indirect tax increases, for example an increase on cigarette taxes, pushes up the Retail Prices Index and increases inflation. A rise in income tax, however, does not raise prices.

▶ **2 The advantages of indirect taxes**

▷ **a** They cannot be avoided easily. Some people can find ways around paying many direct taxes, but it is almost impossible to dodge paying indirect taxes, especially for employees.

▷ **b** You have a choice about whether you pay indirect taxes. You can cut down the amount of indirect taxes you pay simply by cutting down your spending.

▷ **c** Unlike direct taxes, indirect taxes do not put people off working and saving; they do not act as a disincentive to work and saving. People often complain that that it is not worth working harder because you lose so much of any increase in wages in income tax. In addition, you are taxed on any of your income you choose to save.

▷ **d** Indirect taxes can be used to put people off buying certain goods. In 1984, for example, the government increased the price of cigarettes greatly by increasing indirect taxes on them. It was hoped that this would put some people off smoking as well as bring in more money for the government.

**Figure 7.2f**
Why might this miser prefer a tax system that has only indirect taxes?

Unit 7.2 *Government income*

## DATABASE

## Public money, 1986–87: where it comes from (% of total govt. income to nearest %)

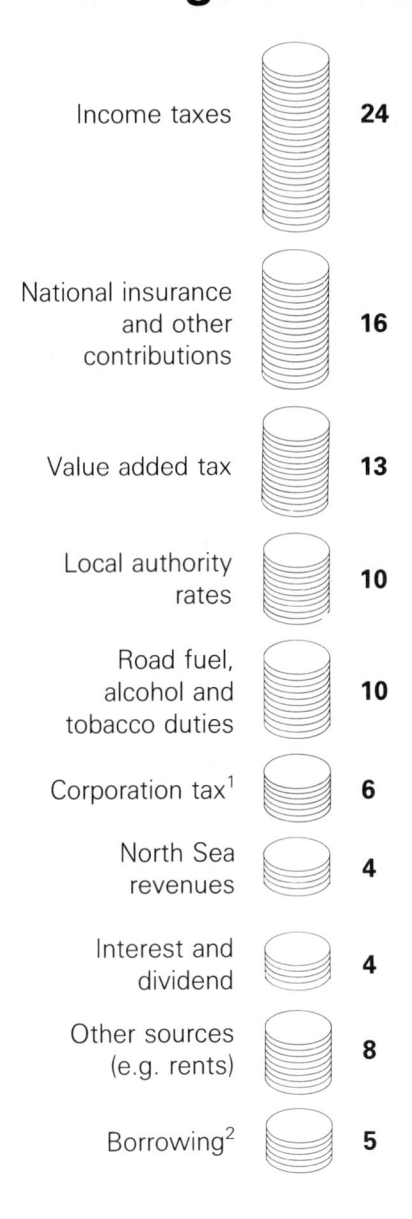

| Source | % |
|---|---|
| Income taxes | 24 |
| National insurance and other contributions | 16 |
| Value added tax | 13 |
| Local authority rates | 10 |
| Road fuel, alcohol and tobacco duties | 10 |
| Corporation tax[1] | 6 |
| North Sea revenues | 4 |
| Interest and dividend | 4 |
| Other sources (e.g. rents) | 8 |
| Borrowing[2] | 5 |

Cash total of revenue £163 billion
[1] excluding North Sea
[2] by central and local government

(Source: *Economic Progress Report Supplement* March–April 1986)

## ACTIVITIES

### SECTION A: FOCUS ON UNIT 7.2

Go back and answer the questions raised in the Focus.

### SECTION B: STEPPED QUESTIONS

1. **a** What name is given to:
   - taxes on income?
   - taxes on spending?
   
   **b** Explain which taxes are paid by the following people and whether they are direct or indirect taxes:
   - Mike earns £12,000 per year. He has a car and likes to eat, drink, smoke and bet on horses.
   - Margaret is unemployed. She can only afford to go out on a Friday night when she has a pint of beer and fish and chips.
   - Anne earns £7,000 a year. She has just bought a car, and has given up smoking to pay for it.
   - Edgar has inherited his father's very profitable business. He likes to buy and sell shares. He earns about £60,000 per year.
   
   **c** Imagine that the government decides to end income tax, and increase VAT and all duties by large amounts. Explain how this change would affect:
   - low income families
   - people who spend very little but save a great deal
   - foreign tourists in the UK.
   
   **d** Would you be in favour of the change in **c**? Give reasons for your answer.

2. **a** What is:
   - a progressive tax?
   - a proportional tax?
   
   **b** How do progressive taxes alter the distribution of income?
   
   **c** How are taxes on expenditure regressive?

## SECTION C: DATA RESPONSE QUESTION

### Taxation in different countries

|  | Total tax revenue as % of GDP | |
|---|---|---|
|  | 1970 | 1982 |
| Sweden | 40.7 | 50.3 |
| Holland | 39.9 | 45.4 |
| France | 35.6 | 43.7 |
| Britain | 37.5 | 40.0 |
| Germany | 32.8 | 37.0 |
| Italy | 27.9 | 33.7 |
| USA | 30.1 | 31.2 |
| Japan | 19.7 | 26.9 |

(Source: *The Economist* 3.12.83)

a  What is meant by GDP?
b  In which country in 1982 was the revenue collected by the government over half the value of GDP?
c  What has been the general trend in taxation as a percentage of GDP in all the countries shown between 1970 and 1982?
d  Which country had the smallest growth in taxation compared to GDP over the period?
e  Give *two* advantages and *two* disadvantages of increased taxation.

**EXTENSION MATERIAL**

**Figure 7.2g**
The PSBR in recent years

## The Public Sector Borrowing Requirement

It is rare for the public sector (mainly central and local government, and nationalised industries) to raise enough from taxation, interest on investments, and fees and charges to meet all its spending requirements. As a result the public sector has to borrow from British citizens, and sometimes from overseas, to cover its spending. The amount that the public sector has to borrow in a year is called the **Public Sector Borrowing Requirement**.

In recent years the PSBR has been about £7,000 million to £10,000 million a year, but the PSBR relative to Gross Domestic Product (the value of goods and services produced in the country in a year) has been falling. This is shown in Fig. 7.2g.

| Year | Total | As a % of GDP |
|---|---|---|
| 1979–80 | £ 9.9 bn | 4.9 |
| 1980–81 | £13.2 bn | 5.7 |
| 1981–82 | £ 8.7 bn | 3.4 |
| 1982–83 | £ 9.1 bn | 3.2 |
| 1983–84 | £ 9.4 bn | 3.25 |
| 1984–85 | £10.1 bn | 3.1 |
| 1985–86 | £ 7.0 bn | 2.0 |

The Conservative government elected in 1979 and 1983 pledged to reduce the PSBR. This government believed that both of the two methods they could use to finance the PSBR were unacceptable. The two methods were as follows:

▶ 1 The government can borrow direct from the banking system by selling short-term securities called **Treasury Bills**. The banking system creates new bank deposits to pay for these (this creation of credit is explained later in Unit 7.4), adding to the supply of money in the economy, and adding to inflationary pressures.

▶ 2 The government can sell longer-term securities outside the banking system, drawing on people's savings and not raising the supply of money. However, the government may need to raise interest rates to attract funds because it is competing for them with individuals and businesses, and this can be harmful to business investment.

The government's opposition, especially the Labour Party, have argued that more public borrowing can mean more public spending, more jobs, more taxes, fewer unemployment benefit payments, and ultimately a smaller PSBR. They believe that the government should use public borrowing and increased public spending to offset the effects of a depression by creating employment.

## The National Debt

The National Debt is the total outstanding borrowing of the central government. It is part of the debt of the entire public sector, which includes the borrowing of local government and nationalised industries. In 1984 the National Debt stood at £131,000 million. The National Debt is made up of three main types of borrowing, and these are shown in Fig. 7.2h.

**The 3 Types of Borrowing**

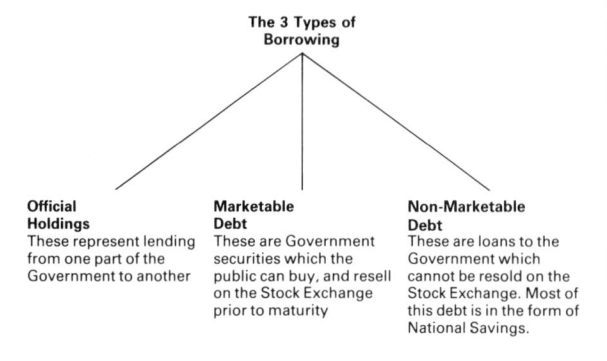

- **Official Holdings**: These represent lending from one part of the Government to another
- **Marketable Debt**: These are Government securities which the public can buy, and resell on the Stock Exchange prior to maturity
- **Non-Marketable Debt**: These are loans to the Government which cannot be resold on the Stock Exchange. Most of this debt is in the form of National Savings.

**Figure 7.2h**
The National Debt

Most of the National Debt is held by large institutions with a great deal of cash to invest, like pension funds, insurance companies and unit trusts.

### Does a rising National Debt matter?

Many people seem concerned that the amount of outstanding debt increases each year. This is not necessarily a problem, for the following reasons:

▶ 1 If the government borrows from one person or group of people within the country, it repays the loan eventually by taxing or borrowing from someone else within the community. The National Debt *transfers* income from one group to another, and does not necessarily make the community as a whole worse off.

▶ 2 If there is inflation, the National Debt becomes easier for the government to repay. If the government borrowed £1,000 for ten years at the beginning of the 1970s, the £1,000 when repaid in the 1980s would be worth about a fifth of its value when it was first borrowed.

▶ 3 If the government borrows from overseas, the country will be better off when the loan is received, because it has extra resources to use, but it will be worse off when the loan is repaid.

It can be seen, therefore, that a rising National Debt does not actually drain resources from the community as whole. It

**EXTENSION MATERIAL 7**

should be remembered, however, that high borrowing in any one year can have undesirable effects. These were described in the earlier section on the PSBR. The government is more likely to worry about the size of the PSBR in any one year than they are about the total outstanding Debt.

**EXTENSION QUESTION 7**

Questions

a What is meant by the PSBR?
b How can the PSBR be financed?
c What are the likely economic effects of a rising PSBR?
d What is the difference between the National Debt and the PSBR?
e Is a rising national debt necessarily a problem? Explain your answer.

# UNIT 7.3 The National Income

**FOCUS**

▶ What is the **National Income**?

▶ What categories of spending make up the National Income?

▶ What methods can be used to measure National Income?

▶ Is the National Income a good measure of general welfare?

## The circular flow of income

The **National Income** is the flow of all the goods and services produced in a country over a year.

The **circular flow of income** is a means of showing in a very simple way how the National Income is created, and how it can be measured. We start off by imagining that the country is made up of only two groups of people. The two groups are called 'households' and 'firms'. A household is any person or group of people who buys consumer goods and services and who supplies factors of production to firms who produce these goods and services. Households are paid wages, interest, dividends and rent for providing labour, capital, enterprise and land. A firm is any person or group of people that owns a private business and sells goods and services to households.

Figure 7.3a shows how the two groups are linked together.

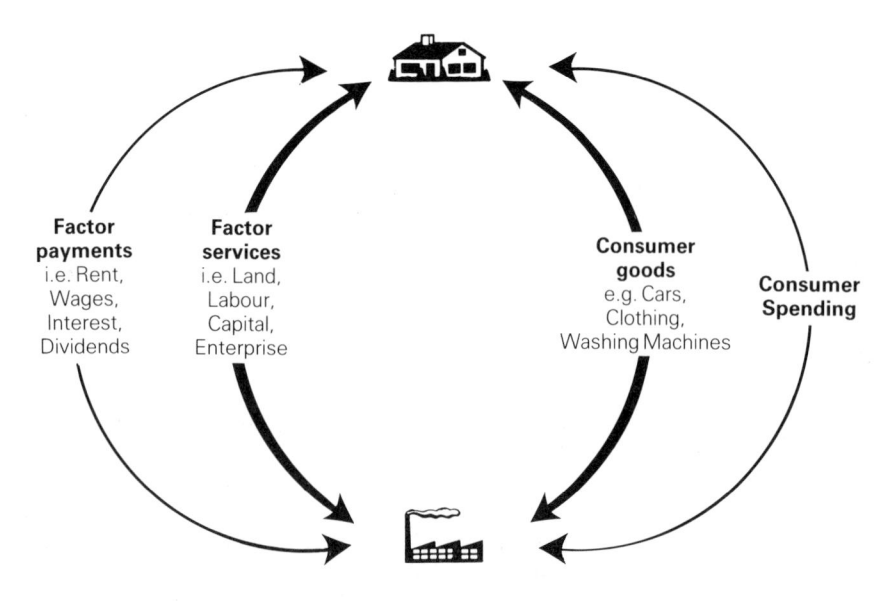

In our simple circular flow you can see the following:
▶ 1 There is no government, and no trade with other countries.
▶ 2 Households spend all their income on buying consumer goods. They do not save or pay taxes.
▶ 3 Firms use all the money earned from selling goods to pay the factors of production. They do not retain any profit for investment, nor do they pay any taxes.

### A more detailed circular flow

The real world does not include just households and firms. Figure 7.3b shows a circular flow which is more realistic. Here are some of the ways in which the real world is different from the simplest version of the circular flow:
▶ 1 Households do not spend their income just on buying goods made by British firms. They spend some of their income on goods imported from foreign countries, they save some of their income, and they pay taxes to the government from their income.
▶ 2 Firms buy capital goods from each other for investment. Firms do not pay all the income they receive to households in Britain for the factors of production they provide. They use some of their income for investment (retained profits), they pay company taxes, and they buy imports from abroad.
▶ 3 The government is involved in the economy, both buying and selling goods and services.
▶ 4 Other countries' citizens buy goods and services from the UK (our exports), and sell goods and services to the UK (our imports).

As a result of all this, you can see from Fig. 7.3b that households will not pass on all their income to firms in the form of consumer spending. Some income is held back from firms, and withdrawn from the circular flow of income. Household savings, taxes and import spending are called **withdrawals** from the circular flow. In the same way, sums of income that firms do not pass on to households are also withdrawals. These withdrawals are retained profits, company taxes, and import spending.

Firms receive some income from other firms

**Figure 7.3a**
The diagram shows households providing factors of production to firms, and receiving factor payments in return. It shows households buying consumer goods from firms, the payments for which are called 'consumer spending'

Factor payments
i.e. Rent, Wages, Interest, Dividends

Factor services
i.e. Land, Labour, Capital, Enterprise

Consumer goods
e.g. Cars, Clothing, Washing Machines

Consumer Spending

# Unit 7.3 *The National Income*

**A More Detailed Circular Flow of Income**

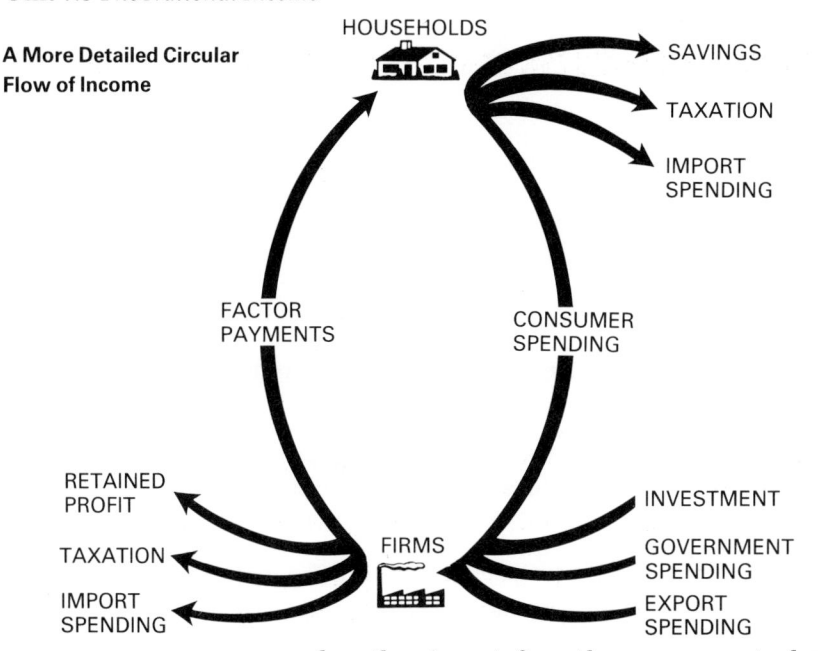

**Figure 7.3b**
A more detailed circular flow of income

when they invest, from the government when it purchases goods and services and from foreign citizens when they buy British goods and services. Incomes that a firm receives from sources other than consumer spending are called **injections**.

### The significance of the circular flow of income

▶ 1 The circular flow diagram shows how National Income can be seen as a 'flow' of goods and services around an economy, and a 'flow' of income to households and firms to pay for goods and services. The National Income is never fixed, but constantly changing.

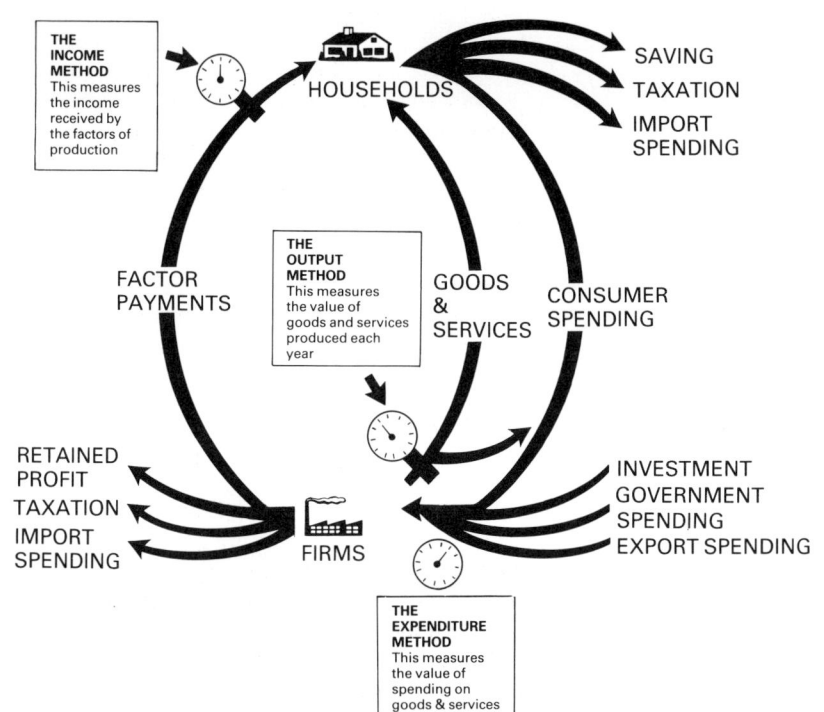

▶ 2 The model shows that National Income can be increased by injecting more into the circular flow by raising government spending, by raising investment, or by raising exports. It shows that National Income can be reduced by increasing withdrawals by increasing saving, taxation or imports.

▶ 3 The diagram shows that National Income will not change if injections equal withdrawals, it will be **in equilibrium**.

▶ 4 The diagram suggests that the government may be able to influence the economy by adopting policies which affect the level of injections and withdrawals.

## Measuring the National Income

In our simple circular flow the value of the goods produced – the National Income – could be measured in three ways, each giving the same result. Figure 7.3c shows the three places we could measure the National Income, and here is a brief explanation of the three methods of measurement:

▶ 1 **The income method**
This method involves asking people what income they earned from providing factors of production to firms.

▶ 2 **The expenditure method**
This method involves finding out what was spent over the year on goods and services.

▶ 3 **The output method**
This method involves finding out from firms the value of goods and services they produced over the year.

In the real world the government uses these three methods of measuring the National Income, but all kinds of adjustments have to be made. The real world is far more complicated than our simple circular flow. The government publishes three figures each year as a result of measuring the National Income:

▶ 1 **The Gross Domestic Product (GDP)**
This is basically a measure of the value of goods and services produced each year by the UK economy, within the boundaries of the UK. So it includes export earnings but excludes income from factories owned by UK citizens abroad.

▶ 2 **The Gross National Product (GNP)**
This is GDP, plus any income earned by UK citizens from overseas investments, but minus investment earnings by foreign citizens in Britain.

▶ 3 **The National Income, or Net National Product (NNP)**
This is basically GNP minus **depreciation**. Depreciation includes goods provided to replace goods which have worn out. These goods do not *add* to the total wealth of the country and are therefore not included in the final National Income figure.

**Figure 7.3c**
The three methods of measuring the National Income

## The National Income and the general welfare

We tend to believe that a rise in the National Income means we are better off because more goods and services are being produced. However, there are some problems that arise in assuming that a country increases its welfare when it increases its National Income. Here are some of them:

▶ 1 If the population rises more quickly than the National Income, then there will be fewer goods for each person in the population. National Income *per head* is a better measure of the welfare of a country than the total national income figure.

▶ 2 A rise in National Income may make just a few people better off, without helping the majority of the population. In some countries, like countries in the Middle East which produce oil, the National Income per head is high, but many people are still very poor.

▶ 3 The National Income is measured in money terms. If prices are rising, the National Income will rise even if the country is not producing any more goods and services.

▶ 4 The National Income can rise as a result of the production of goods and services which do not directly make us feel better off, for example investment goods for industry, or weapons for the armed forces.

▶ 5 The National Income or output of the whole economy is very difficult to measure accurately, so a small change in the National Income may simply be due to inaccurate measurement. Also the figures exclude production in the **black economy** which is not officially recorded, for example cash payments for services which are not recorded to avoid payment of tax.

**Figure 7.3d**
How can a country have a high national income and a lot of poor people?

# DATABASE

## National Income per head

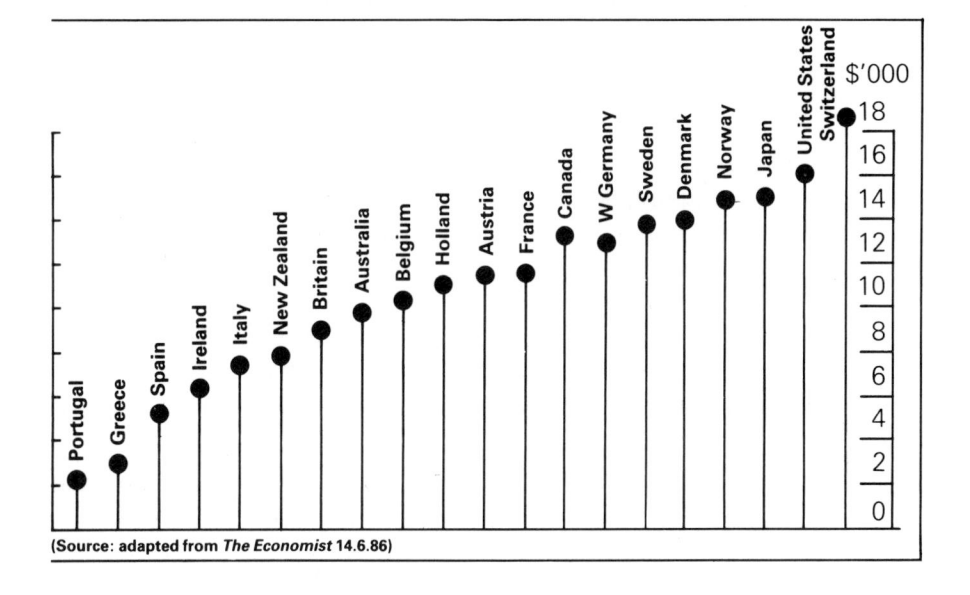

| Country | $'000 |
|---|---|
| Portugal | ~2 |
| Greece | ~3 |
| Spain | ~4 |
| Ireland | ~5 |
| Italy | ~6 |
| New Zealand | ~7 |
| Britain | ~7 |
| Australia | ~8 |
| Belgium | ~8 |
| Holland | ~9 |
| Austria | ~9 |
| France | ~10 |
| Canada | ~11 |
| W Germany | ~11 |
| Sweden | ~12 |
| Denmark | ~13 |
| Norway | ~14 |
| Japan | ~14 |
| United States | ~15 |
| Switzerland | ~18 |

(Source: adapted from *The Economist* 14.6.86)

## ACTIVITIES

### SECTION A: FOCUS ON UNIT 7.3

Go back and answer the questions raised in the Focus.

### SECTION B: STEPPED QUESTIONS

1. **a** If a newspaper headline says 'UK National Income increased last year by two per cent', what does this mean?
   **b** What is meant by 'the circular flow of income'?
   **c** National Income, National Output and National Expenditure should always be equal. Why is this?
   **d** Explain how the circular flow of income works. Include 'injections' and 'withdrawals' in your answer.

2. **a** What is meant by:
   ▷ Gross Domestic Product (GDP)
   ▷ Gross National Product (GNP)
   ▷ Net National Product (NNP)?
   **b** How would a rise in the amount of profits sent to Ford (USA) by Ford (UK) affect the:
   ▷ UK GDP
   ▷ UK GNP?
   **c** Does a rise in National Income always mean that a country's citizens are better off? Explain your answer.

### SECTION C: DATA RESPONSE QUESTIONS

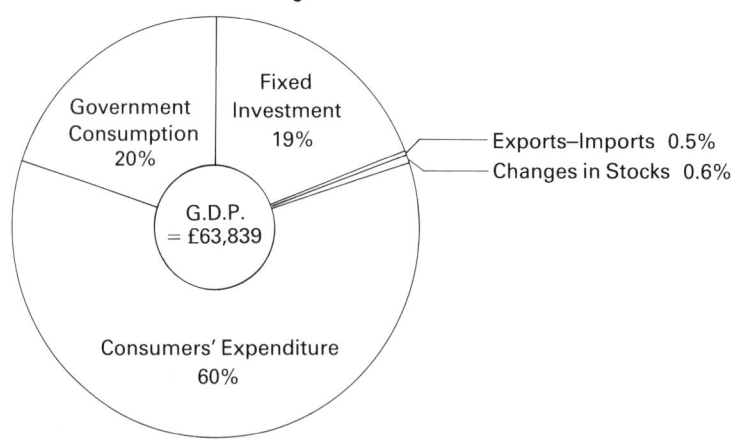

Government Consumption 20%
Fixed Investment 19%
Exports–Imports 0.5%
Changes in Stocks 0.6%
G.D.P. = £63,839
Consumers' Expenditure 60%

(Source: *EPR* 1986)

**a** Over what period of time were these figures calculated?
**b** Into which category would the following fall?
  ▷ the purchase of a British-made fridge
  ▷ the purchase of stationery from a UK firm for use in schools
  ▷ the purchase of a Japanese personal stereo set by a household
  ▷ the building of a new hospital by the government.
**c** Which was the greater, imports or exports? Explain your answer.
**d** Which *two* categories consist only of spending on capital goods? Explain your answer.
**e** Explain how a rise in the following would affect national income:
  ▷ investment
  ▷ income taxes
  ▷ savings.

## Unit 7.3 The National Income

**EXTENSION MATERIAL**

### Factor incomes

This section considers what determines the rewards or **returns** earned by each factor of production.

### Wages

Wages are the price that an employer pays for employing labour. Wages are the 'return' to the factor of production called labour. Like other prices, they are determined by the demand and supply for the commodities and services being traded, the service in this case being the factor service of labour. This is shown in Fig. 7.3e.

**Figure 7.3e**
The wage rate in a particular industry

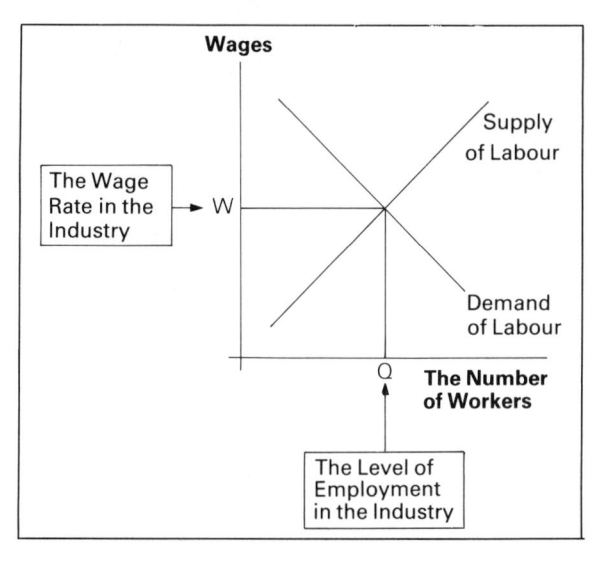

### The demand for labour

The demand curve for labour for a particular industry slopes down and to the right. It shows that employers are willing and able to hire more workers as wages fall. The industry will employ workers as long as the employment of each worker adds more to total revenue than to total cost. Figure 7.3f shows that as wages fall

**Figure 7.3f**
The effect of a fall in the wage rate

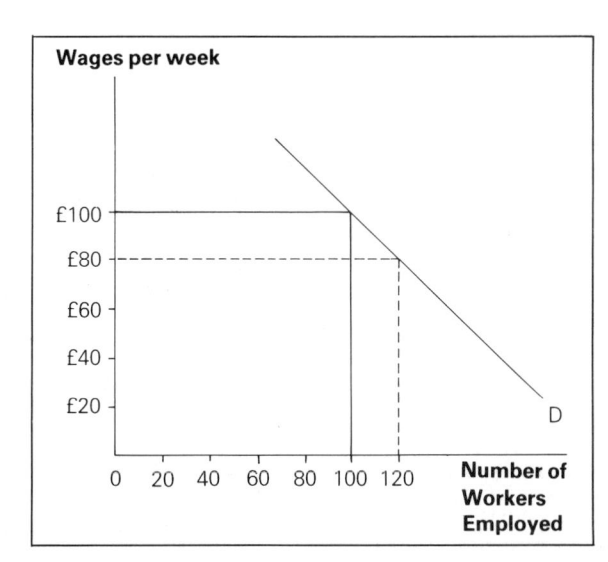

from £100 a week to £80 a week, the industry is willing to employ another 20 workers. This means that each of the workers between the 100th and 121st adds more than £80 a week but less than £100 a week to the industry's total revenue when they are employed. It becomes profitable to employ them at £80 a week, but not at £100 a week.

A change in wages causes a movement *along* the demand curve for labour. There are two main factors which cause a movement *of* the curve:

▷ **1** *A change in the price of the goods and services produced* Labour is a **derived demand**. This means that it is directly related to the demand for the product it makes. If there is a rise in demand for the goods and services produced by labour, there will be a rise in the price of the goods and services. This will increase the revenue generated by employing each worker, and the industry will be willing and able to employ more workers at each wage rate. The demand curve for labour will shift to the right.

▷ **2** *An increase in productivity* If workers produce more goods and services per hour worked, there is said to be a rise in **productivity**. Productivity could be increased by new working practices, or by new machinery. A rise in productivity will increase the revenue generated by each worker's activity, and will cause a rise in demand for workers at each wage rate. The demand curve for labour will shift to the right.

**Figure 7.3g**
A rise in demand for labour will mean that the industry could be willing to employ more workers at the original wage of £100 a week, or they could be willing to increase the wages of the existing workforce by £20 a week.

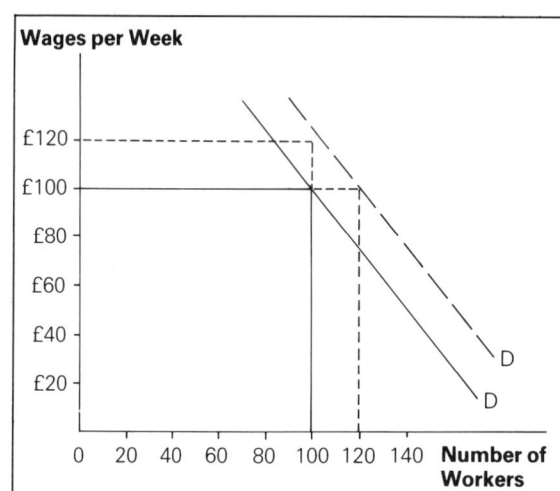

### The supply of labour

The supply curve for labour to a particular industry slopes up and to the right because more workers will be more willing to work in the industry as wages rise.

**EXTENSION MATERIAL**

A change in wages causes a movement *along* the supply curve for workers. The *elasticity* of supply and *position* of the supply curve will be determined by how easily workers can join an industry: by their **mobility**. If workers are able easily to join an industry, the supply curve will tend to be more elastic, indicating that a small rise in wages will attract a considerable number of extra workers. If workers are not easily available, the supply curve will tend to be more inelastic, indicating that a large rise in wages will be needed to attract even a small number of extra workers to the industry.

### The wage rate in a particular industry

The wage rate in a particular industry is determined by the supply and demand for labour in the industry. Figure 7.3h shows the wages of highly skilled workers in an expanding industry. High demand coupled with limited and therefore inelastic supply leads to high wages. Figure 7.3i shows the wages of unskilled workers in a declining industry. Low demand coupled with a potentially large, elastic supply of labour leads to a low wage rate.

**Figure 7.3h**
The wage rate for highly skilled workers in an expanding industry

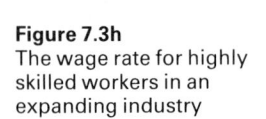

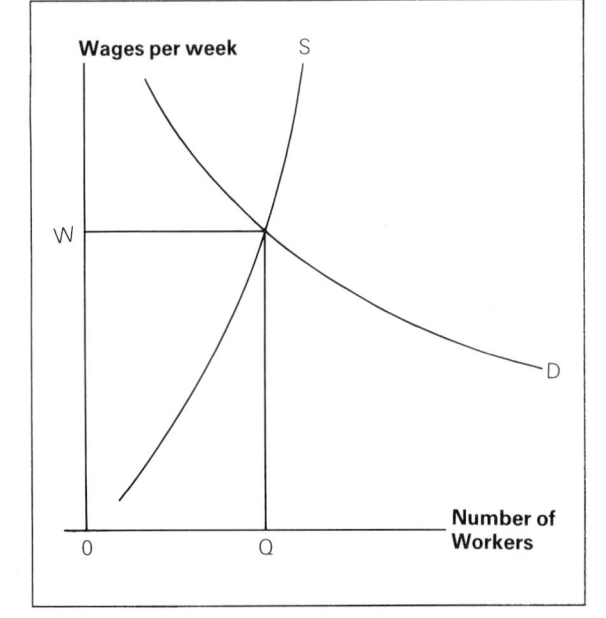

**Figure 7.3i**
The wage rate for unskilled workers in a declining industry

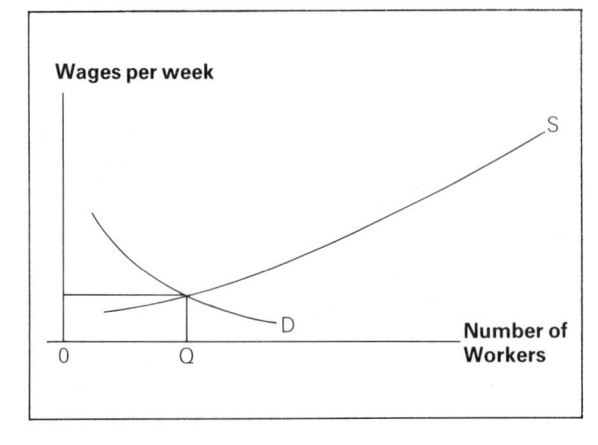

### Rent

Rent is the price of land. It is the return to the factor of production, land. The rent on a piece of land is determined by the supply and demand for land. The area around the Bank of England, for example, is in particularly high demand, causing rents to be over twice as high as other sites just a few miles away.

### Economic rent

Economic rent is an economic idea that can be related to any factor of production, not just land. Economic rent is the surplus earnings of a factor of production over and above the minimum needed to keep the factor in its present use. The amount needed to keep a factor in its present use is called **transfer earnings**, and economic rent is therefore the earnings of a factor above transfer earnings. Figure 7.3k illustrates this. It shows that the teacher earns £10,000 per year, but he would give up his job and take unskilled work if he were paid £7,000 per year. His economic rent is therefore £3,000. The pop star who earns £50,000 a year would also change jobs if she earned under £7,000 per year. Her economic rent is therefore £43,000 a year. The scarcer the supply of labour to a particular industry, the greater is likely to be the economic rent of the workers employed in it.

Factors with only one specialised use, for example a piece of capital equipment designed for a specific purpose, will earn nearly all economic rent. This is because there will be few or no alternative uses to which they can be put.

### Interest

Interest is the price that borrowers pay to savers for borrowing their money. Interest is the return to the factor of production, capital. In the modern British economy there are a whole range of interest rates. Some savings schemes may pay as little as 6½ per cent per year to savers, while others charge borrowers as much as 35 per cent per year. The interest rate in a particular case is determined by a number of factors. These include: the length of the loan, the size of the loan, and the creditworthiness of the borrower.

In an economy, interest rates tend to rise and fall together, and the general level of interest rates is determined by factors such as the total demand for loans, the supply of money and the level of interest rates overseas.

### Profit

Profit is the sum remaining when total costs have been deducted from total revenue. Part of the profit will be used to reward the entrepreneur for taking the risks involved in establishing and running the business. The rest will be used for investment and paying taxes.

## Unit 7.3 The National Income

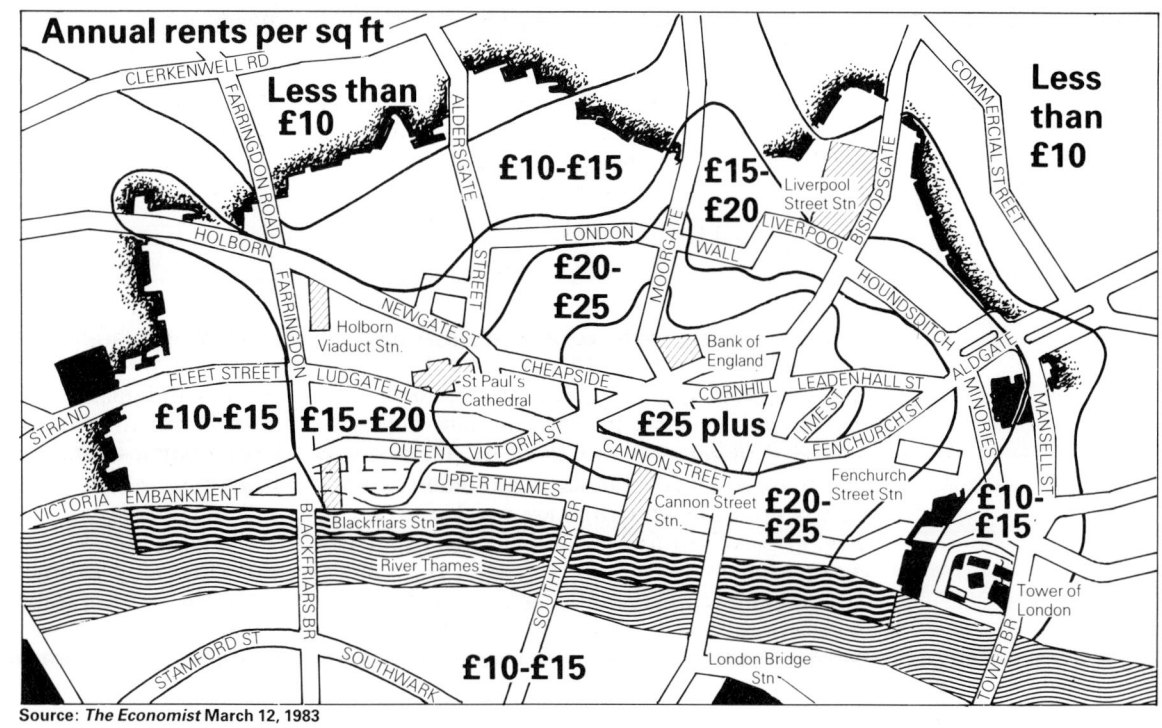

**EXTENSION MATERIAL**

**Figure 7.3j** Rents in London in 1983

Source: *The Economist* March 12, 1983

The amount of profit a firm makes will be affected by the factors which influence total cost and total revenue. These include, on the cost side, the level of wage settlements, the cost of raw materials, and the rate of interest. On the revenue side they are related to the demand for the product, which itself is related to the level of competition, the general state of economic activity, tastes and fashions, and so on.

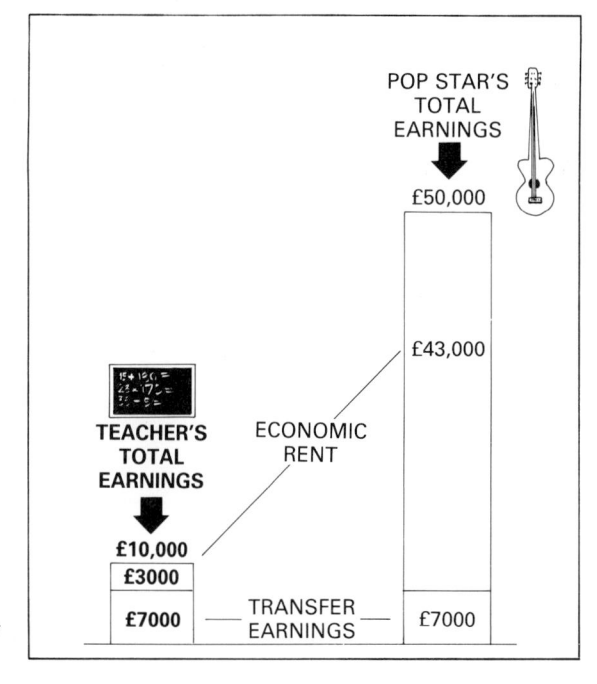

**Figure 7.3k** Economic rent and transfer earnings

**EXTENSION QUESTION**

Questions
1  a  What is a 'derived demand'?
   b  What factors influence the demand for and supply of labour?
   c  ▷ Draw a diagram showing labour demand, labour supply and an equilibrium wage of £80 per week for workers in small textile factories.
      ▷ What factors might cause the wages of these workers to rise?
2  a  Explain what is meant by 'transfer earnings' and 'economic rent'.
   b  What factors might cause the following to change?
      ▷ rents
      ▷ interest rates
      ▷ profits.

# UNIT 7.4 Managing the economy

**FOCUS**

▶ What economic aims can governments have?

▶ What is an **expansionary** or **reflationary** policy?

▶ What is a **contractionary** or **deflationary policy**?

## The economic aims of governments

Every British government of recent years, no matter which political party has been in power, has tried to achieve four basic economic aims. These are a low level of unemployment, a high level of economic growth, a low level of inflation, and a good trading position with overseas countries.

Governments may consider one or two aims as more important than the others. This will depend on their political views, and the seriousness of a particular problem when they come to power.

Labour governments may have a fifth basic economic aim. They may try to reduce the difference in income and wealth between richer people and the less well-off. They may aim to redistribute income and wealth in such a way that it is more evenly spread throughout the population. A Conservative government is unlikely to aim for a further redistribution of income.

**Figure 7.4a**
If the government wishes to reduce unemployment and increase economic growth next year, how might this affect its other aims?

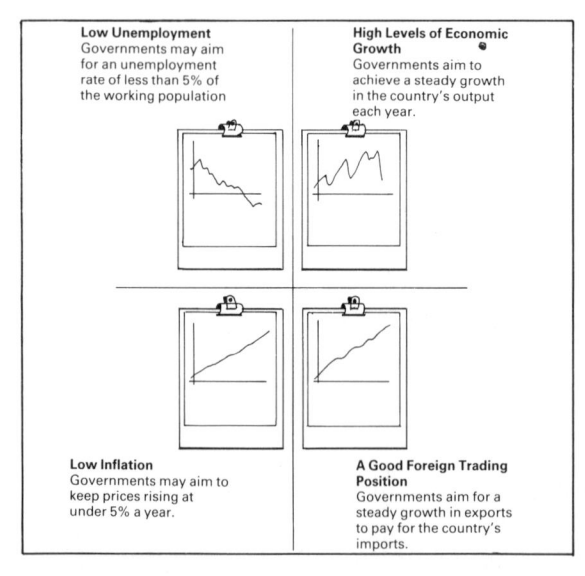

**Low Unemployment**
Governments may aim for an unemployment rate of less than 5% of the working population

**High Levels of Economic Growth**
Governments aim to achieve a steady growth in the country's output each year.

**Low Inflation**
Governments may aim to keep prices rising at under 5% a year.

**A Good Foreign Trading Position**
Governments aim for a steady growth in exports to pay for the country's imports.

## The economic policies of governments

A **policy** is the way in which a government tries to achieve its aims. For example, governments have sometimes tried to keep down wage rises using an incomes policy in order to try and achieve the aim of low inflation.

Although different governments might have the same aims, they often use different policies to try and achieve those aims. Most of the arguments you hear between politicians of different parties tend to be about their economic policies, rather than about their long-term economic aims.

If a government is particularly worried about the rate of unemployment, and the level of economic growth, it may try to increase spending in the economy. More spending can lead to more production and more employment. These policies are known as **expansionary** or **reflationary** policies.

You will notice from Fig. 7.4b that more spending can have bad effects. Some spending will go on imports, which could cause problems for our foreign trade, and there could be shortages of goods and services at home, causing price rises and inflation.

The government can increase spending by cutting taxes, increasing its own spending and by increasing the supply of money in the economy. These methods of raising spending are explained later in the Unit.

If a government is particularly worried about the rate of inflation or the level of imports into the country, it may try to reduce the amount of spending in the economy. If there is less spending in the economy, fewer imports will be bought, and sellers of goods and services will find it increasingly difficult to raise prices. However, less spending could also mean a fall in production and a rise in the level of unemployment.

The government can reduce spending by raising taxes, cutting its own spending, reducing the amount of money in the economy, or by limiting wage rises. The methods of reducing spending are explained later in the Unit. These policies are known as **contractionary** or **deflationary** policies.

Governments can use either monetary policies or fiscal policies to expand or contract the economy. They may also use policies to increase labour mobility and control the growth of incomes to achieve their economic aims.

▶ **1 Policies to control the amount of money in the economy – monetary policies**

Some economists believe that the amount of money in the economy can have a large influence

Unit 7.4 *Managing the economy*

**Figure 7.4b**
What is the opportunity cost of the extra output and employment which may arise from cutting taxes?

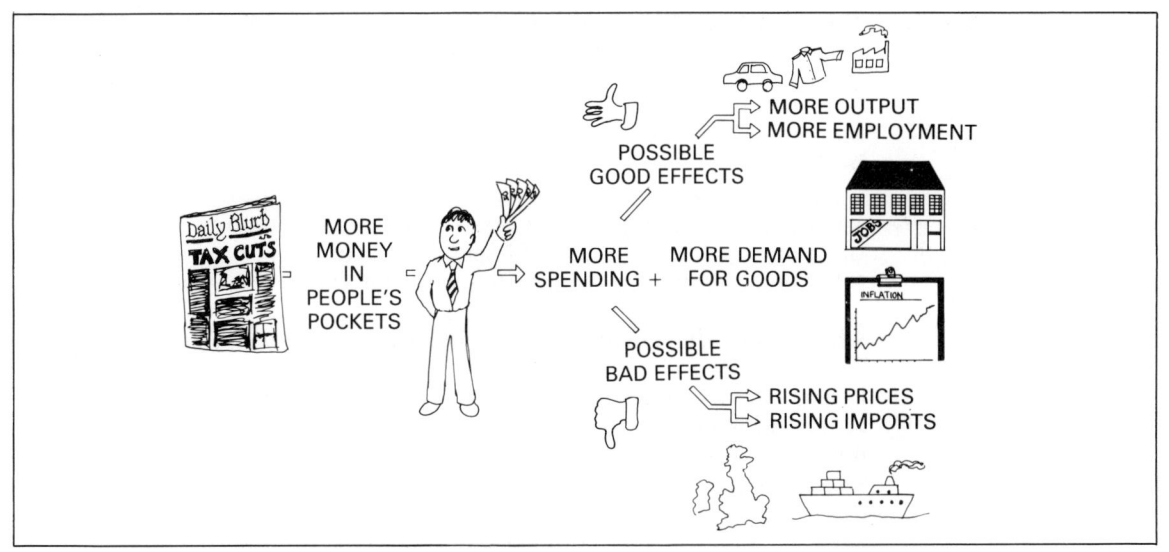

on the level of spending in the economy. The government is said to be using **monetary policy** when it attempts to increase or reduce the amount of money in the economy.

We have seen that the main type of money in a modern economy is bank deposits. Bank deposits are increased when banks lend more, and reduced when banks cut back on their lending. The government can control the amount or supply of money in the economy by controlling bank lending. If the government wishes to reduce the supply of money it can increase interest rates. This will make borrowing more expensive, and fewer people will go to the bank to ask for a loan. On the other hand it can use various methods to reduce the amount that the banks are able to lend, but in the past governments have found it very difficult to do this. Borrowers and lenders have always seemed to find new ways of doing business to get around the controls over lending.

Monetary policy is usually used to reduce spending in the economy in order to reduce inflation and possibly also the level of imports.

**Figure 7.4c**
In what ways can the government control the money supply?

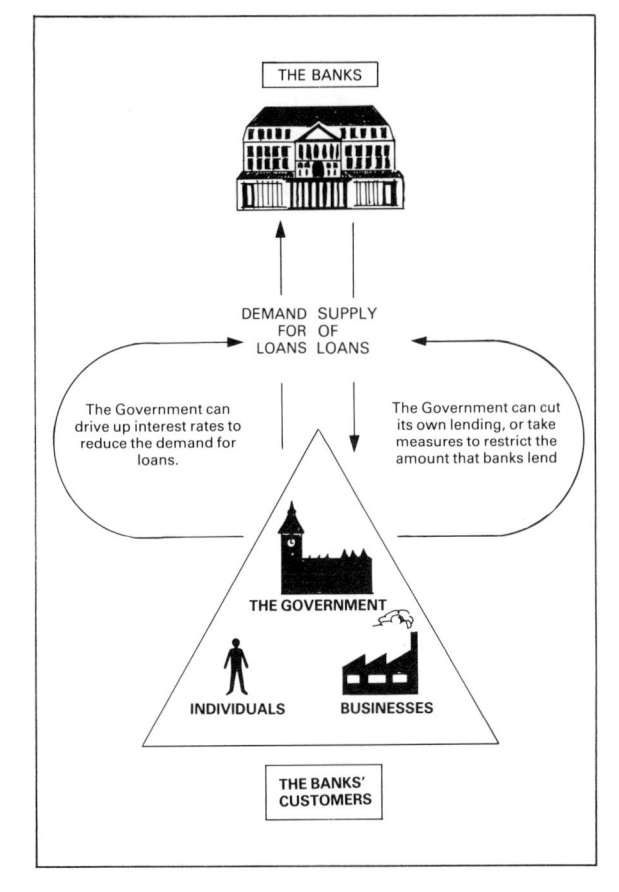

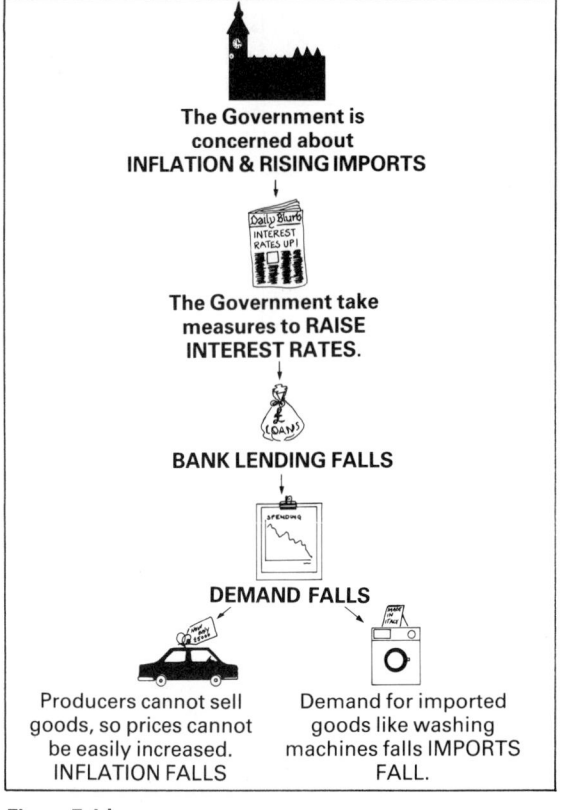

**Figure 7.4d**
How can monetary policy reduce inflation and imports?

### ▶ 2 Policies that involve changing government spending and taxation – fiscal policies

If the government decides to change taxation or government spending in order to achieve its economic aims, then it is said to be using **fiscal policy**.

A rise in government spending using borrowed money rather than increased taxes will expand the economy. More government spending means more employment for people who work for the government, and more work for all the people who supply the government with goods and services. More government spending on education, for example, could affect the whole economy. A cut in taxation, provided government spending is not cut at the same time, will have a similar effect.

A rise in government spending or a cut in taxation may increase production and reduce unemployment, but they may also raise inflation and cause imports to increase. If the government is worried about these problems it may choose to cut government spending and raise taxation. Fiscal policy can be used either to increase or reduce the level of spending in the economy.

Fiscal policy changes are usually made once a year in the **Budget**. The Budget is announced once a year on Budget Day, usually in March or April, by the Chancellor of the Exchequer.

### ▶ 3 Policies to increase the mobility of labour

These are dealt with in Unit 7.5. Successful policies of this type can reduce unemployment and inflation, and increase economic growth.

### ▶ 4 Policies to control the growth of incomes

Wages are usually settled by free collective bargaining between employers and their employees' trade union. At various times in the past the government has stepped in to try and limit the wage rises in the economy. This is called an **incomes policy**.

There have been many different types of incomes policy. Most of them, however, have involved the government setting a maximum percentage by which anyone's wages could rise in a year. Sometimes the incomes policy has been voluntary and has had the backing of the trade union movement. At other times the government has passed an Act of Parliament to limit wage increases. On some occasions the trade unions have insisted that the government controls prices as well as incomes.

Incomes policies have rarely lasted for more than two years because they always seem to run into certain problems. Here are some of them:

▷ **a** An incomes policy involves the government setting an upper limit to the amount of wage increases that workers can receive. Often, however, no union will settle for less than the upper limit, so the upper limit becomes the going rate that everyone expects.

▷ **b** Employers in rapidly growing industries cannot give very large wage rises to attract new workers. Incomes policies may therefore interfere with the mobility of labour.

▷ **c** Employers may be able to give perks and fringe benefits like extra holidays, luncheon vouchers and company cars to make up for lack of large wage rises.

▷ **d** At the end of an incomes policy there tends to be a wage explosion. Everyone tries to get wage rises large enough to make up for any loss of wages during the period of the incomes policy.

## DATABASE

## 1. The government's forecast for the economy after the 1986 Budget

|  | Forecast |
|---|---|
| **A. Output and expenditure at constant 1980 prices** | per cent changes 1985 to 1986 |
| Domestic demand | 3½ |
| of which: | |
|    Consumers' expenditure | 4 |
|    General Government consumption | 1 |
|    Fixed investment | 5 |
|    Change in stockbuilding (as per cent of level of GDP) | 0 |
| Exports of goods and services | 5 |
| Imports of goods and services | 6 |
| Gross domestic product: total | 3 |
|                       manufacturing | 3 |
| **B. Inflation** | |
| *Retail prices index* | per cent changes |
| 1985Q4 to 1986Q4 | 3½ |
| 1986Q2 to 1987Q2 | 3½ |
| **C. Money GDP at market prices** | per cent changes on a year earlier |
| Financial year 1985–86 | 9½ |
| Financial year 1986–87 | 6¾ |
| **D. Balance of payments on current account** | £billion |
| 1986 | 3½ |
| 1987 first half (at an annual rate) | 1½ |
| **E. PSBR** | £billion |
| Financial year 1985–86 | 7 |
| Financial year 1986–87 | 7 |

(Source: *Economic Progress Report Supplement* March–April 1986)

## DATABASE

## 2. Money supply growth and the targets

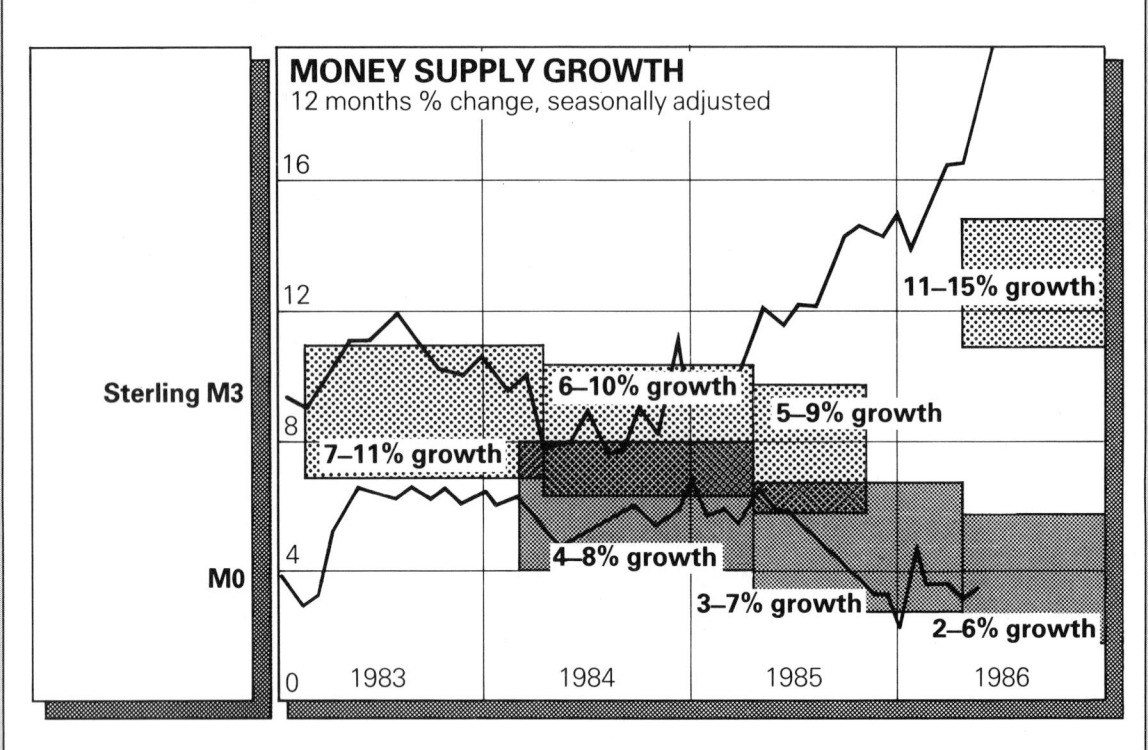

**MONEY SUPPLY GROWTH**
12 months % change, seasonally adjusted

Sterling M3

M0

7–11% growth
6–10% growth
5–9% growth
11–15% growth
4–8% growth
3–7% growth
2–6% growth

1983　1984　1985　1986

(Source: *UK Business Conditions* Royal Bank of Scotland, July 1986 (from government statistics))

# ACTIVITIES

## SECTION A: FOCUS ON UNIT 7.4

Go back and answer the questions raised in the Focus.

## SECTION B: STEPPED QUESTIONS

1. **a** What is the difference between 'reflationary' and 'deflationary' policies?
   **b** State whether the following are expansionary or contractionary, monetary or fiscal policies. For example, increased spending on education: 'expansionary fiscal policy'.
   ▷ an increase in income tax
   ▷ increased spending on infrastructure
   ▷ a reduction in interest rates
   ▷ an increase in value-added tax
   ▷ decreased spending on school textbooks and equipment
   ▷ increased spending on training schemes
   ▷ allowing bank lending to increase
   ▷ printing more money.
   **c** Explain the likely effects of *four* of the policies above on:
   ▷ inflation
   ▷ unemployment
   ▷ economic growth.
2. **a** What is meant by 'incomes policies'?
   **b** Why is it very difficult to make incomes policies work in the long term?
   **c** Explain why economists who advocate expansionary policies think that incomes policies should be used at the same time.

## SECTION C: DATA RESPONSE QUESTION

**The Budget and jobs**
The table below shows the effects of changes in taxation and government spending on unemployment over one year:

|  | Reduction in unemployment |
|---|---|
| £1 billion cut in: | |
|    Income tax | 21,300 |
|    VAT | 17,000 |
|    National Insurance contributions | 16,900 |
| £1 billion increase in: | |
|    Public investment | 38,200 |
|    Current public spending | 65,400 |
|    Special employment measures | 487,800 |

(Source: *British Economy Survey* Autumn 1985)

  a  By how much would unemployment be reduced if income tax was cut by £2 million?
  b  Which is the most effective type of government spending for reducing unemployment in the short term?
  c  What problems might arise from a large increase in spending on special employment measures?
  d  Which type of government spending could produce the biggest improvement in the efficiency of the economy, and so reduce unemployment in the long term? Explain your answer.
  e  Some economists think that cuts in income tax have the biggest effect on the long-term efficiency of the economy. Explain this view.

**EXTENSION MATERIAL**

## The money supply and bank lending

This section looks at how bank lending increases the money supply.

Each bank has a **balance sheet** which is a record of its financial transactions. On the right-hand side of the balance sheet are shown the bank's **assets**. These include cash and claims against other people which could eventually be converted to cash. On the left-hand side of the balance sheet are shown the bank's **liabilities**. These are claims that people have against the bank. Figure 7.4e shows that when someone deposits a sum of cash with the bank it creates

**Figure 7.4e** How credit is created

### BANK BALANCE SHEET.

| LIABILITIES | | ASSETS | |
|---|---|---|---|
| DEPOSITS | £1,000,000 | CASH | £200,000 |
| | | ADVANCES | £800,000 |
| made up of £200,000 worth of accounts for the original depositors of £200,000 cash, plus £800,000 worth of accounts for customers receiving loans | | | |

both an asset and a liability for the bank. The liability is the bank deposit which the bank gives in exchange for cash.

A bank accepts deposits of cash from many thousands of people. It knows that in normal times only a small fraction of deposits will be converted into cash on a given day. The bank can therefore lend out money by creating new bank deposits, without the fear of running out of cash. Figure 7.4e shows the result of lending on a bank's balance sheet. The asset side of the balance sheet shows that the bank has accepted deposits of £200,000 in cash, and given customers bank deposits worth £200,000 in return. In addition, the bank has given loans of £800,000. This lending represents a liability because the customers have a claim on the bank in the form of a bank deposit which, if they chose, they could withdraw in cash. It also represents an asset because the customers will have to repay the bank at some future date.

The ability of the bank to create credit is limited by their need to be prudent. If they lend out too much customers may doubt the bank's ability to convert deposits to cash. This could lead to a run on the bank with everyone rushing to the bank to demand cash. The Bank of England has issued guidelines to banks about the relationship between assets and lending. Lending should be covered by a certain amount of cash, and also by other financial assets which can be converted fairly easily to cash. Assets which can be converted quickly to cash without much loss of value are called **liquid assets**. Figure 7.4f shows that a bank's asset sheet is made up of many different types of asset of varying degrees of liquidity.

### The Main Sterling Assets of UK Retail Banks – Dec 1984

GENERALLY INCREASINGLY LIQUID ASSETS ↑

| | | |
|---|---|---|
| **Notes & Coins** | | £1978 |
| *Balances with the Bank of England | | £525 |
| **Short-Term Loans in the Money Markets** | | |
| – discount houses | | £4177 |
| – other banking sector | | £11079 |
| – certificates of deposit | | £2002 |
| – local authorities | | £1906 |
| – overseas | | 564 |
| **Bills** | | |
| – treasury bills | | £201 |
| – local authority bills | | £410 |
| – bank bills | | £2536 |
| – other bills | | £90 |
| ***Advances | | |
| – UK public sector | | £755 |
| – UK private sector | | £64159 |
| – Overseas | | £4062 |
| **Investments** | | |
| – British government Stocks | | £5120 |
| – other | | £3419 |

GENERALLY DECREASINGLY LIQUID ASSETS ↓

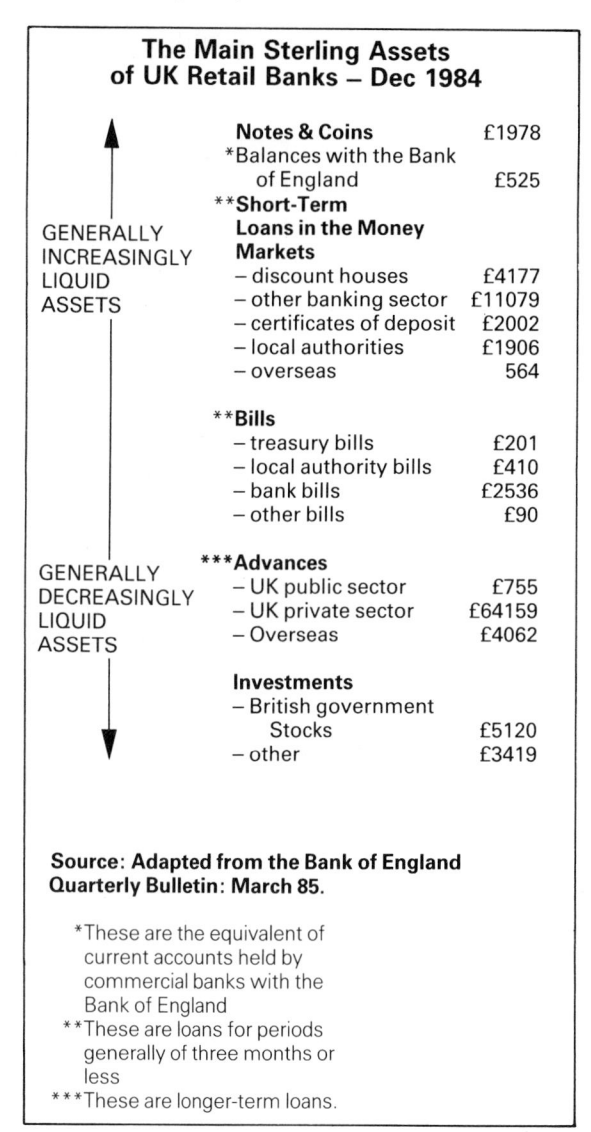

Source: Adapted from the Bank of England Quarterly Bulletin: March 85.

*These are the equivalent of current accounts held by commercial banks with the Bank of England
**These are loans for periods generally of three months or less
***These are longer-term loans.

**Figure 7.4f**
The main sterling assets of UK retail banks – Dec 1984

Banks are sometimes said to have a conflict between liquidity and profitability. A bank needs to keep liquid assets in case there is a sudden demand for cash, but the less liquid the asset, the less interest it will earn for the bank. Banks make most of their profits on interest earned on loans (or advances), but advances are illiquid and cannot be converted to cash before their repayment date.

**EXTENSION MATERIAL**

## Definitions of the money supply

There are many different definitions of the **money supply**, and it certainly can mean more than just notes and coins and bank deposits. Some definitions are said to be 'narrow': these include money held for spending immediately or in the near future. Some definitions are said to be 'broad': these include narrow money, plus assets, usually in the form of savings accounts, which could quickly and easily be converted to cash without much loss of value. Figure 7.4g shows some of the different ways of defining the money supply.

**Figure 7.4g**
Some measures of the money supply

| Narrow measures | |
|---|---|
| M0 | This includes notes and coins in bank tills and in circulation, plus banks' operational balances with the Bank of England. |
| M1 | This includes notes and coins in circulation, plus bank current (or 'sight') accounts. |
| **Broad measures** | |
| Sterling M3 (£M3) | This includes notes and coins in circulation, plus bank current and deposit (or 'time') accounts held by UK citizens in banks. |
| PSL2 | This is basically Sterling M3, plus a number of other liquid assets such as bills and building society deposits. |

In recent years the government, as part of its monetary policy, has set targets for the growth in some of the measures of the money supply. These targets have been set as part of the government's policies to control inflation, which are dealt with in more detail in Unit 7.6. For example, between April 1986 and April 1987 the target for the growth in M0 was between 3 per cent and 7 per cent and the target for the growth of Sterling M3 was between 11 per cent and 15 per cent. In 1985 and 1986 M0 was generally within the target mainly because people were increasingly using non-cash methods of payment. Sterling M3, however, was outside the target mainly because of a sharp growth in bank lending.

## Methods of controlling the money supply

Here are some of the ways in which the Bank of England has tried to control the money supply:

▶ **1 Ceilings on lending**
During the 1960s the Bank of England sometimes simply asked or told commercial banks to put a ceiling on their lending.

▶ **2 Qualitative controls**
During the 1960s the Bank of England sometimes told commercial banks to whom they should lend. They might be told to lend to exporters, for example, but not importers.

▶ **3 The supplementary special deposits scheme ('the corset')**
This system was used in the 1970s. It was a way of penalising banks for over-lending. If they lent over a certain limit laid down by the Bank of England they had to put a sum in a non-interest bearing deposit with the Bank of England. The larger the over-lending, the larger the supplementary special deposit that had to be paid in.

▶ **4 Open market operations**
The Bank of England can sell securities to private individuals and organisations outside the banking sector. The purchasers pay the Bank of England with a cheque, and the sum is taken from the purchaser's bank's balance with the Bank of England. The bank involved suffers a drain on its liquid assets, and it may try to correct this by bidding for other liquid assets like bills. The extra demand for bills could drive up interest rates in the money markets, eventually causing the demand for bank loans, and the money supply to fall. Alternatively, if the bank remains very short of liquid assets in spite of attempts to increase them, it may have to reduce lending directly. If the Bank of England wishes to increase the money supply, it will buy securities on the open market.

▶ **5 Special deposits**
The Bank of England can order banks to place special deposits in a non-operational (i.e. unusable and therefore illiquid) account with it. The banks may need to sell liquid assets to meet the call for special deposits. The last section explained how this could lead eventually to a reduction in lending and the money supply.

▶ **6 Funding**
The government can choose to issue more long-dated securities and fewer short-dated securities. This means that the banks will find themselves with fewer securities coming up to maturity at any one time, and this reduces their liquid assets.

▶ **7 Interest rate controls**
We have just seen that any measure to cut a bank's liquidity may drive up interest rates. During the 1970s the Bank of England used to announce an interest rate called **Minimum Lending Rate** (MLR). It was the rate of interest at which the Bank of England would buy bills from discount houses if the money markets ran short of liquid assets. The shortage was sometimes engineered by the Bank selling securities as part of open market operations. Other interest rates in the economy tended to follow MLR.

**Unit 7.4** *Managing the economy*

**EXTENSION MATERIAL 7**

The present system of monetary control is also based firmly on interest rate control. The Bank of England has an unpublished interest rate band within which it tries to hold money market interest rates. This unpublished band is determined by figures such as monetary targets and exchange rates. The Bank controls interest rates by dealing in the market for bills. The price at which it is prepared to deal in bills determines the interest rate on them, money market interest rates in general, and other interest rates throughout the economy. Minimum Lending Rate can be reintroduced if the government wishes. It was reintroduced for just one day, for example, in January 1985.

**EXTENSION QUESTION 7**

**a** ▷ Draw a grid. Across the top put 'M0', 'M1', '£M3' and 'PSL2'. Down the side put 'Notes and coins', 'Banks' balances with the Bank of England', 'Current accounts', 'Deposit accounts', and 'Saving and building society accounts'. Tick the boxes created by the grid to show which types of money are included in which definitions of the money supply.
▷ Why are such measures of the money supply necessary?

**b** What methods can governments use to control the money supply? Explain how each method is designed to control the money supply.

**c** Why have governments found it difficult to keep the growth of the money supply within its targets?

## Monetarists and Keynesians

Economists and politicians differ about how to run the economy. Those who call themselves 'monetarists', and those who call themselves 'Keynesians' disagree about the kind of economy a mixed economy like the UK should be. In simple terms, monetarists believe that allowing market forces to work freely produces the most efficient economy, while Keynesians believe that the government should intervene to overcome economic problems created by a market economy.

### Monetarism

Monetarists suggest a number of policies to enable market forces to work more freely and, they claim, more efficiently:

▶ **1 Control of inflation**

Monetarists believe that inflation is caused by excessive increases in the growth of the money supply, hence the term 'monetarism'. They suggest that targets should be set for the progressive reduction of the growth of the money supply which should lead to a reduction in inflation. They also suggest that the PSBR should be controlled as government borrowing may increase the money supply.

▶ **2 Labour market policies**

According to monetarists, a major cause of unemployment is the power of the trade unions, which 'price workers out of jobs' by imposing wage levels above the equilibrium wage that would produce full employment (see Fig. 7.4h). They also claim that what they see as a high level of unemployment benefit reduces workers' incentives to accept low-paid jobs. For example, in October 1983 the Economist estimated that a married man with two children, who earned £98 per week after tax and National Insurance, would receive state benefits of £83, taking into account any rent and rate payments, if he became unemployed. They claim that these figures are so close as to provide a disincentive to work.

Monetarists therefore claim that the reduction of trade union power, and the reduction of unemployment benefit would reduce the equilibrium wage and thereby increase employment.

**Figure 7.4h**

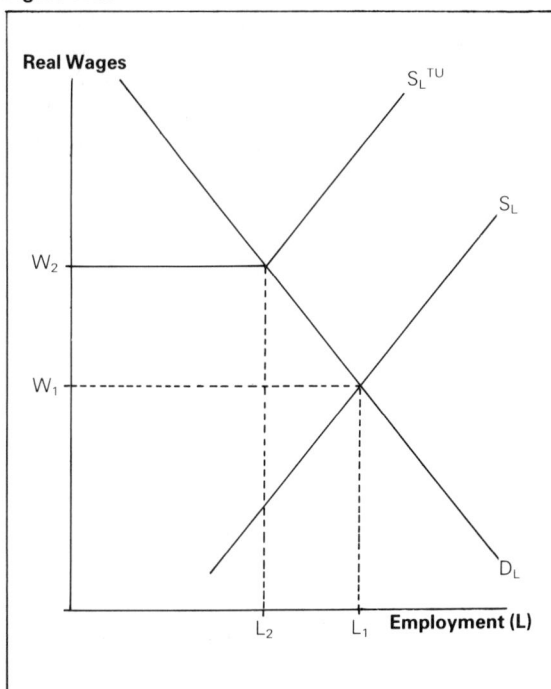

**EXTENSION MATERIAL**

▶ **3 Tax cuts**

Monetarists claim that cutting tax rates, especially income tax, will enable people to keep more of their gross earnings, and will therefore give people a greater incentive to be productive. They claim that individuals and businesses are more able than governments to decide on the most efficient way to allocate resources.

▶ **4 Privatisation**

The monetarist view of privatisation follows on from the last point. Monetarists claim that nationalised industries would be run more efficiently if they were privatised, as the management would be working for the company's own profits. They claim that if a nationalised company is privatised and then faces competition, it will have an incentive to be more efficient. British Gas and British Telecom were privatised as monopolies, while British Airways faces competition from other airlines.

The monetarists' claims for tax cuts and privatisation reflect their general belief that the private sector is more efficient than the public sector, and hence that state spending and intervention generally should be cut. They claim that any increase in government spending will reduce the amount of resources available to the private sector, i.e. that government spending 'crowds out' private spending.

Overall, therefore, the monetarist view is that free market forces, whether in the goods or the labour market, will allow the economy to use resources as efficiently as possible, and will produce a more competitive, dynamic and faster growing economy.

## Keynesianism

'Keynesians' (named after a British economist, John Maynard Keynes) claim that, in a market economy, government intervention is needed to ensure a level of demand that would enable a sufficient number of goods and services to be sold to keep the economy in full employment. However, they also claim that a combination of policies is necessary to ensure that the economy performs efficiently.

▶ **1 Demand management**

Keynesians claim that unemployment is caused largely by a lack of demand in the economy. They claim that a policy of reducing real wages, as suggested by the monetarists, would worsen unemployment as people should have less money to spend on goods and services. Therefore, if there is a recession and substantial unemployment, the government can reduce this by increasing demand in the economy, especially by increasing government spending.

If high inflation and a balance of payments deficit are caused by 'too much' demand in the economy, i.e. where aggregate demand is greater than the amount that can be produced with full employment, then Keynesians claim that the government should deflate the economy.

Therefore, the Keynesian 'demand management (increasing and decreasing demand) approach responds to changes in the economy, while the monetarist money policies concentrate on reducing inflation, while allowing other policies to affect the efficiency of the economy as a whole.

▶ **2 Incomes policies**

If inflation is caused by cost-push factors (see Unit 7.6) such as rapid increases in wages, it can be controlled by placing limits on the growth of wages and salaries, i.e. by an incomes policy. Incomes policies are dealt with in the main text of this Unit.

▶ **3 Government spending on infrastructure, investment and retraining**

If unemployment is caused by declining industries, and lack of competitiveness, Keynesians claim that supply-side measures should be taken, with the government providing essential investment not provided by the private sector or market forces. However, they would advocate more spending on the infrastructure, for example roads, railways, schools, houses, sewers, etc., other government investment, for example in new technology, and retraining. Monetarists would tend to agree that the government has some responsibility for retraining as the economy adjusts to changes in demand, but would claim that the private sector would, on the whole, be best able to decide on and finance training schemes.

▶ **4 Balance of payments policies**

Reflationary policies may produce balance of payments problems by increasing the demand for imports. Some Keynesians claim that devaluation and/or import controls would counteract this (see Unit 8.2).

## Making sense of economists disagreements

It is very difficult to know exactly how effective each of the policies suggested by economists are or could be. However, recent experience does seem to suggest a number of key points:

▶ **1** Experience in the 1960s and 1970s indicates that attempts to increase demand without policies to improve the performance of the supply side of the economy are likely to be inflationary, and to increase imports.

▶ **2** Many economists have claimed that the UK remains uncompetitive, and that tax cuts will increase consumers' demand, but that a large portion of that will be an increase in the demand for imports. While increasing current government spending (especially in increasing the number of public sector workers) may be much more successful in reducing unemployment in the short term, increases in spending on

**Unit 7.4** *Managing the economy*

**EXTENSION MATERIAL 7**

infrastructure are more likely to have an impact on the supply side of the economy, and thus to reduce the inflationary impact of increases in demand.

▶ 3 Monetarists claim that a short-term increase in unemployment may be necessary while restrictions on the money supply reduce inflation. In the long term, they claim that increased competitiveness produced by reductions in inflation and other monetarist policies, will reduce unemployment as more home-produced goods are sold. Critics of the Conservative government from 1979 claim that the pursuit of deflationary policies has simply increased unemployment, and that there seems to be no sign of a significant fall in unemployment while such policies are continued.

▶ 4 The relationship between the money supply and inflation is unclear. The Conservative government from 1979 had great difficulty keeping the growth of the money supply within its targets (see earlier in this Unit), although inflation fell during the period.

▶ 5 Experience in the 1960s and 1970s suggests that the adoption of incomes policies when wage increases and inflation are high only seem to hold down wage increase temporarily.

▶ 6 The economic implications of political decisions cannot be ignored. Monetarism has been more closely associated with the Conservative Party, as it is more consistent with Conservative beliefs in a free market creating a more prosperous, competitive society; reward for wealth creation; and a reduction in trade union rights. Keynesianism is more consistent with government intervention in a mixed economy the greater provision of welfare services and benefits for the less well-off, as practised by the Labour Party.

It is, to say the least, very difficult to separate economic and political policy decisions.

**EXTENSION QUESTION 7**

a What is the difference between monetarists and Keynesians in their view of the role of a government in the economy?
b Compare monetarist and Keynesian policies for reducing unemployment.
c What would be the opportunity cost of each of the policies mentioned in **a**?

# UNIT 7.5 Unemployment

**FOCUS**

▶ What have been the main features of unemployment in the UK in recent years?

▶ What economic and social problems are created by unemployment?

▶ What are the main causes of unemployment?

▶ What measures can the government take to reduce unemployment?

## Unemployment

Unemployment exists when people who are trying to find work cannot do so. In fact all factors of production, not just labour, can be unemployed, but it is the unemployment of labour which is the biggest problem because of the suffering it causes.

The unemployment figure that you see in the newspapers from time to time is the percentage of the working population out of work at any time. If the unemployment rate is given as '13%', this means that 13 per cent of everyone either at work or trying to find work is unemployed.

### Unemployment in Britain in recent years
▶ **1 Unemployment rose very steeply from 1980 to 1983**
Figure 7.5a shows that unemployment was fairly low throughout the early 1970s, but it jumped alarmingly particularly after 1980.

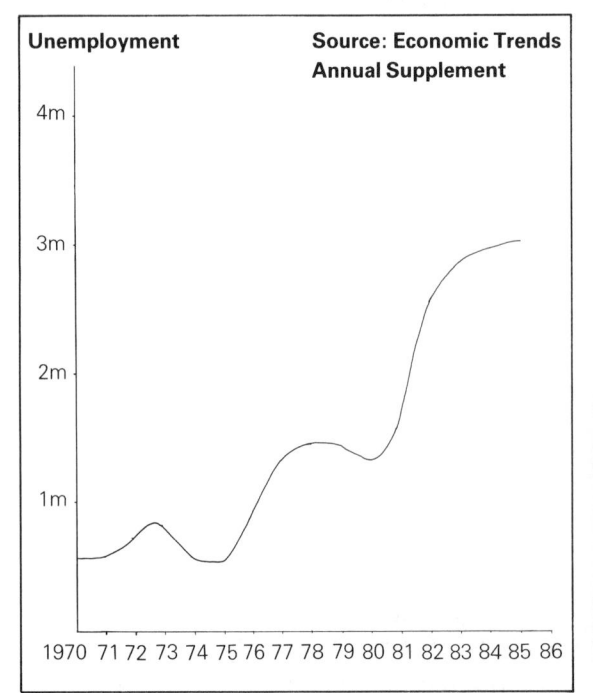

▶ **2 Unemployment has risen particulary steeply in manufacturing industries**
Manufacturing jobs have been disappearing for many years. Between 1970 and 1980, two million manufacturing jobs were lost, whereas over the same period one million jobs were created in service industries. Job losses have been particularly high in metal manufacture, engineering, vehicles and textiles.

▶ **3 Some regions have suffered more than others**
The West Midlands specialises in producing metals and goods made from metals. For this reason the West Midlands has been particularly badly hit by the surge in unemployment after 1980. In 1979 the unemployment rate in the region was about 5 per cent of the working population, about the national average, but by the beginning of 1983 it has risen to 15 per cent, about 25 per cent above the national average. Vehicle producers like British Leyland, engineering firms like GKN, and metal producers

**Figure 7.5a**
UK unemployment 1970–86

**Figure 7.5b**
What type of unemployment is caused when a factory shuts down as a result of a fall in demand for its products?

Unit 7.5 *Unemployment*

like Imperial Metal Industries laid off thousands of workers in the region.

Other regions such as Wales, Scotland, Northern Ireland and the north-east have experienced relatively high unemployment for much longer because of the long-term decline of industries like shipbuilding and steel. For example, in 1976 unemployment in Wales was 7.1 per cent, compared with a national average of 5.5 per cent, and in 1986 it was 16.5 per cent compared with a national average of 13.1 per cent.

▶ **4 Young people have suffered particularly from unemployment in recent years**

One of the saddest things about unemployment is the way in which it affects young people. In 1981, for example, about one in four people between 16 and 19 years of age was unemployed, and youth unemployment was about twice as high as unemployment generally. In some areas of the country, such as Liverpool and Belfast very few school leavers can hope to find work quickly, if at all.

▶ **5 People are remaining unemployed for longer periods**

The length of time people remained unemployed rose in the early 1980s. By 1983, over one million people had been unemployed for over a year.

▶ **6 Many unemployed people do not appear in official statistics**

Many people who may like to work if jobs were available do not register as unemployed. This applies particularly to women who were working but who gave up work for family reasons, and who would return to work if jobs were available.

Almost half a million people in 1984 were on special training and employment schemes paid for by the government, such as the Youth Training Scheme. Many of these people may have preferred to have been in permanent jobs if they were available.

▶ **7 The number of people seeking work has risen in recent years**

Throughout the 1970s and early 1980s the size of the population of working age kept rising. All the children born in the baby boom of the late 1950s and early 1960s grew up and began looking for work. Between 1979 and 1982 the population of working age rose by 436,000. The unemployment problem was made worse by the increase in the population of working age, as shown in Fig. 7.5c.

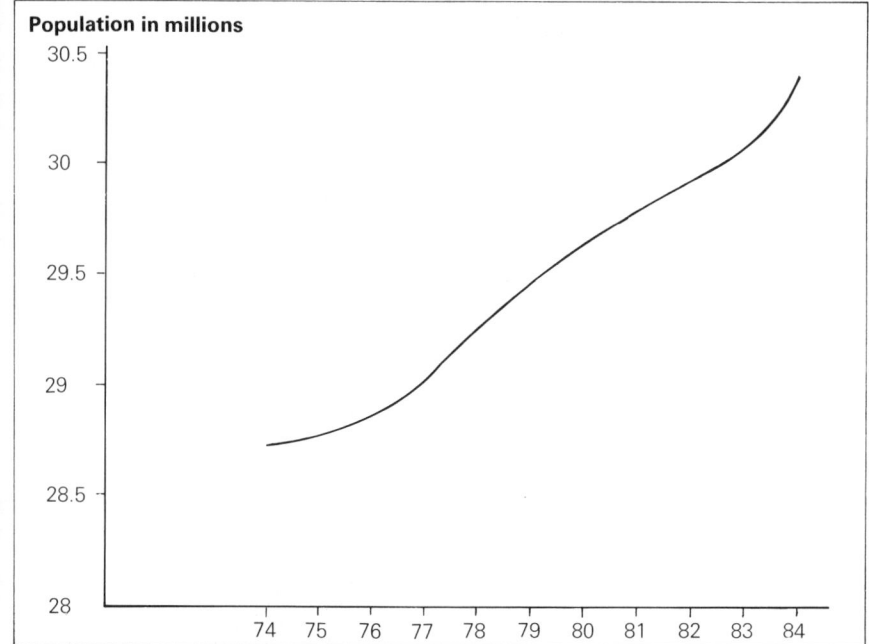

**The problems created by unemployment**

▶ **1 Unemployment wastes resources**

When any factor of production lies idle, it represents a waste of the country's resources. The resources could be used to produce goods and services to improve our standard of living.

▶ **2 Unemployed people can become unemployable**

When people have been out of work for a long period, employers may become less and less willing to employ them. People who are out of work for long periods may forget their skills, and they may become increasingly less able to adjust to having to get up in the morning and go regularly to work.

▶ **3 Some areas of the country become depressed**

We have seen that some regions of the country suffer particularly badly from unemployment. Young, skilled, mobile workers tend to move out, leaving large numbers of young, unemployed people, and also large numbers of older people.

These groups are low spenders, and as spending falls more firms will close down and move out, making the problem even worse.

▶ **4 Unemployment leads to social problems**

Unemployment creates great strains on family life. Men especially tend to lose status when they stop work, and this can lead to them feeling that they are letting down their families. Unemployment can lead therefore not only to a fall in living standards, but also to marital breakdown, physical and mental illness, and even suicide.

▶ **5 Unemployment is expensive for the economy as a whole**

We saw in Unit 7.1 the enormous sums of money that the government pays out each year in social security benefits. In addition, as people become unemployed they pay less in taxes. Unemployment places a great burden on the people in work who have to pay taxes to support the unemployed.

**Figure 7.5c**
The population of working age 1974–84

### Different types of unemployment

These are some of the reasons why people become unemployed, and why they stay unemployed:

#### ▶ 1 Cyclical unemployment

The economy is often said to go from 'booms' to 'slumps'. A boom is a time when there is a great demand for most goods and services, production is high, and unemployment is falling. Two to three years after each boom the economy may suffer from a slump or **recession**. In the slump demand for most goods and services falls, production falls, and unemployment rises. This pattern of booms and slumps is called the **trade cycle**, and the type of unemployment caused by a general fall in demand for most goods and services in a slump is called **cyclical unemployment**.

#### ▶ 2 Structural unemployment

Structural unemployment happens when there is a fall in the demand for the products of one particular industry. In recent years, for example, there has been a great fall in the demand for steel. This has caused structural unemployment in the steel industry. There has been serious structural unemployment in recent years in industries such as textiles, coal, shipbuilding and heavy engineering.

Structural unemployment affects some areas worse than others. In this case it is often referred to as **regional unemployment**. Northern Ireland and the north-east of England, for example, have been affected particularly badly by the fall in demand for ships. Lancashire has suffered greatly from the fall in demand for British cotton textiles. South Wales has suffered from the fall in the demand for coal. More recently the West Midlands has suffered from the decline in demand for cars made in the UK.

#### ▶ 3 Technological unemployment

Nowadays many people are put out of work as the result of the introduction of new machinery. This is called **technological unemployment**. Agriculture is one industry that has suffered particularly from this type of unemployment. In 1928, for example, 156 hours of labour were needed to grow barley on one hectare of land. Nowadays the job can be done using only about 12 hours of labour. The reason is the new machines available to plough, sow and harvest the barley.

#### ▶ 4 Seasonal unemployment

Some people tend to work at some times of the year but not necessarily at others. Agricultural workers, for example, may find more work in the spring and summer than in the winter. An agricultural worker who cannot find work in the winter is said to be **seasonally unemployed**. Workers involved in tourism provide another example of people who may face seasonal unemployment in the winter.

#### ▶ 5 Frictional unemployment

Frictional unemployment is temporary unemployment while people are searching for, training for or simply waiting for work.

### Policies to reduce unemployment

There are great arguments between different economists and politicians about the best way to bring down the level of unemployment. Here are some of the policies that have been used or suggested:

#### ▶ 1 Policies that increase spending – expansionary policies

Some economists believe that an increase in government spending paid for by increased government borrowing is the way to bring down unemployment. This would increase the demand for goods and services and increase the demand for labour. If the increase in spending improves the infrastructure this could improve the efficiency of the economy, leading to higher growth and more jobs. Tax cuts can increase the amount of money people have to spend and this can also increase demand and reduce unemployment. In addition to these expansionary fiscal policies the government could also use monetary policies. Opponents of expansionary policies argue that they could increase inflation in the long term.

#### ▶ 2 Policies to control inflation

The Conservative government that came to power in 1979 believed that the way to reduce unemployment was by first reducing inflation. They believed that unemployment is the result

**Figure 7.5d**
What type of unemployment is illustrated here?

of low investment caused by high inflation. The problem was that the policies used to fight inflation, such as cutting the money supply and government spending, in fact caused unemployment to rise, at least in the first place.

### ▶ 3 Cutting unemployment benefit

Some economists and politicians believe that people will not take jobs they would otherwise take because social security benefits are too high. They say that if social security benefits were cut people would choose low-paid jobs rather than choosing to stay unemployed. If people would work for lower wages, more jobs would be created to employ them.

### ▶ 4 Import controls

Some people believe that much of our unemployment is caused by cheap imported manufactured goods. They say that if we cut down or stopped the import of goods like cars, televisions and computers, more jobs would be created in British manufacturing industry. The advantages and disadvantages of controlling imports is looked at more closely in the next Unit.

### ▶ 5 New ways of working

Trade unions have been fighting for many years for shorter working hours and longer holidays. They say that this will lead to more employment. Employers argue that it may just increase the cost of production and if anything will reduce the number of jobs available.

Some people argue that the work available should be shared out among all the people who want work. They believe, for example, that a job could be done by two people working two-and-a-half days each rather than one person working a five-day week. The problem with job sharing is that none of the people involved may be able to earn enough to support them unless they work a full week.

### ▶ 6 Regional policy

We looked at regional policy in Unit 6.6 and saw how it involved the government trying to encourage firms to move to areas of high unemployment.

### ▶ 7 Policies to increase labour mobility

If people find it difficult to find work, or move from job to job, they are said to be **immobile**. There are two types of immobility: occupational and geographical. **Occupational immobility** refers to a situation where workers cannot take up a job in a different occupation, even if a job is available very near their home. **Geographical immobility** refers to a situation in which workers cannot take up work that is available some distance from their home because they are unable or unwilling to move home.

### ▶ Problems caused by immobility

Immobility can cause many economic problems. Here are some of them:

▷ **a** *Unemployment* If workers are made redundant in declining industries and they are unable to take up jobs in other industries, they may remain unemployed for long periods of time.

▷ **b** *Inflation* If growing industries find it difficult to find new workers because people cannot move easily from declining to growing industries, they may push up wages very high to try and attract workers from rivals. This may put up their costs of production, and put up their prices.

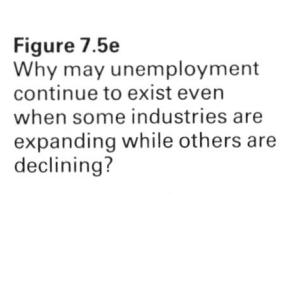

**Figure 7.5e**
Why may unemployment continue to exist even when some industries are expanding while others are declining?

▷ **c** *Low economic growth* Economic growth depends on new industries finding the skilled workers they need quickly. If workers are not available because of immobility of labour, then the production of new goods and services from these industries will be held up.

▷ **d** *Rising imports* If British industry cannot find skilled workers quickly and easily, and cannot produce the goods that people want to buy, then the goods will be bought from firms overseas. One reason why Japan often seems to be ahead of Britain in producing high technology products is because its labour force is more mobile.

### ▶ The causes of occupational immobility and policies to reduce it

▷ **a** *Lack of natural ability* Some jobs, for example in show business, require certain natural talents and abilities. Not everyone has the ability to do every job.

▷ **b** *Lack of training* Training may be expensive, difficult and last a long time. Anything that the government and private employers can do to help people retrain will increase labour mobility. The government hopes that training schemes like the Youth Training Scheme and the Training Opportunities Programme (both described in Unit 2.2) will make it easier for people to move from job to job.

▷ **c** *Trade union and professional restrictions* Trade unions and professions may keep the numbers of workers limited in part of an industry by making it impossible to join the industry without joining the union or the profession. The Conservative government elected in 1979 and 1983 tried to make it more difficult for unions to run closed shops. Closed shops keep out workers who do not want to join the particular union covered by the closed job agreement. Trade unions can also keep workers out of an industry by limiting the number of apprenticeships. Professions can keep down the number of people in the profession by limiting the number of people who are allowed to pass professional exams.

▷ **d** *Discrimination* People are sometimes not chosen for a job because of their colour, race, sex, age, and other reasons that may have nothing to do with how they would carry out the job. The government has passed race relations laws and equal opportunities laws to try and stop this kind of discrimination.

▷ **e** *Ignorance of job opportunities* One reason for immobility is that people do not know about job opportunities that are available. The government runs Jobcentres to try and increase the flow of information between employers and people who want to change jobs or who are out of work.

▷ **f** *Lack of capital to set up a business* In Unit 6.4 you learnt about some of the ways in which the government helps people to start up their own businesses. This kind of financial help increases the mobility of labour.

### ▶ The causes of geographical immobility, and policies to reduce it

▷ **a** *Family ties and social ties* People often do not want to move home because they do not want to move away from their family and friends, or they do not want to take children away from a particular school. There is probably little that the government can do to reduce immobility for these reasons.

▷ **b** *The cost and difficulty of moving* About 30 per cent of people live in council houses. In practice it is very difficult to move from a council house in one area and find one in another area. This is because all councils have waiting lists of people wanting to find houses. To help this problem some councils have decided to keep 1 per cent of their houses for people moving in from outside their area. In recent years councils have begun to sell council houses. This may help mobility because it is often easier to move if you own your own house.

Even if you own your own house, moving can be costly and expensive. As part of regional policy the government sometimes helps with the removal expenses of people moving into assisted areas. Some employers will offer to pay removal expenses for new employees. Because of the geographical immobility of labour, some governments have concentrated on 'moving work to the workers' through regional policy.

Most politicians agree that a more mobile labour force will reduce unemployment, but they often disagree about which of the policies we have studied are suitable. Some politicians have asked for far more money to be spent on training and retraining, while some members of the Conservative government elected in 1983 felt that policies like reducing the power of trade unions and selling council houses may be more important in increasing mobility in the long run.

Unit 7.5 Unemployment

## DATABASE

## 1. Employment in Great Britain (1939–83)

| (thousands) | 1939 | 1949 | 1959 | 1969 | 1979 | 1983 |
|---|---|---|---|---|---|---|
| Manufacturing | 6,815(38%) | 8,229(38%) | 9,169(39%) | 8,181(37%) | 7,053(31%) | 5,346(27%) |
| Construction | 1,310 | 1,438 | 1,509 | 1,415 | 1,252 | 965 |
| Mining + Quarrying | 873 | 875 | 823 | 434 | 347 | 311 |
| Gas, Elect. & Water | 242 | 334 | 374 | 397 | 338 | 323 |
| INDUSTRIAL PRODUCTION | 9,240(52%) | 10,946(50%) | 11,875(51%) | 10,427(47%) | 8,990(40%) | 6,945(34%) |
| National & Local Govt. | 1,385 | 1,392 | 1,307 | 1,432 | 1,564 | 1,495 |
| Distribution | 2,887 | 2,553 | 3,000 | 2,652 | 2,813 | 2,640 |
| Other Services | 3,458 | 5,674 | 6,074 | 7,159 | 8,863 | 8,761 |
| TOTAL "SERVICES" | 7,730(43%) | 9,619(44%) | 10,381(45%) | 11,243(51%) | 13,240(59%) | 12,896(64%) |
| Agriculture, Forestry & Fishing | 950(5.3%) | 1,176(5.4%) | 999(4.3%) | 479(2.2%) | 358(1.6%) | 339(1.7%) |
| EMPLOYEES IN EMPLOYMENT | 17,920 | 21,741 | 23,255 | 22,148 | 22,588 | 20,180 |

(Source: *Economic Review* May 1984)

## DATABASE

## 2. More robots, less workers?

| | Estimated population of robots | | Robots per 10 000 employees in manufacturing (1981) | Industrial production (% change Dec 83 to Dec 84) | Unemployment (% Jan 1985) |
|---|---|---|---|---|---|
| | 1983 | 1990* | | | |
| **Japan** | 16 500 | 67 000 | 13.0 | +8.4 | 2.4 |
| **USA** | 8 000 | 57 000 | 3.9 | +5.1 | 7.4 |
| **W. Germany** | 4 800 | 22 000 | 4.5 | +1.1 | 9.2 |
| **Sweden** | 1 900 | 9 000 | 29.9 | +12.4 | 3.4 |
| **UK** | 1 753 | 11 000 | 1.4 | −1.2 | 13.0 |
| **France** | 1 500 | 6 000 | 1.8 | −1.6 | 11.2 |

*Forecast
(Source: *British Economy Survey* Spring 1985)

**ACTIVITIES**

## SECTION A: FOCUS ON UNIT 7.5

Go back and answer the questions raised in the Focus.

## SECTION B: STEPPED QUESTIONS

1. **a** What is meant by:
   - cyclical unemployment?
   - structural unemployment?
   **b** Explain how each of the types of unemployment in **a** are caused.
   **c** What policies can governments use to reduce these types of unemployment? Explain how the policies you have suggested reduce these types of unemployment.
   **d** What economic problems are involved with the policies you have suggested in **c**?

2. **a** What is meant by:
   - frictional unemployment?
   - technological unemployment?
   **b** Why do some economists claim that cutting unemployment benefit can reduce frictional unemployment?
   **c** Do you think the view in **b** is justified? Explain your answer.
   **d** Would reducing the adoption of new technology reduce unemployment in the long term? Explain your answer (use Database 2 to help you).

## SECTION C: DATA RESPONSE QUESTIONS

# 1. Unemployment in industrialised countries

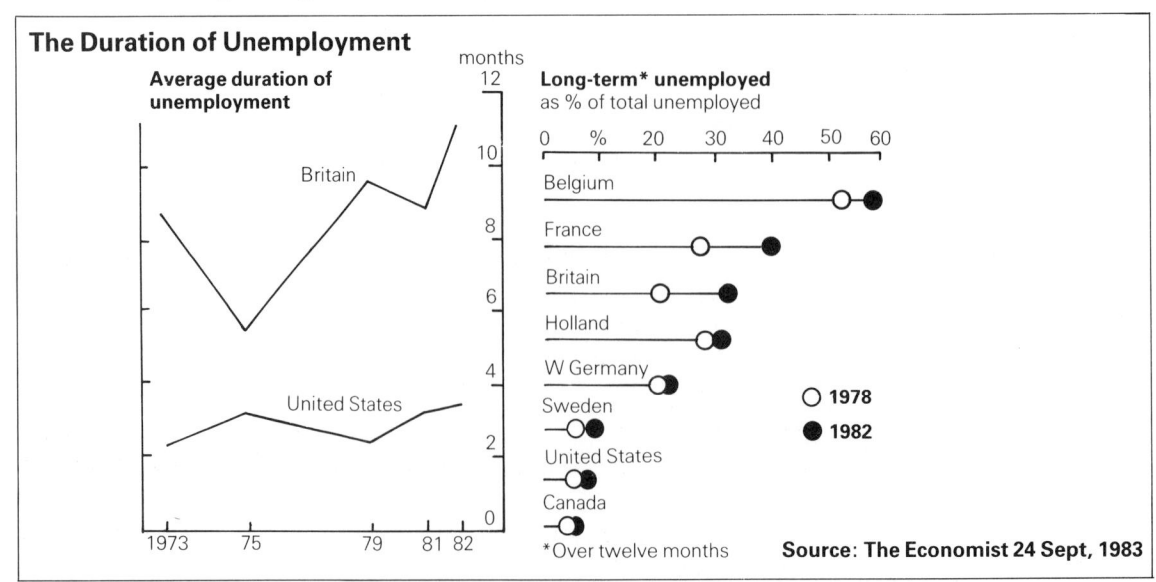

**The Duration of Unemployment**

Average duration of unemployment (months): Britain and United States, 1973–82.

Long-term* unemployed as % of total unemployed (1978 and 1982): Belgium, France, Britain, Holland, W Germany, Sweden, United States, Canada.

*Over twelve months

Source: The Economist 24 Sept, 1983

**a** How long on average were people unemployed in Britain:
   - in 1975?
   - in 1982?

b How much longer on average were people unemployed in Britain than in the USA in 1982?
c What percentage of unemployed people were unemployed for more than a year:
  ▷ in Britain in 1978?
  ▷ in Britain in 1982?
  ▷ in Belgium in 1982?
d What problems may be caused for individuals if they are unemployed for a lengthy period of time while trying to find work?
e ▷ Which type of unemployment increases as the duration of unemployment increases?
  ▷ List *three* ways in which the government could reduce this type of unemployment.

## 2. Unemployment in Watford

### SKILLS SHORTAGE MAY COST JOBS

WATFORD needs to be more flexible if it is to reduce local unemployment and attract high tech industry – and jobs.

This is the message of a special council report on local employment, the *Employment Topic Paper*, which is being used to make changes to the Watford Local Plan. It warns that if certain changes aren't made local unemployment – which has already outstripped the Herts average – could go up. Herts average unemployment is 6.5 per cent compared to Watford's which is 7.6 per cent.

Watford's problem is that since 1971 its traditional industries of printing and publishing have declined dramatically. Accordingly, the number of people actually working in Watford has declined from a peak of 54,460 in 1966 to 42,120 in 1981.

Although high tech and computer firms, as well as financial service firms, have taken up some of the industrial slack there is a mismatch of skills with many Watford people being unskilled or semi-skilled while the new incoming firms are looking for highly skilled people.

The report also looked at the college, as well as government and private agencies, to recognise this need and to train local people to work in these industries and warns that "if the skill shortage in Watford persists, potential new firms may decide to locate elsewhere."

(Source: *Harrow and Watford Focus* 2.8.86)

a What was the percentage unemployment in Watford in July 1986?
b How does this compare with:
  ▷ unemployment in Hertfordshire?
  ▷ the UK national average?
  ▷ unemployment in Wales?
c What reasons does the article suggest for the rise in unemployment in Watford?
d ▷ What does the report recommend should be done about unemployment in Watford?
  ▷ What does the report suggest will happen if these recommendations are not put into practice?
e Explain why the differences in unemployment you found in **b** exist.
f Are policies to reduce unemployment in Watford justified when there are other areas with much higher unemployment? Explain your answer.

# UNIT 7.6  Inflation

**FOCUS**

▶ Why does a rise in inflation cause concern?

▶ What factors can cause a rise in inflation?

▶ What policies might a government use to try and bring down the rate of inflation?

## Inflation

Inflation is a situation in which prices in general are rising from year to year. We looked briefly at inflation in Unit 3.2 and saw how inflation is measured by changes in the Retail Prices Index.

In one month in 1980 the price of the typical basket of goods measured by the Retail Prices Index was 20 per cent above its level in the same month one year earlier. In more recent years the level of inflation has fallen and stayed fairly constant.

### The problems caused by inflation

Inflation can cause difficulties for ordinary people, organisations and the country as a whole. Here are some of the reasons why:

▶ **1 Inflation is unfair to creditors**

Creditors are people who are owed money. If someone lends money at a fixed interest rate, and then prices start to rise, the value of the interest paid will fall. In addition, the money used to repay the loan will be worth less than at the time it was borrowed.

▶ **2 Inflation is unfair on savers**

Unless interest rates are above the rate of inflation, then the value of people's savings will fall in times of inflation. When inflation is high, as in 1979, interest rates tend to be below the rate of inflation. This means that the money someone puts away at the beginning of the year is worth less, in spite of earning interest, by the end of the year.

▶ **3 Inflation causes a fall in investment**

If inflation starts to rise it tends to become unstable. This means that it can alter greatly from one year to the next. Business managers find it almost impossible to work out the future costs and revenues of any investment project they may be planning. Faced with this uncertainty they may decide to put off the investment, and this can have a serious effect on production and employment.

▶ **4 Inflation may cause industrial unrest**

Inflation reduces the purchasing power of wages. Workers may ask for wage rises not only to keep up with past inflation, but also to cover them against inflation they expect in future. If the employers give them the wage rises, it can push up the costs of production, push up prices, and make the workers' fears about inflation come true. This is called a **wage-price spiral** and it is shown in Fig. 7.6a. If employers try to resist the wage demands they could face industrial action.

▶ **5 Inflation may increase imports and decrease exports**

A country may get into difficulty if its inflation rate is above that of its competitors. If prices in Britain, for example, are rising faster than prices in West Germany then British goods will become more and more expensive compared with German goods. This could lead to a rise in imports from Germany, and a fall in exports to Germany. This could lead to a fall in production and a rise in unemployment in Britain.

▶ **6 Inflation could become hyperinflation**

If inflation starts to rise rapidly, people could begin to lose all faith in money. Germany had hyperinflation in the 1920s. By the end of 1923 the German mark was halving in value every hour. The price of a newspaper reached 20,000 million marks! Some countries in recent years like Argentina and Israel have been in a situation where inflation has threatened to get completely out of control.

**Figure 7.6a**
What does this diagram illustrate?

**Figure 7.6b**
How did hyperinflation affect Germany in the 1920s? The picture shows people collecting cash in baskets from the bank.

### The causes of inflation
This is a subject of a great deal of argument. Here are just some of the reasons why inflation happens:

▶ **1 Cost-push inflation**
This is when the price of one or more of the factors of production starts to rise steeply, causing costs of production and prices to rise. There are two main types of cost-push inflation:
▷ **a** *Cost-push inflation caused by a rise in import prices* The price of oil and other basic raw materials leapt up in 1972–73 and again in 1979. This pushed up costs of production in many industries, and led to a large rise in prices in the following years.
▷ **b** *Cost-push inflation caused by a wages explosion* In 1974, and again in 1979, workers received very large pay increases when periods of incomes policies in effect came to an end. Partly as a result of this, inflation rose to 25 per cent in Britain in 1975, (while it was falling almost everywhere else) and to 17 per cent in 1980.

▶ **2 Demand-pull inflation**
This type of inflation happens when the output of the country cannot keep up with the total demand for goods and services. It can happen when the economy is at full employment, and it is not possible to get more output out of the existing factors of production. It can also happen when the economy is at less than full employment and is unable to respond to a rise in demand because of inefficiencies in supply, for example outdated machinery and shortages of skilled labour.

▶ **3 Inflation caused by rapid increases in the money supply**
Some economists believe that inflation is caused by too much money chasing too few goods. They blame inflation on too much borrowing (which raises the money supply) by ordinary people, business organisations, and particularly the government. Since an increase in the money supply can cause a rise in spending, increases in the money supply can also result in demand-pull inflation.

### Policies to deal with inflation
As we have seen, inflation can happen for different reasons. The correct policy to deal with inflation depends on the reason for the inflation in the first place. Here are some of the policies that have been used in the past to reduce inflation:

▶ **1 Monetary policy**
The Conservative government that came to power in 1979 believed that Britain's high level of inflation at the time was caused by too high a growth in the money supply. Interest rates were raised from 12½ per cent at the beginning of 1979 to 17 per cent at the end in order to cut the money supply.

Although inflation fell in the following years, opponents of the government said it was caused by the depression in the economy (causing high unemployment) rather than a cut in the money supply. They said that high interest rates caused business managers to cut production and sell off goods from stocks at low prices.

▶ **2 Fiscal policy**
If a government believes that inflation is caused by very high demand, they may use fiscal policy to try and cut demand. This could involve cutting government spending or raising taxation to take money out of people's pockets. This could reduce government and consumer demand, and so reduce inflation, but it could also increase unemployment, as the reduced spending leads to a reduction in the demand for labour.

▶ **3 Incomes policy**
This policy has been used in the past when wage increases have been a cause of inflation. For example, in 1975 the trade unions agreed a maximum pay rise for the year for all workers of £6 a week, with no increases at all for anyone earning over £8,500 a year. Inflation fell from 25 per cent in 1975 to about 8 per cent in 1978, partly as a result of this policy.

▶ **4 Policies to increase the efficiency of supply**
Inflation can be caused by shortages of labour in key industries, even when there are many people unemployed in the economy. Wages in these industries can rise quickly as firms fight to employ the workers available. Any of the policies to increase labour mobility that we looked at in Unit 7.5 will help to prevent these shortages happening, and it will keep down price rises caused by rapidly rising wages in some industries. A more mobile labour force will help supply to respond more effectively to a rise in demand.

Increases in spending on infrastructure can also increase investment and productivity, and improve the efficiency of supply.

## DATABASE

# 1. Inflation in the UK since the 1960s

*% change on a year earlier*

**General index of retail prices 1960-1986**

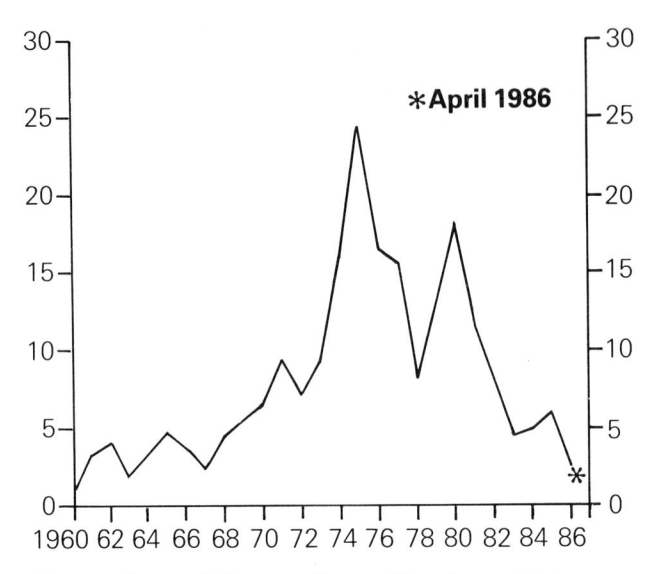

*April 1986

(Source: *Economic Progress Report*, May–June 1986.)

Unit 7.6 Inflation

# DATABASE

## 2. Inflation and its causes

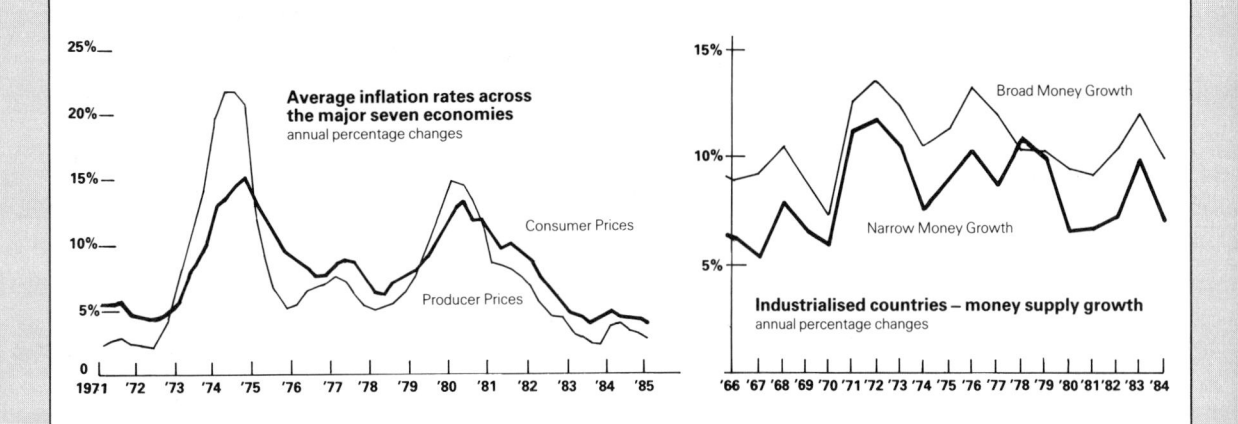

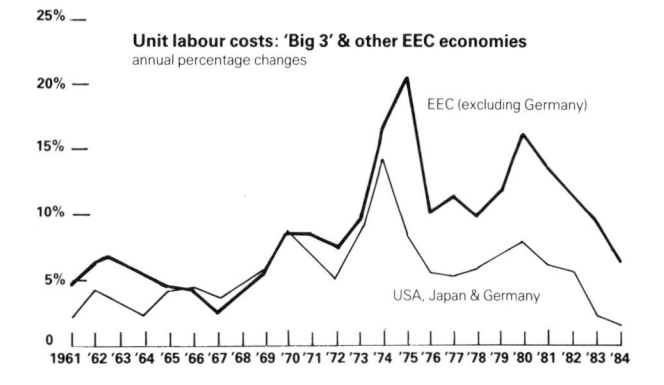

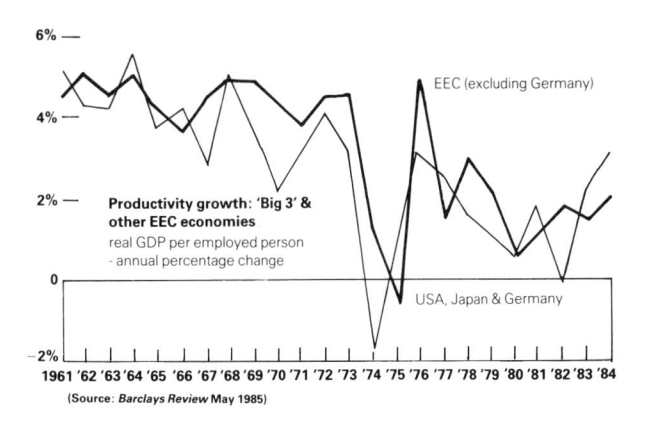

**Average inflation rates across the major seven economies**
annual percentage changes
- Consumer Prices
- Producer Prices
(1971–'85)

**Industrialised countries – money supply growth**
annual percentage changes
- Broad Money Growth
- Narrow Money Growth
('66–'84)

**Unit labour costs: 'Big 3' & other EEC economies**
annual percentage changes
- EEC (excluding Germany)
- USA, Japan & Germany
(1961–'84)

**Productivity growth: 'Big 3' & other EEC economies**
real GDP per employed person – annual percentage change
- EEC (excluding Germany)
- USA, Japan & Germany
(1961–'84)

(Source: *Barclays Review* May 1985)

## ACTIVITIES

### SECTION A: FOCUS ON UNIT 7.6

Go back and answer the questions raised in the Focus.

### SECTION B: STEPPED QUESTIONS

1. **a** What is meant by inflation?
   **b** How can inflation be caused by:
      ▷ cost-push factors?
      ▷ demand-pull factors?
      ▷ rises in the money supply?
   **c** ▷ What policies would be appropriate to reduce inflation caused by *each* of the factors in **b**?
      ▷ Explain *how* each of these policies could reduce inflation.
      ▷ What problems are involved with each of these policies?
   **d** Is inflation the opportunity cost of low unemployment? Explain your answer.
2. **a** How does inflation affect the cost of living?
   **b** Explain why high inflation is unlikely to be considered a problem by the following people:
      ▷ people in strong unions
      ▷ borrowers
      ▷ people with index-linked savings schemes.
   **b** Explain why high inflation is likely to be considered a serious problem by the following people:
      ▷ people in part-time work
      ▷ pensioners
      ▷ business managers.
   **d** Inflation has fallen considerably in the UK since 1981. Does this mean that the UK government need no longer worry about inflation? Explain your answer.
   **e** Is inflation a more serious economic problem than unemployment? Explain your answer.

## SECTION C: DATA RESPONSE QUESTION

**Consumer price inflation in Different Countries (1% per year)**

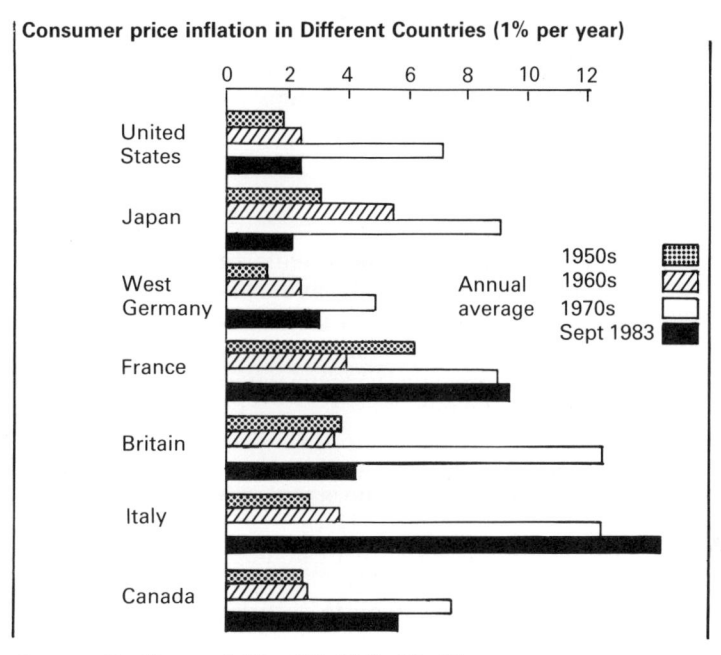

[Bar chart showing inflation rates for United States, Japan, West Germany, France, Britain, Italy, and Canada across four periods: 1950s, 1960s, 1970s, and Sept 1983 (annual average).]

Source: *The Economist* Sept 24, 1983 p23 of Survey

### Inflation in different countries

a For most countries, which was the period in which inflation was lowest?
b Which country had the lowest inflation in 1983?
c What was the average inflation rate in the UK in the:
  ▷ 1950s?
  ▷ 1960s?
  ▷ 1970s?
d Which country has had the worst inflation since the 1960s?
e The worst inflation suffered by most countries was in 1973–4. What happened to cause it?
f ▷ How would you describe Britain's inflation rate in relation to the other countries shown in *each* of the four time periods?
  ▷ How does a high rate of inflation in relation to others affect a country's ability to compete with other countries' products?

# UNIT 7.7 Economic growth

**FOCUS**

▶ What are the advantages of economic growth?

▶ What problems can economic growth cause for a society?

▶ Why has the UK a poor economic growth record compared to other industrialised countries?

## What is meant by 'economic growth'

Economic growth usually means an increase in the production of goods and services by an economy over a period of time, usually a year. Economic growth is usually measured in terms of the percentage increase in GDP or GNP from one year to the next.

### The case for economic growth

People sometimes argue about whether economic growth is good. Here are some of the arguments put forward in favour of economic growth:

▶ **1 Economic growth increases our standard of living**

Economic growth means more goods and services for the country as a whole. This means that more people can live in more comfort, free of financial worries.

▶ **2 Economic growth can make it easier to reduce the difference in income and wealth between rich and poor**

If a country is growing economically, the government finds it easier to collect taxes from the better-off people in the country in order to provide more benefits for poorer people. People do not mind paying extra taxes so much if they can see that their incomes are rising each year. Economic growth helps the redistribution of income and wealth, and this is explained in more detail later in Unit 7.8.

▶ **3 Economic growth means more leisure**

If people find that they are earning more and more each year, they can choose to give up some of their working hours without taking a drop in their living standards. This allows them to enjoy more leisure time. As living standards have risen in the UK, so hours of work have fallen. Male adult workers worked on average

**Figure 7.7a**
How has economic growth helped to change the type of work that has to be done around the home?

# Unit 7.7 Economic growth

47 hours a week in 1970, compared to 44 hours by 1981.

▶ **4 Economic growth can mean more military power**

As a country grows it can afford more powerful armed forces without necessarily cutting back on consumer and producer goods.

▶ **5 Economic growth can mean a healthier environment**

Economic growth can lead to new methods of production which may be cleaner and safer than older methods. Coal mining, for example, is now much safer because of modern methods of supporting mine shafts and cutting coal.

As a country grows it can afford to spend more on building attractive, safe factories which do not belch out unpleasant fumes and spoil the environment.

### The case against economic growth

▶ **1 Economic growth can mean undesirable externalities**

Economic growth can mean external costs on the whole community. Here are some of the possible externalities of economic growth:

▷ **a** Factories produce unpleasant and possibly dangerous smoke and fumes. People are very worried about acid rain which is destroying life in forests and rivers in northern Europe. They say that acid rain may be caused by the smoke from factories throughout Europe.

▷ **b** Large lorries moving too and from factories are noisy, dirty, and destroy the foundations of buildings.

▷ **c** Many industrial developments are unpleasant to look at and destroy the countryside. It is not only the factories themselves that spoil the environment, but also the infrastructure that goes with them like large housing developments and motorways.

▷ **d** Economic growth breaks up communities because younger people keep moving in search of new job opportunities. People who are against growth point out that while a more mobile labour force will increase growth, it will destroy community life.

▶ **2 Economic growth raises expectations**

Some people think that economic growth leads us to want more and more all the time, meaning that we are never satisfied with what we have got. Without economic growth people would not expect their standard of living to keep on rising, and they would be far happier and more contented as a result.

### Britain's growth record

Measuring economic growth is very difficult, and there are several ways of doing it. One way is by measuring the increase in GDP each year. The UK has not been growing at the same rate as other countries with which we do a great deal of trade.

**Figure 7.7b**
Does economic growth lead to a cleaner, healthier environment, or to pollution and the ruin of the environment?

**The causes of Britain's poor growth rate**
This is another topic about which economists argue. Here are some of the reasons that people have suggested for Britain's poor economic performance:

▶ **1 Britain does not invest enough**
New machinery and equipment allows goods to be produced more cheaply and efficiently. The UK invested less per person in the country in 1980 then any of its main trading partners and this a typical situation for the UK. Here are some of the possible reasons for Britain's lack of investment:

▷ **a** British industry has made lower profits than industry in other countries. This has meant fewer funds available for investment. Of course, part of the reason for poor profits has been lack of economic growth!

▷ **b** The government has not helped as much as governments overseas in providing funds for investment. It is argued by some people that Britain will lag behind in microtechnology because our government is unwilling to help on a large enough scale with the enormous cost of investment in this industry.

▷ **c** The trade union movement has resisted the introduction of new machinery and equipment. Some people say that British business managers have put off new investment because they know it will lead to industrial action by trade union members who fear that their traditional skills will no longer be required.

▷ **d** British business managers are not professional. Management training in Britain has lagged behind management training in countries like the USA, and this has meant that our managers are inefficient and amateurish. In addition, British managers sit back when things are going reasonably well rather than planning new investments and new products for the future.

▶ **2 Britain has poor labour productivity**
**Labour productivity** is basically the output per worker. Output per worker has risen much more rapidly in Japan than in the UK in many recent years with the exception of 1982 to 1985.

If our productivity is low, our costs of production will be high, and we will be unable to sell our goods cheaply. Here are some of the reasons for Britain's poor productivity:

▷ **a** Britain does not invest enough in new machinery and equipment. Modernisation of factories is the main way of increasing productivity. The introduction of robots to carry out vehicle assembly in car factories, for example, has meant that more cars can be assembled using far fewer workers.

▷ **b** Trade unions have sometimes resisted working with new machinery. Part of the problem is that many factory workers are members of craft unions. New machinery can threaten old crafts and skills. In addition, when there are craft unions, there tend to be several unions in one place of work. This can lead to demarcation disputes when new machinery and new ways of work have to be introduced.

▷ **c** Scientists and engineers are often poorly paid in Britain, and there is often not enough training for them. Scientists and engineers seem to have lower status in Britain than, say, doctors or lawyers. Over the years this has led to many able people choosing careers not in science and engineering, a shortage of courses for training, in for example, computer science, and the emigration of scientists and engineers in search of better pay and conditions.

**Policies to achieve economic growth**
Since Britain's problem was beginning to be realised at the end of the 1950s, governments have tried various ways of improving our growth record. Here are some of the policies that could help to improve growth:

▶ **1 Policies to increase spending**
The Conservative government that came to power in 1970 tried to increase spending by cutting taxes and increasing government spending. They hoped that the extra spending would make business managers optimistic about the future and they would invest more. The policy was not successful partly because of an oil price crisis in 1973. Some economists now advocate increases in spending on infrastructure which they claim will increase investment, productivity and growth in the longer term.

▶ **2 Policies to reduce inflation**
The Conservative government that came to power in 1979 attempted to reduce inflation in the hope that this would increase investment. They believed that inflation interferes with business managers' expectations about future costs and revenues and makes them less likely to invest. It also reduces demand for British goods overseas and cuts investment in export industries.

▶ **3 Policies to increase the mobility of labour**
We have looked at these earlier in Unit 7.5 and you will have noticed how the achievement of all government economic aims seems connected to labour mobility. The shortage of trained computer staff and experts in microtechnology looks as if it might seriously hold up Britain's economic growth in the future. This is especially unfortunate when there are so many people out of work at the present time.

Unit 7.7 *Economic growth*

## DATABASE

# 1. Comparing productivity

During the 1960s, America's labour productivity in manufacturing grew at an annual rate of 4.3%, which was the slowest of any big industrial country. Japan's productivity in the 1960s grew on average by nearly 12% a year. In 1982-85, gains in labour productivity were more nearly equal across the world. The country with the slowest-growing labour productivity was Italy, with an annual rate of 3.3%. America moved up the ranking and Japan down, so that they stood side-by-side with annual productivity increases of 4.2% and 4.8% respectively. Britain's workers did as well as Japan's. Swedish labour led the pack, with a productivity increase of 5.7% a year.

(Source: *The Economist* 28.6.85)

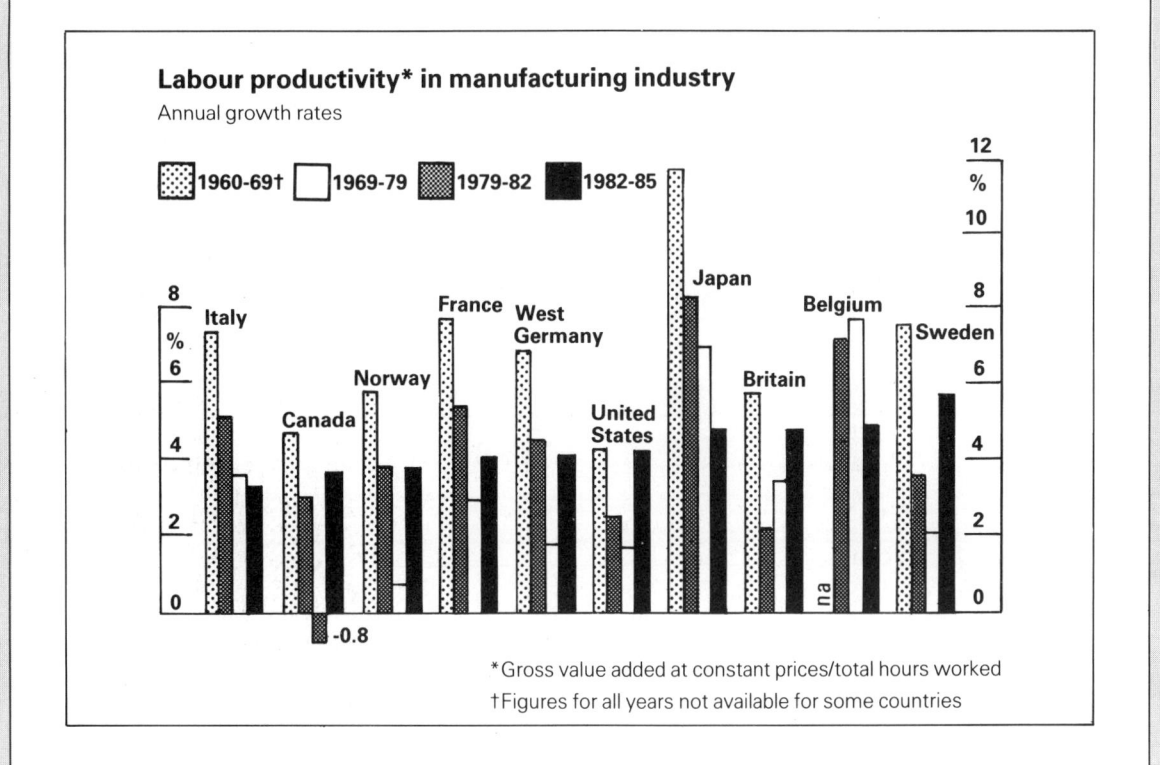

**Labour productivity\* in manufacturing industry**
Annual growth rates

[Bar chart showing annual growth rates for 1960-69†, 1969-79, 1979-82, and 1982-85 across countries: Italy, Canada, Norway, France, West Germany, United States, Japan, Britain, Belgium, Sweden. Canada shows -0.8 for one period; Belgium shows "na" for 1960-69.]

\*Gross value added at constant prices/total hours worked
†Figures for all years not available for some countries

## DATABASE

## 2. Comparing growth

| Year Average<br>% change over previous year | Average<br>1981-85 | Real GNP/GDP Growth | |
|---|---|---|---|
| | | 1985<br>Outturn | 1986<br>Forecast |
| United States | 2.3 | 2.2 | 3.0 |
| United Kingdom | 1.7 | 3.3 | 2.7 |
| Japan | 3.9 | 4.6 | 3.5 |
| W. Germany | 1.1 | 2.3 | 4.0 |
| France | 1.2 | 1.3 | 3.0 |
| Italy | 0.8 | 2.1 | 3.0 |
| Canada | 2.3 | 4.5 | 3.6 |
| Major Seven | 2.3 | 2.8 | 3.1 |

(Source: *Barclays Review* May 1986 (from OECD figures))

## DATABASE

## 3. Investment per head in selected countries (in US $, 1980)

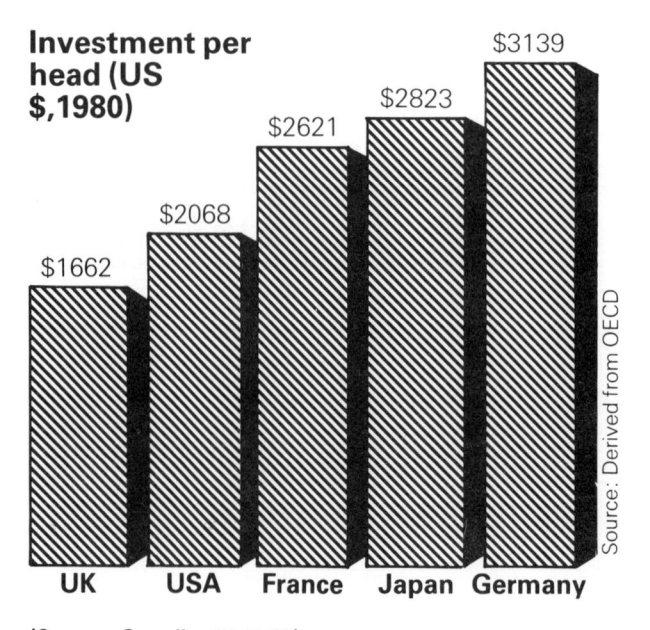

Investment per head (US $, 1980)

- UK: $1662
- USA: $2068
- France: $2621
- Japan: $2823
- Germany: $3139

Source: Derived from OECD

(Source: *Guardian* 17.11.83)

# ACTIVITIES

## SECTION A: FOCUS ON UNIT 7.7

Go back and answer the questions raised in the Focus.

## SECTION B: STEPPED QUESTIONS

1. a What is meant by economic growth?
   b How is economic growth usually measured?
   c One of the results of economic growth is that a country could have the technology and the resources to replace coal-fired power stations by nuclear-powered power stations. Explain some of the advantages and disadvantages that could result from this change.

2. a Give *three* possible reasons for the UK's low growth rate in relation to other industrialised countries.
   b Look at Databases 1, 2, and 3. Give examples of the UK's poor economic performance in terms of:
      ▷ productivity rates
      ▷ growth rates
      ▷ investment.
   c Explain the possible policies governments could use to increase the UK's growth rate.
   d Why do economists disagree so much about policies to increase economic growth?

## SECTION C: DATA RESPONSE QUESTIONS

### 1. Growth is Good!

I think there is enough evidence to suggest that increasing GDP numbers do tell us something about part of increasing welfare. It seems to me inconceivable that one can seriously argue that longer life expectancy, shorter working hours, longer holidays, greater freedom of choice and travel, more telephones and more central heating reduce welfare rather than increase it. As the table shows, we have steadily improved on every one of these fronts and more.

Side-effects can and should be contained, just as the clean air legislation effectively abolished London smogs in the Fifties, or the authorities in more enlightened continental cities have cut congestion by improving and subsidising their public transport. Cleaner air and rivers are another public good which a growing society can provide.

However, growth may not make people happier. Part of the reason growth may not make people happier may be that people increasingly want "positional goods" as they get richer, and the more our basic wants are satisfied, the more we seek jobs with status, or isolated country homes, or exclusive restaurant meals that not everyone else can enjoy by definition.

| | | | | | |
|---|---|---|---|---|---|
| **WHAT GROWTH MEANS** | | | | | |
| Hours of work* | Holidays of 4 weeks + | Life expectancy at 1 year (men) | Households with car | Households with 'phone | Households with central heating |
| 1970  1981 | 1970  1981 | 1901  1979 | 1973  1981 | 1973  1981 | 1973  1981 |
| 47    44 | 7%    86% | 55    70.2 (years) (years) | 54%   59% | 45%   75% | 39%   59% |
| *male manual workers | | | | | |

(Source: Adapted from *The Guardian* 29.12.83)

**a** Give *three* advantages of growth that the writer believes nobody can seriously argue with.
**b** Quote *two* figures that show an improvement in welfare between 1970 and 1982.
**c** What economic term is used in this book for what the writer calls 'side effects'?
**d** Give *two* side effects of economic growth that the writer claims have been reduced in recent years.
**e** As people get richer, how do their wants change?

## 2. Alternative Economics

'The Other Economic Summit (TOES) will take place in London at the same time and in nearly the same place as the meeting at Lancaster House of the Heads of State of the seven richest Western nations. Both events will focus on the world economy.

The Lancaster House Summit, concentrating on how to achieve fuller employment by further industrial expansion, will rely on a conventional economics which is bankrupt of solutions to our present problems and can do little but damage to the prospects for humanity in the future.

A fresh view on economics is needed, and TOES has been organised to express such a view. It will tackle the fundamental issues of our day, the interlocking crises of unemployment, Third world under-development, the arms race, the environment, resources and energy.

TOES will consider these issues in economic terms, in a way that can be recognised as a challenge to conventional economists. It will take a fully constructive position on the issues it addresses, going beyond mere statements of the problems and exploring solutions and their economic implications in detail.

**TOES will bring together economists from all over the world for the conference, many of them pioneers in their field. It will make a major contribution to the development of a new, common-sense economics, that recognises real human needs and the ecological realities within which they must be met, in a context of international social justice.**

Extract from publicity leaflet for *The Other Economic Summit* (TOES) London, June 1984)

- a What important meeting was taking place at the same time as TOES?
- b What does the extract say the Lancaster House Summit would concentrate on?
- c In what ways does the article criticise 'conventional economics'?
- d Is this criticism justified? Explain your view.
- e ▷ What sort of issues does the extract include in 'a fresh view on economics'?
  ▷ What difficulties might be faced by a government trying to deal with these issues?

# UNIT 7.8 The distribution of income and wealth

**FOCUS**

▶ What is the difference between **income** and **wealth**?

▶ Why are some people much wealthier than others?

▶ Why do some people support an unequal distribution of wealth while other people want greater equality?

▶ In what ways does government action reduce inequalities?

## The redistribution of income and wealth

Income is basically the amount that people *earn* whereas wealth is what they *own*. Wealth refers to people's possessions that are worth money (their assets). Wealth can include a house, stocks and shares and insurance policies. Income refers to the money people receive from earnings from work and investments, and from sources such as pensions and social security. Some things that are part of wealth, such as stocks and shares, can earn income.

The redistribution of income and wealth is about whether income and wealth should be spread more evenly throughout the population, and about how governments can achieve this.

Labour governments have tended to believe that income and wealth should be spread more evenly throughout the population, although in practice they have found it difficult to achieve this when they have been in power. Conservative governments tended not to want a greater redistribution of income and wealth.

## The distribution of income and wealth in Britain

In 1983, the highest 20 per cent of income earners received on average a gross income of £19,240 a year, whereas the lowest 20 per cent of income earners received £3,140 a year. Income tax reduced slightly the difference between high and low income earners because high income earners paid a higher percentage of their income in income tax.

Wealth is unevenly distributed in the UK. The wealthiest 1 per cent of the population owned 31 per cent of all wealth in 1971, but this had fallen to 20 per cent by 1983. Half the population, however, owned only 4 per cent of the nation's wealth in 1983.

## Why income and wealth are unevenly distributed

▶ **1 Inheritance**
Wealth can be passed on from one generation to another. Because some forms of wealth earn income, like stocks and shares and land, wealth can go on increasing without anyone having to work to add to it.

▶ **2 Savings**
People who are careful with their money can increase their wealth by saving. If they invest wisely they will see their savings grow, adding to their wealth.

▶ **3 Private business enterprise**
Families often become rich in the first place because someone in the family was very successful in business.

▶ **4 Luck**
A few people become rich through luck, for example by winning the pools.

▶ **5 Skills and talents**
Some people have skills and talents which help them to become very rich. Successful pop stars, for example, can become extremely rich because their talents are in such demand.

▶ **6 Education**
Education can make a great difference to someone's ability to earn high wages. A person's education will depend on the attitude of parents to education, the quality of school that they go to, and many other things. There is no doubt, however, that in general the people who earn higher incomes tend to have more educational qualifications.

## The case for an unequal distribution of income and wealth

Here are some of the reasons why some people would be against government policies which lead to a less unequal distribution of income and wealth:

▶ **1** People have different skills and abilities, and can make different contributions to the general welfare of the community. It is only fair that people who make a more valuable contribution should get higher rewards.

▶ **2** Because people can become wealthier as a result of increasing productivity, there is a great incentive for everyone to work as hard as possible. Everyone ultimately benefits from

Unit 7.8 *The distribution of income and wealth*

this attitude, because the national income increases.
▶ 3 If people are allowed to pass on wealth, this will be a further incentive to hard work.
▶ 4 A more equal distribution of income and wealth will probably mean more government interference in the economy. This, in itself, is undesirable.

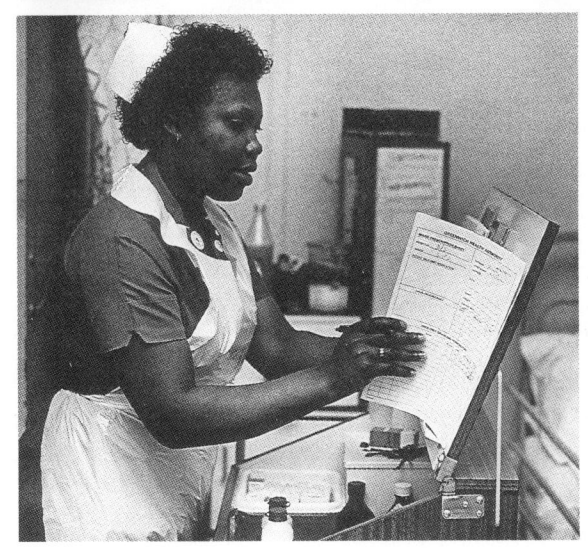

**Figure 7.8a**
Should this pop singer be allowed to earn so much more than, for example, a nurse?

**The case against an unequal distribution of income and wealth**
Here are some of the reasons why people are unhappy that some people seem to be much richer than other people:
▶ 1 It is unfair that some people are very rich without having to work for it. This is a problem caused by allowing people to pass on their wealth to other people when they die.
▶ 2 People should be paid according to need, and not according to the value of their contribution to society. Some people, for example the severely disabled, can never make a significant contribution towards increasing the wealth of the economy.
▶ 3 If everyone has different levels of income and wealth, it will encourage unhappiness, greed and envy. Everyone will try to keep up with people just a bit richer than themselves, and will be dissatisfied with what they have got.

**How income and wealth are redistributed**
Income and wealth are redistributed in the following ways:
▶ 1 **Progressive taxes**
Income tax takes a progressively higher percentage of incomes from people as they get richer. Inheritance tax and capital gains tax work in the same way. All three taxes narrow the gap between people earning different incomes. Inheritance tax reduces the amount that people can leave in their wills and reduces the unequal distribution of wealth.
▶ 2 **Means-tested benefits**
Poorer people are entitled to benefits such as supplementary benefit, and family income supplement. They also can receive benefits like free prescriptions, rent rebates, and legal aid. These benefits mean that poor people are better off than would otherwise be the case.

**Figure 7.8b**
How does the government redistribute income?

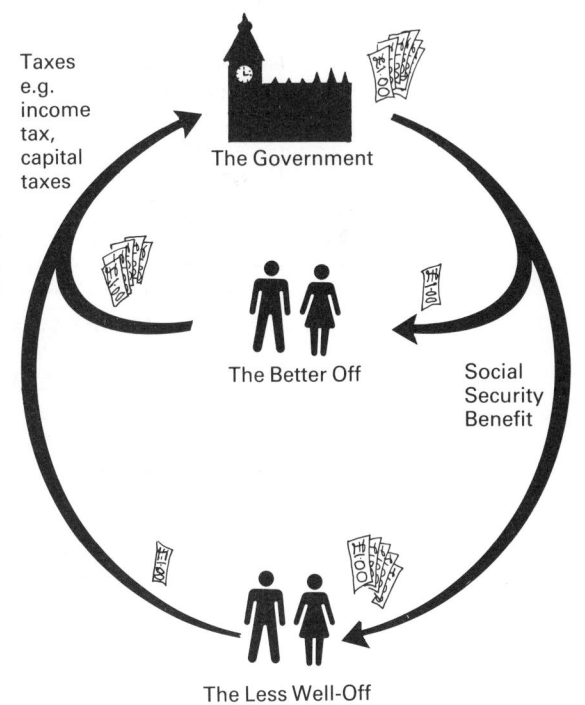

## DATABASE

## 1. The distribution of income 1983

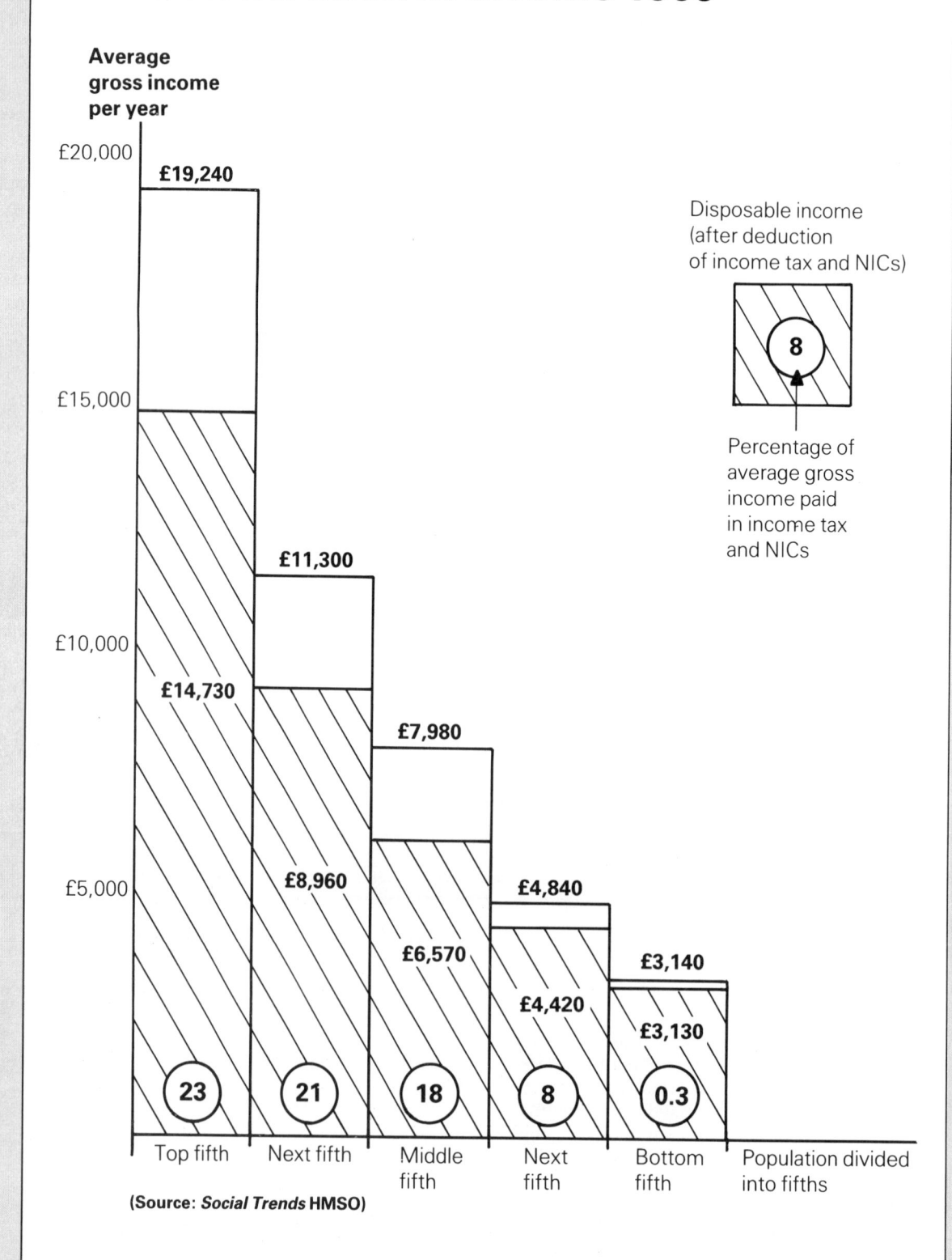

Average gross income per year

- Top fifth: £19,240 (disposable £14,730), 23% tax
- Next fifth: £11,300 (disposable £8,960), 21% tax
- Middle fifth: £7,980 (disposable £6,570), 18% tax
- Next fifth: £4,840 (disposable £4,420), 8% tax
- Bottom fifth: £3,140 (disposable £3,130), 0.3% tax

Population divided into fifths

Disposable income (after deduction of income tax and NICs)

Percentage of average gross income paid in income tax and NICs

(Source: *Social Trends* HMSO)

Unit 7.8 The distribution of income and wealth

**Unit 7.8** *The distribution of income and wealth*

## DATABASE

## 2. The composition of wealth in the UK 1966–1983

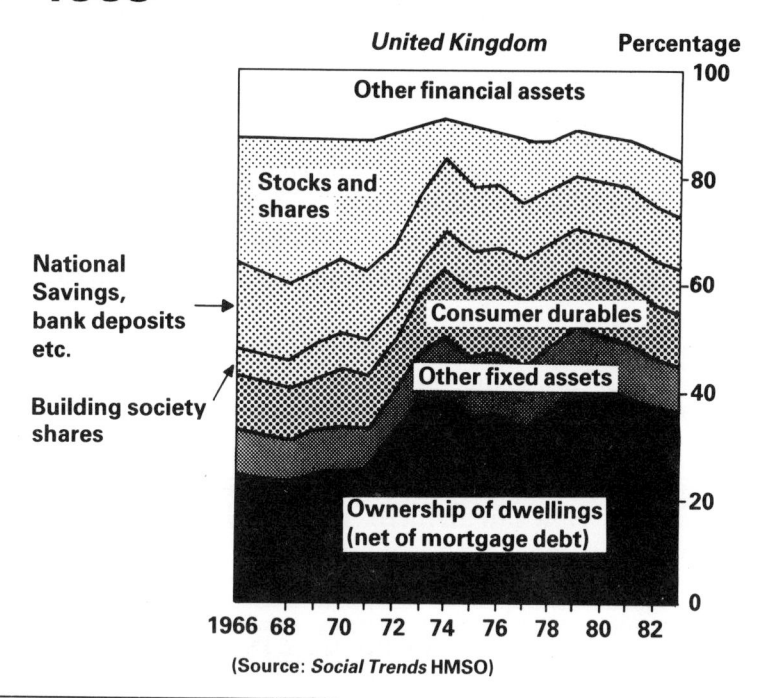

**United Kingdom**

Chart showing percentage composition of wealth 1966–1983, with categories (from top to bottom): Other financial assets; Stocks and shares; National Savings, bank deposits etc.; Building society shares; Consumer durables; Other fixed assets; Ownership of dwellings (net of mortgage debt).

(Source: *Social Trends* HMSO)

## DATABASE

## 3. The ownership of wealth in the UK 1971–83

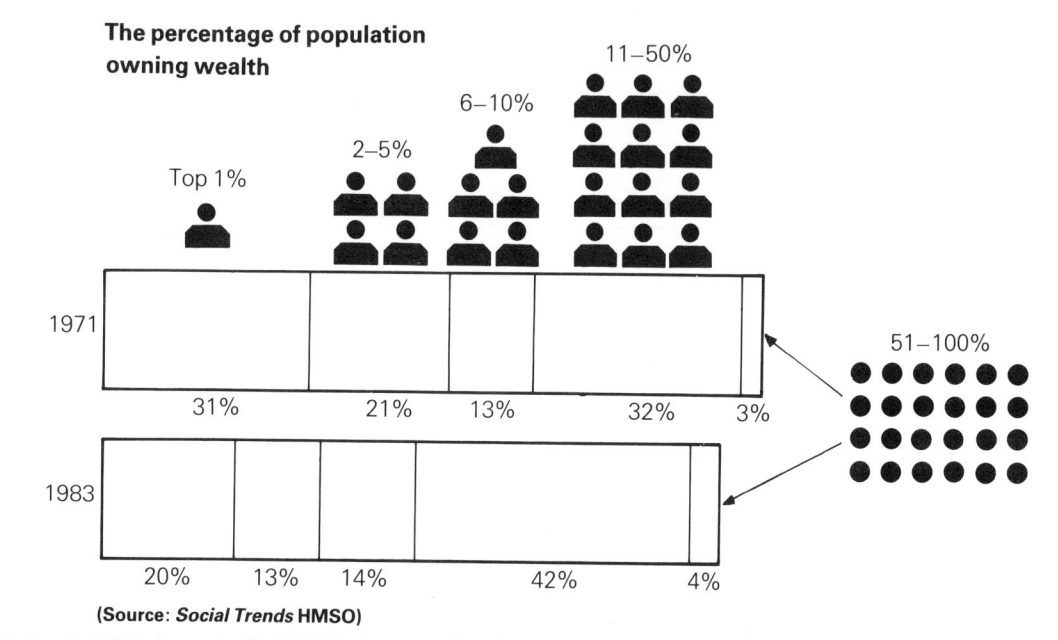

**The percentage of population owning wealth**

Top 1% — 2–5% — 6–10% — 11–50% — 51–100%

1971: 31% | 21% | 13% | 32% | 3%

1983: 20% | 13% | 14% | 42% | 4%

(Source: *Social Trends* HMSO)

## ACTIVITIES

### SECTION A: FOCUS

Go back and answer the questions raised in the Focus.

### SECTION B: STEPPED QUESTIONS

1  a  How much of the nation's wealth was owned by half the UK population in 1981?
   b  What is officially included in 'wealth' in the UK? (Use Database 2 to help you.)
   c  What is meant by 'the redistribution of income and wealth'?
   d  Explain the likely economic effects of a redistribution of income and wealth from the better-off to the less well-off.

2  a  In what ways is income and wealth redistributed using:
      ▷ taxes?
      ▷ social security benefits?
   b  How is income and wealth redistributed by the provision of:
      ▷ free education?
      ▷ free health services?
      ▷ subsidised public transport?
   c  How can an increase in free health services and subsidised public transport benefit the economy?

### SECTION C: DATA RESPONSE QUESTION

**EARNINGS: ANALYSIS BY AGE, SEX & TYPE OF WORK 1985 (FULL-TIME WORKERS ONLY)**

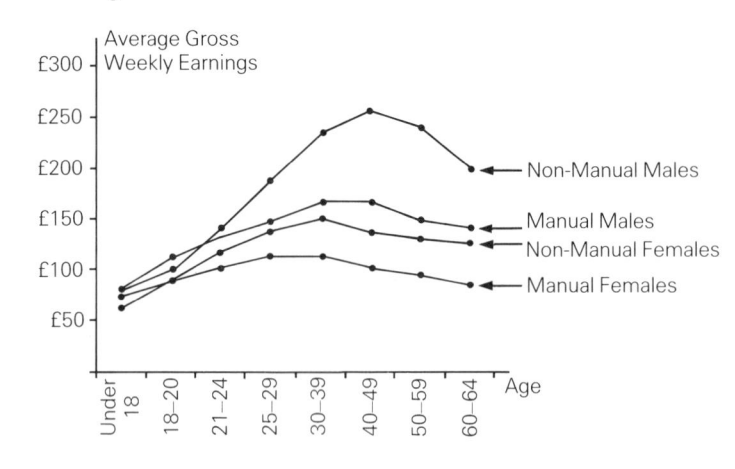

Source: New Earnings Survey DE 1985

Age, sex and pay

   a  Give *two* examples of non-manual jobs, and *two* examples of manual jobs.
   b  How much did manual men aged 18 years earn in 1985? How did it compare with the pay of non-manual men?
   c  ▷ At what age do non-manual men start to earn more than manual men?
      ▷ At what age do non-manual men reach their highest earnings?
   d  How much more were non-manual men at that age earning in 1985 than:
      ▷ manual men?
      ▷ manual women?
   e  Give *three* reasons why women get paid much less than men.
   f  Explain why the pay of non-manual workers goes up throughout their lives, while the pay of manual workers hardly rises after their early 20s.

*Unit 7.8 The distribution of income and wealth*

## COURSE WORK

### PART 7: COURSEWORK SUGGESTION

### TRENDS IN THE UK ECONOMY

1. Keep a copy of articles on inflation, unemployment and economic growth from a good quality newspaper over a period of at least three months.
2. Note any trends, patterns and relationships you can find, and try to find the causes of these.
3. Write a newspaper report on the state of the UK economy over the period you have studied. Support your analysis with evidence from the data you have collected, and use a variety of methods to present it, e.g. line graphs, bar charts, etc.

### DICTIONARY

cost-push inflation
cyclical unemployment
deflationary policy
demand-pull inflation
direct taxes
economic growth
fiscal policy
frictional unemployment
geographical immobility
Gross Domestic Product (GDP)
Gross National Product (GNP)
immobility
incomes policy
indirect taxes
inflation
local rates
monetary policy
National Income
occupational immobility
productivity
progressive taxes
proportional taxes
public sector

redistribution of income and wealth
reflationary policy
regressive taxes
seasonal unemployment
social security
structural unemployment
taxes
technological unemployment
unemployment
welfare state

**Extension**
economic rent
factor incomes
M0
money supply
National Debt
open market operations
Public Sector Borrowing Requirement (PSBR)
transfer earnings
£M3

# Part 8
# Britain and the world economy

# UNIT 8.1   Why countries trade

**FOCUS**

▶ What are **imports** and **exports**?

▶ Why do countries trade?

▶ Why do countries restrict trade?

▶ How do countries restrict trade?

▶ What is the purpose of **GATT**?

## The reasons for trade

Nearly every country in the world sells abroad some goods and services that it produces itself, and buys from abroad some goods and services produced in other countries. Products sold abroad are called **exports** and products purchased from foreign countries are called **imports**. There are two main reasons why countries trade with each other:

▶ **1 Some countries produce goods and services that other countries cannot produce**

Many countries depend on imports that they cannot produce themselves, or that they cannot produce in large enough quantities. For example, West Germany and Japan are two of the wealthiest countries in the world, but they need to import nearly all their oil. The UK has to import raw materials such as copper from other countries.

▶ **2 Some countries produce certain goods and services at a lower cost than others**

Britain could produce all its own oranges, but countries like Spain and the USA can produce them far more cheaply. It is cheaper for Britain to import oranges than to go to the great expense of building, heating and lighting the greenhouses necessary to grow them. If a country imports some goods and services it can use many of its resources to specialise in the goods and services it produces relatively cheaply. For example, Britain specialises in the production of engineering products, and in financial services such as banking. The foreign currency earned from exporting them can be used to buy imports, such as tropical fruit and electronic equipment which may be produced more efficiently elsewhere. Costs of production depend on a country's resources and how well they are put to use.

## Restrictions on trade

In spite of the advantages that countries receive from specialisation and trade in the form of greater output, they often choose to put restrictions on foreign trade. Usually this involves using various methods of keeping out imports. If a country is trying to reduce imports it is said to be carrying out a policy of **protectionism**.

### Some of the ways in which trade is restricted
▶ **1 Tariffs**

A tariff is a tax on imports. It pushes up the price of imports and makes home-produced goods look more attractive by comparison. Customs duties are a sort of tariff.

▶ **2 Quotas**

A quota is an upper limit on how much of a good can be imported. For example, a country might be told that it will be allowed to sell no more than 100,000 cars in a year in another country.

**Figure 8.1a**
Why doesn't the UK grow all its own lemons even though it could do so?

### ▶ 3 Exchange controls

Before someone can import something they must change their own country's currency into the currency of the foreign country. If the government wants to cut down on imports it can put a limit on how much foreign currency an importer is allowed to have. Exchange controls in Britain were ended in 1979, and importers are now allowed to change as many pounds into foreign currency as they like.

**Figure 8.1b**
Which method of controlling imports is shown here?

*"SORRY, YOU CANNOT SELL THIS CAR IN OUR COUNTRY. THE DOOR HANDLES STICK OUT 2CM TOO FAR, THE HEADLIGHTS ARE TOO DIM, THE WINDSCREEN IS MADE OF THE WRONG TYPE OF GLASS, THE..."*

### ▶ 4 Standards

A country may put health or safety standards on imports that foreign firms find it difficult or expensive to comply with. For example, in 1983 Britain tried to limit the import of French milk, saying that it did not meet British health regulations. France said that Britain was just finding excuses to keep out French milk which was cheaper than most British milk.

### ▶ 5 Red tape

Before a good can be imported many forms will have to be filled in, and many regulations complied with. A country can make it very difficult and expensive for another country to sell its goods by increasing the 'red tape' involved in importing goods.

### ▶ 6 Subsidies

A government can pay money to its own country's firms to help them keep prices down and make imports seem less attractive. These payments are called subsidies. Most countries subsidise their steel industries, for example.

### ▶ 7 Government contracts

Governments often place important contracts, for example for weapon systems for its armed forces, with firms in its own country. This is another important way of keeping imports down.

## The reasons for restrictions on trade

Here are some of the reasons why governments sometimes choose a policy of protectionism:

### ▶ 1 Supplies of imports are sometimes unreliable

Most countries are afraid to rely on other countries for certain very important imports in case supplies are threatened for any reason. For example, Britain could not have built as many tanks and aircraft during the Second World War if it had relied on steel supplies from the rest of Europe or Japan.

### ▶ 2 A high level of imports can cause balance of payments problems

If a country imports a higher value of goods and services than its exports, it will have balance of payments problems. The balance of payments is explained in Unit 8.2.

### ▶ 3 Trade restrictions can protect 'infant industries'

When an industry starts up in a country, its costs of production are often higher than those of long-established industries in other countries. This is because the new industry will be small and unable to benefit from economies of scale. Governments often protect these 'infant industries' by means of tariffs and subsidies in order that they can sell their products in the early years of the industry.

### ▶ 4 Cheap imports can raise unemployment

Industries such as the cotton textile industry in Lancashire have faced years of decline because their costs and prices have often been much higher than those of overseas competitors. Representatives of employers and unions in declining industries often ask for the government to place import restrictions on cheap foreign goods because they are worried about the unemployment caused by British firms closing down.

### ▶ 5 Import restrictions may increase demand for home-produced goods in a depression

When demand for goods and services in general is low, and unemployment is rising, it is very tempting for a government to place restrictions on imports so that people have to turn to home-produced goods. Protectionism tends to increase in all countries during a depression.

## The case against restrictions on trade

### ▶ 1 If trade is restricted, specialisation may be reduced

We saw earlier how specialisation by countries could lead to greater efficiency. If the country restricts imports, it may need to start producing goods which it does not make very efficiently, using resources that could be put to better use elsewhere.

▶ **2 Consumers face a restricted choice of goods**
Free trade means a large variety of goods available to consumers. It gives people more choice about how to spend their income.

▶ **3 Foreign competition increases the efficiency of British firms**
The Rover Group needs to produce high quality, reasonably priced vehicles in order to survive fierce competition from Japanese and European firms. If the Rover Group did not face such competition, it may not try to improve its range of models.

▶ **4 Trade restrictions lead to retaliation**
If a country keeps out the exports of another country, it may find that the other country retaliates by blocking imports from that country.

### The General Agreement on Tariffs and Trade

In 1948 a group of countries set up the General Agreement on Tariffs and Trade (GATT) to try and reduce trade restrictions. The nations (there are now 88 members) meet from time to time and hold rounds of talks. The Geneva Round ended in 1982. Some rounds are more successful than others. The Geneva Round took place at a time of world-wide depression and increasing protectionism, and very little was achieved.

**Figure 8.1c**
How might import restrictions limit consumer choice?

## DATABASE
## 1. UK exports and imports 1984 (£ million)

→ EXPORTS  ← IMPORTS

**MANUFACTURED GOODS**

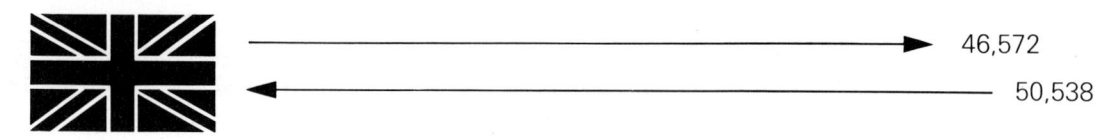

→ 46,572
← 50,538

**FOOD, BEVERAGES, TOBACCO**

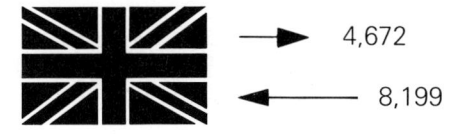

→ 4,672
← 8,199

**BASIC MATERIALS**

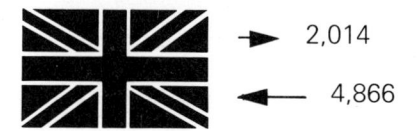

→ 2,014
← 4,866

**MINERAL FUELS & LUBRICANTS**

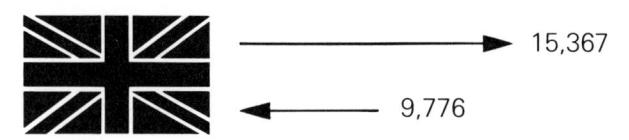

→ 15,367
← 9,776

**SERVICES**

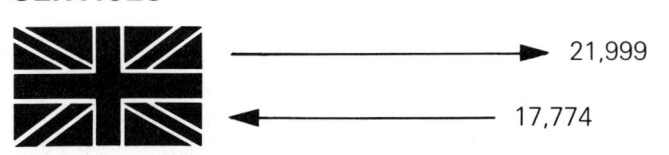

→ 21,999
← 17,774

(Source: *Economic Trends UK Balance of Payments* CSO)

**DATABASE**

## 2. UK trade balances – manufactured goods and services (1985)

**1. MANUFACTURED GOODS** (£ million)

(a) Semi-manufactured goods

| | |
|---|---:|
| Chemicals | +2,508 |
| Textiles | −1,331 |
| Metal goods | +1,237 |

(b) Finished manufactured goods

| | |
|---|---:|
| Mechanical machinery | +1,978 |
| Electrical machinery | −2,316 |
| Road vehicles | −2,891 |
| Clothing and footwear | −1,435 |
| Scientific instruments | +31 |
| TOTAL MANUFACTURES | −5,774 |

**2. SERVICES** (£ million)

| | |
|---|---:|
| General government services | −1,267 |
| Sea transport | −1,077 |
| Civil aviation | +373 |
| Travel | +574 |
| Financial and other services (e.g. banking, insurance) | +7,630 |

(Source: *Economic Trends, Monthly Review of External Trade Statistics*)

Unit 8.1 *Why countries trade*

**ACTIVITIES**

## SECTION A: FOCUS ON UNIT 8.1

Go back and answer the questions raised in the Focus.

## SECTION B: STEPPED QUESTIONS

1. **a** Draw two columns headed 'Exports' and 'Imports'. Put each of the following into the appropriate column:
   - ▷ Japanese cars sold in the UK
   - ▷ British clothing sold in Canada
   - ▷ the earnings from French tourists visiting the UK
   - ▷ German sausages sold in Scotland
   - ▷ Scottish whisky sold in Germany
   - ▷ the payments made by the British government to the Danes to help run an embassy in Denmark.
   
   **b** Use Database 1 to find:
   - ▷ in which categories imports are greater than exports. Give *two* examples of imports in this category.
   - ▷ in which categories exports are greater than imports. Give *two* examples of exports in this category.
   
   **c** How would an economist explain your answers to **b**? Use Database 2 to support your answer.

2. **a** Using a magazine or colour supplement, draw a table showing a list of products advertised that are imported, and the countries from which they come.
   
   **b** What types of goods are imported mainly from industrialised countries like West Germany, Japan and France, and what types of goods are imported mainly from less developed countries like India, China and South Korea?
   
   **c** Explain your answer to **b**.

## SECTION C: DATA RESPONSE QUESTION

### Rigging the Rag Trade

Textiles and clothing have long been protected industries. The first agreement to restrain exports "voluntarily" was signed by Japanese textile producers with America as far back as 1936. Since 1973, three Multifibre Arrangements have rationed imports into developed countries by quotas and tariffs. Their supposed aim has been to give these countries' industries time to adjust to compete with lower-cost producers—mostly in Asia.

Tariffs on textiles and clothing in industrial countries are between two and three times higher than tariffs on manufactured goods as a whole. Moreover, the tariffs tend to be higher on more highly finished goods, like clothing, than on fibres and cloth.

(Source: *The Economist* 28.7.84)

1. What is meant by:
   a protected industries?
   b quotas?
   c tariffs?
2. Why have industrialised countries like the UK tried to limit imports of manufactured goods like textiles, but not of raw material like cotton?
3. a Tariffs on textiles and clothing coming into industrialised countries differ from those on manufactured goods as a whole. Which tariffs are highest, and by how much?
   b Explain the reasons for the differences in the tariffs in **a**.
4. How might developed countries 'adjust to compete with lower cost producers'?
5. Who would benefit and who would suffer, and why, if the UK ended all restrictions on the imports of textiles and clothing into the UK?
6. Explain, giving reasons, *two* other manufactured products imported into Britain which might be suitable for protection using import controls. Explain *two* possible undesirable effects of such a policy.

**Unit 8.1** *Why countries trade*

**EXTENSION MATERIAL**

## The principle of comparative advantage

This section looks further at the advantages of specialisation. It will be assumed, in order to make the explanation simpler, that there are just two countries in the world, called Upland and Highland. In each country just two products need to be available, rice and cars. Both countries can produce both products, and resources used to produce one product can easily be transferred to produce the other product.

If one country was more efficient at producing one product (i.e. it used fewer resources), and the other country was more efficient at producing the other product, then we would say that each country has an **absolute advantage** in the production of that product. If each country specialised totally in the good that they made more efficiently, output of both products would be maximised. The countries could then trade, and have more rice and more cars than they would have done if they had, say, put half their resources into rice and half into cars.

However, specialisation and trade are beneficial to both countries even if one country is more efficient at the production of both products. We will assume that both Upland and Highland have the same level of resources, but they are far better organised in Upland. Before politicians in the two countries start reading economics textbooks there is no trade between them. Each country devotes half its resources to each product, and the position is as shown on Fig. 8.1d.

Now even though Upland is more efficient in the production of both rice and cars, Highland has an opportunity cost or **comparative cost** advantage in the production of cars. For each car produced on Highland, only ten tons of rice have to be sacrificed. The opportunity cost of producing a car on Upland, however, is the loss of fifteen tons of rice. Upland, on the other hand, has a comparative cost advantage in the production of rice. Upland has to sacrifice only one car for every fifteen tons of rice produced, whereas Highland has to sacrifice one-and-a-half cars in order to free the resources to

**Figure 8.1d**
Output before specialisation

Upland: 3000 BAGS OF RICE + 200 CARS
Highland: 1000 BAGS OF RICE + 100 CARS

OUTPUT OF EACH COUNTRY WITH HALF THEIR RESOURCES USED TO PRODUCE EACH PRODUCT

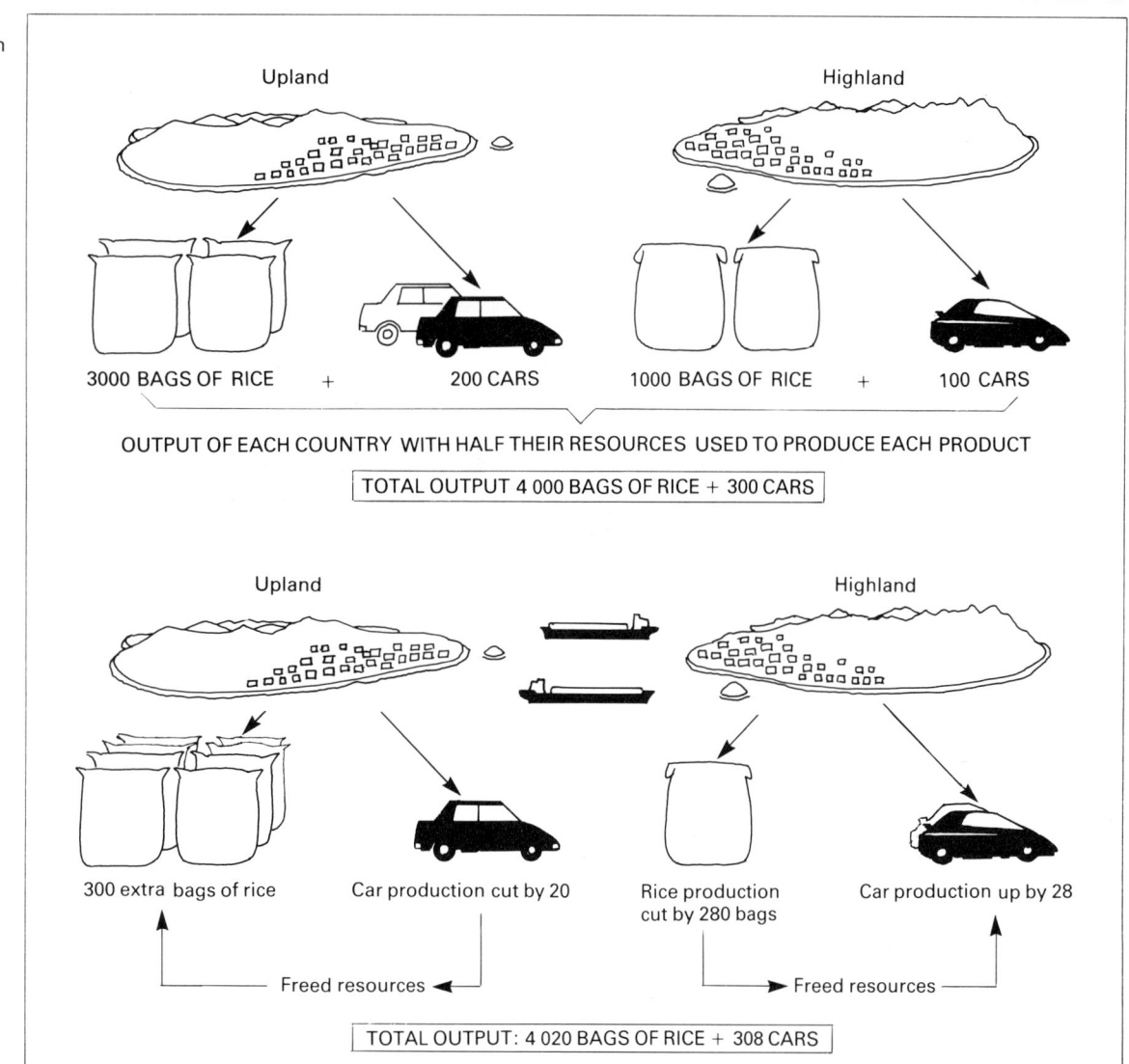

TOTAL OUTPUT 4 000 BAGS OF RICE + 300 CARS

**Figure 8.1e**
Output after specialisation

Upland: 300 extra bags of rice ← Freed resources ← Car production cut by 20
Highland: Rice production cut by 280 bags → Freed resources → Car production up by 28

TOTAL OUTPUT: 4 020 BAGS OF RICE + 308 CARS

produce the same amount of rice. The **Principle of Comparative Advantage** says that production of *both* products will be increased if each country specialises to some extent in the products in which they have a comparative cost advantage. In other words, although Upland is more efficient in the production of both rice and cars, it should nevertheless specialise in the production of rice.

Figure 8.1e shows what happens if Upland decides to cut back on car production in order to release resources to produce more rice, and Highland does the opposite. You can see that total world output rises and, following trade between the two countries, both countries will enjoy higher standards of living with increased amounts of both products.

There are several problems with the Principle of Comparative Advantage when applied to foreign trade in the real world. Here are some of them:

▶ **1 Resources lose efficiency as they are transferred from one industry to another**

As resources are released from one industry to another, they will not keep yielding the same levels of output in the other industry. For example, if Highland kept releasing increasingly hilly land for car production, the number of cars produced for each ton of rice sacrificed would soon start to fall.

▶ **2 Specialisation can lead to economies of scale**

As economies specialise, they may gain economies of scale. This increases the efficiency of production and therefore the benefits of specialisation.

▶ **3 Specialisation can lead to vulnerability**

Countries usually cannot rely on continued supply of an imported product in the long run to the same extent that they can rely on their own production. In our example, for example, Highland may not wish to rely too heavily on Upland for its basic foodstuff.

## EXTENSION QUESTION 7

### QUESTIONS

a Explain, using the Principle of Comparative Advantage, how countries can benefit from free trade between them.
b Why does complete specialisation and free trade not exist in reality?

# UNIT 8.2  The UK's balance of payments

**FOCUS**

▶ What is the **balance of payments**?

▶ How are the **balance of trade**, **current account**, and **capital account** worked out?

▶ What are the UK's major exports and imports, and how have these changed?

▶ How and why has the UK's balance of payments changed?

▶ How can the balance of payments be improved?

## The balance of payments account

A country has to keep a record of its trade with other countries, and in Britain's case, this is called the **balance of payments account**.

Figure 8.2a shows the main parts of the balance of payments account for the UK. Each section will now be explained in more detail.

### The current account
This section records the value of our exports and our imports. It is divided into two parts:

▶ **1 The visible account**
This section of the current account shows the value of exports and imports of goods as opposed to services. Because goods can be seen and touched they are called **visibles**. When the value of our visible imports is taken from the value of our visible exports, we are left with the **balance of trade**, or **visible balance**. For example, if we export in a year £5,000 million worth of goods but import £5,100 million worth of goods, the balance of trade equals −£100 million.

▶ **2 The invisible account**
This section of the current account shows the value of service exports and imports. Services cannot be seen or touched, and this is why they are called **invisibles**. When the value of our invisible imports is taken from the value of our

**Figure 8.2a**
The main components of the balance of payments account

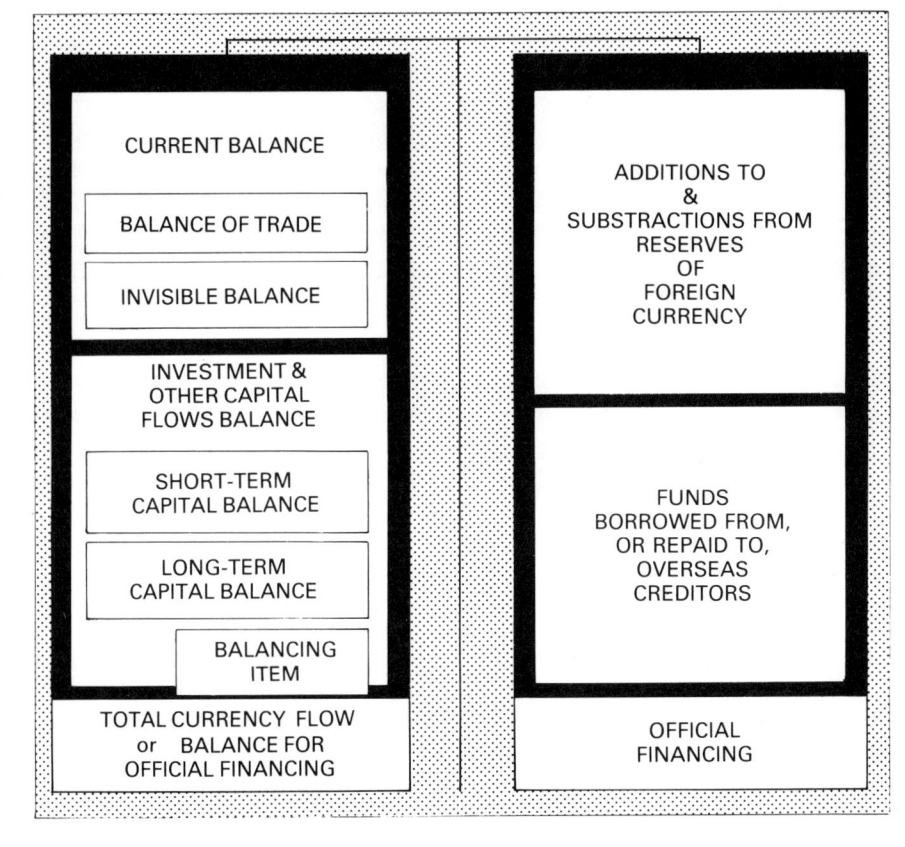

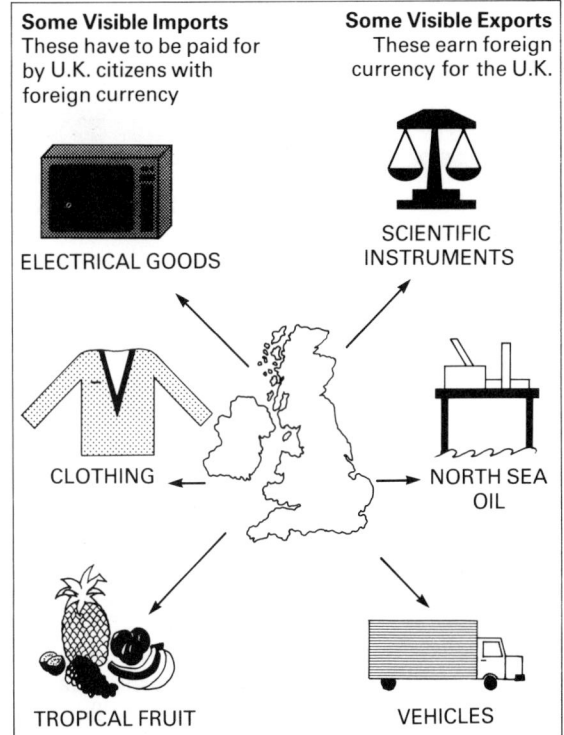

[Diagram showing:
- CURRENT BALANCE
  - BALANCE OF TRADE
  - INVISIBLE BALANCE
- INVESTMENT & OTHER CAPITAL FLOWS BALANCE
  - SHORT-TERM CAPITAL BALANCE
  - LONG-TERM CAPITAL BALANCE
  - BALANCING ITEM
- TOTAL CURRENCY FLOW or BALANCE FOR OFFICIAL FINANCING
- ADDITIONS TO & SUBSTRACTIONS FROM RESERVES OF FOREIGN CURRENCY
- FUNDS BORROWED FROM, OR REPAID TO, OVERSEAS CREDITORS
- OFFICIAL FINANCING]

**Figure 8.2b**
Some of the UK's visible imports and exports

**Some Visible Imports**
These have to be paid for by U.K. citizens with foreign currency
- ELECTRICAL GOODS
- CLOTHING
- TROPICAL FRUIT

**Some Visible Exports**
These earn foreign currency for the U.K.
- SCIENTIFIC INSTRUMENTS
- NORTH SEA OIL
- VEHICLES

**Figure 8.2c**
Some of the UK's invisible imports and exports

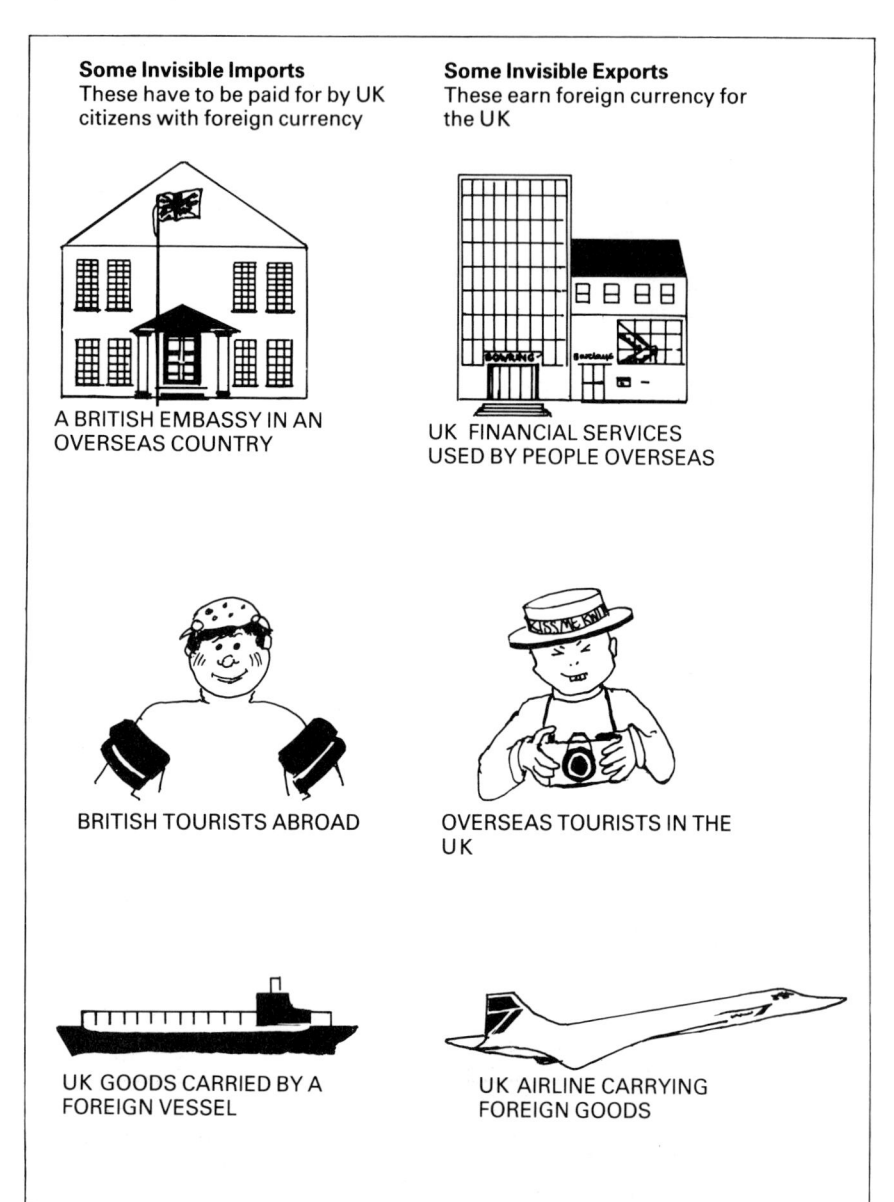

invisible exports we are left with the **invisible balance**.

The current account balance is found by adding together the balance of trade and the invisible balance.

**Some Invisible Imports**
These have to be paid for by UK citizens with foreign currency

A BRITISH EMBASSY IN AN OVERSEAS COUNTRY

BRITISH TOURISTS ABROAD

UK GOODS CARRIED BY A FOREIGN VESSEL

**Some Invisible Exports**
These earn foreign currency for the UK

UK FINANCIAL SERVICES USED BY PEOPLE OVERSEAS

OVERSEAS TOURISTS IN THE UK

UK AIRLINE CARRYING FOREIGN GOODS

### The investment and other capital flows account

Some flows of funds between countries are not immediate payments for goods and services provided, and they do not appear on the current account. For example, if British citizens buy shares in a French company, they do not receive goods and services directly in exchange. The flow of funds from Britain to France is recorded in the **investment and other capital flows section** of the balance of payments account. We can divide the flows of funds that appear in this section in the following way:

▶ **1 Short-term capital flows**
Governments and large firms often hold large sums either in bank accounts, or in some other form that can easily be exchanged for money. These funds can be moved around very quickly, and they are often moved when, for example, interest rates change. These funds are called **short-term capital**, or **hot money**.

▶ **2 Long-term capital flows**
Governments and large firms often move funds to foreign countries for longer periods of time. These funds may be tied up for many years, and they are called **long-term capital**. There are three types of long-term capital:
▷ **a** *Investment in capital projects* Some funds flow from one country to another to be invested in factories, machinery and equipment. They are tied up in capital goods.
▷ **b** *Investment in financial assets* Some funds flow from one country to another to be invested in financial or 'paper' assets such as government securities, and stocks and shares.
▷ **c** *Loans* Some funds are lent by one country to another.

All the capital flows into Britain are taken away from the capital flows out of Britain to give the **balance on investment and other capital flows**, or just **capital balance**.

If investment overseas at some future date leads to earnings or income to someone in Britain, the income counts as an **invisible export** and is recorded in the current account. If, for example, a business manager buys shares in a French company, and the shares earn a dividend at some future date, the dividend will appear as an invisible export. If foreigners are paid interest, profits and dividends on their investment in Britain, this counts as an invisible import, and is recorded on the current account.

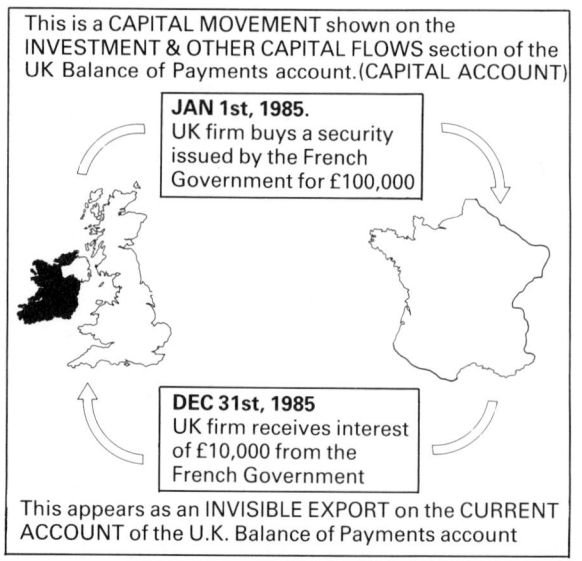

This is a CAPITAL MOVEMENT shown on the INVESTMENT & OTHER CAPITAL FLOWS section of the UK Balance of Payments account.(CAPITAL ACCOUNT)

JAN 1st, 1985.
UK firm buys a security issued by the French Government for £100,000

DEC 31st, 1985
UK firm receives interest of £10,000 from the French Government

This appears as an INVISIBLE EXPORT on the CURRENT ACCOUNT of the U.K. Balance of Payments account

**Figure 8.2d**
How can a transaction on the capital account, which is a minus, lead to a rise in invisible exports in the future?

# Unit 8.2 The UK's balance of payments

### The balancing item
The government has to collect thousands of pieces of information from hundreds of organisations in order to work out the final balance of payments figure. It can check its final figure against the Bank of England's record of flows of funds in and out of the country. If the two figures are not the same, the government knows that some of the information it has collected is not complete or not correct. The balancing item shows the extent to which its information is incorrect. For example, the government's information might show that £800 million more left Britain than came into Britain in a particular year. The Bank of England might say, however, that the figure is just £400 million. The government will record in the balance of payments all the figures that make up the £800 million, and then subtract a balancing item figure of £400 million to show that the figure is not correct.

### The balance for official financing
This figure is the final balance of payments total. It is the difference between all the funds that have left Britain and all the funds that have come into the country over the year. It is the current account balance, the investment and other capital flows balance, and the balancing item added together. It is usually identical to a figure called **total currency flow**.

### The official financing section
At the end of the year the balance for official financing will show either that more funds have left Britain than have entered Britain, or the opposite. The official financing section shows what happened to any surplus funds when the balance for official financing figure was positive and more funds came into the country than left it. It shows where the extra funds were found if the total currency flow figure was negative and more funds flowed out of Britain than into the country. Basically, surplus funds are either paid into the country's reserves of foreign currency, or they are used to repay loans from overseas. If more funds left Britain than entered it, the extra funds will either have come out of the reserves of foreign currency, or they will have to be borrowed from overseas.

### Why the balance of payments always balances
When we talk about the balance of payments account always balancing, we are talking about the fact that the balance for official financing figure is always the same as the official financing figure, but with the opposite sign. This is always the case because the official financing section simply explains how the balance for official financing figure was financed, using borrowing, lending and changes in reserves.

| | |
|---|---|
| Visible exports | £78,072m |
| Visible imports | £80,140m |
| Balance of trade | −£2,068m |
| Invisible exports | £81,074m |
| Invisible imports | £75,243m |
| Invisible balance | +£5,831m |
| Current account balance | +£3,763m |
| Investment & other capital flows | −£3,207m |
| Balancing item | +£243m |
| Total currency flow (Balance for official financing) | +£799m |
| Official financing | |
| Borrowed from other countries | +£959m |
| Added to reserves | −£1,758m |
| Official financing total | −£799m |

(Source: *Economic Trends* HMSO)

**Figure 8.2e**
The UK balance of payments 1985

### Balance of payments surpluses and deficits
The different sections of the balance of payments account can be **in surplus** or **in deficit**. If a section is in surplus, it means that more funds have entered the country than have left it. If the section is in deficit, it means that more funds have left the country than have entered it.

We will look at the importance of deficits on the two main sections of the balance of payments account.

### Deficits on the current account
If the balance of trade is negative (as in 1983), there is said to be a **trade deficit**. It means we have sold a lower value of exports of goods abroad than we have purchased. If the invisible balance is negative, there is said to be an **invisible deficit**. This means we have sold a lower value of exports of services abroad than we have purchased. In Britain we often have a trade deficit, but we usually enjoy an invisible surplus. Depending which is larger, we either have an overall surplus or an overall deficit on the current account. When the current account is in surplus, it is said to be 'in the black'. If it is in deficit, it is said to be 'in the red'.

If the current account is in the red, it means that the value of imports is greater than the value of exports. For a time this can benefit the economy. It can mean that consumers are enjoying a relatively high level of imports which increases living standards. In the long-run, however, it can lead to problems. It means that we are not earning enough from selling exports to pay for our imports. It may also show that many of the UK's products are not competitive with other countries' products.

### Deficits on the investment and other capital flows account

A deficit on current account is generally considered to be a problem that needs solving. This is not always the case with a deficit on the investments and other capital flows account. Deficits on this account can mean that British people are investing heavily overseas, and these investments may, at some future date, earn profits, interest and dividends which will show up as invisible exports. On the other hand, heavy investment overseas can mean fewer funds for British industry. In the past governments have sometimes used exchange controls to stop funds leaving the country on a large scale, hoping that they will then be invested in British industry.

## The pattern of Britain's trade

Foreign trade is very important to Britain. Each month over £6,000 million of goods are exported, and about the same value imported. Millions of jobs in Britain depend upon our sale of exports, and the standard of living of consumers is greatly increased by the purchase of imports. This section looks at changes in our exports and imports over the years.

### Visible trade

In the earlier part of this century Britain imported mostly non-manufactured goods like food and raw materials. The raw materials were made into semi-manufactured goods like steel, and finished manufactured goods like clothing, and sold all over the world. Nowadays manufactured imports have become as important in percentage terms as manufactured exports. We now import vast quantities of goods like cars, washing machines, office equipment and clothing. Fifty years ago imports of such goods were almost unknown. This is partly due to the fact that UK products have often been of poor quality and over-priced compared to foreign goods. Economists say that these products are 'uncompetitive'.

Over the last ten years the most important change in visible trade has been the growth in the importance of North Sea oil as a major export. This is shown in Fig. 8.2g.

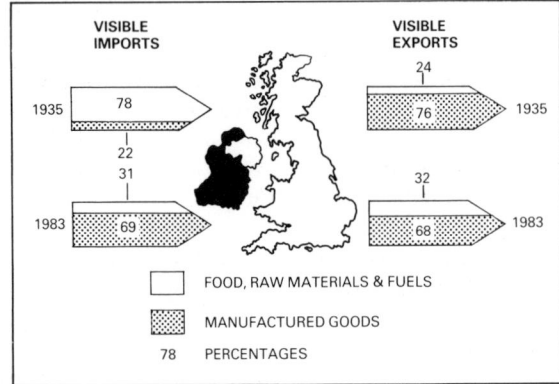

**Figure 8.2f**
How has the composition of the UK's trade changed between 1935 and 1983?

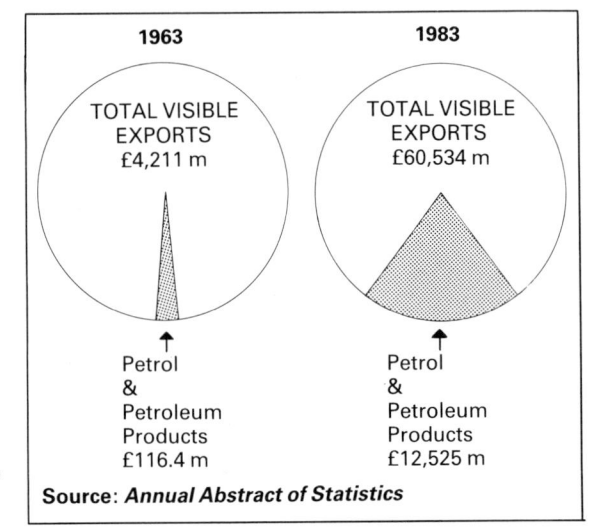

**Figure 8.2g**
The importance of North Sea oil exports to the UK balance of payments

Over recent years there has been a change in importance in the countries with which we trade. In general, a far higher percentage of our trade is now with industrialised countries than was the case in the past. Figure 8.2h shows that most of our trade is with the US and Canada, and with western European countries like West Germany and France.

### Invisible trade

Figure 8.2e shows the importance of invisible trade to the UK. You can see that the UK had a surplus of £5,831 million on invisible trade in 1985 and Fig. 8.2i shows that in recent years the invisible balance was always in surplus. Without the surplus we would not have been able to afford many of our visible imports such as videos, cars, and tropical food. About half our export earnings come from invisibles.

The major items of invisible trade are services such as sea transport, civil aviation, tourism, financial services like banking and insurance, and various government services. Interest, profit and dividends are included in the invisible balance. The major reason why the UK is enjoying such large surpluses on invisible trade is thanks to financial services and the surplus on interest, profits and dividends. Many foreign

Unit 8.2 *The UK's balance of payments*

firms, for example, have insured their ships, aeroplanes and even space rockets with Lloyds of London whereas few British firms insure overseas. The huge surplus of interest, profit and dividends follows the ending of exchange controls in 1979 and a steep rise in investment overseas by institutions like pension funds, insurance companies and banks.

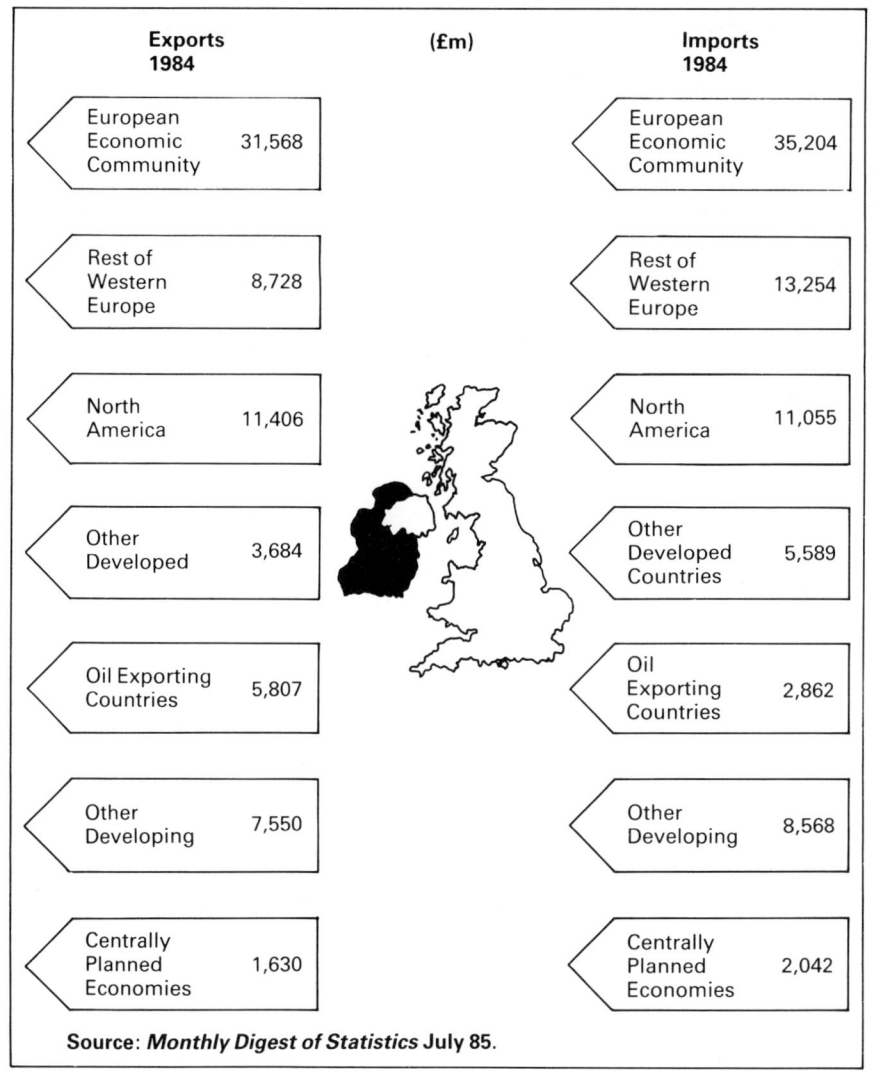

**Figure 8.2h**
Britain's trading partners 1984

| Exports 1984 (£m) | | Imports 1984 (£m) | |
|---|---|---|---|
| European Economic Community | 31,568 | European Economic Community | 35,204 |
| Rest of Western Europe | 8,728 | Rest of Western Europe | 13,254 |
| North America | 11,406 | North America | 11,055 |
| Other Developed | 3,684 | Other Developed Countries | 5,589 |
| Oil Exporting Countries | 5,807 | Oil Exporting Countries | 2,862 |
| Other Developing | 7,550 | Other Developing | 8,568 |
| Centrally Planned Economies | 1,630 | Centrally Planned Economies | 2,042 |

Source: *Monthly Digest of Statistics* July 85.

## Changes in the UK balance of payments

Figure 8.2i shows that the last time the UK current account was seriously in deficit was in the mid-1970s. This was mainly due to a sharp rise in the price of oil and other commodities, and a sharp rise in demand in the whole economy between 1972 and 1974. The late 1970s saw an improvement due to the effects of the recession on the demand for imports although there was a brief deficit in 1979 following another large rise in oil prices. The current account surplus has generally continued into the 1980s as North Sea oil became an increasingly important visible export.

One of the other main features of the balance of payments since 1980 has been the decline in the UK manufacturing industry. A deficit on manufactured goods was recorded for the first time in 1983, and there was still a deficit in 1986. As a result of this, the current account surplus declined from 1981, and in the last few years oil revenues have begun to decline, which could make the situation worse. The fall in the price of oil in 1986 further reduced oil revenues and contributed to a small current account deficit in 1986.

### Reducing a current account deficit
As we saw earlier in this Unit, a large current account deficit creates considerable problems for an economy, and the government may try to reduce it. Here are some of the ways it can do so:
▶ **1 Protectionism**
Increased tariffs and quotas will certainly reduce imports, but they will not deal with the underlying problem of uncompetitive products.
▶ **2 Policies to reduce spending**
Government spending cuts, tax increases, cuts in the money supply, and incomes policies have all been used in the past to try and reduce spending on imports. These are often called 'deflationary' policies. The problem with these policies is that they also reduce spending on home-produced goods, leading to falls in investment and economic growth and rises in unemployment.

**Current account balance of payments 1970-85**

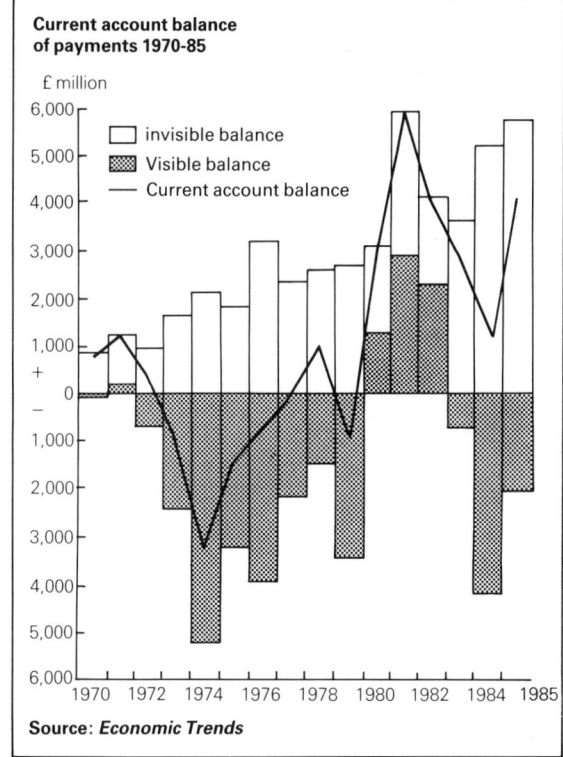

Source: *Economic Trends*

**Figure 8.2i**
Current account of the balance of payments 1970–1985

### ▶ 3 Devaluation

If the government takes action to cut the value of the pound in relation to other currencies (e.g. from £1 = $1.50 to £1 = $1.00), this will make imports more expensive and exports cheaper. The reason for this is dealt with in Unit 8.3. These price changes will reduce the demand for imports and increase the demand for exports. Providing the demand for imports and exports changes sufficiently, the current account of the balance of payments will improve.

### ▶ 4 Policies to make exports more competitive

In the long term it will be difficult to turn a current account deficit into a surplus unless a country's home-produced goods seem at least as attractive as foreign goods. Policies which successfully encourage investment and growth will improve the quality and competitiveness of a country's goods in the long term. There is much disagreement between economists about which policies are best to achieve long-term growth and competitiveness.

In the 1960s deflationary policies and devaluation were the main policies used to try to reduce the current account deficit. In the early 1970s the value of the pound fell following the steep rise in the price of oil and rapid inflation, and the government was able to do little to correct the current account deficit that followed. In 1976 the value of the pound reached a record low. This, coupled with deflationary policies, led to an improvement in the current account which was back in surplus by 1978, the first surplus since 1972. In the 1980s until 1986 the current account was generally in surplus and therefore the government did not have to take specific action to improve the balance of payments. However declining oil revenues and rising imports of consumer goods suggest that the government may have to pay more attention to the balance of payments again in future.

## DATABASE

## Area Analysis of World Trade
Percentage share of the value of World Exports & Imports

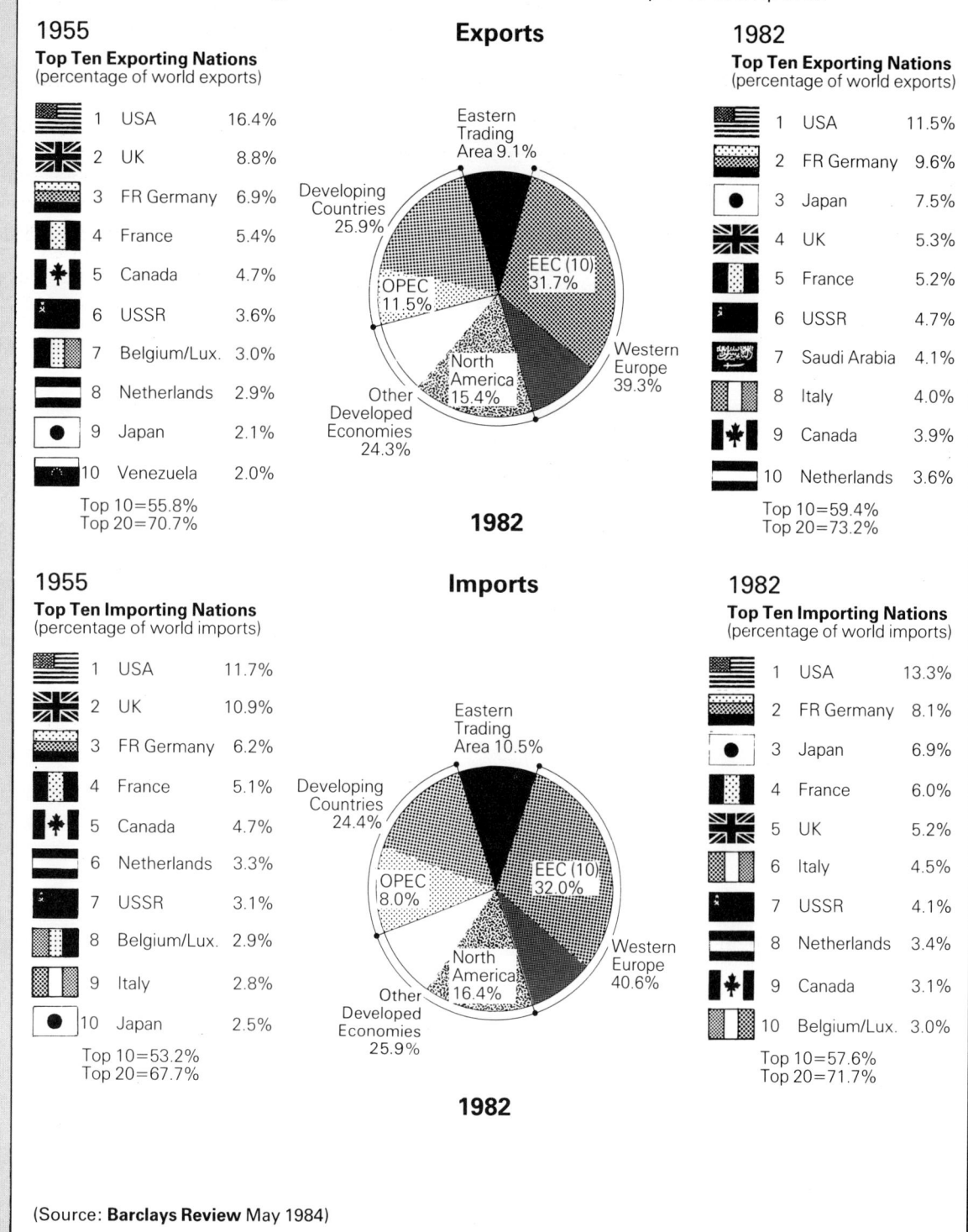

### Exports

**1955**
**Top Ten Exporting Nations**
(percentage of world exports)

| | | |
|---|---|---|
| 1 | USA | 16.4% |
| 2 | UK | 8.8% |
| 3 | FR Germany | 6.9% |
| 4 | France | 5.4% |
| 5 | Canada | 4.7% |
| 6 | USSR | 3.6% |
| 7 | Belgium/Lux. | 3.0% |
| 8 | Netherlands | 2.9% |
| 9 | Japan | 2.1% |
| 10 | Venezuela | 2.0% |

Top 10 = 55.8%
Top 20 = 70.7%

**1982** (pie chart)
- Eastern Trading Area 9.1%
- EEC (10) 31.7%
- Western Europe 39.3%
- North America 15.4%
- Other Developed Economies 24.3%
- OPEC 11.5%
- Developing Countries 25.9%

**1982**
**Top Ten Exporting Nations**
(percentage of world exports)

| | | |
|---|---|---|
| 1 | USA | 11.5% |
| 2 | FR Germany | 9.6% |
| 3 | Japan | 7.5% |
| 4 | UK | 5.3% |
| 5 | France | 5.2% |
| 6 | USSR | 4.7% |
| 7 | Saudi Arabia | 4.1% |
| 8 | Italy | 4.0% |
| 9 | Canada | 3.9% |
| 10 | Netherlands | 3.6% |

Top 10 = 59.4%
Top 20 = 73.2%

### Imports

**1955**
**Top Ten Importing Nations**
(percentage of world imports)

| | | |
|---|---|---|
| 1 | USA | 11.7% |
| 2 | UK | 10.9% |
| 3 | FR Germany | 6.2% |
| 4 | France | 5.1% |
| 5 | Canada | 4.7% |
| 6 | Netherlands | 3.3% |
| 7 | USSR | 3.1% |
| 8 | Belgium/Lux. | 2.9% |
| 9 | Italy | 2.8% |
| 10 | Japan | 2.5% |

Top 10 = 53.2%
Top 20 = 67.7%

**1982** (pie chart)
- Eastern Trading Area 10.5%
- EEC (10) 32.0%
- Western Europe 40.6%
- North America 16.4%
- Other Developed Economies 25.9%
- OPEC 8.0%
- Developing Countries 24.4%

**1982**
**Top Ten Importing Nations**
(percentage of world imports)

| | | |
|---|---|---|
| 1 | USA | 13.3% |
| 2 | FR Germany | 8.1% |
| 3 | Japan | 6.9% |
| 4 | France | 6.0% |
| 5 | UK | 5.2% |
| 6 | Italy | 4.5% |
| 7 | USSR | 4.1% |
| 8 | Netherlands | 3.4% |
| 9 | Canada | 3.1% |
| 10 | Belgium/Lux. | 3.0% |

Top 10 = 57.6%
Top 20 = 71.7%

(Source: **Barclays Review** May 1984)

## ACTIVITIES

### SECTION A: FOCUS ON UNIT 8.2

Go back and answer the questions raised in the Focus.

### SECTION B: STEPPED QUESTIONS

1. **a** What is shown by:
   - the balance of trade?
   - the invisible balance?
   - the balance of payments current account?
   
   **b** Are the following items visible exports, visible imports, invisible exports, invisible imports, or capital flows?
   - Austin Metros sold in France
   - the payment of dividends by British firms to their shareholders in West Germany
   - the sale of Japanese televisions in Britain
   - the building of new factories in Britain by foreign firms
   - British insurance companies selling policies to foreign residents?
   
   **c** How will the current account be affected by a *rise* in each of the examples in **b**?

2. **a** Describe the main trends in the UK current account of the balance of payments since 1970.
   
   **b** Explain the main reasons for the changes in the balance of payments since 1970.
   
   **c** How would an economist suggest that a balance of payments deficit could be reduced?
   
   **d** Explain, giving reasons, which policy or policies you would recommend.

## SECTION C: DATA RESPONSE QUESTIONS

### 1. UK balance of payments 1984

|  | (£) |
|---|---|
| Visible exports | .......... |
| Visible imports | 74,758m |
| Balance of trade | −4,391m |
| Invisible exports | 77,192m |
| Invisible imports | 71,239m |
| Investment and other capital flows (net) | −7,184m |

a What was the value of visible exports?
b Calculate the current account balance for 1984.
c Why are UK invisible credits usually greater than invisible debits?
d ▷ Calculate the balance for official financing.
  ▷ What does 'official financing' mean?
e ▷ What does the minus figure for investment and other capital flows mean?
  ▷ How might this affect the current balance in future?

### 2. North Sea oil and the balance of trade

| (£ millions) | Balance of trade (overall) | Balance of trade in oil | Balance of trade in other visibles |
|---|---|---|---|
| 1975 | −3,333 | −3,057 | −276 |
| 1976 | −3,929 | −3,947 | +18 |
| 1977 | −2,284 | −2,771 | +487 |
| 1978 | −1,542 | −1,984 | +442 |
| 1979 | −3,449 | −731 | −2,718 |
| 1980 | +1,361 | +315 | +1,046 |
| 1981 | +3,360 | +3,111 | +249 |
| 1982 | +2,331 | +4,643 | −2,312 |
| 1983 | −835 | +6,976 | −7,811 |
| 1984 | −4,391 | +6,937 | −11,328 |
| 1985 | −2,068 | +8,163 | −10,231 |

(Source: *Economic Trends* HMSO)

a Which was greater in 1980, exports of goods or imports of goods?
b Describe what happened to the balance of trade in oil between 1976 and 1985.
c Explain the trend you have found in **b**.
d ▷ Why was the balance of overall trade in goods in deficit from 1983 to 1985, even though the balance of trade in oil was in surplus?
  ▷ Explain why this occurred.

**EXTENSION MATERIAL 7**

### The terms of trade

The terms of trade are a way of measuring how successfully a country's exports are buying up a country's imports. The terms of trade are found by using the following formula:

$$\text{Terms of trade} = \frac{\text{Index of export prices}}{\text{Index of import prices}} \times 100$$

The government chooses a base year, and assigns an index number of 100 to both export prices and import prices. In the base year the terms of trade always equal 100:

$$\text{Terms of trade in the base year} = \frac{100}{100} \times 100 = 100$$

In the years following the base year changes in export prices and import prices are monitored. If, in the year after the base year, export prices rise by 10 per cent and import prices rise by 5 per cent, the terms of trade would change as follows:

$$\text{Terms of trade in year 2} = \frac{110}{105} \times 100 = 104.76$$

Export prices have risen relative to import prices. When this happens, and the terms of trade rise, there is said to be a 'favourable movement' in the terms of trade. If the terms of trade fall from one year to the next, there is said to be an 'unfavourable movement'.

#### The significance of changes in the terms of trade

A favourable movement in the terms of trade means that a given quantity of exports can now earn enough foreign currency to buy more imports than it could in the previous year. Another way of putting it, is that the country does not have to sell as many exports in order to buy the same quantity of imports. An unfavourable movement means that the country has to export more to earn enough to buy the same level of imports.

A favourable movement in the terms of trade does *not* necessarily improve the current account of the balance of payments, in fact it could worsen it. If, for example, a rise in the price of exports leads to a dramatic fall in the demand for exports (their demand is elastic), earnings from exports will actually fall. If, at the same time, the fall in import prices leads to a dramatic rise in the demand for imports (their demand is elastic), then spending on imports will rise. The combination of a fall in export revenue and a rise in import expenditure will worsen the balance of payments current account. In the same way, an unfavourable movement in the terms of trade need not necessarily worsen the balance of payments current account. Once again, it depends on the extent to which the demands for imports and exports change as a result of a change in their prices.

**Chart 1** Terms of trade (1980 = 100)

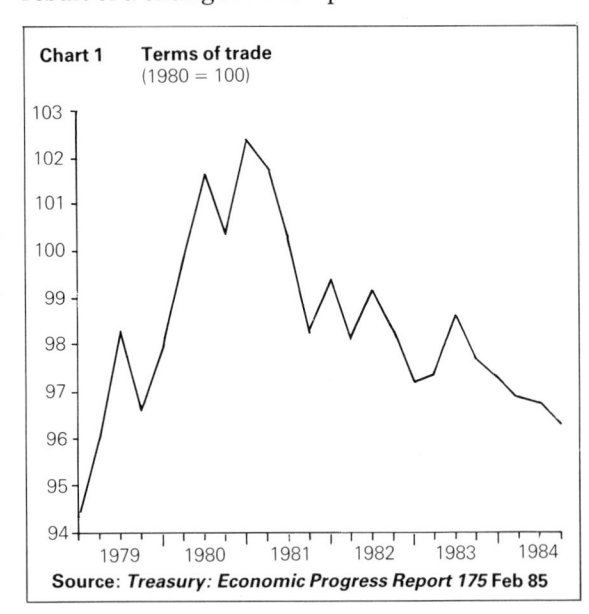

Source: *Treasury: Economic Progress Report 175* Feb 85

**Figure 8.2j**
The UK terms of trade 1979–1984

**EXTENSION QUESTION 7**

### QUESTION:

A country finds that the prices it is receiving for its exports have fallen, on average, by 5 per cent, while the prices of its imports have risen, on average, by 10 per cent:
a What has happened to the terms of trade for this country?
b How would these changes affect the economy of the country?
c Give some examples of countries that have suffered in this way, and name the products involved.

# UNIT 8.3  The value of the pound

▶ What is an **exchange rate**?

▶ Why do people exchange currencies?

▶ What factors can cause exchange rates to change?

▶ What are the effects of exchange rate changes?

## Exchange rates

An exchange rate is the price of one currency in terms of another. For example, if £1 = $1.30, you would have to pay £1 at a bank in order to purchase $1.30.

### Why currencies are exchanged
There are two main reasons why people go into banks and exchange one currency for another currency:
▶ **1 Currency is exchanged by people importing goods and services**
Figure 8.3a shows why importers need foreign currency. The British business manager is importing a car from the US. The car dealer in the US wants $10,000 for the car. In order to buy the car the business manager must go into a bank to change pounds to dollars. If £1 = $1.30, she will need to change £7,692 into dollars.

When people travel abroad they change pounds for foreign currency. The money spent abroad by British tourists counts as an invisible import as far as Britain is concerned.

**Figure 8.3a**
How is currency exchanged in foreign trade?

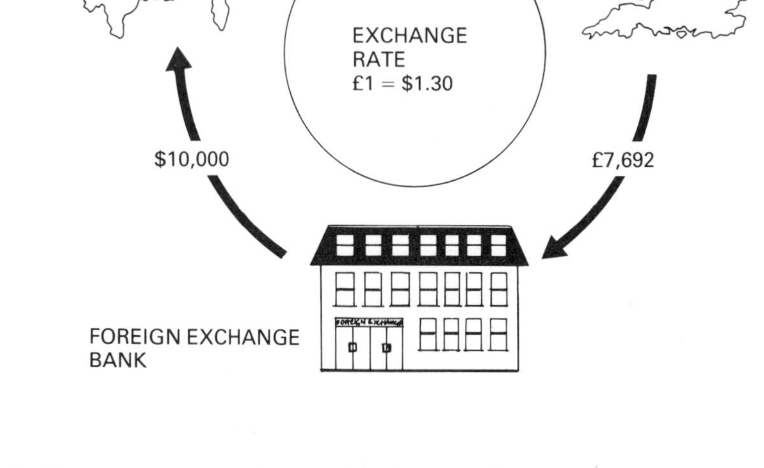

▶ **2 Currency is exchanged by speculators**
Speculators are people who buy and sell currencies in the hope of making a profit when exchange rates change. For example, if a speculator believes that the value of the pound will fall from £1 = $1.30, he or she might choose to change say, £10,000 into $13,000. If the exchange rate of the pound then falls to £1 = $1.28 the speculator can then change the $13,000 for £10,156, making a quick profit of £156.

### The reasons for changes in the exchange rate
You will have heard on the news that the value of the pound changes almost daily when compared to the dollar and other currencies. This is because the exchange rate of the pound is affected by the demand and supply of pounds. For example, if there is a rise in demand in the US for British cars, this will increase the demand for pounds and will cause a rise in the value of the pound. Here are some of the things that can cause a change in the demand or supply of a currency, and a change in the exchange rate:
▶ **1 Interest rate changes**
In 1984, US interest rates climbed steeply compared to interest rates in Britain. Speculators exchanged pounds for dollars in order to put dollars into US banks and earn high interest. The rise in the demand for dollars pushed up the exchange rate of the dollar against the pounds. In January, 1984 you needed 69p for every dollar purchased from a bank, but by August, 1984 you needed 77p. In early 1985 the UK government allowed interest rates to rise to stop the value of the pound going below one dollar. Interest rate changes have a great effect on exchange rates.
▶ **2 Balance of payments problems**
When a country has a deficit on its current account over a long period of time its exchange rate may fall. This is because the number of pounds being exchanged to buy imports is greater than the number of pounds that people in other countries are exchanging to buy the

**Figure 8.3b**
How can high imports and low exports lead to a fall in the exchange rate?

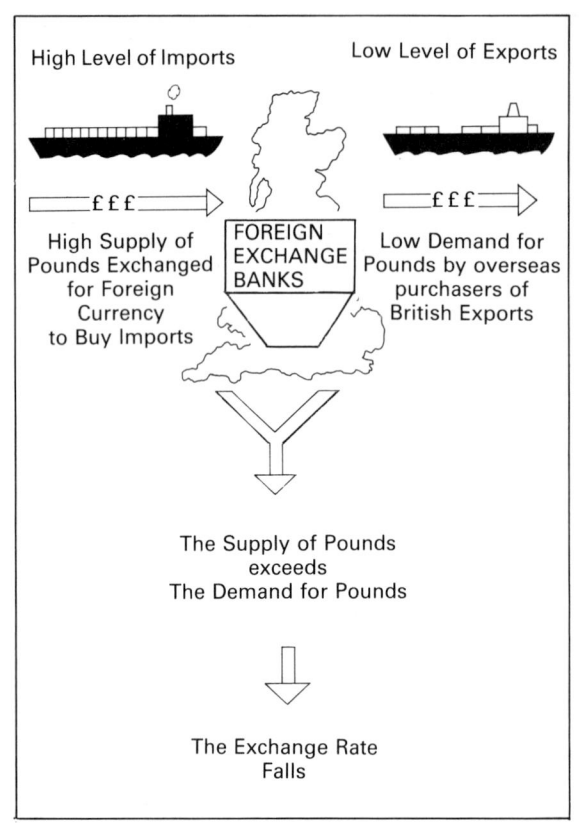

country's exports. This is shown in Fig. 8.3b.

▶ **3 Political and economic changes**

Certain political and economic changes can lead to speculators putting funds into a country or taking them out of a country. For example, a change in the government at a general election usually leads to a rise or fall in the value of a currency. Serious strikes, such as the miners' strike in Britain in 1984–85, can cause a fall in the exchange rate.

▶ **4 Inflation**

If a country has a higher rate of inflation than its trading partners, its exchange rate will fall. This is because its exports will be rising rapidly in price while import prices rise more slowly. This may cause a deficit to appear on the current account, and the exchange rate to fall.

**The effect of changes in the exchange rate**

If you have travelled abroad you will know that a fall in the value of the pound makes it more expensive to travel abroad. A fall in the currency makes foreign goods and services more expensive, so imports (including foreign travel) become less attractive. At the same time the fall in the value of a currency makes a country's exports cheaper. For example, if the exchange rate of the pound falls from £1=$1.30 to £1=$1.00 the American car costing $10,000 in the example at the beginning of this unit would cost £10,000 as opposed to £7,692 and the demand for American cars in the UK would fall. A British car costing £10,000 would cost $13,000 in the US before the fall in the value of the pound and $10,000 after the fall, and the demand for British cars in the US would rise. Therefore, in general, a fall in the exchange rate leads to a rise in the price of, and a fall in the demand for, imports and a fall in the price of, and rise in the demand for, exports. A rise in the exchange rate would have the opposite effect. Providing that the demand for imports and exports change sufficiently, a fall in the value of the pound should improve the balance of payments current account and a rise in the pound should worsen it.

**Changes in the exchange rate of the pound**

The value of the pound against a 'basket' of currencies representing all our major trading partners is known as the **effective exchange rate**. The value of the pound in terms of dollars is known as the **sterling-dollar exchange rate**. The effective exchange rate tended to fall against other currencies like the dollar, the deutschmark and the yen between 1972 and 1976. This was because of a sharp fall in the UK balance of payments current account due to a rapid rise in oil prices and inflation. Between 1976 and mid-1980 the value of the pound rose because of North Sea oil and high UK interest rates. Between 1981 and March 1985 the value of the pound fell slowly, initially because of the decline of manufacturing industry and some fall in relative interest rates, and then steeply in 1984–85 because of the effect of the long-term dispute between the National Coal Board (now British Coal) and the National Union of Mineworkers. Since then the sterling-dollar exchange rate has generally risen, mostly because of the weakness of the dollar whereas the effective exchange rate has remained more or less stable around 70 per cent of its 1975 value.

**Unit 8.3** *The value of the pound*

## DATABASE

The exchange rate of the pound

# 1. The effective exchange rate from 1972–1984

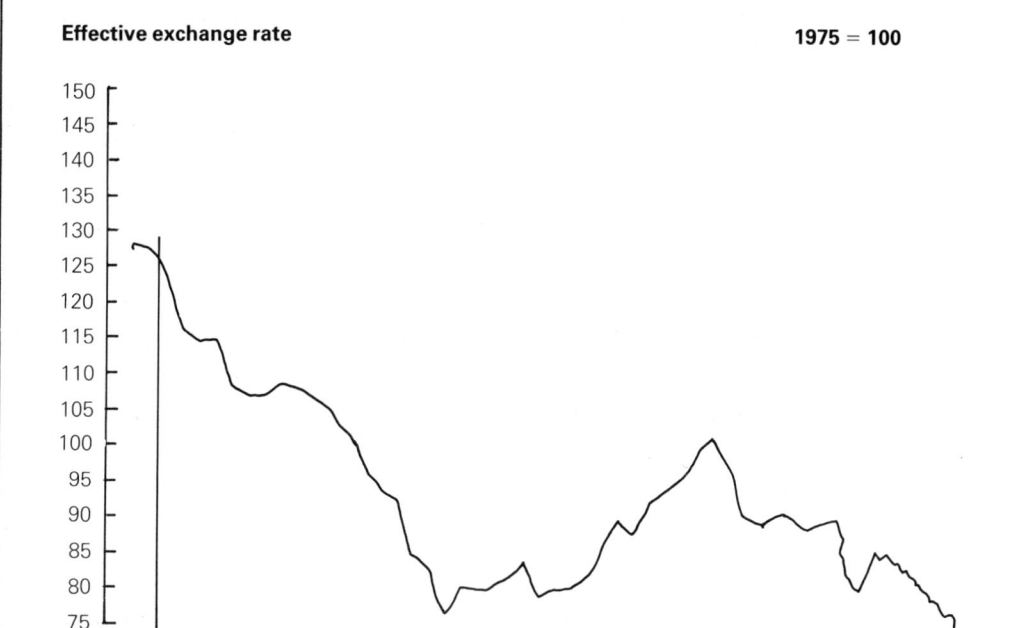

**Effective exchange rate**  1975 = 100

(Various sources)

## DATABASE

# 2. The value of the pound 1983–1986

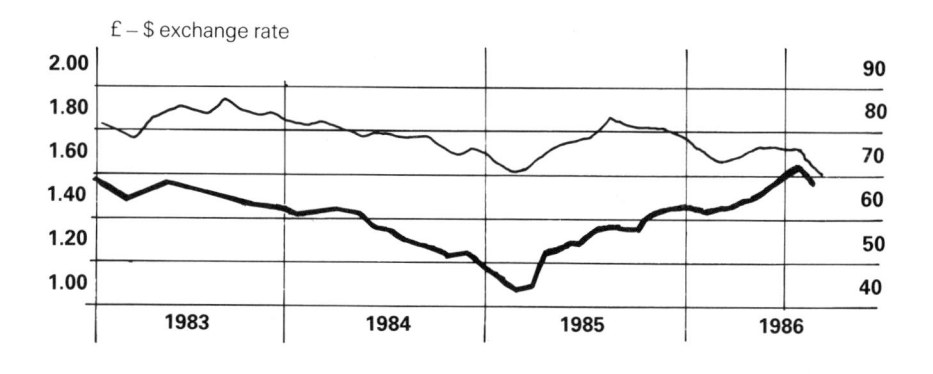

£ – $ exchange rate

Effective exchange rate (1975 = 100)

Key —— Effective exchange rate
      —— £ – $ Exchange rate

## ACTIVITIES

### SECTION A: FOCUS ON UNIT 8.3

Go back and answer the questions raised in the Focus.

### SECTION B: STEPPED QUESTIONS

1 This question refers to a Jaguar saloon, price £10,000 in the UK and a Nissan Sunny, price 1,500,000 yen in Japan.
   a What is the price of the Jaguar in pounds and in dollars:
      ▷ if the exchange rate is £1 = $1.50?
      ▷ if the exchange rate of the pound falls to £1 = $1?
   b How will the change from £1 = $1.50 to £1 = $1 affect the demand for Jaguars in the US?
   c What will happen to the demand for Nissan Sunnys in the UK if the pound changes in value from £1 = Y300 to £1 = Y200? Explain your answer.
   d What will be the effect of the change in c on the UK balance of payments? Explain your answer.
2 a Using the Database, describe what has happened to the value of the pound since 1972.
   b Explain why the value of the pound:
      ▷ rose between 1977 and 1980
      ▷ fell after 1981.
   c Explain why a rise in interest rates can lead to a higher exchange rate.
   d Is a high pound good for the UK? Explain your answer.

## SECTION C: DATA RESPONSE QUESTION

**The exchange rate of the pound against the dollar**

**Surging dollar dampens hopes**

The prospect of a fresh fall in interest rates receded yesterday in the wake of a fresh surge in the dollar, disappointing money supply figures, and the likely continuation of the coal dispute.

The dollar rose sharply on foreign exchanges against all major currencies, sending sterling to a new all-time low of $1.2910 before it recovered slightly to close 1.15 cents down at $1.2915. The main reason was a belief that dollar interest rates could rise still further after US construction industry figures which showed that economic growth may not be slowing as much as expected.

(Source: *The Guardian* 5.9.84)

    **a** What was special about the exchange rate of the pound against the dollar recorded during the day on 4th September 1984?
    **b** What happened by the time trading on the foreign exchanges ended for the day on 4th September 1984?
    **c** Had the pound fallen against all currencies other than the dollar? Explain your answer.
    **d** Why did the increasing strength of the dollar mean that interest rates in the UK were unlikely to fall?
    **e** Why was the rise in the dollar expected to continue?
    **f** Explain the possible effect of the rise in the dollar on:
      ▷ UK imports from the US
      ▷ UK exports to the US
      ▷ inflation in the UK.

**EXTENSION MATERIAL**

### Different types of exchange rate
There are two basic exchange rate systems, a floating exchange rate system and a fixed exchange rate system.

#### ▶ 1 Floating exchange rates
In a system of floating exchange rates the forces of supply and demand are left to act freely to determine the exchange rate. The government takes no action to stabilise or alter the exchange rate. Figure 8.3c uses supply and demand diagrams to illustrate how a change in the demand for imports or exports can change the exchange rate. It is important to note that the action of speculators also affects the supply and demands of pounds, and effects the exchange rate.

If a currency increases in value under a floating system, it is said to 'appreciate' in value. If it falls in value, it is said to 'depreciate' in value.

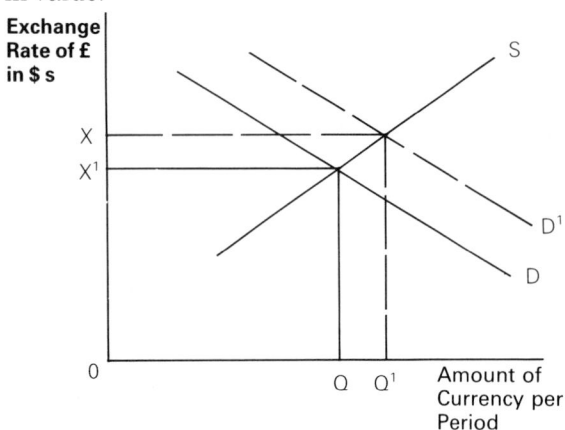

**Figure 8.3c**
A rise in demand for UK exports leads to an increase in the demand for pounds by foreigners wishing to buy UK goods.

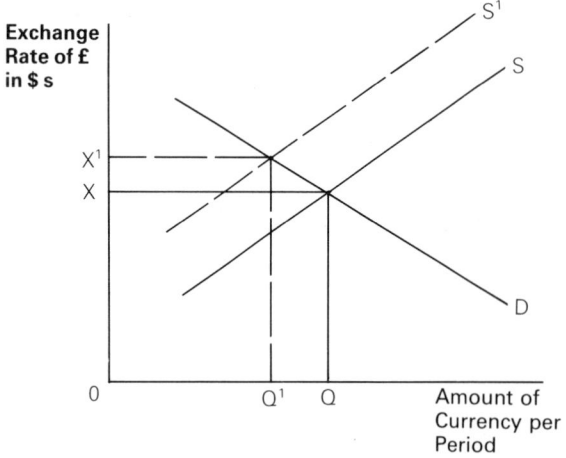

A fall in the demand for imports leads to a fall in the supply of pounds on foreign exchange markets as UK citizens are changing fewer pounds into foreign currency.

*The advantage of floating exchange rates* Some people say that floating exchange rates are desirable because, in theory, they correct balance of payments deficits automatically. This is shown in Fig. 8.3d.

*The disadvantages of floating exchange rates* There are several possible problems with floating exchange rates. They can cause uncertainty for business managers because they will be unsure about the future price of their exported goods, and they will be uncertain about the future price of imported resources. This problem can be overcome, however, because currency can be bought in what is called the **forward market**. Currency can be purchased for collection at some future date at an exchange rate agreed in the present. A fee has to be paid for this service, but it reduces uncertainty for business managers.

There are other problems. These include the fact that even with floating exchange rates balance of payments problems do not appear to correct themselves automatically. This is because the adjustment process shown in Fig. 8.3d can be very slow, and because all kinds of other factors, including government economic policy, affect the balance of payments.

#### ▶ 2 Fixed exchange rates
Under a fixed exchange rate system the central bank of the country uses its reserves of foreign currency to keep the currency at some agreed exchange rate. If, for example, the demand for exports falls and the demand for the country's currency falls, this will put a downward pressure on the exchange rate. The central bank will immediately use some of its foreign reserves to purchase its currency, cancelling out the fall in demand.

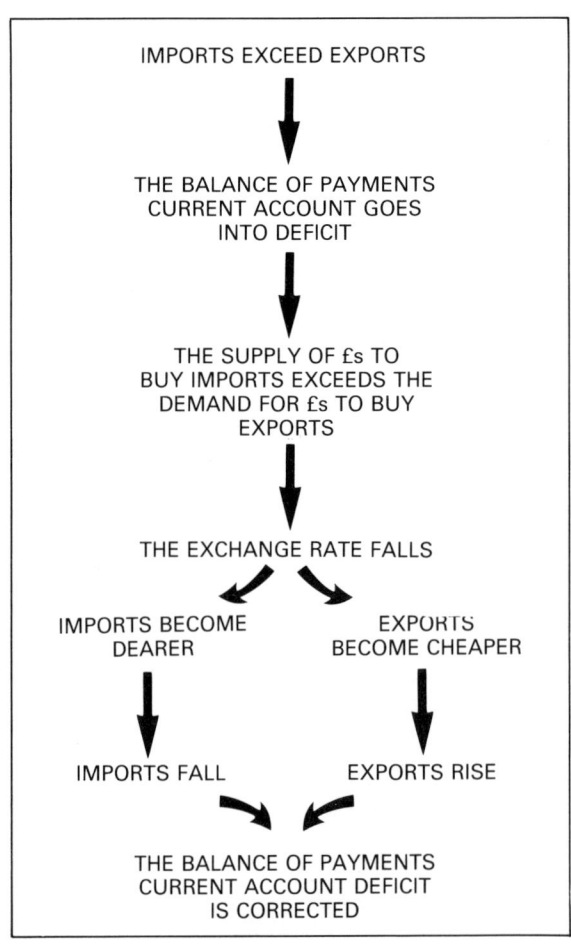

**Figure 8.3d**
How floating exchange rates may correct a balance of payments current account deficit

## EXTENSION MATERIAL

Fixed exchange rate systems in practice usually allow for changes in the exchange rate under exceptional circumstances. If a government decides to raise or lower the value of its currency it will instruct the central bank to buy or sell its own currency. Figure 8.3e shows how a currency's exchange rate can be lowered. If the currency is increased in value under a fixed exchange rate system, it is said to be 'revalued'. If it is decreased in value it is said to be 'devalued'.

*The advantage of a fixed exchange rate* Under a fixed exchange rate system business managers engaged in foreign trade can make reasonably certain predictions about future export and import prices. This certainty may provide a secure basis for investment and increased foreign trade.

*The disadvantages of a fixed exchange rate* Under a fixed exchange rate system there is no automatic correction of a balance of payments current account deficit. The government will need to take some of the measures described earlier in this Unit to deal with the problems. Other problems include the fact that fixed exchange rates are difficult to maintain in times of inflation, and that to maintain a fixed exchange rate the central bank must hold a large fund of reserves.

▶ **3 Other exchange rate systems**

▷ **a** *The Adjustable Peg System* From 1947 to 1972 many countries were on a system of exchange rates called the Adjustable Peg System. Countries were required to keep their currencies fixed against the dollar which, in turn, was fixed against gold. A small fluctuation each side of the agreed exchange rate was allowed. If a country's currency was considered by the International Monetary Fund (which operated the system) to be persistently overvalued, the country could devalue. Britain devalued in 1967.

▷ **b** *The European Monetary System* Several countries in Europe have linked their currencies together with each currency allowed just a small fluctuation each side of an agreed exchange rate. The group of currencies floats as a whole against other currencies like the dollar and the yen. Some economists have argued that the UK should join the EMS as it would prevent large changes in the value of the pound when speculators buy or sell pounds. However, other economists think that having to keep the pound inside the limits of the EMS would stop the UK government from freely deciding its economic policies.

▷ **c** *Managed floating* This probably best describes the UK's exchange rate system since 1972. The pound is free to float, but the Bank of England will intervene to smooth out particularly sudden rises or falls in the value of the pound.

The present world system is a mixture of floating exchange rates, and systems like the EMS.

**Figure 8.3e**
Devaluation under a fixed exchange rate

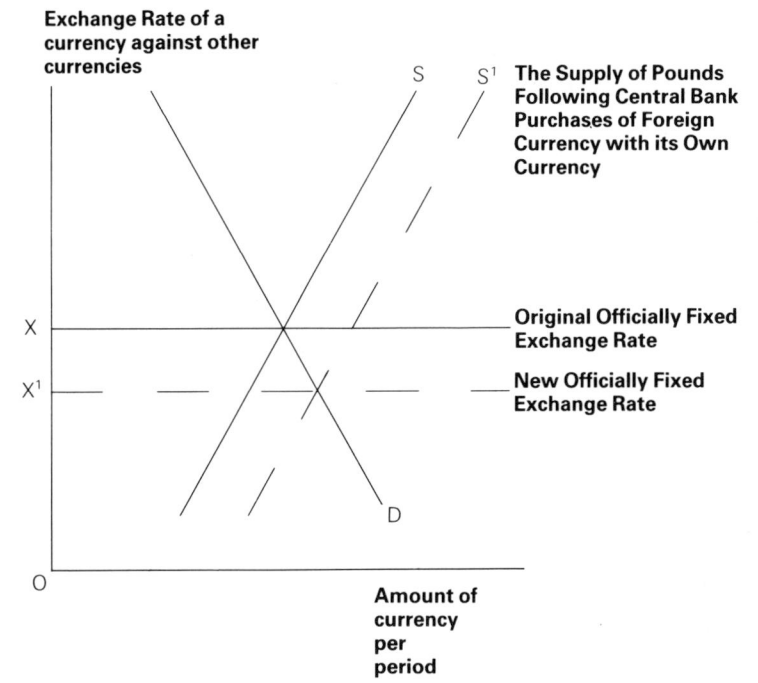

## EXTENSION QUESTION

### QUESTION

a  Explain the difference between fixed and floating exchange rates.
b  What is the difference between a 'devaluation' and a 'depreciation' of a currency?
c  What would be the economic effects of the UK adopting a fixed exchange rate system?
d  Which do you think would most improve the UK's ability to compete in world markets: devaluation, revaluation, or joining the EMS? Explain your answer.

# UNIT 8.4 Trade agreements and the EEC

▶ What types of trade agreements can countries make with each other?

▶ What are the major purposes and policies of the EEC?

▶ What economic effects does EEC membership have on the UK?

## Trade agreements and the European Economic Community

Countries often get together to sign agreements covering all kinds of matters relating to foreign trade. We have already seen that eighty eight countries have signed the General Agreement on Tariffs and Trade. This Unit looks at some other agreements concerned with foreign trade.

### Free trade areas
Countries that belong to a free trade area agree to end all trade restrictions between themselves. In other words, goods can move between one country and another without restrictions like tariffs, quotas, and subsidies.

### A customs union or common market
Customs unions (also called 'common markets') are free trade areas with common trade restrictions on goods and services coming into the customs union from countries outside it. Britain and France are in the same customs union, the European Economic Community. Goods entering Britain from, say, Japan, must in theory have the same tariffs and other trade restrictions on them as the same goods entering France.

**Figure 8.4a**
Countries in the EEC and EFTA

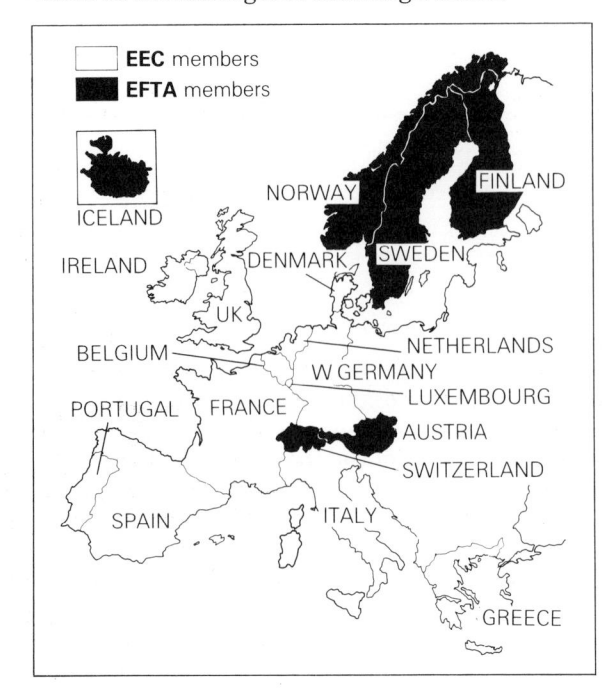

## The European Economic Community (EEC)
In 1957 six countries signed the Treaty of Rome to set up the EEC. The UK joined in 1973, and by 1984 there were ten member countries. Portugal and Spain joined on 1st January, 1987. The members of the EEC in 1987 are shown in Fig. 8.4a.

The EEC is a customs union. It is often called 'The Common Market'. Over the years restrictions on the movement of goods and services, including factors of production like labour, have been reduced, and common trade restrictions on imports from outside the EEC have been introduced. There is still a long way to go before all the aims have been achieved.

### How the EEC is organised
▷ 1 *The Council of Ministers* This group of people decide policy for the EEC. Each country has one seat on the Council, and usually each country has to agree to a proposal before it becomes EEC policy.
▷ 2 *The Commission* The EEC Commission suggests policy to the Council of Ministers, and then make sure that countries in the EEC carry out the policy. Commissioners are supposed to represent the EEC as a whole rather than the countries from which they come.
▷ 3 *The European Parliament* The Parliament discusses EEC policy and watches over the activities of the Council and the Commision. Many people complain that the Parliament, the only directly elected group of people involved in running the EEC, has very little power in practice.
▷ 4 *The Court of Justice* The Court has one judge from each member country. It decides whether members of the EEC have broken its laws and agreements.

### How the EEC raises and spends its finance
**The ways of raising finance**
The EEC raises finance in three main ways:
▷ 1 *VAT* Member countries of the EEC all raise revenue from value-added tax. Up to 1 per cent of this revenue must be paid to the EEC, and this makes up over half of all EEC funds.
▷ 2 *Agricultural levies* Imports of many agricultural products are not allowed into the EEC at prices lower than the same product produced in the EEC. The EEC places a levy – a sort of tax – on the agricultural products entering the EEC

**Figure 8.4b**
How might farmers suffer when there is a good harvest?

to bring them up to EEC prices.
▷ 3 *Customs duties* Duties are also a sort of tax on imports, and about a third of EEC funds are raised by duties.

### How the EEC spends its funds
About two-thirds of all EEC funds are spent on agriculture. The various policies of the EEC on which most of their finances are spent are explained in the next section.

### Some EEC policies
▷ 1 *The Common Agricultural Policy* We have seen that most of the EEC funds in any year are spent on agriculture and in particular on a policy called the **Common Agricultural Policy** (CAP). The purpose of the policy is to make sure that the people in the EEC receive regular supplies of food at reasonable prices. At the same time it tries to make sure that farmers receive a good income and have an incentive to invest and become more efficient.

The reason why the EEC is involved so much in farming is because the laws of supply and demand can work differently in farming to nearly every other industry. If farmers received no help from governments they may end up being rewarded by high prices and high incomes when they produce little, and being punished by low prices and low incomes when they have good harvests. This is because the demand for food remains more or less the same year after year. If food prices fall, people do not rush out and buy lots more food, nor do they cut down greatly on what they eat if food prices rise. Figure 8.4b shows the problem that this causes farmers.

Under the CAP the EEC sets a guaranteed minimum price for many farm products. If farmers have a good harvest the EEC allows farmers to offer for sale to the public only enough to stop the price falling below the agreed minimum. The EEC then uses a special agricultural fund to buy up the surplus. The surplus has to be stored, sold off outside the EEC, or, if there is no alternative, destroyed. If there is a bad harvest the EEC puts some of the surplus back on the market to stop prices rising steeply.

In addition to buying up agricultural surpluses, the EEC uses levies to stop imported food selling in the EEC at below EEC prices. It also uses funds to buy out inefficient farmers, and to help other farmers modernise their farms and reduce their costs of production.

▷ 2 *The regional policy* The European Regional Development Fund provides financial help for regions with severe economic problems. For example, it has provided funds to help with road building in South Wales, a region suffering severely as a result of a fall in employment in industries like coal mining and steel production.

▷ 3 *The social policy* The European Social Fund helps to provide funds for rehousing and retraining workers who are made redundant.

### The advantages of the EEC to Britain
Before Britain joined the EEC, and right up to

the present time, people have argued about whether EEC membership is good for Britain. Here are some of the arguments for British membership, and they are followed by some of the arguments against:

▷ **1** *A larger market* EEC membership means that British firms can sell to over 300 million people with few restrictions on trade. If Britain left the EEC, EEC countries might put trade restrictions on our goods.

▷ **2** *Greater efficiency and economies of scale* Firms from all over the EEC can sell their goods without restriction in Britain. This forces British firms to work efficiently to develop attractive new products at low costs and low prices. In addition, costs should be lowered by economies of scale because firms are producing on a larger scale for a larger market.

▷ **3** *A plentiful supply of food* Since joining the EEC, Britain has rarely run short of food. This has been an advantage of the CAP to British consumers.

▷ **4** *A greater say in world affairs* Over this century Britain has gradually lost its position as a major political and economic power. As a member of a larger group Britain can have a greater say in world affairs.

### The disadvantages of the EEC to Britain

▷ **1** *A decline in British manufacturing industry* As a member of the EEC, the government cannot prevent cheap imports from other EEC countries entering the country. This has led to the closure of many British manufacturing firms.

▷ **2** *A loss of cheap supplies of food* Some agricultural products, like butter, are produced and sold more cheaply outside the EEC than within it. Since joining the EEC Britain has lost the opportunity of purchasing some food products on the cheapest markets.

▷ **3** *The high cost of membership* Throughout its membership Britain has tended to pay more into the EEC than it has taken out. The only other country in the same position in recent years has been West Germany. British governments has protested that this is unfair because Britain has one of the lowest incomes per head in the community. There have been negotiations, and many arguments between Britain and the rest of the EEC to try and settle this matter.

▷ **4** *A loss of power by the British government* The EEC Commission issues many directives which member countries have to follow. Some people say that this takes away power from the Houses of Parliament and the British government.

### The European Economic Community and the rest of the world

The EEC has entered special trading agreements with many of world's poorer nations, particularly those that used to be colonies of EEC countries in the past. These countries are often allowed to sell many of their goods in the EEC without restrictions.

In 1984 the EEC removed all tariffs and quotas on its trade with the European Free Trade Association (EFTA). EFTA is a free trade area made up of seven western european countries. Unlike the EEC, it has no large organisation to run it, and it is not a customs union.

**Figure 8.4c**
What problem of the CAP is illustrated here?

**Figure 8.4d**
What problems does UK membership of the EEC create for UK manufacturers of consumer durables?

Unit 8.4 *Trade agreements and the EEC*

## DATABASE

# 1. The expenditure of the EEC 1984

Common Agricultural Policy £11,543m

Social policy £1,174 m

Other £2,180m

Regional policy £1,161m

Research; energy, industry, & transport £743m

**Total £16,798m**

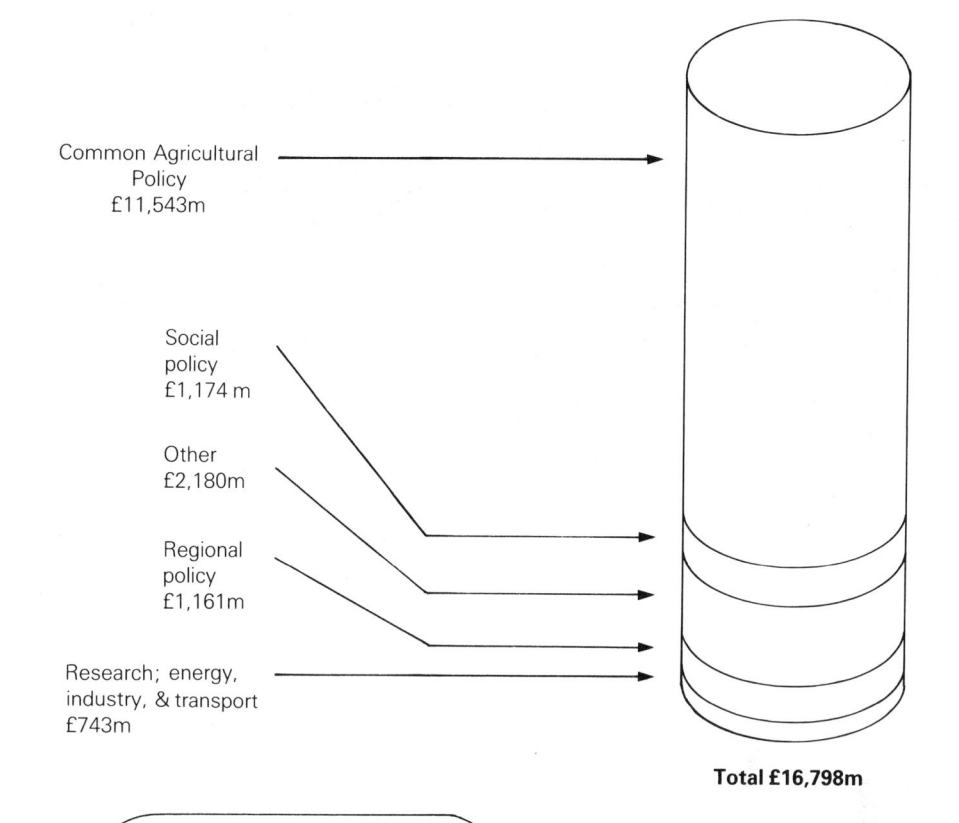

## DATABASE

# 2. The EEC and UK trade

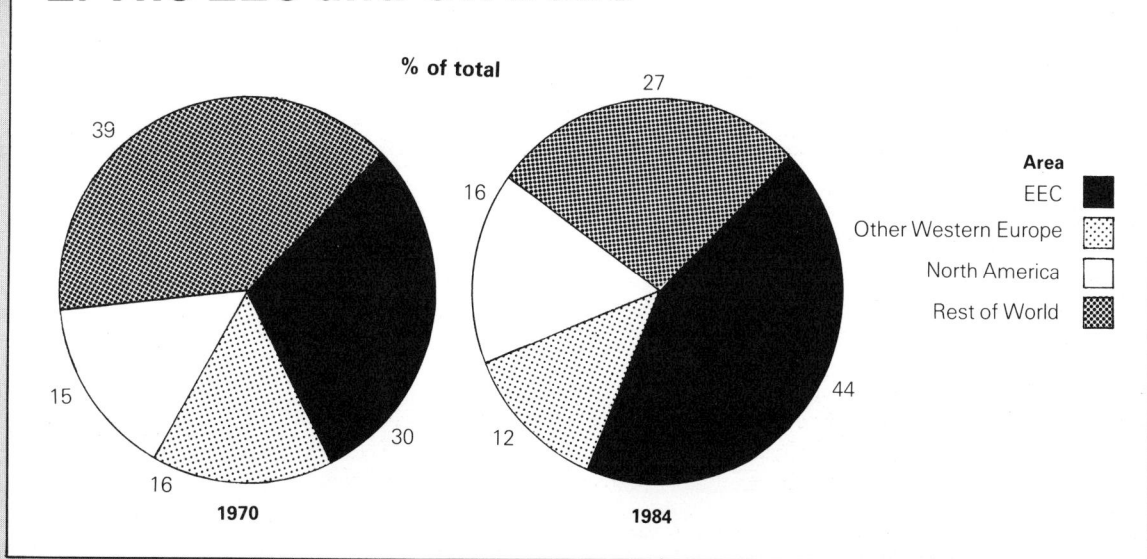

% of total

**1970**
- 39 Rest of World
- 15 North America
- 16 Other Western Europe
- 30 EEC

**1984**
- 27 Rest of World
- 16 North America
- 12 Other Western Europe
- 44 EEC

**Area**
- EEC
- Other Western Europe
- North America
- Rest of World

## ACTIVITIES

### SECTION A: FOCUS ON UNIT 8.4

Go back and answer the questions raised in the Focus.

### SECTION B: STEPPED QUESTIONS

1  a  Explain the difference between a 'free trade area' and a 'customs union'.
   b  Explain why countries in western Europe have decided to try and end trade restrictions between themselves.
2  a  ▷ What does 'EEC' stand for?
      ▷ List the 12 countries in the EEC.
   b  Describe the EEC's main items of spending.
   c  How does the EEC raise finance for its spending?
   d  'Being a member of the EEC means that the UK is unable to stop imports from some of its competitors, and it must put tariffs against other countries it needs to import from.'
      ▷ Explain this statement.
      ▷ Do you think this is good enough reason for the UK to leave the EEC?
   e  Does the decision whether or not to be a member of the EEC illustrate that economic decisions sometimes involve consideration of factors that are not purely economic?

## SECTION C: DATA RESPONSE QUESTION

**Farming surpluses in the EEC**

### EEC Makes a Hash of its Salad Days

Missing the chance of making the biggest and most expensive fruit salad in the world, the EEC farm authorities last year bought and destroyed 206,350 tonnes of apples, 123,107 tonnes of oranges, 120,290 tonnes of lemons, and 10,861 tonnes of pears.

Vast quantities of tomatoes, peaches, and mandarins were also dumped or ploughed back into the ground, after being bought from Community growers at guaranteed prices.

In the farm year 1982-83 the EEC was destroying, every minute: 866lb of apples, 41 cauliflowers, 1,648 lemons, 1,358 oranges, 438 peaches, 755lb of tomatoes, 46lb of pears, and 51lb of mandarins.

In addition, 2,304lb of apples, and 175lb of pears were distilled every minute into alcohol.

(Source: *The Guardian* 14.5.84.)

a How many lemons and cauliflowers was the EEC destroying every minute in 1982–1983?
b Which policy of the EEC is responsible for the huge surplus of fruit?
c Why do farmers produce as much as they can, even if demand by consumers is well below the amount that they are supplying?
d ▷ Describe *two* ways mentioned in the passage that the EEC is using to dispose of surplus fruit.
▷ Describe *two* other ways in which surplus goods are disposed of by the EEC.
e Explain *two* ways in which the EEC is trying to improve farming efficiency.

# UNIT 8.5 Developing economies & world economic organisations

**FOCUS**

▶ What are the main characteristics of **developing countries**?

▶ What problems are faced by many developing countries that may be less of a problem for more industrialised countries?

▶ What economic relationships exist between developing and industrialised countries?

▶ How have these relationships affected developing countries?

▶ What are the main world economic organisations other than GATT and the EEC?

## Developing countries

Developing countries are countries with low incomes per head of the population. In 1983 countries tended to be called developing countries if their GNP was below US$5,000 (about £3,500) per person. Many developing countries are far poorer than this, and several countries, particularly in the north of Africa, have GNPs per person as low as US$300 (about £200) a year.

Developing countries are sometimes also called 'less developed countries' (LDCs), 'Third World countries', or 'the South'. In fact it is almost impossible to lump together countries in this way because there are such great differences between them. Nevertheless, by calling some countries developing countries, it helps us to understand and talk about many of the problems faced by countries on lower incomes throughout the world. Countries on higher incomes tend to be called 'developed' or 'industrialised' countries.

### The problems of developing countries

Here are some of the problems faced by many developing countries. Not all the problems are faced by all the countries, and some countries suffer the problems more severely than others:

▶ **1 Rapidly rising populations**
Figure 8.5b shows that birth rates tend to be much higher than death rates in developing countries. Although both are falling, birth rates are still much higher, and this leads to rapid population growth. In many developing countries 50 per cent of the population is under the age of fifteen.

**Figure 8.5a**

### North and South: some of the differences

NORTH-SOUTH is a very simple way of showing how the world divides into rich and poor countries. Countries in the rich NORTH are those in North America, Europe, USSR, Japan, Australia, and New Zealand. Countries in the poorer SOUTH are most of Asia, Africa, and Latin America.

Countries of the SOUTH are sometimes called the 'Third World' or 'developing' countries because they are generally poorer.

**NORTH:**
- ¼ of the world's people
- ⅘ of the world's income
- person can expect to live on average more than 70 years
- most people have enough to eat
- most people are educated at least through secondary school
- over 90% of the world's manufacturing industry
- about 96% of world's spending on research and development, nearly all the world's registered patents
- dominates most of the international economic system and institutions of trade, money and finance

**SOUTH:**
- ¾ of the world's people
- ⅕ of the world's income
- person can expect to live, on average, to about 50 years (in the poorest countries, ¼ of children die before the age of 5)
- ⅕ or more of the people suffer from hunger and malnutrition
- ½ of the people still have little chance of formal education

According to the Brandt Report, about 800 million people (40% of the South) are barely surviving. Most of these live in the poorest countries of Sub-Saharan Africa and South Asia. About ⅔ of the world's very poorest people live in Bangladesh, India, Indonesia, and Pakistan.

Source: North-South: Our Links With Poorer Countries

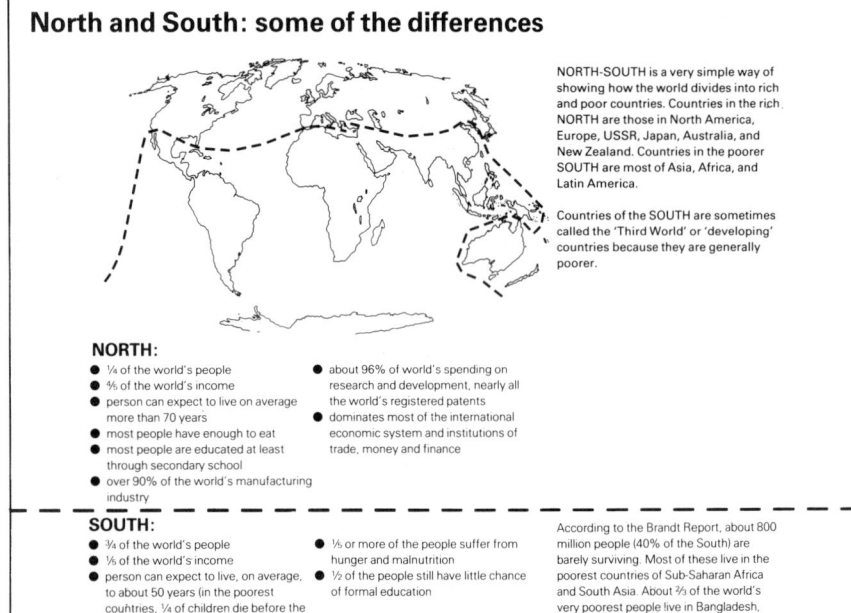

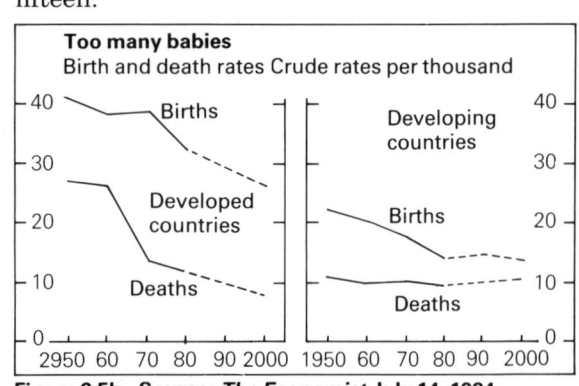

**Too many babies**
Birth and death rates Crude rates per thousand

*[Graph showing Developed countries: Births declining from ~25 to ~15, Deaths around 10, from 1950-2000]*
*[Graph showing Developing countries: Births declining from ~40 to ~25, Deaths declining to ~10, from 1950-2000]*

**Figure 8.5b** Source: *The Economist* July 14, 1984

▶ **2 Poor climate, and poor soils for farming**
Most developing countries are in hot, dry parts of the world, or in other areas where it is difficult or impossible to grow crops cheaply and easily. The world's poorest countries are found in hot desert and grass land areas of the Sahara and Sahel in northern Africa.

### 3 Little capital investment

If a country is very poor, it may be unable to spare the resources necessary to buy vital capital equipment like tractors and electric water pumps. These goods usually need to be imported, and any foreign currency earned by a developing country from selling its exports usually goes to pay for immediate needs like grain and oil.

### 4 A dependence on one or two exports

Many developing countries rely on just one or two exports, usually of basic primary products (commodities). For example, about 90 per cent of Zambia's exports are copper, and about 80 per cent of Cuba's exports are sugar. Primary product prices change very rapidly from one year to the next, and this can lead to sudden falls in export earnings. For example, in just three months in the middle of 1984, the price of soyabean products fell by about 25 per cent and the prices of tea, coffee, copper and zinc all fell by over 10 per cent. The price of imports to developing countries, however, very rarely falls.

### 5 A foreign debt problem

Many developing countries owe huge sums to foreign governments and banks. At the end of 1983, for example, Mexico owed £93,000 million. This is because many poorer countries borrowed heavily in the early 1970s when commodity prices were high, but since then commodity prices have fallen and so have the developing countries' export earnings. Many developing countries see no hope of ever repaying many of their loans, and some cannot even afford to keep up interest payments.

### 6 Extreme poverty

In developing countries the majority of the population live on farms which grow barely enough food to support them, and in shanty towns around large cities which can offer very little work for the millions of people that live in them. In many developing countries bad harvests can lead to mass starvation, as was the case when drought killed millions in Africa in 1984.

## Developing countries and the developed world

In recent years much has been written about the relationship between developing countries and the wealthier countries of the world, particularly in western Europe and North America. Two of the most important reports are called the 'Brandt Reports':

### 1 Brandt Report: 'North-South: A Programme for Survival'

The first Brandt Report said that developed countries could not cut themselves off from the problems of the developing world. It pointed out that the industrialised world depends on developing countries for its supplies of basic materials. The developed countries need developing countries as markets for their manufactured goods. The attitude of the report can be summed up in a quote from the report:

'The world is a unity and we must begin to act as members of it who depend upon each other.'

The report made many recommendations. Here are just some of them:

▷ 1 There must be an emergency programme of help for the very poorest countries.

▷ 2 More funds must be spent on agricultural improvement to end mass hunger and malnutrition.

▷ 3 Funds and skills being put into arms production must be channelled into peaceful needs.

▷ 4 Developing countries should be encouraged to manufacture goods from raw materials, and sell the finished products. At the present time industrialised countries will allow the import of products like sisal, which their own firms use to make string, but they often block imports of string itself because it threatens their own industry. Protectionist measures prevent developing countries increasing the value of their exports and selling a wider range of products.

▷ 5 Aid flows should be increased so that richer countries are giving at least 1 per cent of their GNP in aid by the year 2000.

**Figure 8.5c**
Why does this kind of appeal have to be made regularly, when some countries destroy food surpluses?

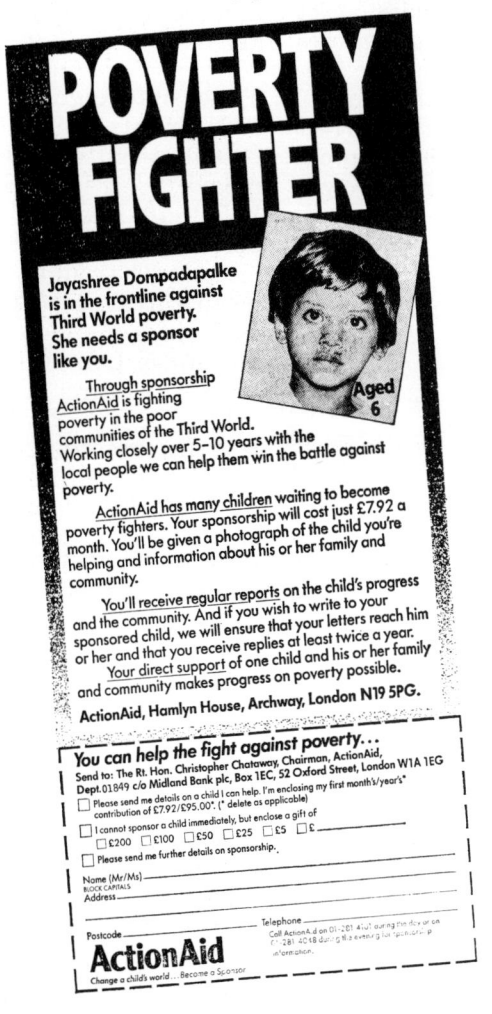

▷ 6 The international monetary system should be reorganised so that poorer countries can borrow funds more easily with easier conditions and lower interest rates.
▷ 7 More attention must be paid to educating public opinion and the young especially about the importance of international co-operation.

▶ 2 **Brandt Report: 'The Common Crisis'**
The second Brandt Report was written and published when there was particular concern about the foreign debt crisis in the Third World. The second report again suggested that more help in the form of grants and easy loans should be given from the developed to the developing world, and that the North must end restrictions on imports from the South.

### Criticisms of the Brandt Reports
Some people criticise the Brandt Reports for suggesting that the developed countries should simply go on pouring more money into the developing world. They point out that much of the existing money is spent on, for example, the armed forces and expensive government buildings. They say that aid does not encourage poorer countries to sort out their own economic difficulties such as high inflation and economic and political corruption. They believe that financial help should be given under strict conditions, for example that developing countries cut government spending and decrease unnecessary imports. They suggest that if countries like Britain and the USA take the correct measures to sort out their own economic problems, this will lead to more economic growth generally which will benefit both the richer and the poorer nations of the world.

## Foreign aid

### Why aid is given
Higher income countries may give aid to developing countries for a number of reasons. Here are some of them:

▶ 1 **Reasons of conscience**
Many people believe that richer nations should help poorer nations because it is right and just for them to do so. Developed countries have often become wealthy because of cheap imports of basic commodities from poorer countries.

▶ 2 **Political self-interest**
Much aid is given because one country wants the political support of another country, and they do not want the government to fall into the hands of parties that do not support them. This is the reason for much of the aid given by the US to El Salvador, and the Soviet Union to Cuba.

▶ 3 **Economic self-interest**
If an industrialised country gives aid to a developing country, the developing country may spend it on the exports of the industrialised country. The industrialised country gains (or, at least, does not lose) as a result of giving the aid.

### Types of foreign aid
▶ 1 **Grants**
Grants are gifts of money that do not have to be repaid.

▶ 2 **'Soft' loans**
Soft loans are loans carrying very little or no interest. The country receiving the loan may be given a great deal of time to repay it.

▶ 3 **Gifts of goods**
Sometimes gifts such as food and blankets will be sent to poorer countries, especially if there has been a major disaster such as an earthquake.

▶ 4 **Information, advice and training**
Developed countries often provide experts in areas like population control, agriculture and engineering to help and advice with development in developing countries. Places are often provided at colleges and universities in developed countries for students from the developing countries.

▶ 5 **Tied aid**
Sometimes an industrialised country will give a poorer country a grant or loan only if the money is spent on goods produced by the 'donor' country (the country giving the aid). This type of aid is called 'tied aid', and in 1981 about 30 per cent of British grants and loans to developing countries were 'tied'.

▶ 6 **Bilateral and multilateral aid**
Bilateral aid is aid given by one country to another. Multilateral aid is aid given by more

**Figure 8.5d** Bilateral aid and multilateral aid

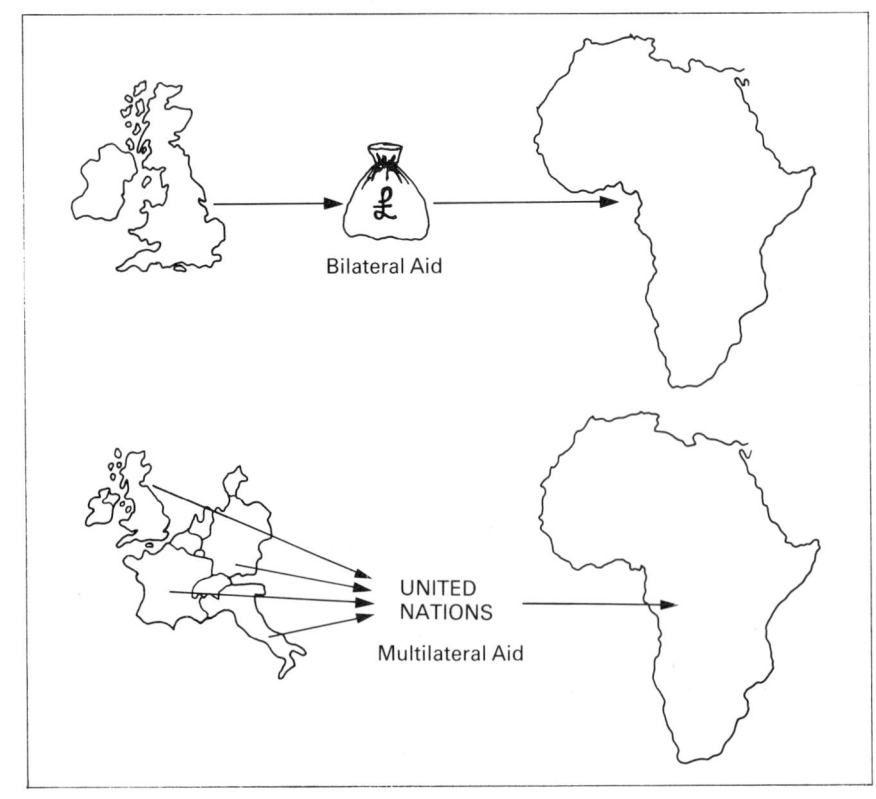

than one country to a developing country. Multilateral aid is usually given through an organisation like the United Nations.

## World economic organisations

World economic organisations can generally be divided into two groups: trading areas and groups, and worldwide organisations.

### Trading areas and groups

We have already seen in Unit 8.4 how countries have agreed on trade policies in the EEC. COMECON (the Council for Mutual Economic Assistance) is in many ways the equivalent of the EEC for centrally-planned economies. Most of the COMECON countries are in eastern Europe although Mongolia, Cuba and Vietnam are also members. There are many other free trade areas and customs unions in areas such as Latin America and southern Africa. OPEC (Organisation of Petroleum Exporting Countries) is slightly different in that it aims to control the prices of crude oil. OPEC is a cartel since it can restrict the supply of oil in order to increase prices. The first major oil price rise caused by OPEC was in 1973, which had considerable economic effects.

### Worldwide organisations

As we have seen in Unit 8.1, countries from different areas of the world have tried to get together to agree on trade policy in GATT. There are many other worldwide economic organisations set up for different purposes. We will look at three of the main ones:

▶ **1 The International Monetary Fund (IMF)**
146 countries belong to the IMF. They all provide it with funds. And they can usually borrow from it when they have severe balance of payments difficulties. In recent years the IMF has given assistance to countries with severe debt problems but it has usually demanded that they use policies that it approves of, for example anti-inflationary policies.

▶ **2 The International Bank for Reconstruction and Development (IBRD)**
The IBRD is also known as the **World Bank**. It obtains its funds from subscriptions from member countries and by borrowing. It provides loans for projects to increase economic development. It was felt that 'soft loans' on easier terms should be provided for such projects to developing countries. This led to the formation of the IDA (International Development Association) which is basically part of the World Bank. It provides loans specifically for economic development projects in developing countries, often at no interest.

▶ **3 United Nations Conference on Trade and Development (UNCTAD)**
This was set up to promote policies to help economic development in developing countries. It is held every four years, most recently in Belgrade in 1983. It has been used by developing countries to bargain with developed countries, particularly in trying to get higher prices for their exports. They are realising that they are less vulnerable if they act together, as the developed world depends on many of them for raw materials.

**Unit 8.5** *Developing economies & world economic organisations*

## DATABASE

# 1. Indicators of world development

**Gross national product, 1982, at market prices**

- Less than $10 billion
- $10 billion to less than $50 billion
- $50 billion to less than $100 billion
- $100 billion and more
- No data

**The Distribution of GNP per capita, 1982**
*Shares of world population living in countries having different levels of GNP per capita*

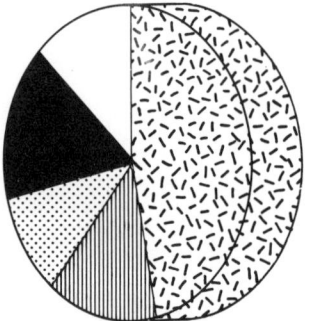

- $400 and less
- $401 to $1,635
- $2,636 to $5,500
- More than $5,500
- No data

**Infant mortality rate, 1982[1]**
*Shares of world population in countries having different infant mortality rates*

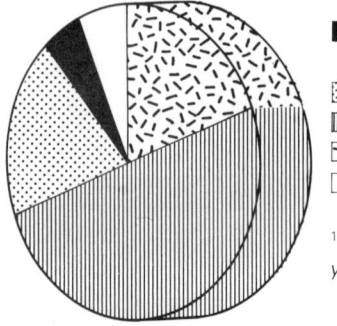

- Less than 10 per thousand live births
- 10 to less than 50
- 50 to less than 100
- 100 and more
- No data

[1] *Deaths in the first year of life.*

(Source: IMF *Finance and Development* June 1985)

## DATABASE

## 2. Who gives aid, and how much?

### Ranking of 17 largest donors of aid, 1984[1]

| | Volume of aid (in millions of US dollars) | | | |
|---|---|---|---|---|
| | Amount | Share (Percent) | Percent of GNP | |
| 1. United States | 8,698 | 30.4 | 1. Netherlands | 1.02 |
| 2. Japan | 4,319 | 15.1 | 2. Norway | 0.99 |
| 3. France | 3,790 | 13.2 | 3. Denmark | 0.85 |
| 4. Germany | 2,782 | 9.7 | 4. Sweden | 0.80 |
| 5. Canada | 1,625 | 5.7 | 5. France | 0.77 |
| 6. United Kingdom | 1,432 | 5.0 | 6. Belgium | 0.56 |
| 7. Netherlands | 1,268 | 4.4 | 7. Canada | 0.50 |
| 8. Italy | 1,105 | 3.9 | 8. Germany | 0.45 |
| 9. Australia | 773 | 2.7 | 8. Australia | 0.45 |
| 10. Sweden | 741 | 2.6 | 10. Finland | 0.36 |
| 11. Norway | 526 | 1.8 | 11. Japan | 0.35 |
| 12. Denmark | 449 | 1.6 | 12. United Kingdom | 0.33 |
| 13. Belgium | 434 | 1.5 | 13. Italy | 0.32 |
| 14. Switzerland | 286 | 1.0 | 14. Switzerland | 0.30 |
| 15. Austria | 181 | 0.6 | 15. Austria | 0.28 |
| 16. Finland | 178 | 0.6 | 16. New Zealand | 0.27 |
| 17. New Zealand | 59 | 0.2 | 17. United States | 0.24 |
| **Total** | **28,647** | **100.0** | | |

[1] Preliminary estimates.

(Source: IMF *Finance and Development* March 1986)

## ACTIVITIES

### SECTION A: FOCUS ON UNIT 8.5

Go back and answer the questions raised in the Focus.

### SECTION B: STEPPED QUESTIONS

1. **a** Name *six* ways in which the UK is different economically from a developing country like India.
   **b** What are the possible economic causes of underdevelopment?
   **c** Explain the possible economic effects of underdevelopment.
   **d** The British government gave just over £1,000 million in overseas aid out of total government spending of £140,000 million in 1986–87. Do you think that the amount given should be increased? Explain your answer bearing in mind the economic decisions involved.
   **e** For what economic reasons do you think that it is likely that the problem of starvation will continue?
2. **a** Name *three* world economic organisations.
   **b** Explain briefly the economic purpose of each of them.
   **c** Explain the possible economic effects of each organisation's activities on the international economy.

## SECTION C: DATA RESPONSE QUESTION

### Britain's 6 pc aid cut defies rising trend

**By Christopher Huhne,**
**Economic Editor**

Britain has cut its aid to Third World countries by an average 6 per cent a year in real terms over the past six years, while most other advanced industrial countries have increased their aid by an annual average of 4 per cent.

Only two other countries in the 18-member OECD development committee, New Zealand and Sweden, cut their aid budgets during the period from 1978-9 to 1983-4. Unlike Britain, they made small cuts – New Zealand by 0.6 per cent a year and Sweden 0.3 per cent.

The figures, released by the Paris-based Organisation for Economic Co-operation and Development, show that Britain's aid fell again in real terms in 1984.

The figures are calculated in constant prices and exchange rates to allow for currency and price fluctuations.

In 1984 the average rise was 6.3 per cent in real terms but Britain's aid contribution fell by 3 per cent. The OECD points out that six other countries cut aid, but that the figures in 1984 were influenced downward by the appreciation of the dollar.

The organisation says that the 1984 decrease in British aid was caused by a drop in bilateral grant assistance and accidental declines in multi-lateral contributions.

As a share of national income, British aid has dropped below the average figure of 0.36 per cent to 0.33 per cent. In 1978-9, Britain gave 0.49 per cent of national output to the third world compared to an average of 0.35 per cent.

In theory, the advanced countries are committed to building up their aid to 0.7 per cent of their output. In 1984, only Sweden, Norway, Denmark the Netherlands and France had surpassed this figure.

(Source: *The Guardian* 12.8.85)

**a** What does OECD stand for?

**b** ▷ What was the annual average increase in Third World aid in real terms over the six years?

▷ What was the annual average percentage change in Britain's Third World aid in real terms over the six years?

**c** Does your answer to **b** necessarily mean that the actual amount spent by Britain on aid fell?

**d** What are 'bilateral' and 'multilateral' aid?

**e** ▷ How large a contribution to aid are developed countries supposed to be committed to, and how many countries have given more than this?

▷ What economic changes do you think could cause developed countries to increase their aid in real terms?

## COURSEWORK

## PART 8: COURSEWORK SUGGESTION

### IMPORT PENETRATION IN THE UK

1. Make a survey in your own and at least two other homes to find out where items found commonly around the home were made, e.g. food, kitchenware, consumer durables, etc.
2. Group the items by the type of countries from which they came, for example those made in the UK, those made in other industrialised countries, and those made in developing countries.
3. Imagine you are a government minister. Write a report for the Prime Minister on the extent of import penetration in UK homes. Use a variety of methods to present your information, e.g. line graphs, bar charts, tables, etc. Conclude the report with the list of the benefits and disadvantages to the consumer and to the economy as a whole of such import penetration.

### EXTENSION COURSEWORK

4. Look in the *Annual Abstract of Statistics* (HMSO), which is available at main libraries, for figures on import penetration, and incorporate an analysis of your research into the report.

## DICTIONARY

Here are some more words and phrases for your Dictionary of Economic Terms. Remember to look for each word or phrase in the text and then write your own definition for it.

balance for official financing
balance of payments
balance of payments deficit
balance of payments surplus
balance of trade
Common Agricultural Policy (CAP)
common market
Council for Mutual Economic Assistance (COMECON)
current account
customs union
developing country
effective exchanger ate
European Economic Community (EEC)
exchange controls
exchange rate
exports
free trade area
General Agreement on Tariffs and Trade (GATT)
imports
International Bank for Reconstruction and Development (IBRD – World Bank)
International Monetary Fund (IMF)
investment and other capital flows

invisible trade
Organisation of Petroleum Exporting Countries (OPEC)
protectionism
quotas
sterling-dollar exchange rate
subsidies
tariffs
Third World
trade restrictions
United Nations Conference on Trade and Development (UNCTAD)
visible trade

**Extension**
absolute advantage
appreciation
comparative advantage
depreciation
devaluation
European Monetary System (EMS)
fixed exchange rate
floating exchange rate
managed floating
revaluation
terms of trade

# Index

**A**
absolute advantage   271
Acts of parliament
  Competition Act   171
  Consumer Credit Act   99, 188
  Consumer Protection Act   188
  Fair Trading Act   171
  Food and Drugs Act   188
  Restrictive Practices Act   171
  Sale of Goods Act   187
  Supply of Goods and Services Act   188
  Trade Descriptions Act   188
  Weights and Measures Act   188
Adjustable Peg System   289
advantage
  absolute advantage   271
  comparative advantage   272
advertising   11, 179–186
  informative advertising   182
  persuasive advertising   182
  point-of-sale advertising   182
advertising media   182
Advisory, Conciliation and Arbitration
    Service (ACAS)   47
age-sex pyramid   124
aging population   124
agreement
  credit sale agreements   97
  service agreement   83
aid
  bilateral aid   298
  foreign aid   298–299
  multilateral aid   298
  tied aid   298
allocation   10, 21, 22
annual general meetings (AGMs)   143
Annual Percentage Rate of charge (APR)   99
annuities   106
apprenticeships   39
arbitration   47
assets
  liquid assets   229
assisted areas   174
assurance
  life assurance   105
automated teller machines (ATMs)   67

**B**
baby boom   119
balance for official financing   275
balance of payments   232, 265, 273–282
  current account   282
  deficits   275
  surpluses   275
balance of trade   273
balancing item   275
banks   66, 91, 112, 156
  bank deposits   57

bank lending   229
bank services   66–68
  clearing banks   69
  functions of banks   66
  merchant banks   69
  National Savings Bank   89
  Trustee Savings Bank   69
bank accounts
  budget account   67
  current account   66
  cheque account   66
  deposit account   68, 91
  savings account   68, 91
bank statements   68
Bank Giro   66
banking   55–73
banknotes   56–
Bank of England   69
barter   32, 56
basic pay   77
benefits
  external benefits   84, 137
  fringe benefits   78
  means-tested benefits   199, 257
  National Insurance benefits   198
  private benefits   83, 137
  social benefits   84, 137
  social security benefits   76, 197
  supplementary benefit   199
  unemployment benefit   237
Big Bang   158
bilateral aid   298
bills
  finance bills   69
bills of exchange   69
birth rate   118, 119, 120
black economy   216
block release   39
board of directors   144
bonus
  productivity bonus   77
borrowing   89, 97–102
Brandt Reports   297, 298
British Electrotechnical Approvals
    Board   190
British Standards Institution   189
broker   158
  insurance broker   104
budget   82
Budget   224
budget accounts   67, 98
budgeting   82, 83, 85
building societies   69, 91, 112
building society accounts
  share accounts   91
bulk buying   163
bulk-decreasing industries   172
bulk-increasing industries   172

305

Business Expansion Scheme 157
Business and Technician Education Council (BTEC) 38
buying
  bulk buying 163
  impulse buying 181

## C

capital 5
capital flows 274
capital gains tax 206
capital goods 6, 136
capital-intensive industry 127
careers service 37
careers teachers 37
cash dispenser 67
Census of Population 118, 119
centrally-planned economy 22, 23
Certificate in Pre-Vocational Education (CPVE) 38
chain of production 136
chain stores 180
  variety chain stores 180
charge cards 98
cheques 66
  travellers' cheques 68
cheque account 66
cheque guarantee cards 66
choice 3
circular flow of income 214–215
Citizens Advice Bureaux (CAB) 189
City and Guilds of London Institute (CGLI) 38
clearing banks 69
Clearing House 69
clearing system 69
closed shop 47, 48, 238
coins 56
collective bargaining 46, 47
COMECON (Council for Mutual Economic Assistance) 299
Common Agricultural Policy (CAP) 291, 292
common market 290
companies 143
  co-operatives 145
  insurance companies 104, 112
  multi-national companies 145
  organisation 144
  private limited companies 143
  public companies 151
  public limited companies 143
comparative advantage 271–272
competition 22, 171
  law and competition 171
Competition Act 171
competitive demand 11
competitiveness 278
complements 11
complementary goods 18
concentration of industry 171
  economies of concentration 174

conciliation 47
conditions of demand 11, 12
conditions of supply 12
Confederation of British Industry (CBI) 48
  director-general 48
conglomerate integration 165
consumers 9, 21, 118
Consumer Advice Centres 189
Consumers Association 190
consumer councils 150, 189
Consumer Credit Act 99, 188
consumer durables 83
consumer goods 6, 136
consumer protection 99, 187–194
  laws for consumer protection 187–190
Consumer Protection Act 188
consumer sovereignty 171
consumption 2
convenience stores 181
co-operatives 145
  producer co-operatives 145
  retail co-operatives 145
  worker co-operatives 145
Co-operative Wholesale Society (CWS) 145
corporations
  public corporations 151
corporation tax 206
costs 31, 136–141
  external costs 84, 137
  fixed costs 82, 83, 137, 138
  long-run costs 138
  marginal cost 138
  opportunity cost 6
  private costs 83, 137
  short-run costs 138
  social costs 84, 137, 151
  total costs 137, 138
  variable costs 83, 137, 138
cost of living 61
cost-push inflation 243
craft unions 44
credit 11, 97–99
  deferred payments 97
  direct credit 66
  trade credit 156
credit cards 57, 98
credit rating 97
credit sale agreements 97
creditworthiness 97
cross elasticity of demand 18
current account 66, 273, 277
Customs and Excise duties 207, 291
customs union 290
cyclical unemployment 236

## D

day release 39
dealer 158
death rate 118, 120
debentures 157

debit
　direct debit　67
deductions from pay　77
deferred payments　97
deficit　275
deflationary policy　277
demand　10–20, 21, 22
　competitive demand　11
　conditions of demand　11, 12
　cross elasticity of demand　18
　demand for labour　219
　derived demand　219
　extension in demand　13
　income elasticity of demand　18
　joint demand　11
　price elasticity of demand　17, 18
demand curve　10
demand management　232
demand-pull inflation　243
demarcation disputes　44
department stores　180
dependent population　126
deposit accounts　68
depreciation　83
derived demand　219
Design Centre　190
devaluation　278
developing countries　296–298
developing economies　296–304
Development Areas　174
direct credit　66
direct debit　66
direct sales　181
direct taxes　205, 208
directors
　board of directors　144
　managing directors　144
Director-General of Fair Trading　171
discount houses　69
discount stores　180
diseconomies of scale　164
disposable income　77
disputes
　demarcation disputes　44
distribution of goods　179–181
distribution of income　256–261
　redistribution of income　248, 256–257
distribution of population　124, 126, 127
distribution of wealth　22, 256–261
　redistribution of wealth　248, 256–257
diversification　165
dividends　143, 157
division of labour　31, 32
　limitations of division of labour　32
durable goods　17
duties
　Customs and Excise duties　207

**E**

earnings　76
　transfer earnings　220

economic decisions　2–9
economic goods　2
economic growth　222, 248–255
economic organisations
　world economic organisations　296–304
economic problem　2–9
　basic economic problem　2–4
economic rent　220
economic resources　5
economic system　1–28
economies of concentration　174
economies of scale　138
　external economies of scale　165, 174
　internal economies of scale　163, 165
economists' disagreements　232–233
economy
　Britain and world economy　263–304
　centrally-planned economy　22, 23
　free-market economy　21–22, 23
　government and the economy　195–261
　managing the economy　222–233
　mixed economy　22–23, 196
　model economy　21
　types of economy　21–28
EEC　174, 290–295, 299
effective exchange rate　284
elasticity　17–20
　cross elasticity of demand　18
　income elasticity of demand　18
　inelasticity　17
　price elasticity of demand　17, 18
　price elasticity of supply　17, 19
　unit elasticity　17
employees　30, 76
employers　30, 43–53
employers associations　48
employers federation　48
employment　19, 30, 37. 76
　self-employment　76
employment agencies　38
endowment assurance　106
endowment mortgages　112
enterprise　5, 6
Enterprise Zones　166, 174
entrepreneur　6
Environmental Health Departments　189
equilibrium price　12–13
European Free Trade Association
　(EFTA)　292
European Monetary System　289
evening classes　39
exchange
　bills of exchange　69
　foreign exchange　69
exchange controls　265
exchange rates　283–284, 288–289
　effective exchange rate　284
　fixed exchange rates　288
　floating exchange rates　288
　sterling-dollar exchange rate　284
expansionary policies　222, 236

expenditure 82
exports 264, 284, 297
extension in demand 13
extension in supply 13
external benefits 84, 137
external costs 84, 137
external economies of scale 165, 174
external migration 118, 120
externalities 137, 151, 249

## F
factor incomes 219–221
factors of production 4–6, 12, 19, 21, 22
  capital 5
  enterprise 5
  labour 5
  land resources 5
fair trading
  Director-General of Fair Trading 171
  Office of Fair Trading 189
Fair Trading Act 171
faith
  utmost good faith 103
finance 156–162, 165
finance bills 69
financial system 66–73
Financial Times (FT)
  FT 30 Share Index 159
  FTSE 100 150
firms 3
  aims of firms 142
  financing firms 156–162
  large firms 163–171
  location of firms 172–178
  organisation of firms 142–145
  private sector firms 142–148
  small firms 163–171
fiscal policies 224, 243
fixed costs 82, 83, 137, 138
fixed exchange rates 288
floating
  managed floating 289
floating exchange rates 288
Food and Drugs Act 188
footloose industries 173
foreign aid 298–299
foreign exchange 69
forward market 288
free goods 2
free-market economy 21–22, 23
free trade areas 290
fringe benefits 78
fully comprehensive insurance 105

## G
General Agreement on Tariffs and Trade (GATT) 266
general unions 44
geographical immobility 237

goods
  capital goods 6, 136
  complementary goods 18
  consumer goods 6, 136
  demand for goods 10
  distribution of goods 179–181
  durable goods 17
  economic goods 2
  free goods 2
  inferior goods 11
  merit goods 22, 23
  price of goods 12–13
  private goods 23
  producer goods 136
  public goods 21, 22, 23
  supply of goods 11–12
government 3, 21, 22, 195–261
  economic aims of government 222
  economic policies of government 222–224
  government income 205–213
  government spending 196–204
  local government 196
government spending 196, 250
grants
  Rate Support Grants 206
  Regional Development Grants 174
Gross Domestic Product (GDP) 196, 215, 248
gross income 205
Gross National Product (GNP) 215, 248
gross pay 77
growth
  economic growth 222, 248–255

## H
hire purchase (HP) 97, 156
holidays 84–85
horizontal integration 165
housing 111–116
  buying housing 111–116
  renting housing 111–116
  running a house 82–83
housing associations 111
hyperinflation 242
hypermarkets 180

## I
immobility 127
  geographical immobility 237
  occupational immobility 237, 238
imports 264, 265, 277, 284
  visible imports 276
import controls 237
impulse buying 181
income 11, 82, 224
  circular flow of income 214–215
  disposable income 77
  distribution of income 256–261
  factor incomes 219–221
  government income 205–213
  gross income 205
  money income 78

National Income 214–221
  real income 78
  redistribution of income 248, 256–257
  taxable income 205, 206
income bonds 92
income elasticity of demand 18
incomes policy 232, 243
income tax 77, 90, 205, 206
indemnity 103
independent retailers 179
index
  FT 30 Share Index 159
indirect taxes 207, 208
infant industries 265
informative advertising 182
industrial action 47, 48
industrial inertia 172
Industrial Revolution 127
Industrial Training Boards 39
industrial unions 44
industry 33
  bulk-decreasing industries 172
  bulk-increasing industries 172
  capital-intensive industry 127
  concentration of industry 171
  footloose industries 172
  infant industries 265
  localised industries 174
  location of industry 172
  manufacturing industry 277
  primary industry 33, 126
  secondary industry 33, 126
  service industry 127
  tertiary industry 33, 127
inelasticity 17
infant mortality 120
infant mortality rate 120
inferior goods 11
inflation 61, 92, 98, 222, 231, 236, 242–247, 250, 284
  cost-push inflation 243
  demand-pull inflation 243
  hyperinflation 242
infrastructure 173
inheritance tax 206
injections 215
insurable interest 103
insurance 103–110
  certificates 105
  claims forms 105
  life assurance 105
  motor insurance 105
  National Insurance 76, 77, 103, 206
  policies 105
  premiums 104
  principles of insurance 103–106
  proposal form 104
  renewal notices 105
insurance broker 104
insurance company 104, 112
integration 164
  conglomerate integration 165
  horizontal integration 165
  lateral integration 165
  reasons for integration 165
  vertical integration 165
interest 90–91, 220
  insurable interest 103
interest rates 230, 283
Intermediate Areas 174
internal economies of scale 163, 164, 165
  buying economies 163
  financial economies 163
  managerial economies 163
  marketing economies 163
  risk-bearing economies 164
  technical economies 163
internal migration 118
International Bank for Reconstruction and Development (IBRD) 299
International Development Association (IDA) 299
International Monetary Fund (IMF) 289, 299
investment 76, 242, 250, 274
investment accounts 91
investment and other capital flows account 274, 276
Investors In Industry (3i) 156
invisibles 273
invisible trade 276

**J**
Jobcentres 37
joint demand 11

**K**
Keynesianism 232
Keynesians 231–232

**L**
labour 5
  demand for labour 219
  division of labour 31, 32
  labour market policies 231
  labour productivity 250
  mobility of labour 224, 237, 243, 250
  supply of labour 219
land resources 5
lateral integration 165
laws
  law and competition 171
  consumer protection laws 187–190
leasing 156
lending
  bank lending 229
less developed countries (LDCs) 296
liability
  limited liability 143
  unlimited liability 142
life assurance 105
  annuities 106
  endowment policies 106

term policies 106
whole life policies 105
limited companies
  private limited companies 143
  public limited companies 143
limited liability 143
liquid assets 229
living
  cost of living 61
  standard of living 30, 61, 248
loans
  personal loans 68, 97
Loan Guarantee Scheme 157
local authorities 112
Local Authority Consumer Advice Centres 189
Local Authority Environmental Health Departments 189
Local Authority Trading Standards Departments 189
local government 196
localised industries 174
location of industry 172
long-run costs 138

## M

mail order 181
Malthus, Thomas 123
managed floating 289
managing directors 144
Manpower Services Commission (MSC) 37, 39
manufacturing industry 277
marginal cost 138
marginality 4
markets 10–20
  forward market 288
  labour markets 231
  Unlisted Securities Market (USM) 159
market maker 158
market mechanism 10, 21, 22, 23
market power 165
market price 12–13
market stalls 181
marketing 145
means-tested benefits 199, 257
media 38
  advertising media 182
merchant banks 69
mergers 164, 171
  Monopolies and Mergers Commission 171
merit goods 22, 23
migration 119
  external migration 118, 120
  internal migration 118
mixed economy 22–23, 196
mobility of labour 220, 224, 237, 243, 250
model economy 21
Monetarism 231
Monetarists 231–232
monetary policy 69, 222, 243

monetary targets 230
money 55–73
  development of money 56–57
  functions of money 57–58
  managing money 75–116
  purchasing power 61
  qualities of money 57
  value of money 61–65, 283–289
money income 78
money supply 229, 230–231, 243
monopolies 171
  natural monopolies 150
Monopolies and Mergers Commission 171
monopolistic practices 171
monopoly power 171
mortality
  infant mortality 120
mortgages 111, 112
  endowment mortgages 112
  repayment mortgages 112
motor insurance 105
  fully comprehensive 105
  Road Traffic Act 105
  third party 105
  third party, fire and theft 105
multilateral aid 298
multi-national companies 145
multiple stores 180

## N

National Debt 69, 212–213
National Girobank 67, 69
National Income 214–221
  measuring National Income 215
National Insurance 76, 103
National Insurance benefits 198
National Insurance contributions 77, 206
National Savings Bank 89
  income bonds 92
  investment account 91
  ordinary account 91
  premium bonds 92
  yearly plan 92
National Savings Certificates 91
National Savings Scheme 91
nationalisation 150
nationalised industries 149–155
  Select Committee on Nationalised Industries 149
Nationalised Industries' Consumer Councils 189
natural monopolies 150
negotiation 47
Net National Product (NNP) 215
net pay 77
North Sea oil 276, 277

## O

occupational immobility 238
off-the-job training 39
Office of Fair Trading 189

oil
  North Sea oil   276, 277
on-the-job training   39
OPEC (Organisation of Petroleum Exporting Countries)   299
opportunity cost   6
optimum population   123
ordinary accounts   91
ordinary shares   143
overdrafts   68, 97
overheads   138
overpopulation   123
overtime pay   77

**P**
partners
  sleeping partners   143
partnerships   143
pay   43, 76–81
  basic pay   77
  deductions   77
  gross pay   77
  net pay   77
  overtime pay   77
  piece rate of pay   77
  take-home pay   77
  time rate of pay   77
Pat As You Earn (PAYE)   206
pay packet   77
pensions   76
perks   78
personal loans   68, 97
personal services   165
personnel   145
persuasive advertising   182
picketing   47
point-of-sale advertising   182
pooling of risk   103
population   11, 117–133, 296
  age distribution of population   124
  aging population   124
  Census of Population   118, 119
  dependent population   126
  geographical distribution of population   127
  natural decrease in population   118
  occupational distribution of population   126
  optimum population   123
  overpopulation   123
  population change   118–123
  population immobility   127
  population size   118–123
  population structure   124–133
  regional distribution of population   127
  sex distribution of population   126
  theories of population   123
  underpopulation   123
  working population   126
Post Office   69, 91
pound sterling
  value of pound   283–289
preference shares   143

premium bonds   92
price   10–20, 21
  equilibrium price   12–13
  market price   12–13
  share prices   159
price elasticity of demand   17, 18
price elasticity of supply   17, 19
price mechanism   10
price system   21
primary industry   33, 126
primary products   297
private benefits   83, 137
private costs   83, 137
private goods   23
private limited companies   143
private sector   196
privatisation   149–155, 232
producers   6, 21, 118
producer co-operatives   145
producer goods   136
products
  primary products   297
production   2, 135–194
  chain of production   136
  costs and benefits of production   137–138
  factors of production   4–6, 12, 19, 21, 22
production line   30
Production Possibilities Curve (PPC)   6
productivity   219
  labour productivity   250
productivity bonus   77
professions   238
Professional and Executive Recruitment   37
profit   138, 142, 220
  retained profit   156
progressive tax   207, 257
proportional tax   207
proprietors
  sole proprietors   142
protectionism   264, 277, 297
public goods   21, 22, 23
public companies   151
public corporations   151
public limited companies   143
public sector   196–204
Public Sector Borrowing Requirement (PSBR)   69, 212

**Q**
quotas   264

**R**
rationalisation   165
rates   206, 207
rate-capping   207
Rate Support Grant   206
real income   78
reflationary policies   222
Regional Development Grants   174
Regional Fund of the European Economic Community   174

regional policy   157, 174, 237, 291
Regional Selective Assistance   174
regressive tax   207
rent   220
  economic rent   220
renting housing   112
repayment mortgages   112
research and development   144
resources   2, 5
  allocation of resources   21, 22
restrictions on trade   265
restrictive practices   171
Restrictive Practices Act   171
Restrictive Practices Court   171
retail co-operatives   145
Retail Prices Index (RPI)   61, 91, 242
  problems with the RPI   62
retailers   179
  independent retailers   179
retailing   179–186
retained profit   156
revenue   138
  total revenue   17, 138
risk
  pooling of risk   103
Road Traffic Act insurance   105

## S
salary   77
sales
  control of sales   165
  direct sales   181
Sale of Goods Act   187
sandwich courses   39
saving   89–96
  interest on savings   90–91
  places to save   91–92
  reasons for saving   89
savings accounts   68
scale   163
  diseconomies of scale   164
  economies of scale   138, 163, 165, 174
seasonal unemployment   236
secondary industry   33, 126
securities   157
  Unlisted Securities Market   159
Select Committee on Nationalised Industries   149
self-employment   76
services
  demand for services   10
  personal services   165
  price of services   12–13
  supply of services   11–12
service agreement   83
service industries   127
shares   157, 159
  ordinary shares   143
  preference shares   143
share accounts   91
share prices   159
shareholders   143
  annual general meetings (AGM)   143
shop steward   45
short-run costs   138
shortage   12
Skillcentres   39
sleeping partners   143
small firms   165
Small Workshop Scheme   166
social benefits   84, 137
social costs   84, 137, 151
social policy   291
social security benefits   76, 197
social security system   76, 197–199
sole proprietors   142
sole traders   142
specialisation   31, 32, 264, 265, 271
speculators   283, 284
spending
  government spending   196–204, 250
  planning spending   82–88
standard of living   30, 61, 248
standing orders   67
statement
  bank statement   68
sterling-dollar exchange rate   284
stocks   157
Stock Exchange   92, 157–159
Stock Exchange Automated Quotations (SEAQ)   158
stores
  chain stores   180
  convenience stores   181
  department stores   180
  discount stores   180
  multiple stores   180
strikes   47
structural unemployment   236
subsidies   12, 265
substitutes   11, 18
supermarkets   180
supplementary benefit   199
supply   10–20, 21, 22
  conditions of supply   12
  control of supply   165
  extension in supply   13
  money supply   229
  price elasticity of supply   17, 19
  supply of labour   219
supply curve   11, 31
Supply of Goods and Services Act   188
surplus   12, 275

## T
take-home pay   77
takeovers   164
targets
  monetary targets   230
tariffs   264
taxable income   205, 206
taxation   12, 205–208